BALTIMORE

The Nineteenth Century Black Capital

Leroy Graham

UNIVERSITY
PRESS OF
AMERICA

"To those who are and do good"

ACKNOWLEDGMENTS

        I wish to thank those, who, in the least bit, helped make this possible; that includes the libraries and staffs at the Maryland Historical Society and Enoch Pratt Free Library, both of Baltimore; Hall of Records, Annapolis; Friends Library, Swarthmore College, Swarthmore, Pennsylvania; and, of course, Morgan State University Library, Baltimore. This project was first taken up at Morgan State University in 1972, while earning the M.A. degree. Since then, as with most meager theses topics, both the range and scope have widened. On a personal note, I wish to thank, in the order as they helped: Dr. Benjamin Quarles, for his books were excellent models; Dr. Thomas Cripps, for the criticisms, some finally sunk in; Mr. Samuel Hopkins, for his enthusiasm for the subject under study; Mrs. Phyllis Hathaway, for her sympathetic ear was always present; Dr. Sandye McIntyre, II and Carleen Leggett for helping me to get a Fulbright; and last, but not least, Mrs. Harold Manakee for her encouragement while at the end--many meanings intended. Also, I would like to express my appreciation to my typist Charlotte Schisler.

v

ABBREVIATIONS

A.C.S.   American Colonization Society papers, Library of Congress, Manuscripts Division, Washington, D.C.

H.S.P.   Historical Society of Pennsylvania, Manuscripts Division, Philadelphia, Pennsylvania.

M.H.S.   Maryland Historical Society, Manuscripts Division, Baltimore, Maryland.

TABLE OF CONTENTS

FOREWORD

This work recounts mainly the efforts of four remarkable men who devoted themselves to an unprecedented degree to make Baltimore a just and livable city for blacks. They were Elisha Tyson, William Watkins, George Alexander Hackett, and Isaac Myers. Their endeavors were of such dimensions as to be noticed by the nation. In fact, they made the city throughout most of the nineteenth century a focal point in black history--the nation's unofficial black capital.

Elisha Tyson, born into a Quaker family, was conditioned early to the rigor of the unconventional life. When he advocated the cause of the blacks, here again, Tyson was not merely just drifting with the mainstream of public behavior either. Indeed, the firm, forthrightness of his stance on behalf of blacks made Tyson the foremost Quaker abolitionist of his day. As a man of wealth and industry and leader of a large family, and several associates of like attainments, he helped make Baltimore one of the most important commercial centers in the nation; and, this accomplishment, itself, is intimately part of the reason for his success on behalf of black emancipation.

At the time of Tyson's death in 1824, much had improved in Baltimore from earlier days when he arrived in the City in 1781, when Baltimore was rightly considered an ornament in slavery's crown of thorns, to the days helped into existence by Tyson, when some thought it the "headquarters" of free blacks from throughout the country. The blacks to follow Tyson, also, did much to strengthen the vitality of Baltimore's black community.

The first of these, William Watkins, born into a free family around the time the century of Enlightenment, the 1700s, faded from view, enjoyed what advantages and comforts were to be had growing up in Baltimore at this time--especially its just-beginning-independent church and school organizations around the Sharp Street church. In so doing, he accomplished outstanding things. He was a fine writer and certainly a careful teacher, a minister and, as well, as one of his former students said, a kind of counselor to blacks throughout the nation. He was, in addition, a sometimes student of medicine, businessman, and father of a family of sons who followed in his footsteps.

ix

George A. Hackett emerges as an acknowledged leader around 1840 and derived great benefit from being a son of his father. His parents were probably free, also of the "best" society; and, in turn, he married into the best of black Baltimore society. He travelled extensively as a seaman in his youth, broadening his view of the world and, through continued diligence, developed his mental and oratorical talents fully. After his seafaring days, he succeeded in business and, with tremendous courage, pursued plans of black-uplift to his death in 1870 in the city on a par with the attainments of Tyson and Watkins. His life is more of a contradiction of most of what has been known, written, thought, or believed about nineteenth century free black life than perhaps any other man of his era.

Referred to in his last years as Captain Hackett, George A. Hackett deeply affected associates, especially those belonging to his own church, Bethel African Methodist Episcopal Church. One of these was Isaac Myers. After Hackett's death, the free-born Myers proceeded swiftly, not only to assume a leading position in the various aspects of black life in Baltimore, but in the nation as well. He ranged over all the issues and fields—labor, politics, education, religion, business, literature, and society. Myers, indeed, was a fitting culmination and heir to the legacy of the foregoing three, and making it correct to view Baltimore as the nineteenth century black capital.

Chapter I

FIRST STEPS, FIRST

Sometime in the latter third of the seventeenth century, William Penn converted Elisha Tyson's great-grandfather to the Quaker faith before he departed his lower Rhine home in Krefeld for Pennsylvania. Penn, an Englishman, had received from the King of England a huge tract of land in North America, which he wanted his fellow Quakers to settle. Reyner Tiesen, Elisha Tyson's great-grandfather, and other relatives and friends, sailed to America aboard the <u>Concord</u> in 1683 and founded the settlement of Germantown, Pennsylvania. Daniel Pastorious, more noted before the embarkation as a classical scholar, served as leader of these pioneers. On the whole, the passengers were skilled craftsmen and farmers; and, almost from the outset, the community was a beacon which attracted further German migration to America.[1]

In 1688, though barely established, the founders of Germantown served as pioneers in another respect. They were the first noteworthy group to protest the practice of Negro slaveholding amongst their neighboring fellow Quakers, most of whom were English. In this effort, also, Pastoriuous was the principal leader. In this "Germantown Protest," the Krefeld Quakers evidenced a strong adherence to the biblical "Golden Rule," which commanded one treat others as one wished to be treated. The enslavement of blacks, mainly to the exclusion of others, and the harsh, beastial treatment they sometimes received was, in the view of the protesters, a gross sin against God, which had to be, must need be abandoned. The Germantown Protest is not only significant for being the most significant first effort among Quakers to ameliorate the condition of blacks in bondage among themselves, it is also one of the first most significant first steps among all those efforts by all kinds of peoples soon to be directed toward bettering the lot of the abused African.

Reyner Tiesen's signature did not appear on this 1688 protest petition because it is believed at this time that he could not write. Though perhaps unable to write, Tiesen, in the judgment of his peers, was a "weighty Friend," one noted for his piety. His house often served as a kind of public meeting place. He was elected to official positions in the overall community government of the township for a long while. Amongst

1

his own sect, in 1695, he was appointed an overseer of the Germantown Quaker Meeting, and, by 1725, had been appointed an elder in his Meeting in Abingdon. An elder was one step removed from the highest Quaker position, that of minister. Elders served as advisors to their local ministers and travelling companions to them when they visited outside of their jurisdictions. Generally, elders became the conservators of the traditions and customs of the sect. Usually, only after showing the notable gift of impromptu, inspired speech-making for the Lord, was one certified as a minister. In keeping with its unconventional ways, the high officialdom in the Quaker faith served without pay in contrast to most others.[2]

Members of the Society of Friends, from the inception of the group in England around the 1650's, believed themselves set apart from other people to give a more visibly profound testimony to what they considered righteous living to be as based on their biblical reading and understanding. On the surface, distinctive speech and clothing made it rather easy to identify the group. Dressed in dark clothing, the ever-present hat, unremoved before anyone, regardless of his supposed higher rank, as was the custom; likewise, the disinclination to use titles, no matter to whom speaking and the use of "thou" and "thee" instead, made it rather easy to recognize a Quaker. The silence in assembled worship was another rather unique characteristic of Quakers.

Friends believed that the quality of divinity within each person, his soul, could be inspired to speak the words of the Divine Presence in assembled worship, if one waited in silence, patiently, for the message or revelation. Naturally, the more one became attuned to know the Divine Will or Mind, the purer one's life became, and the better one was qualified to lead others. Consequently, Friends were noted for valuing simplicity, frankness, and exacting probity. Others at times viewed their social manners as being too austere and reserved. They believed in living peaceable lives, doing good deeds without recourse to force or coercion. Many willingly suffered violence, rather than respond violently, even when justly provoked. In keeping with this latter belief, there gradually evolved amongst them a practice of refusing to pay taxes designated for war. To them, life was too precious to be snuffed out in war; and, on the other hand, too meaningful to be wasted away slowly in pursuit of unbridled or indecent pleasure such as found in playhouses, bearpits, ostentatious playthings, and too much strong drink.

2

Quakers were further strengthened in their distinctiveness by the way they arrived at decisions or made precedents for themselves. By developing a general consensus, a rather slow process at times that could take years, were most major decisions reached. As such, members were strictly expected afterwards to adhere to decisions arising out of the General Will. So ingrained was this practice in Elisha Tyson's day, that it was not uncommon for Quakers to feel uneasy when joining with others to decide matters by majority vote, even on so vital a question as bringing about the abolition of slavery. After most or all had agreed, then was a matter considered decided.

Similarly, with an eye to their reputation in the community, Quakers avoided being party to judicial proceedings, members of juries in which their vote might decide the outcome of something which they had advocated as disinterested persons. This, as so much of their lives, was evidence of their implicit faith in God to be the final arbiter in matters sufficiently aired in the light of day. That is to say, in their view, a prophet's warning and call to repentance was sufficient, but God would make the final decision, if man did not heed the warning--do what was just. When Quakers reached decisions amongst themselves, however, a member who refused to carry out a prohibition or prescription decided upon faced disownment, removal from the membership list.[3]

At the age of 86, Reyner Tiesen died in 1745; and, according to one account, Elisha Tyson was born four years later, in 1749, in a house standing on the site of his great-grandfather's original homestead in Germantown. An obituary printed at the time of Elisha's death in February 1824 states, however, that his birth was in 1748 in Montgomery County, Pennsylvania, a county in which Reyner Tiesen did own some land. Regardless of the truth in this matter, as it relates to his birth, Elisha Tyson apparently was heir to much that his great-grandfather represented. Elisha's father was Isaac Tyson; his mother, Esther Shoemaker.[4]

The propensity of his foreabears for hard work apparently enured Elisha Tyson and other Tysons to the same regimen. As the original settlers of Germantown were either good farmers or competent craftsmen, their overall industry made Germantown noteworthy in another regard. The city became known as Pennsylvania's first "distinctly manufacturing town," dense with mills of all kinds-grist, fulling, oil, and paper-run by water power.

Following in the family's footsteps, Tyson was apprenticed to a craft, the milling business, while young.
Upon reaching maturity, Elisha Tyson was about six feet
tall and possessed extraordinary strength. Tyson's immense physical strength was a decided advantage in handling the burdens of his trade--the bushel baskets of
wheat and barrels of flour.[5]

Elisha Tyson grew to maturity in the volatile years
before the outbreak of the American Revolution in the
region around Philadelphia which produced four of the
foremost public critics resolved in the belief of the
urgent necessity for the abolition of slavery. The
quartet consisted of Benjamin Lay, Ralph Sandiford, John
Woolman, and Anthony Benezet, all Quakers. Like the
Krefelders, they believed slavery to be a heinous sin,
for which severe Divine chastisement could surely be expected unless repentance and reformation were huriedly
decided upon.

The agitation of this quartet was reminiscent of
the ways of the prophets of the Bible as well, such as
in the splattering of a blood-colored substance on
slaveowners to denote their virtual and actual participation in murder in order to get and keep their slaves.
As a result, in part of the persistent criticism of the
four during the Revolutionary era, Quakers throughout
the United States, but first in Pennsylvania, finally
adopted the position of the founders of Germantown, making slaveholding amongst its members an offense, worthy
of dismissal from the sect. Before this, during the
time of the French and Indian Wars (1754-1763), Quakers
had denied their ministers the right to hold slaves.

Of the quartet of Quaker abolitionists, Tyson was
probably acquainted on a personal level, if at all, with
the activities of only Anthony Benezet, whose reputation
was international in scope. The other three were dead
by the 1780s but then still remembered, expecially Benjamin Lay, whose likeness was said to hang in practically every Quaker home in and around Philadelphia.
Benezet, at one point in his life, taught at the school
started in Germantown by Daniel Pastorious. Later,
Benezet headed a school for blacks in Philadelphia, having among his more accomplished pupils Richard Allen,
the first bishop of the African Methodist Episcopal
Church; and James Forten, rich sailing loft owner and
general leader in the community and Absalom Jones,
first leader of St. Thomas Episcopal Church.

Toward the end of his life, Benezet helped to
organize the first abolition society founded anywhere,

4

which included Quakers, as well as non-Quakers. Although first organized in 1775, the body did not accomplish much until the conclusion of the American Revolution. In 1784, the year of Benezet's death, or thereabout, Elisha Tyson began in earnest to devote himself to the abolition of slavery and the betterment of the lot of free and slave alike in Baltimore.[6]

Prior to settling in Baltimore, however, as a young man of 24, in 1773, Elisha Tyson moved from Pennsylvania to Jericho Mills, Maryland, which was located near Joppa Town. At Jericho Mills, Elisha Tyson and his brother Jacob established themselves in the milling business with the purchase of a tract of land consisting of 280 acres. At the time of his arrival, Joppa Town was steadily being displaced by Baltimore as the political and business center for the extensive area of land known as Baltimore County. Baltimore Town was some 15 miles south of Joppa Town, laid out on the Patapsco River.

Elisha Tyson's move to Maryland took place just before strife between Britain and her colonies exploded into actual war; a war which posed a dilemma for Tyson. He was in the midst of building a new grist mill on his property when the Fourth of July Declaration of Independence was issued by the colonies. Despite the Quaker stance against making or contributing to war, Tyson sent a letter dated June 28, 1776, to the Council of Safety, the Revolutionary Governmental body in the state, proposing to alter his plans and, instead, build a powder mill if he could receive compensation.

One of his neighbors, David Lee, who had recently moved from Bucks County, Pennsylvania, had already converted a flour mill into a flint lock manufactory and had received compensation from the Council to do so. The decision of the Council on Tyson's offer is not known. Yet, despite this lapse in Quaker belief against aiding war, some time later, when Tyson refused to become an active combatant, his horse worth twelve pounds was confiscated by Revolutionary authorities in Harford County, a county carved out of Baltimore County.

In a few months after the letter to the Council of Safety, Elisha married Mary Amos with the blessing of the Gunpowder Monthly Meeting. William Amos, Mary's father, had been one of the organizers of the Gunpowder Meeting. Within a short while, the Tyson family increased as Isaac was born in 1777. The increase in family seemed coupled with an increase in wealth.[7]

Realizing the business advantages to be gained from being a resident of booming Baltimore, in late 1781, Tyson moved to Baltimore, settling on Gay Street. In doing so, he placed at public auction his substantial property in Harford County. The property consisted of two or three flour mills, a sawmill which he thought capable of doing as much cutting as any in the state, and other necessities to carry on the milling trade, as well as a blacksmith shop, meathouse, and springhouse. Tyson described his mills as being one of French Burr, one of Cologne, and one of country or local stone. He said that in the area of this property, wheat was plentiful and stave timber and hoop poles for making the barrels were produced in abundance by local artisans. Water transportation was within easy reach, not more than two or three miles away. His terms were: one-third being due within a month's time, the other two-thirds payable in easy installments, and payable with tobacco or flour.

Tyson offered the property for sale, secure in the knowledge he had title to it. His claim was soon counterclaimed, however, by William Gwin in a newspaper advertisement issued on March 12, 1782. To say the least, Tyson's reputation and ability to do business could have been seriously impaired if Gwin's accusation had proved true.

About two weeks after Gwin's attack, Tyson had the following printed in a newspaper, addressed to "Neighbor Gwin."

Thou hast, amply made me satisfaction for the unjust aspersion thou curious Advertisement had levelled at my veracity, by an act of generosity at these times not to be expected even from a friend, much less from thee; to one who thou averest was offering to public sale, lands and mills to which thou had indefeasible title; I think it therefore obligatory on me, to make this public acknowledgment of thy boundless and unparalleled generosity, by candidly owning, in the fore of day, that, very lately, and since the appearance of thy advertisement, thou hast been so obliging as to give me good bonded security for the payment of two thousand eight hundred pounds specie, six hundred and twenty of which are to be paid the 14th of June next, for suffering thee to remain in peaceable possession of those lands and mills & c. to which thou

6

advanced that I had no <u>title</u>, either <u>legal or equitable.</u>

As indicated by the frankness in the opening lines and the underlined portions, the notice seemed written with suppressed anger.

Also, it seems Tyson had allowed Gwin to use his mills for some time without having received any compensation; and, if true, indicates the depth of generosity he was willing to practice, even to a competitor. Some months later, however, Gwin appeared not satisfied and accused Tyson of not living up to their agreement by putting him in legal possession of the land. Whatever may have been the land Tyson sold in Harford County at this time, part of his holding there remained in the family well into the nineteenth century.[8]

In 1781, the year of Tyson's settlement in Baltimore, the town ranked as the tenth largest in the colonies, with most of its black population being slaves. Geographically, the city stood at the center of the United States. By the 1790s, it would become a successful rival to Philadelphia and New York as the country's trading, financial, and political focus. Because of the long, ever-narrowing entrance to its harbor, Baltimore was secure from British attack during the Revolutionary years. This fact was not lost on Revolutionary leaders who used the town as a supply and distribution center for the Continental armies. For a while, the Congress was even headquartered there. This recognition of the city's importance during the war, further strengthened its growing acquisition, since the 1760s, of the tobacco and flour trade that used to go to Philadelphia.

Three parts constituted Baltimore at Tyson's arrival. These were Baltimore Town proper, Fells Point and Jones Town, also known as Old Town. Established in 1729, Baltimore Town was laid out on the western edge of the harbor area; the Jones Falls River, which rose about ten miles north of the city, emptied itself into this portion of the harbor. The other two communities were older settlements located around the harbor. The entire harbor area, on the whole, had several advantages over other eastern ports--it was not subject to freshets, icing-over in winter, or wood-eating worms in the summer.[9]

As a businessman, Tyson arrived in a city that had much respect for its men of commerce. Businessmen had been in charge of the Revolution, and so it was after the Revolution. Members of this group were conspicuously forward to welcome George Washington when he passed through the city in September 1781. They offered thanks to him and Heaven for what it was then perceived as a certain success. A year later, the same types repeated almost the same ceremonies in welcoming the entrance of Count de Rochambeau, commander of French troops, to the city. Doubtlessly, however, many of these men of affairs, as slave owners, were a little less restrained in their greeting for Rochambeau. On several occasions, the Count had shown a reluctance to hand over blacks within his lines who claimed to be free or who proved to be useful to his troops. This, of course, encouraged slaves to flee to his camps as the word spread, perhaps upsetting routine plantation rigor.[10]

Baltimore's prosperity was dependent upon its strategic setting in an area producing an abundance of grain and tobacco in fields to the west, north, and south, and in a landscape with sufficient streams and rivers for mill sites to make much of the magnificent yearly harvests. These natural benefits were not enough, however. Roads had to be built and much of it was done in the 1780s and most, if not all, under the direction of certain private groups, men of means whose petitions before the General Assembly for the right to build the improved path through the agricultural heartland and near some mill centers were favorably received. Several of the more important roads passed by Ellicott Mills, an advanced milling center, established by Quakers who had come to Maryland in 1772 from Bucks County, Pennsylvania. In the end, however, all roads eventually led to Baltimore.[11]

Within the city, road and street improvement was not neglected as well, and here efforts were made by different private groups to bend road terminals to certain parts of the city. Indeed, a rather serious situation developed around the time of Tyson's arrival, as each section of the greater area looked after its own interests to the detriment of the common good. The situation seemed utterly bewildering to farmers who were eager to deliver their goods to Baltimore and derive the financial benefits the entire city offered.[12]

Whereas the desire for a greater share of the produce and prosperity rolling and sailing into the city pitted the community against itself, one project directed at improving traffic conditions engaged all in a spirit of unanimity. The court house, located on a promi-

8

nent hill, blocked the busy Calvert Street approach to the harbor. In 1784, Leonard Harbaugh, a master builder and inventor, in a plan offered for public approval, proposed both to save the court house and clear the obstruction. His plan called for digging underneath the court house and underpinning the structure with three arches, large enough for the growing traffic to pass beneath. The central arch stood 18 feet high, another 20 feet, and the other reached 28 feet. Harbaugh calculated the costs to be less than 1,100 pounds and not to exceed 13 months to complete. He and his associates were willing to pay up to 4,000 dollars in penalties, if unsuccessful. They asked for no new tax to pay for the project. The work was successfully completed and became one of the city's wonders.

In a few years, this structure on stilts would witness numerous legal fights instituted by Tyson on behalf of blacks seeking their freedom. When the court house, a few years after its renovation, acquired a striking clock which could be heard for three or four miles all around, at every peal of its bell; doubtlessly, depending upon the circumstances of the hearer, the bells' tolling was either one striking a reminder for liberty won or enslavement better fastened.[13]

For the most part, as much as the court house scheme united the community, other worthwhile undertakings, in those years when dynastic families in Baltimore were to be founded, proved divisive. This was especially so with the attempt to establish a new market house. A great commercial advantage and power would be placed in the hands of the commission empowered by the General Assembly to make decisions relative to the new market--from the buying of the land, naturally affecting the prices of land and property in the neighborhood, to the handling of fees and dispensing of privileges in the new structure. As time progressed, even blacks would open stalls in Baltimore's markets, even the central one; they becoming, in turn, people of means themselves.[14]

While some worthwhile projects in the opening years of the 1780s stirred intense activity, others caused little. Such was the case relative to establishing well-run and regulated coffeehouses, a primitive meeting place for business and pleasure. Even later, founding a well-regulated exchange to give firmer order to the way business was conducted in the city which, for the longest time, was conducted on the streets, seemed forever in the planning and talking-up stage. In addition, the completion of well-adorned churches or meeting houses was, in the opinion of one critic, not exactly firing people to great effort, either.[15]

In contrast to some, a few years after Tyson's arrival, saw him very active in building a new Quaker meeting house of its usual plain, rather rectangular design in Old Town. He was one of the co-signers of the loan taken out to finance the project. Gradually, other denominations built more elaborate churches with steeples and organs. As Quaker services took place without musical instruments and singing, having no organ was not such a calamity.

As much as there were too few pew seats in the early 1780s, there were also equally too few burial places present at this time. Keepers of the public conscience urged the various congregations to remedy this situation, and gradually, this, too, was accomplished.[16]

If from the early 1780s there were few well-appointed churches, there existed somewhat understandably, few well-qualified ministers. In this regard, the same could be said for other professionals, such as lawyers and teachers. Teachers, in these years, were virtually nonexistent. Noah Webster, who later became famous for the dictionary he constructed, during this time in Baltimore, wanted to be well-known for his teaching. In one instance, he offered to teach music "scientifically" at a church. More substantial educational improvements in the form of regular, well-run academies were to come a little later for those with the means to pay. Yet, the situation for the children of the poor would take much longer to improve. In fact, some fifteen years after Tyson's arrival, someone, possibly Tyson himself, critically compared what Baltimore did for its poor, with what had been the case in Germantown, Pennsylvania. This critic condemned the money wasted on plays and the like which could have done more good by enriching the minds of the poor than the money chests of managers of frivolities.[17]

From the days of Tyson taking up residence in the city, however, in three substantial movements, the more important men of affairs spared no effort to bring these projects to successful conclusions. The merchant princes vigorously supported attempts to get the national and state governments moved to Baltimore, and to have a charter enacted for the city.

The competiton to select the nation's permanent capital, was mostly a competition between New York, Philadelphia, and Baltimore. The newspapers in Baltimore continually extolled the virtues of the city in late 1789, until the contest was finally settled more than a year later. The merchants of Baltimore were willing to underwrite the entire cost of a removal of the national government to the city. No matter the amount of financial burden the city leaders were willing to bear, Baltimore lost out in this effort, mainly because not all of Maryland's delegation in the House of Representatives believed enough in her possibilities. Those who did not vote for the city supported locating a capital on the Potomac.

The move to transfer the state government to Baltimore was similarly blocked by those refusing to give their consent to an effort which would enhance Baltimore. Perhaps the slower pace suited those accustomed to Annapolis, especially those many delegates coming from rural areas.[18]

The struggle to incorporate the city, thereby doing away with its loose governmental structure of boards and commissions, commenced also from the days of Tyson settling in the city, with success not coming until more than 15 years later. Many of these earlier attempts were based upon proposals narrowly drawn to suit some particular business interest. They died aborning. Some were thought so tyrannical in intent as those recent British efforts to hold and tax the colonies in "bondage" without representation.[19]

The proposal of 1793-94, in particular, was repulsive to those believing in equality as Tyson because it seemed bent upon denying citizenship rights to blacks. This particular proposal was ridiculed in a unique poetic rebuttal--part of which reads as follows:

This monster of a corporation, said Ralph,
would ruin half the nation;
Have I not, therefore, giv'n the wink
For men to look about and think;
Call'd boldly the Addresser Calf;
Who hop'd to catch old Birds with Chaff?
Have I not told, without offense,
What arrant fools are men of Sense,
And mar'd their labour'd work, with Dots
To shew the ignorant its Spots?

Have I not prov'd thy reasoning fair,
The right of Negroes to be <u>Mayor</u>?
Or limb of City Legislature,
Like any other human Creature;
Or <u>Judge</u> of Court, styl'd <u>Crim</u> or <u>Civil</u>
Though black as Chimney-Sweep or D_l;
And that we're <u>bound it should be so</u>,
By an Oath, as ye well know?
It follows, therefore, Clear as Light,
This Attempt is 'gainst the White;
For Council might resolve it smack,
Who were not <u>standard white</u> were black.
Hence, your <u>White Mayor</u> is a mere trick,
Contriv'd by men Aristocratic;
I therefore move to strike out white,
This said, the many hemned'd applause,
And Ralph took up another Cause.[20]

Such broadmindedness was rarely to be expressed so succinctly in newspaper accounts throughout the remainder
of the eighteenth century and even rarely so during the
entire nineteenth century.

Incorporation became a reality in 1797, but this
did not resolve all--by making city government entirely
authorized to care for the total or near total needs of
the environ and its population. As was the case when
Tyson settled there in 1781, much still had to be done
by individuals and collectives of individuals. This was
so with regard to most matters relating to the poor,
which included many blacks and this was also the case
with regard to the functioning of the fire companies.

Looking closer at the fire companies, they were
disjointed and served under no single subordinating authority for the longest time, even well into the nineteenth century. Periodically, however, Tyson and his
associates attemped to remedy this situation.

Tyson belonged to one of the oldest fire companies,
the Union Fire Company, founded by residents of Howard's
Hill in 1782. Tyson was often delegated to do important
duties by other members of the Union Fire Company. When
Engelhardt Cruse brought his newly invented fire engine
out for public inspection, Tyson was one of those given
authority to investigate the new apparatus. Tyson, also
periodically kept the keys to the engine house. At one
point in his life, it is related that he gave a fire
engine and carriage house to the public. At times,
Tyson was appointed to try to urge other fire companies
to adopt rules similar to those of his own company. In

December 1789, as several of the more important fire companies sought better cooperation among themselves, the Union was, naturally, well represented.

Doubtlessly, Tyson's involvement in poor relief work and with the activities of the fire companies gave him contact with all types of people and made his access to these same ones easier when he took to advocating a better treatment of blacks.[21]

During his first years of living in Baltimore, although Tyson invested time in numerous activities to promote the commonweal, yet he did not neglect his personal advancement to build further on that measure of wealth he had earned in Harford County. As a merchant-miller, it took him approximately twelve years to reach the rung of the very rich, and, as he himself described it, place himself beyond "the frowns of the world." Without question, in 1793, he was considered one of the richest men in Baltimore.

At this point in his life, Tyson was recorded in an English diarist account of a visit to Baltimore which took place in October 1793. In the diary, the traveller writes of how he and his companion were just about to cross an enclosed turnip garden, when an unknown voice, later found to belong to Tyson, called out to them not to trespass. The two men did as told and afterward had a most interesting conversation with Tyson. He spoke to them about many things including the operation of the poorhouse near his patch of turnips. During the conversation, the two Englishmen pointed out to Tyson the lack of scenic landscapes in Baltimore. The town looked half-baked, as it was. Land had been rapidly cleared to handle the booming business needs and population increases--thus, much was disfigured and not completed. At this juncture in the conversation, Tyson invited the two men home to stay the night and promised to show them, as the diarist said,

> . . . some curious flour mills on a new construction in which he is concerned, and also a country romantic and beautiful to that degree, that he did not doubt but we should be pleased with the expedition.[22]

These mills served for some time as the base of operations for Tyson's prosperity.

Several years later, when these mills, which were located on the Jones Falls river, had been finished, one observer described one of them as three stories high and quite elegant. It had two pairs of six-feet stones, two water wheels, and normally was capable of grinding out seventy thousand bushels of grain per year, but as a testimony to Tyson's industry and stamina, once ground eighty thousand bushels of wheat in an eleven-month period.

Besides noting his mills and wealth, the English diarist was extremely complimentary of Tyson's gracious hospitality. He said rarely had he and his companion been paid such careful attention in all their travels throughout America. Many travelers had become dependent upon the hospitality of strangers during these times of underpopulation and slight or nil public lodging conditions. Indeed, many believed it nearly their "inalienable" right that a stranger should open his door to them while traveling. Finding someone not so open and free led one man to send a letter to a newspaper to complain about being denied access to the bed and board of a gentleman. The slight was the more appalling felt by the traveller, as he had to seek shelter in a more lowly dwelling amongst Negroes. Whether true or not, but probably in keeping with the prevailing prejudice, the man added he got little sleep the whole night, being in constant fear of being robbed or having something worse happen.

Tyson's hospitality, however, was a genuine trait throughout his life and extended to all. His obituary stated some thirty years after the English diarist, when innkeeping and the population had increased, filling in some of the void by then, that

> To his hospitable board, were admitted, without distinction, the advocates of christianity (sic) whether rich or poor, bond or free, whether their complexions indicated them as descended from the frigid or torrid zone.

For a man who risked his life on many occasions for blacks, anything less would have been out of character or niggardly in a very peculiar manner.

Having reached the top rung of his business in the 1790s proved that Tyson knew how to give much of himself, both physically and spiritually. The milling business consisted of, besides involving the physically demanding operation of grinding, sorting and packing flour; also, for those like Tyson, merchant-millers, it

14

entailed bartering, shipping, and managing money as a banker. Other physical aspects of the business required a miller to diligently secure his right to water at his mill seat along streams and rivers that nobody really owned, but which anybody could interfere with. The stones from which the wheels were made to grind the wheat were of vital importance as well; and in the 1780s, it seemed the best kinds were from Europe--French or Cologne burr. Good stone did not overheat, causing fires--an occupational hazard--especially at the height of the harvest season. The best stone, also, did not deposit particles in the flour or discolor it. Not until after the Revolutionary War did local stones become popular and plentiful. All in all, however, milling was very profitable, when profitable, and, at times, even taxes could be paid in wheat at designated mills.

Tyson seems to have conducted most of his business from the time of his arrival in Baltimore to around 1785 at his flour store on Cheapside Dock, near the County Wharf in the basin area of the harbor--the western extremity. In addition to trading in flour, at times he dealt in such items as bar iron, fish oil, rum, Narraganset cheese, mackeral, cider, herring, salt, port, sugar, and boat boards. While he bought or sold the above items, he also on occasion offered for sale ships with their entire cargo. Once the brig Bald-Hill with all its goods was put up for sale. She was laden with 151 tons of cargo. A couple of days later he asked for 4,500 barrels of flour to fill the hull of the Bald-Hill, bound for the West Indies; apparently, no one bought the ship. Other ships which Tyson may have had some interest in were the sloop Polly, captained by a Mr. Sweet from Rhode Island, and the schooner Matilda, captained by Moses Pierce, also of Rhode Island.

Upon his arrival in Baltimore, it appears that at first Tyson went into business, much on his own; but, not too long afterward, he operated in several partnerships. One of his earliest business associates was the Quaker Joseph Anderson, who came from Bucks County, Pennsylvania. Another major partnership was with Thomas Hough, also of Bucks County, Pennsylvania, and likewise a Quaker. The two firms respectively were called Tyson & Anderson, and Tyson, Hough and Company. Tyson also held a share in two other concerns. These two seemed to operate mainly in his old base in Harford County. With John Dickinson, he was associated in Dickinson & Tyson and with his brother, Jesse, in Jesse Tyson and Company.[23]

Being an active miller, Tyson came to know the others in his trade in the Baltimore area and especially those of prominence--many of whom were Quakers. Of this group, the most prominent were the Ellicotts, natives of Bucks County, Pennsylvania, and founders of Ellicott Mills about ten miles outside of Baltimore in 1772. They, as did the Tysons, earned most of their wealth after the Revolutinary War. Taking advantage of the excellent business climate in Baltimore, the Ellicotts maintained family representatives in the city. Other Quaker millers associated with Tyson in Baltimore were the Stumps, who at first operated around Deer Creek, Harford County, and the Wilsons, whose base of operations had been in the area of Bel Air, also in Harford County. The Hollingsworths were the most important non-Quaker millers in Baltimore with whom Tyson had contact.

As it seems the more successful millers were not individual millers, but families of millers; so it was the case with the Tysons. Elisha Tyson was the oldest child in his family and, as such, took an interest in seeing his brothers and relatives prosper. Nathan, the third eldest, had from early 1789, at least, operated out of a flour store on Cheapside Dock, prior to a move to Ellicott's Wharf in September 1792. In addition to flour, he sold much St. Domingo Coffee. Also, he seems to have dealt with New York firms and, perhaps, specialized in discounting New York notes. He also seems to have handled more dried Indian cornmeal than wheat. George Tyson operated out of Mexico Mills, sometimes known as Onion Mills after its owner, John Onion. It was on the Little Falls of the Gunpowder. George Tyson also dealt in kiln-dried Indian cornmeal and had a store in the city on County Wharf. The youngest brother, Jesse, was very active and seems to have been about as successful, if not more so, than his brother, Elisha. He took over Elisha's property in Harford County. Jacob, second oldest, seems to have had no sustained interest in milling after helping Elisha get started in the 1770s.[24]

Other relatives and in-laws got a helping hand from Tyson, as well. It was at the family's property in Harford County that Moses Sheppard, a first cousin, got his business experience in the milling trade. Indeed, Elisha's brother-in-law, John Mitchell, and Sheppard, had a very active partnership in the flour business. Edward Norris, who married into the Amos Family as did Tyson, received assistance from Elisha. Thereafter, the Norrises and Tysons paths crossed several times in the milling business and in marriage relationships.[25]

As Tyson prospered, so did his participation in matters that gave evidence to his success and worth in the business community. In 1786, he joined with other businessmen to set a rate of exchange for Maryland's money, particularly its copper coins because of the disadvantages the Maryland currency suffered in money markets in surrounding states. In 1790, he was authorized with some others by the General Assembly "to lay out a road not exceeding forty feet wide from their mill seats on Jones Falls to Baltimore Town."

In 1791, Tyson was to the fore when the issue of public vendue was taken up. It was the general complaint that the General Assembly granted a few, exclusive rights for a fee to auction certain merchandise being imported. The protesters thought this monopolistic, against free trade, and plainly forbidden by the 39th article of the State Constitution. Of the approximately 170 firms protesting the vendue offices, Tyson's was third from the top and many of his associates were there as well.

Interestingly enough, some years later, the family continued to be opposed to vendue offices. In an 1800 campaign, Mitchell and Sheppard, operating a dry goods and grocery business, headed a list of some 72 companies who joined together to try to have the public vendues abolished. These two, Sheppard and Mitchell, with a few others, served as monitors of the others, seeing to it that the association formed to resist the public vendues, lived up to their agreement not to buy from these agents unless for the benefit of underwriters or insolvent debtors.[26]

As for himself, Elisha Tyson, toward the end of the eighteenth century, had removed himself far from the ranks of the insolvent debtor. He joined with the other well-off residents to petition for an exclusion of roaming herds of hogs within the city because they tended to destroy improved property—blight the accomplishments of those who had worked the last twenty years to build up Baltimore. It was also in this time frame that Tyson was beginning to withdraw from an active day-to-day concern with milling, turning over this part to his sons and partners.

With so strong a tie, and ever-increasing tie to the community of Baltimore, as represented by the Tyson clan's heavy participation in businesses of the city; Elisha, as chief amongst them, was a person with whom to be reckoned in all that was of concern to him in

Baltimore--no matter whether the nature of that concern dealt with fire companies, the poor, or the betterment of the condition of the blacks. Even before he was very wealthy, however, Tyson served as the heart of a group of like-minded men of means from the various denominations of the city who were interested in the abolition of slavery and other improvements in the community as well. In 1789, these men joined together to form the first abolition society in Maryland. Key personages to this endeavor were some other Tyson family members, of course, and numerous other Quakers in and outside of the milling trade. Some of the more important Quakers were Joseph Townsend, James Carey, and the Evan Thomas family.[27]

Joseph Townsend, who served as secretary throughout the existence of the society, was the person most responsible for organizing the society. In the late 1770s, he moved from Chester County, Pennsylvania, to Harford County, and taught in a Quaker school there; and, by 1783, Townsend had settled in Baltimore. In one of his other more important promotional concerns outside abolitionism, he was chief organizer of the Baltimore Equitable Society, a mutual fire insurance company, and served as chief executive officer of that company for 47 years. Elisha Tyson was one of the original forty-nine subscribers to the Equitable Society which notified the general public of its existence on January 21, 1794 in the local newspapers.[28]

James Carey, a Quaker convert, was one of the wealthiest shippers in Baltimore. In 1785, he married an Ellicott, and as such stood near the center of the benevolent-spirited-happenings in Baltimore. Carey was also an organizer and later president of the first bank in Maryland, Bank of Maryland.[29]

Evan Thomas, before moving to Baltimore, was a Quaker minister from Montgomery County, Maryland, who freed his slaves and gave them land. Afterward, he was noted for preaching against slaveholding. His son, Philip Evan Thomas, who had a very successful hardware business, was also a worthy opponent of slavery who served in positions of trust among his fellow Quakers, often as a clerk. He was, as well, entrusted with responsibility in the community-at-large, at various times being secretary or treasurer on many projects involving the entire community. In the late 1820s, he and his brother promoted the initiation of commercial railroading in the United States. In this regard, Philip served as the first president of the Baltimore and Ohio Railroad, the first incorporated railroad in the United States.[30]

18

From amongst the other prominent men of the city to associate with Tyson in the founding of the first abolition society and assist him in his many other worthwhile projects, and initiate some of their own, many came from the evangelical sects; they mostly were Methodists, German Evangelical Reformists, and Baptists.

Adam Fonerden was one of the most active Methodists in the concern of this, so to speak, abolitionist-minded, benevolent directorate; this group of willing workers, whose names appeared on the subscription lists of most public-spirited projects, and which revolved around Elisha Tyson. From a business point, and at various times, Fonerden was a blacksmith, shoe store owner and, later, having earned some money, an active investor. He participated in the establishment of the first Methodist church in Baltimore and in 1776 was appointed a trial minister in his denomination. Three times he served as president of the abolition society; in addition, he also helped to organize and became first president of the Baltimore Mechanical Society, an organization of craftsmen and artisans. At times he worked as an energetic member, along with Joseph Townsend, of the Board of Health.

A similarly active and benevolent-minded Methodist who also was a flour miller and owner of one of the oldest wharves in the city was Jesse Hollingsworth. Without compensation, and at risk to his own life during the Revolutionary War, Hollingsworth supplied bread to American prisoners held in Philadelphia by the British. Hollingsworth was such a central figure in poor relief work, along with Peter Hoffman, another Tyson associate, that as efforts in 1811 to relieve the poor got underway unusually late, one observer said:

> May we not indeed with truth exclaim Hollingsworth and Hoffman are dead! Yes, ye poor of Baltimore, these faithful, constant friends of yours, are dead!

As old men, the strenuous manner in which Hollingsworth and Hoffman worked to preserve the City Springs as a fresh-water supply, was said to have contributed to their deaths by 1811. Their endeavors in ths project led the city to erect a monument on the spot at which they had given, perhaps, too much of themselves.[31]

From the German Evangelical Reform Church, founding members of the abolition society included Leonard Harbaugh and Peter Hoffman. These men had also been founding elders of their church. Harbaugh was an architect, builder, and inventor. He built many houses, churches, taverns, warehouses, and bridges in Baltimore. Hoffman was a prominent dry goods merchant who served the city as a selectman before its incorporation in 1797, and as a city councilman afterward. He also served as well as trustee of the almshouse and Female Humane Association Charity School.[32]

David Shields, a master hatter; George Presstman, a tradesman; and Nathan Griffith, a tavern owner, were among the founders of the Baptist church in Baltimore, who as well were charter members of the state's first abolition society. Indeed, sometimes the abolition society held its meetings at Griffith's tavern. By the 1790s, Griffith changed the name of his place to "Rights of Man," an indication of where his heart lay with regard to oppression in general.[33]

Before the coalition of these and many other "respectable" gentlemen in 1789 to form the abolition society, the struggle to rid the state of slavery was well underway, but perhaps in a less organized fashion. As early as 1784, the Society of Friends in Maryland took up the concern of some of its members who, ignorant of the laws of the state which forbade the manumission of slaves, had freed some blacks, but, who then desired to petition the General Assembly to make it certain their former slaves would not be reenslaved. At the same meeting in which the above problem was discussed, Friends appointed a committee to accompany several Negroes who were eager to present a petition of their own before the Legislature in Annapolis. In 1787, a more significant abolitionist campaign took place, as Samuel Chase led an all-out attempt to secure enactment of a bill of emancipation in the Maryland General Assembly. Chase had just taken up residence in Baltimore in 1787, in time to be immediately elected to the General Assembly. When the abolition society was organized, he became an honorary counsel of the organization.

In 1788, Maryland Quakers renewed efforts before the Legislature on behalf of blacks. At the Baltimore Yearly Meeting, held at Third Haven on June 7, 1788, reports of the previous year's efforts on behalf of blacks read rather dismally. Those appointed to attend the Legislature informed the rest of the Meeting that the petition for emancipation had been voted down, but the committee was prepared to renew the petition the following year. It is not known if Tyson accompanied the 1788 delegation to Annapolis, but the group designated to journey to the state capital in 1789 included Jesse Tyson.

Hand in hand with the petitioning of the Legislature and the personal pleading of some for slavery's abolition, in the few years prior to 1789, many letters to the editor appeared in local newspapers criticizing slavery and its incongruity in America, a land just freed from what some were too willing to term British "slavery." Supposedly some of these pieces, and perhaps broadsides as well, were written at the behest of Elisha Tyson, who, according to his nephew, wrote little himself but relied upon others to be his amanuensis, incorporating his thoughts in literary productions. Some of the correspondents took the pen names of "Justus Americanus," "Benevolus," "Othello," and "Philanthropos."

"Justus Americanus" observed, in a communication, that neither arts nor science would flourish in a state where so many of its residents were slaves. In a later opinion, the same writer thought it an outrage that slavery should be continued because some feared business stagnation--in his opinion, slavery already contributed to a depresssion in the economy. "Benevolus" appeared on the scene about the same time as "Justus Americanus" and generally supported his views. The pieces of "Othello" came in response to the National Constitutional Convention held in Philadelphia in 1787 which failed to do something about what this writer thought even worse than slavery itself--the international slave trade.[34]

After the establishment of the Maryland Society for the Abolition of Slavery in 1789, the struggle for equal rights had near immediate notable successes. One success was in attracting William Pinkney, an excellent orator and member of the House of Delegates from Harford County, to the cause. Tyson, himself, may have been mainly responsible for this as the two men were previously well acquainted with each other. Pinkney's efforts in the General Assembly brought about the repeal of the act of 1753 which severely restricted the rights of individuals to manumit their slaves. Another success of the society involved having Granville Sharp, the leading English emancipationist from the 1760s, to his death in the early 1800s, as an honorary member of Maryland's society. He provided them with advice and the prestige of his name. It is worthwhile to note that after a leading British abolitionist toured the United States in the 1840s and reflected on the history of abolitionism in America, some twenty years after Tyson's death, he referred to Tyson's preeminence in the struggle for abo-

21

lition by calling him "the Granville Sharp of North America."[35]

How true it was that Tyson deserved such a comparison with Sharp, perhaps, can be seen in the range of intensity and geography which was present in the society's fight to free two Indian slaves. Tyson belonged to the most important committee of the abolition society, the Acting Committee. As such in 1790, he, along with a few others, took under consideration the plight of two allegedly illegally enslaved Indians named Simon and Fortune, whose mother had lived in Florida, New York. In Maryland it was supposedly against the law to hold Indians in slavery. The effort to establish these two men's claims to freedom took Maryland abolitionist investigators to places in Pennsylvania, New Jersey, and New York. The abolitionists pursued this case with such tenacity that it brought down upon their heads the condemnation of the General Assembly, controlled by slaveholders.

Tyson, for his part, raised money and gave a great deal of his own to pay the unusually high cost of court in a losing trial with the alleged owners of the Indians. The abolitionists had the right to appeal the judgment and would have, however, had not a law been passed by the Legislature at the insistence of the Indians' court-confirmed owners, which made it illegal to reinstitute a court suit unless judgments of a previous suit were carried out and court costs paid up. Having exhausted the treasury of the society, and with Tyson at that time in the midst of dissolving his flour business partnerships to go into business on his own, and as such, probably not sure of his own financial situation, no money would likely be forthcoming if the Indians' appeals were lost in a second trial. As legal action seemed unwise, and with no other recourse, it was claimed by the Indians captured that Simon and Fortune were encouraged by abolitionists to run away. Perhaps Tyson was one of those so urging. 36

As the abolition society became firmly established, providing for the formal education of blacks, especially free blacks, became essential to plans devoted to their elevation. On July 7, 1792, the society appointed a committee to secure subscriptions for erecting a permanent school for blacks. Before this time, blacks were fitfully educated, if at all, by kind-hearted individuals, as indicated in the following advertisement which appeared in the 1780s.

22

> A person of a liberal Profession is desirous
> of trying a benevolent Experiment, by in-
> structing an ingenious Negro Lad in a Business
> that will give him if ingenious and docile, an
> accurate knowledge of the English language,
> and besides rendering him really a rational
> Creature, will enable him in due time, to earn
> handsome Wages.[37]

In addition, it is quite possible that before 1792,
through some of Baltimore's abolitionist-minded mechanics and tradesmen, other blacks as apprentices received
a rudimentary education. With Adam Fonerden occupying,
at times, both the presidencies of the abolition society
and the mechanics society, it is highly likely that he
may have encouraged such an approach amongst the men he
knew.

Whatever the extent of the individual efforts at
educating blacks may have been, this was not enough and
the abolition society continued to plan for a permanent
school. While the funds were still being solicited to
build the school, it seems that the society employed
Jonathan Coates, a Quaker, to open a temporary school at
the end of James Jaffrey's brick warehouse, near the
central market. But, the subscription collection continued to move rather slowly; not until January 27,
1794, had a committee, consisting of Jamey Carey and
some others, been appointed to purchase a suitable plot
of land for the building. Eventually, the money
directed to purchase the land was saved when Carey gave
the ground upon which the building was to be raised.

The African Academy was finally completed by June
1797. When completed, it was probably one of the first
such substantial structures raised by abolitionists in
the United States from the ground, especially dedicated
for educating blacks. Other Negro schools, particularly
those in New York and Philadelphia, were renovated
buildings, except for one seemingly much smaller school
in Philadelphia. The building also served as a place of
worship and a general meeting place for the black community. 38

Elisha Tyson had an important part in the establishment of the first African school structure. He took
it upon himself to promote its acceptance in the community, at first extremely hostile to the idea of blacks
being taught to read and write, being given an opportunity to be something other than virtual, helpless de-
pendents. No doubt the fear that blacks would write

passes for slaves or instruct the slaves in understanding and valuing freedom and equality was too unsettling for some to contemplate. Perhaps this is the essential reason for the long time it took for the project to come to fruition, about five years after the proposal was first introduced. Tyson's brother, Jesse, was a trustee of the Academy. Later, Elisha Tyson, himself, gave other visible support to this struggling school-church complex by deliberately moving to the block where the building stood. He either bought or had built houses for himself and four of his children on the same street as the Academy. Indeed, the four houses of his children were immediately across the street from the building. Up the street from the Academy lived Moses Sheppard and, in general, surrounding the building were those abolitionists most committed to its survival.[39]

Baltimore's abolitionists, and especially the Ellicotts, were interested in another way in promoting the idea that blacks were full men, more than brutes, with minds capable of reasoning; and thereby justly entitled to their freedom in terms of all of the prevailing - philosophic sentiments of the day. Benjamin Banneker, a free black with little formal education, a genius in the raw, was ably assisted in several endeavors that eventually made him the most widely known Negro of the 1790s. He resided near Ellicott Mills. His fame as America's first black scientist rests mainly on an almanac he calculated; although, other achievements, such as making a clock and being a part of the survey team that mapped out the land which became the nation's capital, were notable accomplishments in themselves.

In 1791, Thomas Jefferson received a manuscript copy of Banneker's first to-be-published almanac. The intent was to change Jefferson's well-publicized opinion that belittled the intellectual capacity of blacks. Banneker had received some assistance from George Ellicott with his calculations and was encouraged by other local abolitionists in the publication of the work. He completed several other almanacs that were distributed, like his first, throughout Maryland, Pennsylvania, Delaware, and Virginia.

Banneker's work may or may not have influenced Jefferson, but it is known to have affected the international scene. In a letter dated February 3, 1792, sent from an Englander to a Philadelphian at the time of the debates on the suppression of the African slave trade in the British Parliament, the writer thanked his correspondent for copies of Banneker's almanac. The effect of Banneker's little book caused many in the Parliamentary debates to abandon frank expressions about the lack of intellectual capacity amongst blacks. With so much attention coming to Banneker, it has to be believd that his life was inspirational to other black Baltimoreans.

In addition to Banneker's uniqueness, in 1792, another black Baltimorean responded to the liberalizing atmosphere being promoted by Tyson and his associates. Thomas Brown, a free black, decided to run for one of the two House of Delegate seats allotted the city. In a day when blacks were not even enfranchised in some states; or, if enfranchised in others, custom forbade many from voting, not to mention running for office, Brown's decision to run for office was probably unique as well. Even in Maryland, the February prior to Brown's decision to run for office, the State Legislature passed a billed to disfranchise blacks. But it seems that in Baltimore, at least, up to 1811, some Negroes were still voting.[40]

Brown served as a soldier in the War of Independence and also served by appointment in some public office. He promised, if elected, to promote the Union and root out of office any remaining Tories or antifederalists. In his campaign statement to the people of Baltimore, Brown stated his reason for running despite the attitude of some against black involvement in politics. He said the liberal climate of Baltimore caused him to:

> ....conceive that justice and equality will excite you to choose one Man of Colour to represent so many hundreds of poor Blacks as inhabit this town, as well as several thousands in the different parts of the state.[41]

Not much else is known about this interesting man.

In considering the few, but significant activities of Banneker and Brown, and one other remarkable Baltimore black, Joshua Johnston, perhaps the nation's most substantial black portrait painter of this period, one has some indication of the quality of abolitionism in Baltimore that was somewhat supportive of free black life. The quality of abolitionism in the city in the 1790s was, however, only the beginning or foundation phase of a process that eventually made Baltimore have the largest concentration of free blacks by the time of the Civil War; and made it, unofficially, the nation's black capital, most vital black community throughout most of the nineteenth century.[42]

Whatever may have been the distinction of Banneker, Brown, and Johnston, their fame did not affect much, the most horrendous manner in which blacks were treated by the average white. This scandalous behavior was not hidden, either, but was there for any to see. In a letter to a newspaper editor in July 1795, as the nation had just revelled and exalted in self-praise for the extension of freedom it had brought to the world in defeating the British a few years before, "Parisienne" reminded the public of its unfinished tasks. The writer spoke of the dastardly way other free blacks, who were not of Banneker's stature, whom he mentioned by name, were being robbed of their freedom at times with the connivance of public officials. He wrote of the case of one justice of the peace destroying a free black's freedom papers, then bringing him before a court, where he was subsequently confined as a runaway slave, and eventually sold out for hire to pay his jail expenses, with the justice getting part of the profit.

"Parisienne" also found regrettable, that so many black revolutionary soldiers were similarly subject to the worst kind of treatment, though they had contributed a share to giving birth to the country. A week later, after "Parisienne's" article appeared, his sentiments were seconded by "A Philanthropist," who thought free blacks unduly harassed if found without their freedom papers and thought they should be indemnified for being falsely arrested too often, instead of being made to pay for the cost of their maintenance in jail as was the practice. 43

The plight of the freed black and those justly entitled to their freedom was a problem of immense proportions which Elisha Tyson vigorously tried to correct. Indeed, he expended so much energy in that regard that at his death in 1824, his obituary stated:

.....so widespread was his fame among the colored people of Baltimore, that all who consider their liberty endangered, or improperly withheld, flew to him for protection.

Those he helped to obtain their freedom and prevent from illegal enslavement ran into the thousands. In this regard, his obituary said:

To no private individual, in Europe or America, it is believed, can be traced an equal number.

Tyson never sought publicity or extracted praise from those he helped, for he considered his activities a duty owed God, and

....having effected the deliverance from slavery, by legal means, of fellow beings, when he considered them capable by their own industry to support themselves, he dismissed them with a suitable admonition, touching their future conduct, and...if children, his care did not relax until he placed them by indenture under suitable guardians.[44]

Tyson's activities on this score consumed an inordinate amount of time, and explains why he eventually had to retire from business.

With a willingness to come between a man and his slave, Tyson naturally incurred the wrath of men who thought they were entitled to hold their property with a tight grip, especially as the highest national documents regarded property rights as near sacrosanct. There are a few recorded instances when this interference was openly criticized. In one case, in particular, Tyson seemed to have stirred the ire of Christopher Hughes. The case involved Negro Jim, 6'2" a bricklayer by trade, who had formerly belonged to widow James, who lived near Charlestown at the head of the Chesapeake Bay. Hughes put up a $50.00 reward for the return of Jim who had abandoned him. Judging from what he placed in the advertisement, one would think that Hughes did not really want his slave returned.

Jim was described in the advertisement as being awkward, ugly, and disgusting. Being property, however, he cost so many dollars, and this was, after all, the heart of the matter. Hughes further stated:

The subscriber would have advertised him sooner, but was informed by a certain Elisha Tyson, that the Abolition Society, or that a deputation or committee of the Abolitionists had the fellow in keeping, to get him his freedom. The subscriber told Mr. Tyson that he held in abhorrence holding any person in improper bondage and bid him or his associates bring the fellow forward to claim his freedom in a legal matter. It is hard to be deprived

27

of the labor of my negro (sic) for whom I paid four hundred dollars, without receiving one month's service from him.[45]

What was implicated in Hughes' advertisement may actually have been the case; Tyson probably aided fugitive slaves to escape to freedom; because Hughes added he believed Jim was sulking about Charlestown.

The matter of assisting slaves to run away was also on the mind of a Maryland representative in the United States Congress in December 1796 when the House dissolved to meet as a committee of the whole at the suggestion of a congressman from Delaware to consider remedies to stop the rampant practice of the kidnapping of free blacks by means of sea conveyances. The congressman from Maryland, however, mindful of his slaveholding constituency, turned the intent of the meeting on its head. He insisted, instead, that the House consider the problem of those who assisted slaves to become free--aided slaves to run away.

This Free State representative objected to the strict law which hindered a slave owner obtaining too easily the proper degree of proof that a person assisted one of his slaves to abscond. Likewise, he thoughts it too hard to obtain damages from those easily suspected of assisting the slave to abscond. Furthermore, he said, with surely feigned ignorance, that he did not understand the meaning of the word "kidnapping". He did not know whether it applied to those abolitionists running off slaves as it did apply to those persons illegally depriving blacks of their freedom. Assisting slaves to run away from Maryland was, so the Maryland congressman thought, of a grave magnitude. He said the business:

....had been greatly encouraged by the false philosophy and misplaced philanthropy of the advocates of emancipation.[46]

This congressman had in mind, no doubt, Elisha Tyson and friends.

About a couple of years later, Tyson was again publicly accused in so many words of harboring runaway slaves. Ruth Norwood on Belair Road had several slaves abscond, and with this in mind she described her people, saying,

These Negroes were seen at the house of a Mr. Tyson, in Hanover Street, a few days since, and are at this time, supposed to be concealed near the turnpike gate, on the road to Hook's town.[47]

In that same year, 1801, a reward of $10.00 was offered for Milly, about twenty-one, five feet high, yellowish complexion, who formerly belonged to John Oldham of Baltimore. Her present owner wanted her back and said, cautiously, that it seems she had lived with Tyson last summer.[48]

It seems likely that blacks in the vicinity of Tyson's house were a part of such efforts as the Maryland congressmen said, of "kidnapping to make free," because one slave owner accused those blacks in that area of harboring his property and that, in fact, the slave, was lured away from his house by some "miscreant," one of abolitionist sentiments, no doubt.

Because not many could withstand the tremendous pressure to conform to the wishes of the strong slave power in the state or resist the lure of a notion that represented slavery as beneficial and necessary for prosperity and controlling an "alien", dangerous element in the community, at the turn of the century, abolitionism and the abolition society in Baltimore were practically dead. As an indication of this, toward the end of 1798, Upton Bruce, an abolitionist-miller, and member of the House of Delegates from Frederick County, introduced a bill in the Legislature calling for gradual emancipation that created such a howl it had to be withdrawn. Although Bruce withdrew his bill, he declared his intention to bring the matter up again in the following year. If he did so, it is now known. The abolition society in Baltimore was dead at the turn of the century. Tyson and some few others, however, were to remain active in promoting the betterment of blacks in the next century as Baltimore became the black capital of the nineteenth century.[49]

NOTES

Chapter I

[1]William I. Hull, William Penn and the Dutch Migration to Pennsylvania (Baltimore: Genealogical Publishing Co., 1970, c. 1935), pp. 221-222; E. T. Kidder, "The Tyson Family (n.p.), p. 3.

[2]Thomas E. Drake, Quakers and Slavery in America (Gloucester, Mass.: Peter Smith, 1965, c. 1950), pp. 13, 77, 78, 82, 115.

[3]See, in general, Sydney V. James, A People Among Peoples: Quaker Benevolence in Eighteenth-Century America (Cambridge, Mass.: Harvard University Press, 1963; Howard H. Brinton, Friends for 300 Years (Wallingford Pa.: Pendle Hill Quakerback, 1965); Peter Brock, Pioneers of the Peaceable Kingdom (Princeton: Princeton University Press, 1968).

[4]Lawrence B. Thomas, Genealogical Notes (Baltimore: Lawrence B. Thomas, 1877), p. 150.

[5]Samuel W. Pennypacker, The Settlement of Germantown, Pennsylvania, and the Beginning of German Emigration to North America (Philadelphia: William J. Campbell, 1899), p. 3; American, February 28, 1824, p. 2; Ella K. Barnard, "Elisha Tyson, Philanthropist and Emancipator," The Journal of the Friends' Historical Society, 9 (April 1912):108-112.

[6]See, Thomas E. Drake; Robert Vaux, Memoirs of the Lives of Benjamin Lay and Ralph Sandiford (Philadelphia: Solomon W. Conrad, 1815), p. 50; Brightwen Roundtree, "Benjamin Lay," The Journal of the Friends' Historical Society, 33 (1936):3; George S. Brookes, Friend Anthony Benezet (Philadelphia: n.p., 1937), p. 27.

[7]William B. Marye, "Place Names of Baltimore and Harford Counties," Maryland Historical Magazine, 8 (March 1958):50; Harford Land Records, JLG, No. A 1777 to 1778, P. 77; Kidder, pp. 3-4; Milton Wright, Our Harford Heritage (n.p.: C. Milton Wright, 1967), p. 200; Minutes of Baltimore Meeting for Sufferings, 1791.

[8]Maryland Journal (Supplement), January 15, 1782, p. 1; February 12, 1782, p. 2; March 12, 1782, p. 1; March 26, 1782, p. 3; (Extraordinary) September 24, 1782, p. 1.

[9]Johann D. Schoepf, Travels in the Confederation, 1783-1784, translated by Alford Morrison (Philadelphia: William J. Campbell, 1911) II, p. 326; Ronald Hoffman, A Spirit of Dissension: Economics, Politics, and the Revolution in Maryland (Baltimore: The Johns Hopkins Press, 1973), pp. 74-80; David T. Gilchrist, ed., The Growth of the Seaport Cities, 1790-1825 (Charlottesville, Va.: Published for the Eluterian Mills-Hagley Foundation by the University Press of Virginia, 1967), pp. 62-67.

[10]Maryland Journal, September 18, 1781, p. 2; July 30, 1782, p. 2; August 6, 1782, p. 1; Lee Kenneth, The French Forces in America, 1780-1783 (Westport, Conn.: Greenwood Press, 1977), p. 156.

[11]See, in general, Ceclia M. Holland, Ellicott City, Maryland, Mill Town, U.S.A. (Chicago: Ceclia M. Holland, 1970); Maryland Journal, April 2, 1782, p. 3.

[12]Maryland Journal, April 30, 1782, p. 3, July 23, 1782, p. 4.

[13]Henry Harbaugh, Annals of the Harbaugh Family in America, from 1736 to 1856 (Chambersburg, Pa.: M. Kieffer & Co., 1856), p. 95; Maryland Journal, October 8, 1784, p. 2; December 29, 1789, p. 3; April 16, 1790, p. 3; June 29, 1790; July 13, 1789, p. 3; Maryland Gazette (Baltimore), July 24, 1789, p. 3.

[14]Maryland Journal, October 9, 1781, p. 3; October 16, 1781, P. 3; September 3, 1782, p. 3; October 8, 1782, p. 3; December 19, 1782, p. 2.

[15]Maryland Journal, May 26, 1778; March 20, 1781, p. 1; September 3, 1782, p. 3; October 15, 1784, p. 2; Federal Gazette, April 28, 1800, p. 2.

[16]Baltimore Meeting of Suffering, 1784, p. 41; Maryland Gazette (Baltimore), August 20, 1784, p. 2.

[17]Maryland Journal, August 3, 1784, p. 3; December 7, 1784, p. 15; May 27, 1785, p. 3; July 19, 1785, p. 2. Maryland Gazette (Baltimore), January 10, 1786, p. 3; Federal Gazette, March 2, 1796, p. 3.

[18]Maryland Gazette (Baltimore), January 14, 1786, January 27, 1786, p. 1; February 3, 1786, p. 3; February 7, 1786, p. 2; February 28, 1786, p. 3; Maryland Journal, February 10, 1789, p. 2; February 13, 1789, p. 2; Maryland Gazette (Baltimore), June 25, 1790, p. 4.

[19]Maryland Journal, April 2, 1782, p. 3; November 16, 1784, p. 2; March 7, 1786, pp. 1-2; March 10, 1786, p. 2.

[20]Maryland Journal, February 10, 1794, p. 3

[21]The Union Fire Company Book, 1782-1805, M.H.S. Maryland Gazette (Baltimore), December 1, 1789, p. 3.

[22]Correspondence from Wook Nook (n.p., n.d.), p. 13; American, February 28, 1824, p. 4; Harriet P. Marine for Dr. William I. Hull, Chart Tyson Family of Pennsylvania and Maryland, 1930, p. 2; Maryland Journal, April 9, 1790, p. 3.

[23]Maryland Journal, October 28, 1785, p. 1; November 1, 1785, p. 3; December 30, 1785, p. 1; July 11, 1786, p. 3; October 13, 1786, p. 3; August 4, 1789, p. 3; November 1, 1791, p. 3; Baltimore Land Records, W.G., No. G.G., 1791, p. 218; Martha E. Tyson, A Brief Account of the Settlement of Ellicott's Mills (Baltimore: Maryland Historical Society, 1865), pp. 33-34, 40, 42.

[24]Maryland Journal, December 1, 1789, p. 3; November 1, 1791, p. 3; September 7, 1792, p. 3; July 23, 1793; Baltimore Daily Repository, September 25, 1793, p. 1; Federal Gazette, March 27, 1795, p. 3.

[25]Lavens M. Thomas, Moses Sheppard, 1775-1857 (n.p.: 1941), p. 10; See, in general, Bliss Forbush, Moses Sheppard: Quaker Philanthropist of Baltimore (Philadelphia: J. B. Lippincott, 1968), p. 44; Federal Gazette, May 2, 1798, p. 3; January 29, 1799, p. 1; February 24, 1801, p. 3; March 8, 1802, p. 3; June 29, 1809; Telegraphe, February 4, 1817, p. 3; May 3, 1800, p. 3.

[26]Maryland Journal, January 11, 1791, p. 3; Federal Gazette, October 30, 1798, p. 3.

[27]Maryland Journal, September 22, 1789, p. 3; Baltimore Gazette, October 2, 1789, p. 4; December 15, 1789, p. 3.

[28]Joseph Townsend, Some Account of the British Army Under the Command of General Howe, and of the Battle of Brandywine on the Memorable September 11, 1777 (Philadelphia: Press of the Historical Society of Pennsylvania, 1846), p. 15; Federal Gazette, January 25, 1794, p. 1; June 26, 1797, p. 3.

[29]James Carey, Biographical File, Maryland Room, Enoch Pratt Free Library, Baltimore, Maryland.

[30]Lawrence B. Thomas, p. 151.

[31]James E. Armstrong, History of the Old Baltimore Conference from the Planting of Methodism in 1773 to the Division of the Conference in 1857 (Baltimore: King Bros., Printers, 1907), pp. 18, 30; Louis P. Henninghausen, History of the German Society of Maryland (Baltimore: W.E.C. Harrison & Sons, Booksellers and Stationers, 1909), p. 48; Maryland Journal, February 12, 1793, p. 3; July 26, 1793, p. 2; January 29, 1794, p. 3; January 28, 1795, p. 2; Jesse Hollingsworth, Biographical File, Maryland Room, Enoch Pratt Free Library, Baltimore, Maryland; Maryland Gazette, January 17, 1811, p. 3.

[32]A.W. Drury, The Life of Rev. Phillip William Otterbein, Founder of the Church of the United Brethren in Christ (Dayton, Ohio: United Brethren Publishing House, 1884), pp. 165, 182, 184, 251, 288, 291, 372; History of the Baltimore City and County Almshouse, 1820, Vertical File, M.H.S.

[33]J. F. Weishampel, History of Baptist Churches in Maryland Connected with the Maryland Baptist Union Association (Baltimore: Author, 1885), pp. 31, 33.

[34]Minutes of Baltimore Meeting for Sufferings, 1784, pp. 39-40; Maryland Journal, December 16, 1785, p. 2; January 3, 1786, p. 2; January 17, 1786, p.2; September 14, 1787, p. 3; September 21, 1787, p. 3; September 28, 1787, p. 3; October 5, 1787, p. 2; April 15, 1788, p. 2; May 6, 1788, p. 1; May 16, 1788, p. 1; September 23, 1788, p. 2; (Extraordinary) October 4, 1788, p. 1.

[35]John Tyson, pp. 21, 23; Granville Sharp, Letter from Granville Sharp, Esq., of London, to the Maryland Society for Promoting the Abolition of Slavery (Baltimore: The Society, 1793), pp. 3-5; Joseph Sturge, A Visit to the United States in 1841 (New York: Augustus M. Kelley Publishers, 1969, c. 1842), p. 10.

[36]Maryland Journal, May 18, 1790, p. 3; February 10, 1792, p. 1; February 14, 1793, p. 1; Letter, Joseph Townsend to James Pemberton, November 14, 1790, H.S.P.

[37]Maryland Journal, January 18, 1785, p. 3.

[38]Extracts of Minutes of the Maryland Abolition Society, September 19, 1789, H.S.P.; _Maryland Journal_, July 20, 1792, p. 3; _Federal Gazette_, June 26, 1797, p. 3; Richard H. Townsend, _The Diary of Richard H. Townsend_ (Baltimore: Enoch Pratt Free Library, 1937), I, 25.

[39]John S. Tyson, pp. 56-57; Lavens M. Thomas, p. 23.

[40]See, in general, Silvio A. Bedini, _The Life of Benjamin Banneker_ (New York: Charles Scribner's Sons, 1972); _Maryland Journal_, April 20, 1792, p. 2.

[41]_Baltimore Daily Repository_, September 26, 1792, p. 1.

[42]See, in general, J. Hall Pleasant, _An Early Baltimore Negro Portrait Painter: Joshua Johnston_ (n.p.: The Walpole Society, 1940).

[43]_Telegraphe_, July 29, 1795, p. 3.

[44]_American_, February 28, 1824, p. 2.

[45]_Federal Gazette_, February 4, 1796, p. 3.

[46]_Federal Gazette_, January 3, 1797, p. 2.

[47]_Federal Gazette_, January 2, 1801, p. 2.

[48]_Federal Gazette_, November 3, 1801, p. 3; September 6, 1803, p. 3.

[49]_Telegraph_, January 2, 1798, p. 2; _Federal Gazette_, December 19, 1798; December 20, 1798, p. 1.

Chapter II

ELISHA TYSON, PRESIDING ELDER

Having earned sufficient wealth by 1800, Elisha Tyson retired from the active, physical participation in the milling business, to devote the remainder of his life mainly to affairs of a benevolent nature. He remained, however, a businessman, but more so in the role of an investor and advisor. Whatever his activity in Baltimore in these years, Tyson served as or acted as a kind of presiding elder. He was actually an elder in his Quaker Meeting. Then, too, he was senior brother of a large family generating itself. As time went by, diminishing the number of his associates, he stood alone and was senior-most person in the operation of the benevolent directorate, which was at the center of most community-wide projects of a philanthropic nature. Finally, he was the most valued and oldest patron of blacks in the city. Tyson was the Presiding Elder of Baltimore.

The financial bases for the Tysons' fortunes rested on that money earned in the milling business. As they prospered, money was invested in other businesses, such as the Union Bank, whose charter ratification was guided through the General Assembly, by the efforts of Andrew Ellicott, a son of one of the founding brothers of Ellicott Mills. The Union Bank, at its incorporation in 1804, was the state's largest bank, capitalized at $3,000,000. Elisha's eldest son Isaac was the Tyson to take the most active part in promotion of this project. He was selected as one of the original directors and served in that position for a very long time. Isaac, no doubt was nominated by his father and other family members to so involve himself here. Naturally, Elisha favored the Union Bank, and at his death, he left each of his four sons 100 shares of the bank's stock. He also left 76 shares of stock in the Mechanics Bank which had been promoted by many Tyson allies. By 1821, Elisha, Jr., was a director and Philip Evan Thomas, by then an in-law by marriage, was president of the Mechanics Bank. The Union and Mechanics Banks were just two of the several supported by the Tysons. The Farmers and Merchants Bank, founded in 1810 had both Jesse Tyson and his first cousin Moses Sheppard heavily interested in its organization.[1]

After the banks, fire insurance companies were especial enterprises entered into by the Tysons and their associates. Specifically, Elisha Tyson and his brothers were involved in the founding of the Equitable Society in 1794 and had a great deal of property insured by the organization. In 1808, when the Baltimore Fire Insurance Company emerged, its charter was drawn so as not to conflict with that of the Equitable Society. Again, probably with the advice and support of his father, Isaac was elected as a director, representing the family's interest. Later, others to be elected to directorships were Moses Sheppard, Philip Evan Thomas, and Peter Hoffman, Jr., son of a long-time Tyson comrade.[2]

During the early years of the nineteenth century, roadbuilding, especially turnpike or toll-road building was just as much a venture capitalist enterprise as founding a bank. Groups came together for such purposes, sought charters, and sold stock to investors who expected a return on their money. It seems that only a few of the same persons were put in charge of these numerous roadbuilding schemes in Baltimore. Again, Isaac Tyson represented the family's interest in most of these undertakings. In 1805, Isaac was one of six managers of the Falls Road Turnpike Company; he became a perennial manager. The Ellicotts, too, were represented and eventually James Ellicott, to whom Elisha rented one of his mills on the Jones Falls, became president of the company. The Falls Road was one of the better and more efficiently built roads in the state, constructed by northern contractors without use of convict labor. The Falls Road was the first in the state not to use such labor. With free labor, the job was accomplished more easily and more quickly. It seemed a very profitable investment.

The Tyson family kept an active hand in the Falls Road for quite some while. By 1813, Jesse Tyson was president, and, of course, Isaac Tyson was there, as well as an Ellicott, as managers. Later on, Elisha, Jr., served as a manager and treasurer.

The Falls Turnpike Road Company was just one of those with which the Tysons were deeply connected. Through Isaac Tyson, the family, was active in one which built a road west of Frederick Town to Harper's Ferry. This particular project also had an Ellicott, a Hoffman, and Philip Evan Thomas as participants. The Boonsborough and Williamsport Turnpike, when authorized to take subscriptions, showed Isaac Tyson and Thomas Ellicott as being a part of the enterprise. The Cumberland Turnpike Road Company, responsible for blazing a trail to the west, when this company opened its subscription books, it did so at the Union Bank Headquarters; it showed also as managers Isaac Tyson, two Ellicotts, a Hoffman, Upton Bruce, and a Hollingsworth.[3]

The prosperity of the community, as well as the continued growth in individual wealth were motivating factors behind the Tyson involvement in establishing banks, insurance companies, and turnpike road companies. Yet, with the incorporation of the Baltimore Water Company, the entire community stood to benefit from this project in a direct and immediate way. The charter enactment of this company in 1804 was guided through the General Assembly, as were those of the Union Bank and Road Companies, by Andrew Ellicott. The Baltimore Water Company was established in order to bring a constant supply of fresh water into the city, by this time unsupportable by water gotten only from wells and the like. The Tysons had a hand in the project from the beginning, but the Ellicotts were even the more deeply involved. A committee set up to draw up plans for the project included Elias Ellicott; and, from the earliest days of the company's existence, it was generally thought that Jonathan Ellicott would be selected its president. Yet, some others considered Jonathan's brother, James, not a bad alternative to head the organization. In general, the Ellicotts were very inventive and mechanically minded. Eventually, Jonathan was elected president.

Not long after his election, Jonathan Ellicott resigned from the presidency of the Water Company, when others questioned the plans he wanted instituted; these persons suspected the Ellicott-Tyson mills on the Jones Falls would benefit too much in a pecuniary way from their introduction.[4]

The advice or opinion Elisha Tyson may or may not have given Jonathan Ellicott with regard to his difficulties while head of the Water Company is unknown, but in another situation, when the honor of the Ellicotts was attacked, Tyson defended them most heartily. The incident involved had significance for the nation at-large. It essentially was a dispute over who invented or made certain inprovements in milling machinery. Oliver Evans, originally from Delaware and later from Philadelphia, was the other party contending in the dispute. Evans demanded royalties of all millers who used what he claimed were his inventions. Many millers in Baltimore believed that the improvements had been made by the Ellicotts who had sought no patent rights for their works but allowed other millers to use them gratis. The improvements came in the 1780s, with the dispute arising more than twenty years later, and lasting another ten years in court trials, eventually going as far as the Supreme Court of the United States which decided in favor of the Ellicotts. Throughout the wrangle, Evans saw Elisha Tyson as his strongest opponent, who refused to pay judgments in early decisions won by Evans. In general, Tyson seemed prepared to share his wealth with the poor of the world throughout his life; but, having earned it, he must have felt no compunction to hand it over to those he suspected in dealing in sharp practices.[5]

As much as Elisha Tyson's money and disinterested concern led him to be considered an elder in the community-at-large, whose advice and means were sought at various junctions to further certain projects; he also, because he was father of several children and senior brother in a large family, doubtlessly, took a decided interest in the success of his relatives. He naturally was keenly concerned at the marriage of his children. William, his second oldest, in 1803, married Sarah, a daughter of Jonathan Ellicott. In 1804, Isaac, his eldest, married a daughter of Evan Thomas and sister of Philip Evan Thomas. A grandson of this marriage, Philip Evan Tyson, was a chemist and first president of the Maryland Academy of Science. Isaac and Nathan both married in 1815, Isaac for the second time in June, in Philadelphia, to Patience Marshall; Nathan for the first time to Martha Ellicott in September of that year. This latter marriage was a further cementing of a relationship between the two leading milling families in Baltimore. Nathan was more into his flour business than any other concerns although he did serve as a director of the Baltimore and Ohio Railroad. He also was to become first president of the Baltimore Board of Trade, the city's early chamber of commerce. His wife, Martha, was a Quaker minister and principal founder of Swarthmore College in Pennsylvania. Elisha Tyson had two other children to reach maturity, Mary and Elisha, Jr., the youngest, who as such had a life considerably different from his older brothers and sister.

Elisha, Junior, in 1816-1818, made the Grand Tour of Europe. The diary of his travels reveals how much he was like his father. Before setting sail, he received quite a bit of practical information and advice from Evan Thomas, Junior, brother of Philip Evan Thomas. While in England, amongst other things, such as visiting the old abolitionist Thomas Clarkson, and listening to Parliament in session, he also saw the socialist-utopian

Robert Owens and his progressive millworks system at New Lanark. He met Joseph Lancaster while in Great Britain, who told him of his plans to come to America. Lancaster, a Quaker, and abolitionist-minded, was, along with Johann Pestalozzi of Switzerland, the best-known pedagogue of the Western World for his time. Lancaster came to the United States and eventually chose to settle in Baltimore.[6] When settling in the city, Lancaster operated two schools--one for children and one for teachers.

When young Tyson returned from his broadening experience in Europe, one newspaper announced his return, saying that Elisha, Junior,

> ... has kindly favoured the Editor of the Patriot with papers, letter and a minute shipping list up to the 10th ult. from which every item of moment has been selected. In regard to the state of the markets, the following is the latest date and most authentic.[7]

Elisha Tyson, Senior, was indeed the presiding elder over a remarkable brood of his own, while several of his kinsmen were noteworthy as well.

The other most significant of the Tyson brothers was Jesse whose first wife, a Hopkins, had, according to her obituary, lived a very praiseworthy life. Their children were John Shoemaker and Isaac, Junior, so named to distinguish him from Elisha's son named Isaac. John was a lawyer and politician whose eloquence supported his uncle's many public concerns, even his abolitionism. After his uncles' death, he still had the liberal spirit and was a key supporter of the Jewish Emancipation Bill in 1826. Isaac, Junior, became a pioneer metallurgist in the country, eventually being greatly responsible and quite rich off the improvements he brought about in the chrome industry.[8]

There were other significant members of the Tyson clan or group who lent their support to Elisha Tyson's endeavor to abolish slavery and uplift blacks and other downtrodden peoples. Moses Sheppard, who never married, very much admired his cousin Elisha. He prospered and left his money to found a mental hospital. Another man affected by the Tyson legacy happened to be Johns Hopkins, whose aunt married Jesse Tyson. Hopkins, also, who never married, was a benefactor to a hospital and university. He also left provisions in his will for supporting a black orphan asylum, urged upon him by

Isabella Tyson, a cousin, and Elisha Tyson's granddaughter; but, unfortunately, these provisions of the
will were never carried out. Quite possibly, Thomas
Wilson was of the same Quaker family from Harford County
which Elisha Tyson's sister married into. Wilson willed
his money to maintain Maryland's first sanitarium and
the Thomas Wilson Fuel Fund for assisting poor people to
buy fuel.

Lastly, Enoch Pratt, the library founder, though
not a relative in any sense, was seriously affected by
the Tyson tradition of concern. Pratt served as a
pallbearer at Nathan Tyson's funeral and so admired
Moses Sheppard that he gave money to the Sheppard-
endowed hospital. Pratt also was an initiator of the
Cheltenham Reformatory for Black Youth. Before the latter institute's establishment, black youth were treated
as adult offenders. The only biography of Elisha Tyson,
Elisha Tyson, the Philanthropist, perhaps, accurately
points out his most outstanding attribute which apparently some were willing to imitate.[9]

The health and welfare of the poor, regardless of
race, and the means for relieving their conditions, were
the particular province of Baltimore's benevolent directorate, at whose center, Elisha Tyson was a mainstay-
ing presence. As a result of the disastrous yellow fever epidemic of 1800, 978 adults and 219 children died,
with most of the victims being residents of Fells Point,
one of the poorer sections of the city. Throughout the
ordeal, two Tyson associates, Adam Fonerden and Joseph
Townsend were the only Health Commissioners to remain in
the city to supervise relief efforts. The other commissioners probably fled the city as many other wealthier
inhabitants had done.

Since many of those who died were poor, some of
these, doubtlessly, were buried in the potters' fields
purchased sometime earlier for the poor by the benevolent-minded. Those who had participated in the potters'
field project included Joseph Townsend and Elisha Tyson.
Before the purchase of the two potters' fields, it had
been the practice of the poor to bury their dead in certain streets and alleys. As a great many blacks probably could be counted among the poor, they probably
benefited greatly from those purchases.

Because of the death of both parents of some of the
poor children in Fells Point, Fonerden and Townsend com-
mandeered the African Academy to house those who had
been so completely orphaned. Susanna Ellicott acted as

a matron at the Academy, supervising nurses employed to care for the children. As the epidemic spread to other areas, the Academy sheltered orphans from these sections as well. As late as November 17, 1800, about twenty children still remained in the school although the contagion had almost spent its course.[10]

Indeed, when the epidemic had finally finished, lasting remedies were sought to provide medical care for the poor. Elisha Tyson and several of his friends initiated one effort, the Baltimore General Dispensary. At this time, establishing general dispensaries was in full bloom in Europe and other large American cities. On Friday, January 9, 1801, those interested in assisting Tyson organize the Dispensary attended a meeting at Evan's Tavern. About a couple of weeks later, the rules of the organization appeared; and, in about two months more time, the Dispensary was fully operational, when a schedule of doctors was posted at its office located at 127 Baltimore Street. The Dispensary was incorporated in 1807 and persevered for many years beyond the lives of its founders.[11]

When first established, the Dispensary required that any person wanting medical aid, had to be recommended by a contributor to the organization. In part, because of this fact, in 1803 a controversy ignited that could have crippled the organization's annual fundraising campaigns. Richard Lee, a contributor, in a newspaper complained that he sent a black man to seek assistance for his brother who had been badly burned, but concluded because of all the unreasonable delay in attending the patient's foot, that this was due to his being black. Lee made other complaints besides this one, but this was potentially the most damaging. The resident apothecary replied to the charges, asserting that he gave the victim's brother a prescription for the burn and a note for him to see a doctor attending poor patients in the pertinent ward. According to the records kept, the victim never presented the note to a doctor. Nevertheless, realizing the seriousness of the complaint for drying up future financial assistance from Tyson and like-minded persons, if a charge of racial discrimination could be sustained against those left to manage the Dispensary's daily operations, the resident apothecary said:

> I would only observe...that persons should forbear to bring a charge of this nature, unless after the most cautious investigation of facts lest they should unintentionally injure

so beneficial an institution.

The matter proved to be not of that magnitude, however.

Yet, the controversy would not subside and, eventually, nothing less than an investigation of Lee's charges would clear the air. The managers of the Dispensary appointed a committee to examine those involved in the dispute. Although a manager of the Dispensary, it appears that Elisha Tyson appeared at the initial hearing only as an interested observer. As the victim's brother was unaware of the correct meeting time, a second one was set. At this meeting, the truth, as determined by the panel, was that no racial discrimination occurred and that, possibly, the victim's brother misled or even lied to Richard Lee about the extent of the abuses he suffered.[12]

Being thoroughly involved with the health and welfare needs of the poor, both black and white, Tyson and his friends had a prominent part in promoting the establishment of a house of industry, a place where the destitute poor could be housed and taught trades which later would permit them to earn their own keep. The house of industry plan was initiated in Baltimore in 1804. The concept of the house of industry, like so much else, came from Europe. As the Tyson group got moving in this direction, a successful house of industry had already been started in Philadelphia by a woman. Operating a food kitchen, patterned after the one founded by Count Rumford in Munich, Germany, was a key feature of the plan. The kitchen provided prepared food to the poor, inexpensively. A job training program vital to the house of industry concept, was not realizable that year.[13]

Nevertheless, from 1804, throughout the remainder of Tyson's life, various attempts were made to fully actualize the house of industry concept. Philip E. Thomas, in fact, during those years, was secretary to the trustees of the proposed institution. In 1817, efforts were directed to organize Baltimore's institution on a plan similar to one operating in Hamburg, Germany. Baltimore, at that time, experienced the same kind of dislocation caused by large prospering cities in the early phase of industrialization. The poor, both adults and children, in the Hamburg set-up were studiously observed, inspected and cared for, in terms of food and instruction. In Baltimore, the Hamburg plan was never realized, but along the way various amounts of money were raised to bring the project to fruition. The idea was not efficiently carried forward or completed, until the erection of the house of Refuge several decades later.[14]

As much of the house of industry idea had been an attempt to establish a permanent solution to the perennial woes of the poor, the practice of forming annual ad hoc relief committees to handle emergency situations of the poor thrown out of work because of inclement weather or some other disaster, also was a concern of Tyson and the men surrounding him.

In 1810, as in previous years, Elisha Tyson was involved with soliciting items for the poor and the distribution thereof. The year 1810, however, proved to be a momentous year for that type of benevolence in Baltimore. Tyson, a prohibitionist of sorts and supposedly the first man in Baltimore not to allow liquor to pass through or be stored in his warehouses, in 1810, with others, complained of the disastrous effect immoderate drinking had in reducing and keeping people in poverty. That year an investigating team sent out under the authority of the poor relief committee visited 1,113 poor families and found many of them:

...in a most deplorable state of suffering and misery, crouded (sic) into small open houses, and utterly destitute of fuel or food and, in many instances, afflicted with disease, which rendered them unable to make any kind of effort for their own relief.[15]

In its report to the public, the committee of poor relief noted with pleasure the fact that the mayor and city council proposed to do something about excessive whiskey consumption, by closing down many of the taverns whose only function was to serve alcoholic drink. For some of the poor relief committee, it seemed that every year it was necessary to waste more relief expenditures on the unworthy drunkard, who did not consider his responsibility to his family, but wasted his small earnings intemperately.

The aid from the public treasury neither materialized as had been expected nor, apparently, were the number of places dispensing liquor reduced. In 1817, an investigation of poverty-causing conditions revealed that drinking was responsible for nine out of ten cases of poverty.

In 1811, Tyson and friends were again called upon

to provide for the poor, and at the group's assembled meeting in the mayor's office, the female societies were much applauded for their work with the poor. Amongst these were the Impartial Free School Society, the Benevolent Society, and the Aimwell Charitable Society. The latter had its location on Camden Street between Charles and Hanover Streets, an area in which Tyson and several of Tyson's friends lived. In fact, the house of Elisha's son, William, may have served as a place where the group on occasion met. In certain aspects of annual poor relief committee activities, the woman had an integral part such as in visiting the poor and sick to ascertain their wants and needs.[16]

The care of the poor was the province of Tyson and company whether in peacetime or in time of war. In 1814, during the British attack on the Chesapeake Bay, in addition to the annual poor relief committee, on August 31, the local Committee of Vigilance set up another relief committee to administer to discomforts of the general public, as well as the poor, experienced because of the unsettled conditions resulting from war. This other committee included, amongst others, Elisha Tyson, James Ellicott, and Joseph Townsend as secretary. One listing of donations showed Tyson to have made one of the largest contributions.[17] At a meeting it indicated he chaired the proceedings.

Because of an incident that happened early in the year, it can be imagined the abolitionist presence in poor relief work in 1814 was more appreciated than ever before by blacks. A member of the seventh ward had let it be known in the beginning of the year that his attitude would be different this time as a collector for the poor in his ward. In his statements to the public, he claimed that most of the poor taking advantage of the annual poor relief were free Negroes,

> ... who are not entitled to it, in as much (sic) as they are continually idling away their time, and will not work unless they get double pay for their labor, &c, &c. [18]

This particular seventh ward collector hoped others would do as he and some others were asked to do, which was essentially, not to give aid to the free blacks. This request, except in cases of individual blacks, probably received no worthy reply from Tyson and his cohorts.

Oddly enough, in the same year of his work with the special relief committee set-up in response to the British activities around the Bay, Quakers were attacked by the Democratic Press of Philadelphia for what one writer thought traitorous conduct at their last Philadelphia Yearly Meeting. Tyson, having attended that meeting with other Baltimore Friends, denied these charges in public print. As to what conduct was not patriotic, this was not fully aired by the accuser or the Quaker rebuttal.[19]

In time, the concern for the poor led many of the benevolent directorate to be responsible for the opening of the Savings Bank of Baltimore on March 6, 1818. Those abolitionist-minded paricipants who served as directors included Thomas W. Griffith, Isaac Tyson, Evan T. Ellicott, and Moses Sheppard. Sheppard, in fact, served briefly as president of the bank in 1827. In the first year of the Bank's establishment, it interested itself in encouraging blacks to become savers. In an early advertisement, prominently displayed to attract savers, it was stated that a black cordwainer had already put $400 in the Bank. Blacks did indeed save at this Bank and, by the 1890s, it supposedly held most of the savings of black Baltimoreans; and, the president at that time, Archibald Sterling, Senior, and his son Archibald, Junior, were significant supporters of blacks in their various undertakings after the Civil War.

Two other societies were founded at about the same time as the Savings Bank with the intent of helping the poor--The Baltimore Economical and Soup Society, and the Baltimore Society for the Prevention of Pauperism. Both group were greatly influenced by Elisha Tyson's associates; and, naturally, their efforts would tend to benefit the poor blacks of Baltimore as well.[20]

As distressing as poverty was as a constant consideration of the benevolent-minded of Baltimore to combat, providing adequate fire protection was an even-more taxing matter to contemplate. In this regard, Elisha Tyson and his friends were actively involved with the volunteer fire companies, especially the Union and Mechanical Fire Companies. Blacks seemed to have been members of some of the fire companies and performed admirably at times, as a description of a fire occurring at Jacob Meyers' property in 1803 indicates. Meyers was a former leading member of the first abolition society, operating throughout the 1790s and benefitted, it seems, from that past association. The article stated:

> The people of Colour last evening deserved much praise. They were generally found at the

'post' of labor, while hundreds of those who have property to defend and liable to like misfortune looked on with apathy.[21]

In 1822, when an effort was made to establish an all-white fire company came up for approval in the City Council, the bill was defeated. This was a measure, perhaps, of the kind of influence Tyson's long life of advocacy of true democracy in Baltimore had in some circles of the city.

Elisha Tyson presided and advised in becoming fashion after 1800 as a philanthropist in his church, amongst his family and circle of associates, and to the poor. In general, his activities were to have a profound affect on blacks. In addition to this, after the turn of the century, he reached out to help the Indian population, who more and more were being parted from and pushed off their ancestral lands; their lives being made miserable by the movement of whites westward. The Quakers had an Indian Affairs Committee, as they had one that handled matters relating to blacks. Baltimore Quakers had shown a keen interest in Indians in the Midwest as early as the 1790s; and, in particular, George Ellicott, father of Martha, daughter-in-law of Elisha, displayed as deep a concern for the Indians as Tyson did for blacks. Ellicott made several arduous trips to the Midwest to urge the Indians there to settle down to an agricultural life. He taught them how to use farm implements the Baltimore Quakers had provided. In 1797, he advised the Wyandotes, Shawnees, and Delawares on the selection and erection of mill sites in their territory. Also, in 1804, he made another trip west on which Tyson was supposed to accompany him, but for some reason did not go.

The Quakers had assiduously lobbied before national authorities to restrict the sale of alcoholic beverages to the Indians who were not accustomed to such drinks, and which were rapidly undermining their social structure. These efforts culminated in success in 1807, and, again, with George Ellicott being a big factor in this outcome. Also at this time, the Quakers sent help to instruct the Indians in the use of implements partially purchased by an annual grant furnished by the national government.

In 1808, Elisha Tyson went west to the Miami and Pattowatomie; he was accompanied by James Gillingham. The hazardous journey on horseback, to one of the furthest-out military posts of the United States, almost cost Tyson his life. After arriving at Fort Wayne, he spoke with the important chiefs of the region, and continued to urge the Indians to persist in the arts of agriculture and an abstinence from alcoholic beverages.

By the 1840s, Baltimore Quaker involvement with the Indians was a deep and continuing one. So respected were Baltimore's Quakers in Indian councils, that the Indians of New York made good use of the Baltimoreans, Philip Evan Thomas and Moses Sheppard, when whites tried to swindle them out of their land. Thomas, for his assistance, was made an honorary chief by the New York Indians.[22]

Though Elisha Tyson seemed to be of an older generation of Quaker opinion that eschewed direct mixing in politics, some from the following generations were not of the same opinion. Tyson did, however, serve as one of the original directors of the State penitentiary when first opened in 1811 and as such helped to make it probably one of the most unique of its kind in the United States--it did not practice racial discrimination within its walls with regard to housing its inmates.[23] Similarly, many of Tyson's Quaker associates did participate in a valuable way in governmental affairs. These men's names could be found on commissions to further various public projects. Without question, however, Elisha Tyson and his like-minded Quaker associates had an interest in the outcome of certain political happenings in Baltimore.

In 1818, with Adam Walsh presiding and John Shoemaker Tyson acting as secretary, the first ward examined a report it had commissioned which investigated the then present mayoral administration and found its chief characteristic being "a great want of public economy and an inordinate ambition of power". Because of this finding, a movement to depose the mayor was seen as necessary to save the purses of everyone. The mayor and his "henchmen" had, through bribery, in the opinion of some, gotten enormous taxing power from the state, which they used to put the citizenry under a tremendous burden, with an enormous increase in the tax rate. In addition to being extravagant with regard to public works projects, the mayor and city councilmen had not neglected to allot themselves salaries way out of line with what was the norm for the time in other places. The reform efforts led by the Tysons of the first ward, failed in promoting a former Harford Countian to the mayor's office; however, in the next election, their efforts were crowned with success. Throughout this episode, it is not unlikely that Elisha Tyson had a keen interest in this campaign although he probably demurred to let younger Quakers take charge.[24]

To fight in gladiator fashion for power in the political arena seemed alien to Elisha Tyson, but his intense devotion to helping the less fortunate was indeed all-embracing and his wish to see the general community thrive was quite visibly indicated throughout his life. Yet, abolition and providing protection for the black community were his most readily accepted responsibilities. In the first years of the nineteenth century, Baltimore was to witness the staunchness of Tyson's support for blacks under trying circumstances when support for abolition in organized fashion was declining, not only in the city, but throughout the country. This decline was, in part, because of the turn toward violence on the part of some blacks to obtain their freedom or satisfy themselves vis-a-vis whites as seen in Gabriel Possner's uprising in Richmond in 1800, and in the successful overthrow of French rule in Haiti in 1804. Also at this time, slavery persisted because, simply put, many could not resist the desire to have slaves and the sense of power, wealth, and status it could confer.

It was in the first decade of the nineteenth century that Tyson rededicated himself, with additional fervor, to the plight of the blacks. It was at about this time he began expending some efforts toward helping the Indians in the Northwest Territory, when, as his obituary said:

> He soon perceived that those objects (Indians) could not fail of advocates, as many fellow laborers were in the vineyard; and his active mind was turned to the suffering of the oppressed children of Africa; for whom it appeared that Heaven had yet raised but few efficient advocates.[25]

Tyson proved to be quite adequate to the task in the remaining years of his life.

A great deal of Tyson's time in the latter years was needed to halt an upsurge in kidnapping of blacks, especially free ones, which seemed of epidemic proportions at the turn of the century. At the turn of the century, Elisha Tyson established an underground railroad line, probably one of the first in the country, no doubt, done to counterbalance the conspiratorial and callous manner in which blacks were defrauded of their freedom and denied due process of law to reestablish claim to that freedom. "Underground railroad" was a term applied to the furtive manner slaves were assisted to escape to places where slavery did not exist or where a black could disappear, blend in with the surrounding area.

Although the term "underground railroad" came into being after Tyson's death, his activities were definitely like those famous underground railroad operators of the 1840-to-1860 period. Tyson sent runaway slaves to Jacob Lindley, a minister in the Society of Friends who lived near Avondale, Chester County, Pennsylvania. Lindley was so much like Elisha Tyson in the intensity of his opposition to slavery that his name was remembered and linked with that of Tyson for some time after both of their deaths. From Lindley's place in Avondale, slaves went to two other stations on the Tyson-Lindley underground railroad in Pennsylvania, to Philip Price, East Bradford, north of Strode's Mill; from there they were finally transported to Abram Bonsall's house and neighborhood, who lived near Valley Creek Bridge.[26]

Tyson and Lindley's participation in the operation of an underground railroad line, distinguished them from other well-known friends of the Negro, active before this time. Once, Granville Sharp proposed to Anthony Benezet that American abolitionists should refuse to give up fugitive slaves as the biblical injunction in Deuteronomy 23:15 stated. Having apparently consulted Benjamin Rush on the advisability of adopting that strategy, Benezet concluded it unwise. In fact, Rush said to advocate such a position would be to invite others to "knock us in the head".[27]

Whether in Benezet's day or Tyson's, blacks were an essential part of the operational success of any underground railroad, if only for the reason, they did not alert authorities of what they knew. Yet, they did even the braver and more daring deeds as well, taking an active part in assisting and leading slaves to a free area. So, although kidnapping increased enormously at the turn of the century, it can be said its counterweight of assisting slaves to run away was also in evidence.

At the turn of the century, some of the most feared kidnappers in Baltimore and elsewhere were called "Georgia men" and for good reason, as apparently many kidnappers were thought to be from that state, while some even seemed to have been supplied with money from the Treasurer of Georgia to secure Negroes anywhere, by any means, and without regard to the legality of the transactions. As an indication of their technique, on one spring night in 1801 in Baltimore, the "Georgia men" went roaming the streets with painted faces, snatching every black in sight. In this night rampage, some police seemed clearly implicated, and because of this, a committee of abolitionist-minded thought it time, in viligante-fashion, for private citizens to suppress what they believed to be violations of the laws of God and country. In May 1801, another vigilant abolitionist, possibly Tyson, forewarned that those engaged in these flagrant acts of kidnapping or abetting the same were, indeed, known to the public and would soon be brought to court.

Indeed, vigilant efforts were quite necessary to reduce the success of the kidnappers. An aspect of the kidnapping business, the private dungeons which gangs of kidnappers maintained up and down the East Coast, in which to hold their particular wares as they were moved south, mainly through the efforts of Elisha Tyson, most of these rendezvous facilities in Baltimore were closed down. The fact that Tyson and many of his cohorts lived near the harbor, also, made it easier for them to disrupt at times, the movements of the abductors. A letter to the _Federal Gazette_, dated September 5, 1801, told of how some locally concerned citizens, suspicious of the method used to load several blacks aboard a ship sailing south, upon approaching the ship to investigate, were threatened with death if they came aboard--no doubt a serious indication that the blacks were indeed kidnapped victims. This incident is similar to one recorded as exemplary of the kind of situations Elisha Tyson often confronted. Instead of backing down, however, Tyson usually leaped aboard the ship or went forward and challenged the bullies present to carry out their threat to kill him. They never did and Tyson usually carried back to safety those who had been kidnapped.[28]

That Tyson had to do such daring deeds is understandable because policemen seemed unwilling to risk their lives in such situations. In addition, at times they were implicated in the crimes. Two years after these 1801 incidents, "0", a correspondent to a local newspaper, speaking from personal knowledge of the crimes of kidnapping perpetrated by "Georgia men" with the connivance of police officials, said:

To recapitulate the numberless instances in this city alone, of the free negroes (sic) who have been, without any infraction of law, forcibly dragged before magistrates, under the pretence of their being runaways, would be to write a volume.[29]

The unreliability of local authorities led Tyson and others to initiate dawn-to-dusk patrols in the individual wards to prevent the crimes from ever arising.

The sensitivity of some people to the plight of blacks, in general, at this point in time was commendable. The editor of the American Patriot apologized for criticizing a petition circulating in 1802 because he thought its object was to disfranchise free blacks. He later learned it was to benefit them; with that clarification made, he wished the circulators of the petition success.[30] That same year, the friends of blacks, and Tyson had to be included in that number, were buoyed by the passage of a bill that forbade the sending of term slaves outside of the state, where they could not as easily be protected and, more than likely, might not be released on the day their freedom was due them.[31]

No matter the sensitivity of some to the overall plight of blacks, kidnapping remained an everpresent danger to the free Negroes. The intensity of kidnapping varied at times and, as already mentioned, one intense period was around 1800, another around 1807, and still others around 1816 and 1825. The mass of kidnappings around 1807 inspired some, especially Philip E. Thomas, to attempt to resurrect an organized abolitionist movement in Baltimore. It failed. The apparent noninvolvement of Tyson in a leadership position in this organizational revival may be accounted for perhaps by his increased involvement with the activities of Friends, abolitionist and nonabolitionist activities alike. Significantly, at this time, Quakers were publicly warned by a supporter of slavery not to continue so ardently promoting the betterment of the slave.[32]

In general, matters with regard to kidnapping around 1807 were such that one correspondent, penning his name "Warning" to the editor of the Federal Gazette during the summer of that year, spoke of a gang of "hardened wretches," who were in the business of stealing young Negroes. They had connived with some innkeepers, whose houses were rendezvous places for the kidnappers. This letter writer pointed out a place specifically in the southwest of the city which was guilty of such crimes. In effect, "Warning" wanted to know what the proper authority should do against those whose plans and intents were so obvious. He further stated, "one had only to ask the blacksmith who was tricked into making collars and chains for the detained blacks by the owner of the tavern to know what business they were in."

In the very same issue of this newspaper, a couple of incidents from eye witness accounts appeared in an article entitled "Look to the Villains," in which the writer stated that on the 21st day of July, between 8 and 9, three attempts were made to steal a black boy in an Old Town neighborhood by someone offering the boy money to go with him to a more secluded location. The other outrageous incident by another attempted kidnapper was to throw a slip-noose at the head of a boy as if he were some kind of wild animal. The noose would have choked him into silence, if it had been successful. In conclusion, the writer pleaded that citizens and police, in particular, be more vigilant in order to prevent these crimes as the two above potential crimes had been thwarted.[33]

A day later, "One of the Justices" answered the criticism being aimed at the police force, saying that public disclosure of the practices of the kidnappers at the tavern in the southwest section had allowed them time to make their escape.[34] Afterwards, because partially responsible for this development, "Warning" apologized for having unwittingly assisted the kidnappers to escape. He suggested, however, the best results would be brought about if kidnappers were to be subjected to "hanging". This writer disclosed he had been reassured by officials that the police had a serious eye on the problem. Despite this assurance, "Warning" sent the editor of the Federal Gazette a copy of "A's" plans to organize an association against kidnappers. "A's" closing statement in his plan said:

> Let then every man amongst us, who is a friend of the just and equal rights of man, who is an enemy to tyrany, injustice, and oppression, be his religious opinion, what they may, attend at the place appointed, that we may show to the world the respectability of our numbers. Here is a wide field open for the philanthropist, one, in which the patriot may obtain a crown of never fading laurels.[35]

Apparently, no organization was established and men like Tyson pursued an individual attack on the problem as seen in the following.

In the summer of 1811, T. I. Moses went to Philadelphia, stayed several days, and during his stay,
gained the confidence of a Negro boy named Peter Reuben
Frances Johnson, whom Moses eventually kidnapped by en-
ticing the boy to go with him to New Jersey, supposedly
to pick cherries. From there, young Johnson was taken
to Baltimore and sold into slavery. Somehow his case
came to the attention of Tyson, who wrote his friend in
Philadelphia, Isaac T. Hopper, a Quaker with strong
antislavery sentiments, who was to contact the mother,
to tell her that her son was all right. Hopper was also
to secure someone to come with papers or in person to
indentify the youngster so as to remove him from the
Sheriff's custody. Tyson informed Hopper in his letter
that he also aimed at capturing Moses who had escaped
from the authorities.36

Two weeks later, Tyson was still waiting for con-
firmation of the boy's identity; apparently an uncle who
had promised to come down to Baltimore to identify the
boy had not done so, leaving his nephew still in the
custody of the sheriff. The expenses to be paid to the
sheriff for the boy's upkeep were increasing each day,
which Tyson would, no doubt, have to pay. It was not
long before Moses was apprehended in Philadelphia, and
Tyson wrote a letter informing the people in charge of
matters on that end that the man to whom the boy had
been sold was willing to go to Philadelphia to testify
against Moses, if informed of the trial date.

Actual, as well as possible, kidnappings seemed
never to go out of season, and later that same year,
Elisha Tyson was asked by William Masters of
Philadelphia to look into the city jail to secure the
release of Robert Barkley. Masters sent Tyson Barkley's
indenture papers and $5.00 for expenses. After
investigating, Tyson informed Masters that there was no
such person in the jail, nor, to the best information he
had received, had Barkley ever been in the city jail.

Kidnappings and related incidents were so abundant
that at times Elisha's children were called upon to take
a hand in protecting the free blacks in their rights.
Isaac, his oldest son, investigated the matter of a
group of free blacks, which included Maria Lewis, who
came to Baltimore from Philadelphia for a religious
meeting and were apprehended as runaways and confined to
jail since they were without their freedom papers. From
J. Ridgway in Philadelphia, Isaac Tyson received these
blacks' papers which permitted them to be released, free
of expenses. In a letter to Ridgway, Isaac stated:

It is a matter of astonishment they will go rambling up and down through the country in the manner they do without any papers whatever.[37]

He added that why their cause was not more popularly championed was because "many of them behave very badly". The so-called "misbehavior" of some free blacks had always, rightly or wrongly, been used as a measure of the kind of justice or lack of it, all blacks were to receive or should receive.

Not only did his children assist him, Elisha Tyson was always seconded in his efforts by his Quaker friends, especially at their annual meetings. In 1811, a committee of them went before the State Legislature and got passed an Act that made it unnecessary for a deed of manumission to have two or more witnesses, perhaps, a difficult matter to come by if a man is about to die and wanted to atone for having held his slaves to the near bitter end, but who wanted to release them before he went to receive his own just reward. The same year the committee of Quakers got passed a more definitive piece of legislation forbidding the selling of term slaves out of the state where their rights were probably nonexistent to nil, and where, when their term of slavery ended, they might be kept in bondage.

With the above accomplishments duly reported at the annual meeting of Maryland Friends in 1811, work for the coming year was parceled out, the most important being preparing a memorial to Congress, pleading for the abolition of the internal slave trade. The committee constituted to prepare the petition included Tyson; and, it showed a willingness to accept less then the whole loaf, if the Congress would enact legislation which required Federal certifications to be obtained from custom houses, when a black was transported across state lines. This it was hoped, would diminish the number of kidnapped free blacks being taken south by ship. Naturally, Tyson was amongst those appointed to go to present the petition before Congress. Others who went along included Philip E. Thomas, George Ellicott, Thomas Moore, and William Brown. The memorial was presented and, according to the 1812 yearly Quaker Report, favorable action seemed likely to be taken on the matter.[38]

Although Tyson worked with his Quaker friends, he seemed destined to handle a great deal of the work of abolition, at least the most difficult part, that involving kidnapping, alone. In the summer of 1812, some black people from Philadelphia were sitting in Baltimore City Jail as runaways, but, who were, as so often was the case, not. Tyson took up their case and informed William Masters to send documents supporting the freedom of these blacks. Apparently, the kidnappers of these blacks were in jail in Philadelphia and Tyson wanted someone in Philadelphia to have the Governor of Pennsylvania to demand the extradition of the blacks so they could be used as witnesses against their abductors. Yet, Tyson said in his letter that he still needed documentary evidence to prove the blacks' rights to freedom, even if they were not to be used in a court proceeding against the kidnappers.[39]

A month later, Tyson was to write saying he had tried to get the blacks released but was told by the judge in no uncertain terms, that documents from the Governor had to be sent to demand the return of the blacks as material witnesses in the trial of the kidnappers, if this was still the intention of people in Pennsylvania handling the case on that end. If this was not the case, other documents had to be sent to prove the blacks' right to their freedom. Tyson also further stated he was sorry to hear that one of the kidnappers had escaped from jail in Philadelphia. He declared that Baltimore bench warrants had been issued for the arrest of two accomplices in the crimes.

Yet, in another two and one-half weeks, Tyson informed Masters that Joseph Roach who was believed to have been a partner in the crime of kidnapping the boy Johnson the year before, had been jailed this time for having sold two of the Negroes still being held in jail, regrettably because no documents of their right to freedom had been received. Tyson also reported to Masters that Roach had hired a lawyer to defend himself. At this, Tyson said it was essential that some persons from Philadelphia or Delaware come down to identify Roach and the four blacks, if the prosecution was to have any success in convicting Roach, in that no deposition could be used in a criminal court proceedings in the State of Maryland.

He further stated,

I cannot but indulge the hope that some persons will come as witnesses to prove what I have before stated, and I can also say that they will not be detained one day as the trial will be brought on immediately, there being nothing to prevent it but the arrival of those

witnesses, and on their return they can take
with them the coloured people....[40]

Tyson went on to say that the witnesses would not be out
of any expenses as he would pay that. He stated, too,

> I must entreat thee to send the witnesses on
> as it will be a great Pity (sic) this man
> (Roach) should be acquitted for want of the
> testimony which no doubt can be had.

In a postscript, he added,

> It is not only necessary that those witnesses
> should come on in order to aid the conviction
> of Roach, but it is impossible that the Black
> People can be Released unless Identified.

An ordeal of this nature was the kind of thing Tyson en-
countered a great many times in his endeavors to reestablish the identity of some free blacks who had been
kidnapped--that this was a time-consuming and expensive
process can easily be imagined.

A successful conclusion for this latter case occurred some three months after the last letter, as the
men, Gabriel Jackson, Solomon Luff, Richard Baily, and
Amos Morris were freed by the Judge of Baltimore County
Criminal Court. After their release, Tyson sent the men
off to Philadelphia with a letter to his friends, James
Cammeron and William Masters, explaining the particulars of this case, and at the same time asking, "any
little assistance afforded them (the blacks) will be
very grateful and an Act of Christian Benevolence."[41]

While cooperating with Quakers in Pennsylvania,
Delaware, and elsewhere to stem the tide of kidnappings,
Tyson and Maryland Quakers remained attentive to the
situation under their own jurisdiction. The Maryland
Yearly Meeting in 1814, which had jurisdiction over
Maryland, Washington, D.C., parts of Virginia, Pennsylvania, and the Northwest Territories, solicited its members, who had slaves in their keeping to be manumitted,
to see that their manumission papers included provisions
about the right of the children of such females to be
free. The next year, Quakers sent a memorial to the
State Legislature, renewing their complaint against the
continuing outrages committed by kidnappers. The efforts of the Quakers were directed toward getting stiffer penalties for the kidnapper or to make it easier to
convict such criminals. Their pleas received favorable

treatment from the General Assembly but could not get by
the vote of the full House of Delegates. This did not
deter the Quakers, however, because in 1816, they were
determined to present similar petitions before both the
State Legislature and the Congress.[42]

Many seemed concerned about the intense period of
kidnapping taking place in the fall of 1816. This outbreak sparked several writers using pseudonyms such as
"Wilberforce," "Libertas," "Humanitus," and "Benevo-
lentia" to communicate to the public about this continuing criminality.[43] Perhaps Tyson assumed one of these
pseudonyms, especially that of "Wilberforce". In "Wilberforce's" communication, not only local kidnapping,
but the international slave trade, a species of kidnapping, came in for attack as well. At best, American
laws against the participation of Americans in this business enacted in 1807 were never fully enforced, nor
sufficient provisions made to make it possible for the
law to be enforced, if anyone chose to do so. The accusations under "Wilberforce" were so sweeping that the
Federal Gazette, usually sympathetic to abolitionist
matters, refused to print the piece without verification
of the writer's name and other important facts
surrounding the charges. Nevertheless, another paper
printed the letter which said, in essence, that some
shippers in Baltimore would, through deception, claim to
have sold their ships in Cuba, then proceed to Africa,
presumably under new ownership, and pick up slaves. The
ships returning to Baltimore, by way of Havana, would
revert to the original owners and the slaves aboard
would be claimed as crew members before custom officials
once it docked in the United States. Of course, later
the crew would be sold into slavery.

"Wilberforce" in demanding a stop to the practice,
said,

> Think not that I am ignorant of whom I ad-
> dress, I know you all, and of this you shall
> have fatal evidence, if you do not reform—if
> you do not stay the work of death.[44]

Toward the end of "Wilberforce's" communication, the
same startling resolve was revealed as the idea was repeated again, which would seem to be in keeping with Tyson's determined nature.

> I tell you again, I know you all. I have do-
> cuments which furnish incontestible evidence
> of your guilt: If you do not reform, you
> shall be gibbeted to public abhorrence,
> scorn, and detestation.

Whether Tyson was "Wilberforce" or not is not really de-
terminable, but under Tyson's guidance, with Francis
Scott Key as his lawyer, this type of slave running,
kidnapping, was greatly abated in Baltimore.[45]

So outrageous was the situation in Baltimore by
1816, as far as kidnapping was concerned, that at least
two newspapers, one in the South and one in the North,
applauded efforts just being set in motion to remedy
what was occurring too frequently. With such unkindly
notice being given Baltimore from outside it and the
continuing display of brutality within the city, as in
the incident in which a Negro boy was shot in the head
by his guardian and killed because he wanted to tell his
master that his temporary guardian wanted to sell him to
the "Georgia men," the city was ripe for a new abolition
society, in which Tyson had a predominant hand in bringing into existence. A few days after "Wilberforce's"
publication, the Protection Society of Maryland was
formed in early Fall 1816. Elisha Tyson called together
the meeting that organized the society, but did not attend.

Perhaps Tyson did not attend for several reasons.
First of all, he seemed reluctant to organize abolitionists outside of the Society of Friends. Secondly,
being the grand old man of abolition in Baltimore, he
probably could not have refused an office in the new
body, which went against his self-effacing manner.
Thirdly, when informing Thomas Shipley, an officer in
the American Convention of Abolition Societies, of the
formation of the Protection Society, Elisha Tyson, Junior, described his father as "advanced in life and his
constitution somewhat impaired from a late extreme illness;" and, because of this, he wanted to be relieved of
unnecessary burdens. Not long after the establishment
of the Protection Society in Baltimore, in November, a
similar group was formed at Pipe Creek in Frederick
County, where many Quakers and Dunkards lived. Dunkards
were of German ancestry and very similar in outlook to
the Quakers in their beliefs.[46]

So pressing was the problem of kidnapping around
the time of the formation of the Protection Society,
that even the Grand Jury of Baltimore County felt the

need to investigate the problem. Its report, when issued, in the strongest language condemned kidnapping.
The Grand Jury's report also stated it seemed present
laws were too inadequate to stop these violations of
both law and common decency; and that the private dungeons, frequented by those intent upon kidnapping, were
outside the scrutiny of the law, providing a distinct
advantage to the kidnapper. The report concluded by
saying, the

> . . . alarming frequency of their occurrence
> (kidnappings), their everyday notoriety is
> such, as to shock every spectator that has the
> least regard for mercy or for justice.[47]

In sum, the grand jurors subscribed its name to the various individuals, then demanding stiffer penalties for
the kidnapper, and less obstruction in the way of free-
ing blacks in the grasp of kidnappers.

As the grand jurors, members of the Protection Society were eager to see the arrest and conviction of
kidnappers, but some members of the Society were not interested in advocating general emancipation--something
Tyson thought just. This doubtlessly secured the maxi-
mum cooperation of all in the community. The group organized itself into committees representing the various
wards, and a regularly established patrol system was instituted to augment the police or watch as had been done
in earlier times by Tyson and his friends. A list of
nightly captains was established and probably functioned from around 10 o'clock at night to 5 in the morning, as had been the case with patrols operated by Tyson
and his associates in 1810.[48]

After the Society's founding, even more were to
join in protesting the crimes of kidnappers. At the beginning of the year of 1817, the Methodist Episcopal
Church of Baltimore came out against kidnapping and a
"Justice" from Queen Anne's County lauded the efforts of
Baltimoreans in establishing the Protection Society. He
also noted many on the Eastern Shore were circulating
petitions in behalf of efforts to stop kidnappers. The
latter must be considered quite an achievement, in that
the Eastern Shore was noted as slavery's stronghold in
the state. Yet, despite these noble beginnings, in
1817, kidnapping was such a lucrative and deeply venal
practice that it would not be abruptly halted by petitions and mere public condemnations.[49]

59

In the middle of the year, two instances of the boldness of the Negro stealers were put in a newspaper on successive days. "A Resident of Charles Street" told of how a man with whiskers and the "gallows" look of a kidnapper tried to lure a little black boy away by offering a dollar if he would direct him to a house of someone further away. The boy started to go, but was warned not to. But the persistence of the potential kidnapper was described as indefatigable, but for the boy's sake, without success. "A Resident of Charles Street" said, "if a stop were not put to the vile practice of stealing colored people, by a gang of desperate free-booters who infest our city, the most serious consequences will ensue.[50]

The next day in the same paper, "Observer" related how a black boy at work on Market Street was grabbed, and an attempt was made to make off with him in broad mid-afternoon by someone claiming the child was a runaway. Someone else knew this not to be the case and took the boy from the thief. "Observer" said, "This enraged him (kidnapper) to a degree, and he vented himself in uttering abusive language; but the outrage he had just committed was so flagrant, and so palpably infamous, that he was soon booted and kicked out of the street." "Observer" suggested people should keep their servants in at night, and if one saw a kidnapper, the observer suggested he be beat as the one was on Market Street.[51]

As some individuals continued to be vigilant and heroic, Quakers as a group still persevered with their petitions. By the end of 1817, Quakers in Baltimore sent a petition to Congress to get laws already on the books strengthened to prevent kidnapping, especially the law relative to making sure people did not evade, getting clearance at custom houses before transporting blacks by water. Others at this time also sent petitions from places such as Tennessee, North Carolina, Kentucky, and Virginia. These latter petitioners also wanted something done to prevent kidnapping and supported efforts to colonize blacks in Africa. Indeed, at the end of 1817, the work of the Quakers and Protection Society had been so successful that the General Assembly was more receptive to petitions relating to the subject, and the public seemed willing to vigorously pursue thwarting kidnappers by convicting several that year.[52]

The highlight of the Protection Society's activities for 1818 on the Fourth of July, was an anniversary address given by John Shoemaker Tyson, Elisha's nephew.[53] As he spoke, and only at twenty-one, John Tyson seemed to captivate many with his classical oratorial style. About a month later, he was nominated to run for one of the two seats the city had in the General Assembly. Again, due note was made of his oratorical ability and public service he rendered at community meetings, generally in the role of secretary. In addition, mention was made of his family's standing in the community. A newspaper correspondent said:

> . . . the uniformly patriotic and republican principles professed and practised by his family and connexions from the commencement of the revolution to the present day must procure for him the marked consideration of every consistent democrat.[54]

Not all, of course, were of this opinion. "No Irony," in fact, belittled the Tyson family and its contributions to the community[55]

In 1818, John Tyson did not win the election but he did make a respectable showing. Later, he did succeed in becoming elected to the General Assembly where, among other things, he was one of the forceful advocates of the successful Jewish Emancipation Bill, an effort to remove the restrictions on Jews, preventing their full participation in public life.

The organizational activities of Quakers and the Protection Society were not the only ones operational after the wave of kidnappings around 1816 to come to grips with this recurring problem. A few weeks after the organization of the Protection Society, in October 1816, a new group, the American Colonization Society, was formed in Washington. The American Colonization Society, a body national in scope, had a different solution to the nature of the racial problems, including kidnapping. It hoped that by carrying back to Africa those free Negroes willing to return, much tension between the races would be relieved. The Colonization Society had many slaveholders, and large ones at that, as members, and, thus, brought its motives under suspicion for wanting to remove the free Negroes from the scene—the potential leaders of slaves out of their bondage. Blacks up and down the country were against the Society, and, at first, stymied the group's immediate effectiveness.[56]

Colonizationists in Baltimore received some support from some of the surviving members of the city's benevolent business directorate that coalesced as a unit in the late 1780's, but never did they get the unqualified support of Elisha Tyson in the beginning. Tyson's connection with colonization nevertheless proved to be a most significant one. He was instrumental in getting the Federal Government involved in the American Colonization's acquisition of its first successful colony on the West Coast of Africa, Cape Mesurado. From that point onward, his interest in Liberia, the subsequent name of the colony, was to see it serve as a place for those Negroes genuinely wanting to go there to escape the hostility in the United States; but, also, and more importantly, it could be used as an initial place to forward recaptured Africans--Africans detected before being smuggled into the United States as slaves, by then against the Law of 1807--so that they could eventually find their way to their homes in Africa.[57]

In fact, one of the last deeds of Tyson's life involved getting some recaptured Africans back to Liberia. According to one account, the news of the safe return of these blacks to Africa came forty-eight hours before Tyson's death. His obituary states:

> The dying (Tyson) reanimated by this information, manifested a lively sense of gratitude to the author of all good; in that this humble effort had been crowned with success in his last enterprise, exclaimed, Well, I am glad, now I have done--I have done![58]

Tyson could be more than satisfied to die with having been responsible, in so many ways, including this last act, in affecting so much good for blacks in general, but especially in helping to reduce kidnapping and slave smuggling.

Parallel to the activities Tyson and others undertook to make life better for blacks in the city, the blacks themselves from early on, but especially after the turn of the century, did not fail to contribute their share to the efforts at hand. At the turn of the century, the community-at-large got involved when their numbers were substantial in the ranks of the free blacks and when it surely behooved it to make plans based on its own assessment of its needs, especially as organized abolition at this juncture was on the wane. Many of the needs of the community were met when blacks purchased the African Academy in 1802. The purchase of the Academy seemed to arise out of an incident taking place in 1799.

Not long after the erection of the African Academy, a crisis developed over what direction the school should take. In November, 1799, "Philom," perhaps a pseudonym for a letter written by or at the behest of Tyson, appeared in a newspaper divulging some facts relative to the crisis. Apparently, some free blacks withdrew their children from the Academy with the intent to enroll them in some of the better-operated private schools; but when these private schools refused to allow blacks to attend, these free black children were not being education at all. "Philom" suggested that since the African Academy was vacant or under-utilized because of the blacks' withdrawal, it was necessary for the liberal-minded to rescue the honor of the city and make a new effort to give the blacks an opportunity for receiving the kind of education they desired.

Eventually, another teacher was hired for the African Academy, but it seems that quality and consistent education for blacks did not occur until after blacks bought the Academy building in 1802. Both a school and a church were established at the facility, but it seems that a permanent educational program did not get underway until the arrival of Daniel Coker, generally believed to be the first black teacher in Baltimore and probably one of the best educated blacks of his day in the entire country.[59]

Daniel Coker was born a slave in Frederick County prior to 1800, perhaps around 1785. His mother was Susan Coker, an indentured English woman; his father, Edward, a slave. In his youth, as a companion to his master's son, he learned to read. Sometime around 1801, he came to Baltimore and joined the local black Methodist church. Subsequently, he ran away to New York, read widely, and was ordained a deacon by Bishop Asbury of the Methodist Church. When Coker returned to Baltimore, supposedly four blacks, Charles Hackett, Nicholas Gilliard, George Murray, and John Watts, either bought Coker's freedom from his master or urged John Needles, or John S. Tyson, both Quakers, to purchase Coker, so that he could teach in Baltimore untrammeled. Coker probably returned to the city around 1808. The first contemporary public mention of him in his capacity as teacher at Sharp Street Church School, the new name of the group in control of the former African Academy, occurred a couple of years later.[60]

In January, 1810, "A Spectator," reporting on the African School Exhibition, no doubt the first such grand display of educated black talent to appear before the general public, stated:

> Coker and (George) Collins. . .the present
> teachers presented with three coloured boys,
> their pupils, ample proof of great powers of
> mind and memory. Their references, too, and
> quotations from ancient and modern history,
> were very appropriate and correctly done; and
> the prudent conduct, and elegant matter and
> manner of the whole performance was very cred-
> itable, yea highly honorable to the teachers
> and the children--Could Anthony Benezet and
> William Wilberforce, with other worthy per-
> sons, who have so nobly interested them-
> selves, and so effectually served the cause of
> the great injured Africans, have heard the
> grateful plaudits pronounced on this occa-
> sion, their hearts would have told them, 'we
> have not lived in vain.'[61]

More comments were to come, describing this unique occasion.

A day or so later, another writer submitted his account of the African Exercises. "An Observer" said of
the day set aside to commemorate the ending of the slave
trade, as set forth in the United States Constitution
and the subsequent Law of 1807, that Coker:

> . . . made a few observations on the extraor-
> dinary opinion of some philosophers, that the
> Africans are inferior to the Whites in the or-
> ganization of body and mind; and concluded by
> recommending to the attention of the au-
> dience, the addresses which were to be de-
> livered by his pupils.[62]

The pupils, in their parts, gave an overview of the ori-
gin and progress of the abolition of the slave trade in
England and America.

In speaking of George Collins, Coker's assistant,
"An Observer," said that:

> The exercises were followed by an address from
> the other preceptor (an African) who is him-
> self a complete refutation, if I may so ex-
> press myself, of the theory (black inferior-
> ity) alluded to by his associate. Had he re-
> ceived a classical education, or had the op-
> portunities of improvement which we usually

have, he would undoubtedly have been a conspicuous orator--nature had done much for him. His voice is strong, and harmonious, and he possesses in an eminent degree the power of modulating it, so as to affect the passions, his emphasis is good, and he has all the qualifications requisite for the formation of an orator, except the gracefulness of gesture--his situation in life is the cause of that defect, which admits of correction. In his address, he exhorts his brethren to offer up their gratitude to Providence, and next to him, to their earthly benefactors, for the numerous benefits received from them. He observed that as an Ameriean he was proud to say, that his country had been the first to ameliorate the condition of the blacks: 'When the sons of '76, whose bosoms beat with the enthusiasm of liberty, declared that man was by nature equal, and entitled to the privileges of life, liberty and property, the trembling captive lifted up his hands, bound with the galling fetters of slavery, and exclaimed, I too am a man. Then it was that the noble work commenced; and a provision was made by the framers of the constitution for their redemption.' It would take too much room to enlarge upon his pathetic and truly eloquent address. I need only add, that he concluded by exhorting his brethren to return thanks to God for his goodness to them, and to be obedient to the laws of their country.

That harmonious voice of Collins permitted him to be the first director of the choir of Sharp Street Church and, as such, start a tradition which made the Church's choir superb throughout the nineteenth century. Indeed, Lillie Mae Jackson, famed Civil rights leader of the twentieth century, as a member of the Sharp Street Church, sang in its choir.

More than the school and choir attracted blacks to this church, however. It was a spirit of freedom that prevailed there which even caused one slaveowner, and doubtlessly others, to publicly wonder about the example of such independence being displayed by blacks. Along these lines, in the same year as the auspicious opening to inspection of the African School taught by blacks, Coker had published A Dialogue between a Virginian and an African Minister, which was "humbly dedicated to the People of Colour in the United States of America." The

65

Dialogue is considered one of the earliest discursive antislavery works published by an American Negro. Coker's tract has the ring of being an account of an actual happening. In the Dialogue, a Mr. C. takes notes (this could have been Collins) to protect Coker from being misquoted by the Virginian. In addition, in the Dialogue itself, at the end of the discussion, Mr. C. thinks what has been said should be published.[63]

What transpired in the Dialogue was a skillful defense by Coker of what the Virginian called Coker's advocacy of emancipating by law the slaves the Virginian purchased "under the sanction of law." In a word, the Virginian thought his blacks were like his cattle and horses and should not be taken from him. Coker's defense made use of the terms and philosophy of natural rights, "so explicit and succinctly phrased in the declaration of independence." Coker said men had made men slaves against their will, which was not right. He particularly saw the enslavement of children of slaves as the grossest inequity. Even if those enslaved originally were guilty of crimes, hence the reason for their enslavement, as so many at that time used as an argument to buttress their enslavement of blacks, it was surely not equitable to punish their offsprings. Coker, in fact, believed as many abolitionists of his day believed, that the bulk of Africans sold into slavery were the victims of unjust pillage and plunder by Africans upon Africans; and, if the Africans were the thieves, the Europeans stood ready to receive, knowingly, stolen goods. Both in any moral schemes were equally guilty.

The Virginian, for his part in the discussion, brought in the Bible in defense of slavery. Coker, however, answered the Virginian's inference that those servants bought by Abraham were to serve for life by referring to Leviticus 29:42,54, which explicitly forbids perpetual slavery. Other evidence existed which, to Coker's way of believing, indicated that the slaves Abraham had were to be considered as equally worthy recipients of the goods of Abraham as the free in his camp, they were to be educated and well fed, "and enjoy all of the common privileges of citizens"--something few Negroes, slave or free, could boast of receiving amply. Coker was saying that Abraham was surely above his slaves, but he was not a heartless tyrant over them.

The Dialogue concluded with the Virginian evincing he had been converted to accepting a gradual emancipation plan that would set a date at which all born to slave parents would be born free. On his part, Coker advocated that no more barriers be placed in the way of masters who wanted to free their slaves.

In his opening remarks, the Virginian had indicated that he was aware of the fame of Coker because of the excellence of his education and his use of that education to advocate so skillfully the emancipation of the slaves. Coker taught school for approximately ten years in the city, and he was to have many eminent pupils. Even from outside the city, came pupils. Two daughters of George Bell from the District of Columbia, were taught by Coker; and, afterwards, their father, apparently impressed with the results, built the first black school in Washington. Besides being a teacher, he was an ordained minister who married many free blacks and gave them signed certificates indicating the same; he was, as well, president of the local mutual relief society. He was an invaluable asset to and became a focal point in the black community.

The public attention Coker attracted to himself in 1810, as a result of the schools' success and the publication of his Dialogue, certainly added to deflating arguments that proclaimed the indelible inferiority of blacks. This was, however, just part of Baltimore's contribution that year to deflating those who loudly pronounced the eternal subjugation of blacks. In England during 1810, Tom Mollineux, also from Baltimore and a boxer, challenged English boxers to fights and as one account stated, "threaten to mill the whole race of fighters of the day."--including the champion, Tom Crib.

On December 18, 1810, in the first encounter between Crib and Mollineux, Mollineux lost his battle with the champion; nevertheless, he immediately issued a challenge for a rematch. In his published provocation to Crib, Mollineux said:

> As it is possible this letter may meet the public eye, I cannot omit the opportunity of expressing a confident hope that the circumstances of my being of a different colour to that of a people amongst who I have sought protection, will not in any way operate to my prejudice.[64]

Mollineux fought Crib the following fall in 1811, and was beaten again in a fight in which both men were bloodied beyond belief. Nevertheless, his activities surely must have enhanced his own, plus his race's, and hometown's renown.

The concern caused in slaveholders by the activities of Coker, as was more dramatically the case with Mollineux, that blacks were taking matters into their own hands in Baltimore, as far as organizing and bettering themselves, was alarming to some who thought the liberal attitude toward Negroes, inspired and sustained by Elisha Tyson, was without precedent. In September 1810, the Attorney General of Maryland, Luther Martin, had published a letter disputing a decision of Judge John Scott that freed two blacks as a result of a writ of Habeas corpus and subji cundum. This judicial decision was against the usual practice which demanded free blacks be imprisoned if without freedom papers on their possession. Judge Scott, however, wanted evidence or witnesses to testify that the persons were runaways before having them committed. Being jailed without grounds could eventually, at best, result in selling a free black into temporary slavery to pay for his jail upkeep, if he were poor; or, at worst, having someone fraudulently claim him as their slave without too much difficulty and, thus, condemning that person to potential perpetual slavery.

Attorney General Martin thought the tenor of Judge Scott's decision in allowing the two blacks without their freedom papers to leave prison would draw to Baltimore black incendiaries from all around when the decision became known amongst blacks. It was ever the opinion of some that blacks were responsible for many or most of the fires that occurred, supposedly because it was believed blacks sought revenge for some slight, real or imagined, which they experienced at the hands of their masters. Martin also thought the Judge's decision further disposed Baltimore "to become the headquarters of free blacks and people of Colour, not only from other states of the Union, but from the islands." The possibility of more Negroes coming from the West Indies was positively alarming to Martin, as surely he was aware of the bloody measures blacks of that region were willing to take to gain their emancipation and independence.

To possibly add to Martin's alarm, a few months before Judge Scott's ruling, rumors circulated that the mulatto Haitian General Rigaud was in Maryland. Purportedly, Rigaud had been given a commission by the French Directorate around 1798 to raise a rebellion of slaves in the southern United States, something Martin could have feared Rigaud would then attempt, with Baltimore as the focal point of the rebellion.[65]

Martin submitted to newspapers a rebuttal to Judge Scott's decision which was described by one observer as "indecent." Martin promised to give legal support to any magistrate or constable who continued the old practice of arresting blacks without their papers. He also offered to assist any law officer who had a damage suit brought against him by a black for following this advice. Even in his courtroom appearance, Martin argued with such unbecoming ill will, that after two warnings from Judge Scott, Martin persisted in his uncouth behavior, at which the Judge walked out of the courtroom. Martin suggested in his open letter to the Justices of the Peace and Constables that it was their duty, owed to God, to put in jail any black found without his papers, for as surely as a black was without his papers, he more than likely was a murderer or robber.

Martin's crude language in the letter, perhaps, was evidently of the kind he had used before Judge Scott. He said, as he read the law, Judge Scott's opinion to the contrary, it merely states that a black without his papers was to be considered a runaway. He further stated to the justices, whose duty it was to authorize the commitment of a black, that

. . . since Judge Scott cannot trust their eyes or their nose to determine whether the person thus brought before them is a negro (sic) or a mullato, to swear some person to the fact, to wit'-- whether the person is a negro (sic) or mullato' to the best of his knowedge, skill, judgement and belief.[66]

With this great display of concern for the public interest behind him, Martin, a year later in 1811, offered himself as a candidate for the House of Delegates. As was his advice to the justices and constables, his campaign statement was arrogent, boastful, even condescending.[67]

In the same year of Martin's run for office, however, Judge Scott indicated his views in some respects had not altered as well. In his charge to the Grand Jury of Baltimore in 1811, he requested they look into the conduct of masters toward slaves to determine if the enslaved were being well-fed and clothed and not excessively beaten. When the report of the Grand Jury was presented by foreman Isaac Burneston, a leading Methodist, the report noted the abuses being made against Negroes at the public's expense should be stopped. That is to say, the report suggested it was improper for slave traders to be allowed to confine their slaves at City Jail, especially since it was sometimes likely the group might, perchance, include a black entitled to his freedom--a kidnapped victim.[68]

The concern of some, like Martin, that Baltimore was indeed becoming a center for black life seems fully justified. The Sharp Street School continued to prosper. In December 1811, it held its annual exhibition. Admittance, which was by ticket, was to be secured from certain individuals and from the warehouse of the Impartial Humane Society. In May of the next year, the school hosted a meeting for the wealthy black Quaker Paul Cuffe from Massachusetts as he promoted his Back-to-Africa plans. Cuffe spoke on his subject and afterwards the first chapter of his African Institute, under the leadership of Coker, was established. At this gathering, Elisha Tyson was in the audience.

Cuffe had just come from Washington where he advocated his ideas of colonization before Congress. In essence, his plans were to Christianize and commercialize Africa by and for the benefit of blacks. Cuffe's arrival in Baltimore was announced in the **Federal Gazette** and his endeavors lauded. When he first arrived in Baltimore, Cuffe was a victim of racial discrimination when a tavern refused to serve him supper unless with the servants. In addition, the tavern was unwilling to lodge him for the night, though he certainly had the means to pay. Cuffe quickly found a tavern which would serve him and avoided staying the night at any tavern at all, as he slept a guest in Tyson's house. Having observed Tyson up close, Cuffe recorded in his diary that Tyson was, indeed, a "real" friend of the Negro.[69]

Cuffe left Baltimore without too greatly affecting one way or the other the average black's desire to remain in the city; and, as time progressed into the next few years, the Sharp Street School remained important and central to the active and growing Baltimore free black community. It continued to hold annual exhibitions attracting its friends from throughout the city. It also took seriously its charge to prepare its pupils with a sense of purpose. In 1813, the school needed an additional teacher and advertised for him. As an indication of the ideals to which the school subscribed, it was stated the teacher had to be of good character and understand English grammar completely. Apparently none in Baltimore fit the bill and it was hoped someone outside of the city would venture to settle in Baltimore and contribute to making it that "headquarters" of free black life which people like Tyson furthered and people like Attorney General Martin feared.

The great worry of Martin, and some others, that
blacks in the city were hatching deep, dark plots of
riot and mayhem seems generally not to have been so much
the case in Baltimore as in other places. The efforts
of the abolitionists, especially Tyson, to better their
lot, if only in the particular matter of kidnapping
alone, would seem to stymie any disregard on the part of
the blacks for undoing the modicum of safety and freedom
they enjoyed in the city. In part, the history of kidnapping and in the instance of rioting in the summer of
1812, a little after Cuffe's visit to the city ended,
pointed out the contrary fact: that blacks suffered a
great amount of unjust violence.

The Baltimore riots of 1812 occurred just before
war was declared on Great Britain and acquainted Baltimore blacks, to an unprecedented degree, with the en-
vious and vehement, patriotic wrath of some white Baltimoreans.[70] Supposedly the reason for the riotous abuse
against blacks was laid at the door of a slave from the
West Indies, probably belonging to John Mycroft, gardener at the City Hospital, who supposedly made rather
general threats against whites. Whatever the nature of
this slave's threats, his arrest, and his arrest alone,
seemed easily brought about, and thus there was probably
not too deep a conspiracy involved. Nevertheless, the
riots of June and July were mainly directed at what was
considered the pro-British element of the community
which was thought to include many free blacks. After
killing several pro-British or anti-war whites, some of
prominence, the mob turned its attention to demolishing
two houses belonging to a free black named Briscoe, reportedly because he was in favor of the English and
declared he would "be a king himself."

After destroying Briscoe's property, the rabble
sought, symbolically, it might be said, to decapitate
the black community by destroying Sharp Street Church.
It is believed this end would have been accomplished if
those inside the church had not threatened to use force
to defend the building. Mayor Edward Johnson testified
later in an investigation of the riot that the many
criminal assaults committed against Negroes prompted
him to order a detail of mounted troops, under the command of Colonel Biays, to parade the streets specifically to stop these excesses.

In this period of general unrest, during the War of
1812 years, a group of blacks of Sharp Street Church
withdrew from it to help organize Bethel African Church.
Along with Coker, the others of prominence involved in

this endeavor included the Gilliard family, Charles Hackett, Don Carlos Hall, and Stephen Hill. Coker had married a Gilliard, the daughter of Jacob Gilliard, Junior. On May 9, 1815, the group assembled and selected the name "The African Methodist Bethel Society." With its founding, Bethel Church was probably the first independent Methodist church established in the United States amongst a significant free black population. Baltimore's Bethel Church was established from the beginning, independent of white ecclesiastical control.

The case of other Methodist congregations, especially those in Philadelphia, was not so. In Philadelphia's struggle to secure independence, the leading black Methodist of that city, Richard Allen, kept the Baltimore group informed of its progress. In a letter dated February 18, 1816, Baltimoreans were told of the Philadelphian's legal fight to rid themselves of white ecclesiastical control. Some aspect of the victory must have come some time earlier, however, for Coker preached a sermon on January 21, 1816, about the Philadelphian's success. He selected as a text, Psalm 126, verses 1-4, which drew an analogy between Jewish Babylonian captivity and Negro American enslavement--both peoples fought to restore themselves to the privilege of freedom. In part, he said:

> When the Lord returned to the captivity of Zion, we were like them that dream. Then was our mouth filled with laughter and our tongue with singing; then said they among the heathen, the Lord hath done great things for them. The Lord had done great things for us, whereof we are glad. Turn again our captivity, O Lord, as the streams in the South.

With the full victory of the Philadelphia Bethel becoming known several days later, Coker sent a few verses of his own to Allen:

> The God of Bethel heard her cries,
> He let her power be seen;
> He stopp'd the proud oppressor's frown
> And proved himself a king.
> Thou sav'd them in the trying hour
> Ministers and Councils joined;
> And all that stood ready to retain
> That helpless Church of Thine.
> Bethel surrounded by her foes
> But not yet in despair,
> Christ heard her supplicating cries

The God of Bethel heard.

In addition to all his other talents, it seem Coker was an aspiring poet.[71]

With Philadelphia blacks free of white ecclesiastical control, black Methodists in both Baltimore and Philadelphia were free to make bold plans. In April 1816, Baltimore's Bethel Church members, especially Coker and Stephen Hill, were very instrumental in setting up the first black national organization, The African Methodist Episcopal Church. At the organizing meeting, Coker was chosen the first bishop, but resigned in favor of Richard Allen when some questioned the validity of establishing an "African" Church with someone of Coker's complexion at its head--his complexion was noticeably white. That is one account. The other is that Coker stepped aside for Allen when the latter thought the society too small to support two bishops, one each from the power centers of the New Confession, Philadelphia and Baltimore, which had been the intention of many of those gathering at the organizational meeting. Nevertheless, Coker became an apostle of independence among black Methodists. He even travelled outside Baltimore to preach this new brand of Methodism.[72]

About a year after the organization of the A.M.E. Church and as Coker pursued with vigor preaching engagements to strengthen the new body, he countered a strong opposition to the new church's program at a courthouse meeting in Hagerstown, Maryland, in May 1817. His opponent was a black whom Coker believed had been sent by white Methodists growing fearful of a lessening of their influence among their black members. Yet, in the town, Coker had important allies. He was acquainted with Thomas Kemp of the Episcopal Church, soon to become bishop of his own denomination, but then a resident of Hagerstown. Indeed, Coker, along with Allen, and James Champion, had sought Kemp's advice on a discipline they had written for the African Methodist connection. The previous year Kemp had preached at Bethel Church, in a sense adding his blessing to black Baltimore's independent activities.[73]

The thriving boldness of Bethel in Baltimore was greatly due to the talents of Coker. Coker served as minister and teacher at Bethel as he had at Sharp Street Church. At times assisting him with the teaching duties was John W. Prout.[74] In his capacity as minister, he negotiated with persons such as Dr. Richard Hopkins in

73

1816 to use their land for a religious camp meeting. Hopkins' land was located one mile from Elkridge Landing. Similarly, in September 1817, at the camp meeting held on the road to Washington, five miles from Baltimore, Coker was in charge of these activities as well. After this meeting had ended, some black Methodists who participated in the activities, were accused of helping free two Negro convicts who happened to come by during the service. At least this was the story circulated in the city, so it seems, to damage the image of the new group, for one of those supporting the accusations, "A. B.", let it be known that Coker's Methodists were not under the governance of the white-led Methodist Episcopal Church.

Coker had a reply for the rumormongering printed in a friendly newspaper. He said:

> Seeing a charge of a serious nature in your paper of the 2d inst. relative to the conduct of the people of color at our camp meeting on Sunday last, we felt it our imperious duty to notice it. That an affair such as related, took place, we have strong reasons to doubt and we rest satisfied that a few days will remove every doubt from the public mind--and, had it been the case, we are satisfied that none of our members would have any hand in a crime of such magnitude, as that of causing the guilty to escape the hand of justice. We are of the opinion that hundreds of our respectable white citizens were at the meeting on the Sabbath day, and certainly some of them would have had some knowledge of the circumstances had it been true; and we have conversed with several of them, and they are of the opinion, that the report is false, and justify us in contradicting the same.[75]

There the matter rested except for further rebuttal from "A. B." about having witnesses capable of supporting his account.

In conjunction with this effort to besmirch the reputation of the African Methodists, there was evidence stemming from the officials of the Methodist Episcopal Church, itself, that it regarded the blacks still in their churches with less than a brotherly feeling. At a meeting of the Elders of the church in 1817, a resolution was submitted requesting the blacks to withdraw

74

from the Light Street, Eutaw, and Old Town congregations and join the separate black meetings in the denomination at Sharp Street, Asbury, or Strawberry Alley Churches.

For some blacks and whites in the General Methodist Episcopal Church, however, there was still some collaboration or cooperation in certain matters. In the same year as the Elders made their requests for blacks to leave, earlier that year, J. Kingston, President of the Asbury Education Society appealed for funds for his sabbath school operation that included whites and blacks, both slave and free as participants.[76]

As much as practically everybody, friend and foe, could recognize Coker's contribution to the success of Bethel Church, he was not considered wholly above his congregants--a law unto himself. Sometime in 1818, he was disciplined by his own church and apparently stripped of all positions of importance in the body--for what reason, it is unknown. Nevertheless, he was reinstated and, in 1820, decided to go to Liberia, the African colony founded by the American Colonization Society.

Coker was the most prominent black to go to Liberia in this early period. He set sail on the first expedition of the Colonization Society from New York on February 6, 1820. Initially, whites had been placed in charge of the expedition, but Coker vigorously assumed the leadership position among the colonists as a result of the deaths in transit and the death and sickness visited upon the party after it landed in Sherbro, an unhealthy spot. Ten days out of port, an A.M.E. congregation was formed and ready to operate once the group disembarked. Thus, Coker planted the independent black church in Africa, that is the black American Westernized branch. Eventually, this pioneering group broke up, with some going to the Grandville Sharp inspired British settlement at Sierre Leone.

Coker recorded in a journal the exploits of the founders of Liberia which was published in the United States and sold for 25 cents a copy. He also stayed in touch with his many friends back in the States through letter writing. One enthusiastic letter he sent his wife dated May 26, 1820, from Genoy, Africa, said, among other things, that much good could be accomplished by the free blacks coming over to help enlighten the native African to the good of Christianity and benefits of western ideas and technology. One of the best examples of technology Baltimore was more fittingly able to demonstrate to the Africans was represented in the person of Nathaniel Peck, who had been a miller for an establishment on Falls Road; perhaps he served as such at one of Tyson's mills there. Besides being the miller for the colony, Peck was also president of the Sunday School. In the conclusion of his letter to his wife, Coker gave voice to what all hoped for as he said, "Africa is good land; tell the people to come here and they will be happy if they will be industrious."[77]

Coker's letters and his Journal were considered vital elements of a campaign by colonizationists to get blacks to go to Africa. His Journal was to remain valuable even into the 1830s. Yet his overall value and past service to the community seemed well appreciated by those not colonizationists. Not long after his settlement in Africa, friends of Coker throughout the United States wanted his likeness preserved in an engraving so that it would not be forgotten. Coker wrote to Bishop Thomas Kemp to get one of the paintings of himself owned by Don Carlos Hall, Nicholas Gilliard, Jeremiah Watts, or Alex Murray, and decide with others of his acquaintances which should be engraved.[78]

Meanwhile, back in Africa, as time moved along, Coker became an extensive coastal trader, having several vessels, one of which he commanded in person. His residence was on Sherbro Island and there he lived in great spendor. He died in 1845 or 1846 at an advanced age, leaving a family of several sons and daughters.

Coker was, without doubt, the first black American leader of national significance. He had considerable leadership experience in New York and Baltimore and had been fully acquainted with the black leaders of Philadelphia. When he did decide to go to Liberia in 1820, he stopped in Philadelphia to have a meeting with the influential people there; he apparently tried to influence them to join him in Liberia. Prince Saunders; Richard Allen, Bishop of the African Methodist Episcopal Church; and James Forten, rich sailing-loft owner, and leading laymen at St. Thomas Episcopal Church were amongst those with whom he conferred. James Matthews, another A.M.E. minister, was also present.

After leaving Philadelphia and arriving in New York, Coker described the enthusiasm for the emigration venture saying that 500 could have been taken over to Liberia if there had been room. While in New York, he probably visited his old friend George Collins, his teaching associate in Baltimore, who did not go to Liberia, but who would in about two years be very important in the founding of the other national black Methodist body, the African Methodist Episcopal Zion Church. The throng that witnessed Coker's departure from New York for Africa, Coker estimated to be about 10,000, all of whom were not accommodated in a local black church which opened its doors for those wanting to ask Divine help for the success of the mission.

Although the excitement involved in going to Africa did seem genuine enough, it did not preclude other black Baltimoreans from considering an alternative to African emigration. Some Baltimore-free Negroes organized the Maryland Haytian Company which chartered its first ship, the Dromo, to embark for Haiti from the city on December 4, 1819. As with African colonization, it is possible that the Baltimore effort to colonize Haiti may have been a key part of a national concerted drive by Negro leadership. In May 1819, Prince Saunders had forwarded to the Emperor of Russia, through the President of the American Convention of Abolition Societies, material relative to the feasibility of blacks in the United States colonizing Haiti. Saunders wanted the Russian leader's commendation and support in establishing a receptacle for the emigrating free blacks, whose efforts would, hopefully, change their own condition, but also help bring about the destruction of the international slave trade--how this was to be accomplished was not revealed.[79]

George R. McGill was the leader of Baltimore's expedition to Haiti. McGill was a preacher-teacher at the Sharp Street Church, and an enterprising businessman who operated at times an oyster cellar, messenger service, and other little enterprises. At one point, his place of business was located at No. 3 Calvert, nearly opposite the Mechanics Bank, one looked upon with favor by Tyson. McGill had purchased himself, father, brothers, and sisters out of slavery and was encouraged by both black and white in his endeavors. Around 1809, he married a woman, herself formerly a slave, but set free by her blind lady master she served who, also, left her an inheritance. McGill saw all the important people and presented his commission from the Maryland Haytian Company to the President of Haiti. Falling sick from fever, however, he was prevented from extensively surveying the country as he had wanted. During his stay, misfortune struck. The promise of free transportation to be provided by the Haitian Government was rescinded because of malicious rumors circulated in the United States, disparaging the island nation's level of development, at least, that was an opinion held by some.

Upon returning to Baltimore, McGill, nevertheless, defended the level of attainment which Haiti had achieved, in so short a time, and it was still his recommendation that blacks should look to Haiti for salvation of a kind. In conclusion, McGill said:

> In this land of real freedom, blessed with equal rights and governed by equal laws, which for obedience return security--purified from the defilement of partial degradation; the souls of the black men, bursting the shackles imposed by prejudice, may walk 'abroad in its own majesty,' and by the extent of its attainments may furnish additional evidence to sceptics (sic) that the God of nature never designed that intellectual excellence should be confined to any particular complexion.

McGill never settled in Haiti, but did eventually go to Liberia.

One of George McGill's sons, Samuel Ford, recalled something of the atmosphere some 25 years after the time his father returned from Haiti. He Said,

> I was about five or six years old when my father returned from his visit to St. Domingo, he then made me understand the object of that visit. He used to talk to me about the Haytians, their revolution, its horrors and the final triumphs of the blacks. When six years old I could read, The History of St. Domingo was put in my hands ....It was customary in them (sic) days to have Exhibitions at which the scholars delivered selected speeches, my first was delivered in the old concert Hall on Charles Street;--it was my own selection, from the 'Genius of Universal Emancipation.' I yet remember the opening lines.

> > Republic of Hayti, the Queen of the Isles,
> > The tyrants may frown; tis your Parents who smiles
> > Be youthful and thankfully live to his praise

                    the   Author   of   Life,   The
                    Creator of days.
                    Your bonds he has broken, re-
                    member the hand
                    Which has raised you to Glory
                    and given you this land.[80]

Haiti had a real fascination and was a viable alternative to Liberia for some in the early years after its
revolution against French rule.

    Despite the attempts of some to view colonization
as a solution to the racial tension in the United
States, from late 1819 to early 1820, the Missouri Crisis developed, giving hope to others who sought to destroy slavery and its twin, racial prejudice in the
United States. The essence of the Missouri Crisis, a
national debate over what should be the geographic extent of slavery in the United States, got started when
the Missouri Territory requested admission to the Union
in 1819. Some aroused members of Congress, however, led
by Representative Tallmadage of New York, sought to pro-
scribe perpetual slavery from the State's constitution.
Tallmadge had made a similar attempt to prevent the admission of Illinois to the Union a year earlier because
of its sanctioning of slavery which was a clear violation of the Ordinance of 1787 prohibiting slavery in the
Northwest Territory, out of which Illinois was carved.[81]

    The attitude Baltimoreans would take on this matter
certainly aroused interest elsewhere as the city was the
major emporium of the Southland--it sat as an entrance
to all concerns going to and from between the North and
South, whether these be ideas, goods, slaves or freedmen. After such places as Trenton, New Jersey; New
York; and Philadelphia, had made known their views
against Missouri's entrance into the Union as a slave
state, Elisha Tyson gave notice in the newspapers that a
public meeting would be held on the 28th of December
1819 at four o'clock in the court house, to discuss the
subject of Missouri's request for admission. Inside the
court house meeting a lengthy debate occurred and, afterward, a vigorous newspaper dispute ensued as both
sides realized what was at stake.[82]

    Even before the debate in the court house, Daniel
Raymond, who was an important person in the debates and
a lawyer in petition of freedom suits and involved in
the formation of the Protection Society, had published a
pamphlet, "On the Missouri Question," which was anti-
slavery in tone. To spread his messages, Raymond sent

his pamphlet to such persons as John Jay, first Chief Justice of the United States Supreme Court. Jay replied to Raymond's pamphlet saying:

> The remarks and statements contained in it, place the pernicious influence of slaves on the welfare of our country, in conspicuous and impressive points of view. The obvious dictates both of morality and policy lead us to believe that our free nation cannot encourage the extension of slavery, nor the multiplication of slaves, without doing violence to their principles, and without depressing their power and prosperity.[83]

Raymond's pamphlet was answered on the opposing side from Baltimorean Joseph D. Learned.

About a year after Raymond's pamphlet, he indicated he was not quite finished with the Missouri Question, or dealing with the question of whether the United States was to be a free society with a free economy, or a slave society with an economy moved along only at the point of the lash. Raymond wrote Thoughts on Political Economy, supposedly the first work of an American into the field long dominated by the likes of Adam Smith, incorporating his thoughts on the above subject. The book, like the pamphlet, was well received, especially by John Adams, the former President. It should be considered likely also, that Raymond's uncle, Senator James Hillhouse of Connecticut, a prominent part of the group that fought against the admission of Missouri as a slave state, was doubly proud to make use of the ideas of his nephew in the debates in the Senate in the ensuing couple of sessions.

Needless to say, Raymond's theoretical work was much a part of the debates in Baltimore's court house when it took up the issue of Missouri's entrance in the Union. As a result of the court house meeting in Baltimore, a memorial drawn up by Tyson and his associates, eventually attracted 2,000 signatures and when presented to the Congress, was supposedly the largest such petition against Missouri's admission as a slave state, that it thoroughly astonished other Southerners. It is believed Baltimore's memorial was decisive in the House of Representatives' initial support of Tallmadge's amendment against Missouri.[84]

As the memorial was circulating in Baltimore and being signed, numerous correspondents to Baltimore's various newspapers continued to debate and comment on the issues. Some disputed over whether many or few of Baltimore's elite attended the meeting. One article thought that inside the meeting abolitionists kept a tight control, preventing a postponement of the meeting to make it certain more persons unfavorable to their cause could not be called upon to attend a future gathering. Along those lines was a similar complaint made which suggested the promoters of the meeting deliberately set the meeting at Christmastime, a time, "sacred to the slave-holders"--doubtlessly words pregnant with irony for many blacks and abolitionists, alike.[85]

With the most cursory view of the letters and articles, the main fear of the slaveholders seemed to have been that discussing slavery, at all, somehow tampered with their property rights to their slaves, despite the fact that abolition was only contemplated for Missouri. Doubtlessly, there was a concern that any appreciable rebirth of emancipation sentiment in Baltimore might give others throughout Maryland and the remaining Southern States the idea to bring forth new proposals for general emancipation.

This attitude seems evident in the letter of "A Slave Holder," who said the meeting was a product of the minds of those in the Protection Society which, as he recalled, had once tried to convince others at its founding that it was not advocating general emancipation. This writer held in disdain the presiding officer of the meeting, Mayor Edward Johnson, whom he thought had been duped to sanction the machination of abolitionists. He wrote,

> It is true, he (Mayor) was in the chair, but I believe it is equally true that he had no more to do with the management by which the meeting was got up or conducted than I had. It did not require the keenest vision, to discover the master-spirit, who, though seated in a much humble position, was too conspicuous and too active to escape notice.[86]

The "master-spirit" was Elisha Tyson, or one of his personal representatives.

While Elisha Tyson played a conspicuous part in Baltimore's efforts against Missouri's entrance into the Union, many hoped another Marylander would play as central a role in defeating Missouri's entrance on the national scene. William Pinkney, who became famous in antislavery circles in 1789 for his speech before the House of Delegates, urging abolition and the repeal of the law restricting manumissions by last will and testament, was elected to the United States Senate from Maryland on January 4, 1820. Needless to say, a similar speech in favor of the Missouri restriction was expected by those acquainted with his past. In anticipation of this hoped-for-effort, his speech of 1789 was reprinted in local papers. Such was not the case, however, and Pinkney did a reversal of all he had spoken in favor of in 1789. He became instrumental in resolving the Missouri Question in a compromise, instead of restricting slavery and providing for the emancipation of slaves already in Missouri as abolitionists had hoped. The result of the compromise concluded with hashmarks being placed on maps of the country restricting slavery, in the future, to lands of the Louisiana Purchase, south of the 36 30' parallel. This settlement and the recognition of the limits of slavery was not final as the Civil War proved, being brought about, in part, because of Southern violations of the Agreement of 1820.[87]

Elisha Tyson's involvement in the Missouri Crisis was nearly the last great effort of his life spent as the elder, most distinguished abolitionist in the United States. When he did see death approaching, he did two things relative to what he had considered his Divine Commission. He called together the various elements of the black community and urged them to form a society to collect money and to continue the battle, in court and elsewhere, against the oppression of their brethren; this was probably a unique event in black history, up to that time.

With the organization formed, Tyson next turned his attention to what could be left as a legacy to those blacks in other parts of the country, especially to those living in the Middle States. Tyson's solution was to leave a Farewell Address as evidence of the deep and affectionate solicitude he had for their further advancement. Apparently the affection of blacks for Tyson was reciprocated, as indicated in the thousands who attended his funeral, and heard the Address commemorate an epoch in their history coming to a close. Subsequently, the fact that Negroes, at least in Baltimore and Philadelphia, commemorated annually either his birthday or date of death, further indicated the high regard blacks had for Tyson.

Tyson, aware of his reputation among Negroes, was careful to say in his Farewell Address that throughout his years of effort on their behalf, fame had not been his aim; his desire had been to promote justice and true religion. A piece of advice he wished to leave blacks from his own experience was the necessity of worshiping God with awe, decency, and order; because, ultimately through God had blacks been released and would be released from bondage and elevated by secular and moral instruction provided by the many schools and churches erected to accomplish these ends. This proved to be a sentiment shared by most black reformers that came to prominence after his death.

Tyson suggested that as the free blacks improved and showed themselves capable of living as free men, more and more whites would be led to emancipate their slaves and rid themselves of prejudice. In the end, a free black people in the United States would be accepted as equals among the array of nations which would, he believed, be assembled before God on the Last Day. In saying this, however, Tyson was not justifying their present enslavement. He further stated, in a prophetic vein, that when free blacks conducted themselves with honesty and sobriety, God, Himself, would undoubtedly use them as instruments to show a higher ideal to the world at-large, an ideal practiced by a people that did not render evil for evil. He also envisioned America's blacks would be useful in diffusing the light of a higher morality and knowledge among Africans, whose spiritual benightedness had made it so easy for many Africans and their descendants being found as slaves throughout the world, in the first place, inasmuch as many Africans in many cases were so willing to sell or too weak to prevent other Africans being taken into slavery.[88]

The death of Elisha Tyson was reported throughout the United States, and at a meeting held at Bethel Church in Philadelphia, on March 18, 1824, a month after his death, with Bishop Richard Allen in the chair, and John Allen as secretary, the meeting proclaimed Tyson as:

> ... a very influential and efficient friend of the people of Color, known for his many acts of humanity and hospitality for upwards of forty years.[89]

The Philadelphians resolved to march through the streets on April 1 and afterward hear "an appropriate funeral discourse" to be delivered on the death of "our friend". No more public and appropriate tribute could have been paid a man who openly and zealously stood forth in the light of day for justice and righteousness as no other had.

Tyson was remembered by those whose lives he touched. Samuel F. McGill recalled, thirty years after Tyson's death,

> ... the admiration I felt for the man who brave (sic) the fierce wrath of the slave dealer Woolfolk, who pistol in hand threatened his life for having rescued individuals of my race from his chains. I have stood on the pavements opposite his house, patiently waiting to catch a single glance of his towering form, and felt happy in this distant admiration of the friend of my race; he was too exalted in my boyish opinion for any near approach.[90]

McGill also said, that, in his eyes, Tyson had a "dignity of appearance," and was "a giant in power--because he was struggling with the oppressors of my race." McGill went to Liberia but remained touched by the Tyson legacy as Elisha's cousin, Moses Sheppard, assisted him in many ways to become a doctor and successful businessman.

Some whites, as well, viewed the life of Elisha Tyson with awe because of its great spiritual quality and the courageousness he showed throughout his life. Dr. Bartholomew Fussell, an associate of Tyson who resided in Baltimore at the time of the incident with Woolfolk alluded to above took place, later moved back to his native Pennsylvania, where he acted in a courageous fashion as a conductor of the underground railroad, assisting many slaves to escape to freer Pennsylvania. Fussell's recollection of the Woolfolk incident was of this manner: Woolfolk's agents were dragging a woman up the street on which Tyson lived, when as the party got near Tyson's house, the lady demanded to see "Father Tyson". As a crowd gathered, it, too, demanded she be permitted to see Tyson; and, at this point, Tyson spoke with her. Woolfolk was informed of the situation, whereby he raced to the scene, with pistol in hand, and uttered he would "send him (Tyson) to hell for interfering with his property." Tyson Coolly exposed his breast, telling him that he dared not shoot, and that he (Woolfolk) was in hell already though he did not know

84

it." The woman was found to be entitled to her freedom. Because of this incident, and many other similar ones, Tyson was remembered as the champion, without peer, in the struggle for human rights, full human rights in Baltimore, and his name was known throughout the country. Those that came after him had to be measured by his actions, and not many came even half close.[91]

Chapter II

[1]Federal Gazette, February 24, 1804, p. 2; April 10, 1804, p. 3; October 7, 1805, p. 3; October 8, 1805, p. 3; March 20, 1810, p. 2; Wills of Baltimore (Elisha Tyson), No. 11, W.B. No. 2, 1819-1824, p. 643.

[2]Federal Gazette, February 27, 1794, p. 2; March 7, 1794, p. 1; The North American and Mercantile Daily Advertiser, February 8, 1808, p. 3.

[3]Federal Gazette, February 12, 13, 14, 1805; July 18, 1805, p. 3; October 2, 1805, p. 3; October 30, 1805, p. 3; November 18, 1805, p. 3; December 14, 1805, p. 2; October 2, 1807, p. 3; April 13, 1809, p. 3; October 6, 1813, p. 2; February 16, 1816, p. 3; September 23, 1817, p. 2; October 7, 1817, p. 3.

[4]Federal Gazette, April 21, 1804, p. 3; April 27, 1804, p. 2; May 9, 1804, p. 3; May 22, 1804, p. 3; Martha Ellicott Tyson, p. 34.

[5]Martha Ellicott Tyson, pp. 33-34; Oliver Evans, A Trip Made by a Small Man in a Wrestle with a Very Great Man (Philadelphia, n.p., 1813), pp. 13-14.

[6]See, Elisha Tyson, Jr., "Diaries," M.H.S., Federal Gazette, November 30, 1819, p. 2; December 7, 1820, p. 3.

[7]Frederick Herald, August 1, 1818, p. 2.

[8]Federal Gazette, September 29, 1813, p. 3; June 21, 1804, p. 3; see Collamer M. Abbott, "Isaac Tyson, Jr., Pioneer Mining Engineer and Metallurgist"; Maryland Historical Magazine, 60 (March 1965):15-25.

[9]See in general, Forbush, Moses Sheppard; Helen H. Thom, Johns Hopkins: A Silhouette (Baltimore: The Johns Hopkins Press, 1929); Richard H. Hart, Enoch Pratt: The Story of a Plain Man (Baltimore: Enoch Pratt Free Library, 1935); Thomas Wilson, Biographical File, Enoch Pratt Free Library, Baltimore, Maryland.

[10]Federal Gazette, October 29, 1800, p. 3; Telegraphe, August 2, 1800, p. 3; August 23, 1800, p. 1; October 7, 1800, p. 3; October 9, 1800, p. 9; November 17, 1800.

[11]See, in general, C. Herbert Baxley, A History of the Baltimore General Dispensary Founded 1801 (Baltimore: General Dispensary Foundation, Inc., 1963).

[12]Federal Gazette, January 7, 1802, p. 3; February 17, 1802, p. 3; February 18, 1802, p. 3; February 20, 1803, p. 2.

[13]Federal Gazette, August 18, 1804, p. 2; November 30, 1804, p. 2; November 26, 1805, p. 3; February 6, 1818, p. 2; November 19, 1822, p. 3; Robert R. Allen, "Count Rumford: Behavior Engineer," Social Service Review 46 (December 1972), pp. 597-602; Evening Post, December 16, 1805.

[14]Federal Gazette, February 20, 1817, p. 2.

[15]Federal Republican, February 28, 1810, p. 2; March 7, 1810, p. 3; C. T. Kidder, p. 4.

[16]Federal Gazette, February 5, 1811, p. 3; February 25, 1811, p. 3; February 28, 1811, p. 3.

[17]William D. Hoyt, Jr., ed., "Civilian Defense in Baltimore, 1814-1815: Minutes of the Committee of Vigilance," Maryland Historical Magazine, 39 (September 1944):211-212; Federal Gazette, September 2, 1814, p. 2; December 19, 1814, p. 3.

[18]Federal Gazette, February 21, 1814, p. 2.

[19]Federal Gazette, October 15, 1814, p. 3.

[20]The Savings Bank of Baltimore, The Savings Bank of Baltimore: One Hundred Years of Service, 1818-1918 (Baltimore: Thomsen Ellis Co., 1918), p. 11; Blanche D. Coll, "The Baltimore Society for the Prevention of Pauperism, 1820-1821," American Historical Review, 61 (October 1955):82, 84; American, March 9, 1820, p. 2; Federal Gazette, December 21, 1818, p. 3; November 2, 1819; June 11, 1821, p. 2; September 10, 1821, p. 3; December 27, 1821, p. 3.

[21]The American Patriot, February 24, 1803.

[22]John S. Tyson, p. 62; American, February 28, 1824, p. 4.

[23]Marvin E. Gettleman, "The Maryland Penitentiary in the Age of Tocqueville, 1828-1842," Maryland Historical Magazine, 56 (September 1961):275; Annual Report of

the Directors and Wardens of the Maryland Penitentiary
(Baltimore: Thomas E. Evans Printing Co., 1911), pp.
22-23.

[24]Federal Gazette, February 1, 1803, p. 3; February 2, 1808, p. 3; August 6, 1818, p. 2; September 4, 1818, p. 2.

[25]American, February 28, 1824, p. 4.

[26]Robert C. Smedley, History of the Underground Railroad in Chester and the Neighboring Counties of Pennsylvania (Lancaster, Pa.: Office of The Journal, 1883), pp. 100, 245.

[27]Thomas E. Drake, Quakers and Slavery in America, p. 119.

[28]John Parrish, Remarks on the Slavery of the Black People (Philadelphia: John Parrish, 1806), p. 16; Federal Gazette, May 8, 1801, p. 2; September 5, 1801, p. 3; John S. Tyson, p. 79.

[29]Federal Gazette, August 3, 1803, p. 2.

[30]The American Patriot, November 13, 1802, p. 3.

[31]Federal Gazette, January 9, 1802, p. 3.

[32]Letter, Philip E. Thomas to John Parrish, August 31, 1806, H.S.P.; Federal Republican, December 2, 1816, p. 2; December 13, 1816, p. 2; Federal Gazette, September 20, 1816, p. 2; October 16, 1816, p. 2; December 6, 1816, p. 2.

[33]Federal Gazette, July 27, 1807, p. 2.

[34]Federal Gazette, July 28, 1807, p. 3.

[35]Federal Gazette, August 6, 1807, p. 3.

[36]National Anti-Slavery Standard, October 29, 1840, p. 2; Letter, Elisha Tyson to Isaac Hopper, July 10, 1811, H.S.P.; Letter, Elisha Tyson to William Masters, July 28, 1811, H.S.P.; Letter, Elisha Tyson to William Masters, December 12, 1811, H.S.P.

[37]Letter, Isaac Tyson to J. Ridgway, July 25, 1811, H.S.P.

[38]Minutes, Baltimore Meeting of Sufferings, 1811, pp. 122, 129; 1812, p. 131.

[39]Letter, Elisha Tyson to William Masters, July 1812, H.S.P.

[40]Letter, Elisha Tyson to William Masters, August 20, 1812, H.S.P.; Letter, Elisha Tyson to William Masters, September 4, 1812, H.S.P.

[41]Letter, Elisha Tyson to James Cammeron and William Masters, November 11, 1812, H.S.P.

[42]Minutes Baltimore Meeting of Sufferings, 1815, pp. 144-145; 1816, pp. 146, 149; Baltimore Yearly Meeting, 1814.

[43]Federal Gazette, September 26, 1816, p. 2; September 30, 1816, p. 2; Federal Republican, September 17, 1816, p. 2; September 28, 1816.

[44]Federal Republican, October 2, 1816, p. 2.

[45]Hamilton Owens, Baltimore on the Chesapeake (Garden City, N.Y.: Doubleday, Doran & Co., Inc., 1944), pp. 128, 212-213.

[46]Federal Republican, October 9, 1816, p. 2; John S. Tyson, p. 100; Letter, Elisha Tyson, Jr., to Thomas Shipley, December 5, 1816, H.S.P.

[47]Federal Gazette, October 28, 1816, p. 2.

[48]Federal Gazette, March 19, 1810, p. 3.

[49]Baltimore Patriot, January 7, 1817; January 11, 1817.

[50]Baltimore Patriot, July 25, 1817, p. 2.

[51]Baltimore Patriot, July 26, 1817, p. 2.

[52]Federal Gazette, December 13, 1817, p. 2.

[53]American, July 7, 1818, p. 2; July 10, 1818, p. 2; Federal Gazette, July 15, 1818, p. 2.

[54]Evening Patriot, August 7, 1818, p. 2.

[55]Evening Patriot, October 3, 1818, p. 2.

[56]See, in general, P. J. Standenraus, The African Colonization Movement, 1816-1865 (New York: Columbia University Press, 1961)

[57]John S. Tyson, pp. 110-121; William Innes, Liberia (Edinburgh: Waugh & Innes, 1833), pp. 15-17; William E. B. DuBois, The Suppression of the African Slave Trade to the United States of America, 1638-1870 (Baton Rouge, La.: Louisiana State University Press, 1969, c. 1896), pp. 109-116; Federal Gazette, November 7, 1816, p. 2.

[58]American, February 28, 1824, p. 4.

[59]Federal Gazette, November 5, 1799, p. 2; James A. Handy, Scraps of A.M.E. History (Philadelphia: A.M.E. Book Concern, 1902), p. 14.

[60]David Smith Biography of Rev. David Smith of the A.M.E. Church (Xenia, Ohio: The Xenia Gazette Office, 1881), pp. 25, 32-33, 35; American, September 16, 1894, p. 20.

[61]Federal Gazette, January 2, 1810, p. 3.

[62]Federal Gazette, January 3, 1810, p. 2.

[63]Coker's pamphlet included in Dorothy Porter, ed., Negro Protest Pamphlets (New York: Arno Press and The New York Times, 1969); Carter G. Woodson, The Education of the Negro Prior to 1861 (New York: Arno Press and New York Times, 1968, c. 1919), p. 140.

[64]London Times, August 23, 1810, p. 2; December 19, 1810, p. 3; December 25, 1810, p. 4; September 28, 1811, p. 3.

[65]Federal Gazette, March 28, 1810, p. 1; September 13, 1810, p. 2.

[66]Federal Gazette, September 13, 1810, p. 2.

[67]Federal Gazette, September 20, 1811, p. 3; September 30, 1811, p. 2.

[68]Federal Republican, February 23, 1811, p. 3.

[69]Sheldon H. Harris, Paul Cuffe: Black American and the African Return (New York: Simon and Schuster, 1972), pp. 60, 64, 151-152; Federal Gazette, May 7, 1812, p. 3.

[70]James S. Buckingham, America Historical Statistic, and Descriptive (London: Fisher, Son & Co., 1841), I, p. 430; Federal Republic, July 27, 1812, p. 2; Report of the Committee of Grievance and Courts of Justice of the House of Delegates of Maryland on the Subject of the Recent Mobs and Riots in the City of Baltimore, Together with the Depositions Taken before the Committee (Annapolis: Jonas Green for the Committee, 1813), pp. 42, 100, 149, 163, 186, 201, 307.

[71]Charles Wesley, Richard Allen (Washington: The Associated Publishers, Inc., 1969, c.) pp. 42, 46, 150, 167; Federal Gazette, February 4, 1817, p. 3.

[72]See, in general, Carol V. R. George Segregated Sabbaths: Richard Allen and the Emergence of Independent Black Churches, 1760-1840 (New York: Oxford University Press, 1973); Rodney Carlisle, "Self-Determination in Colonial Liberia," Negro History Bulletin, 36 (April 1873), p. 78.

[73]Letter, Daniel Coker to James Kemp, June 3, 1817, Diocesan Archives, Episcopal Church, Maryland Historical Society.

[74]Federal Gazette, November 20 or 26, 1818, p. 3.

[75]American, September 3, 1817, p. 2; September 5, 1817, p. 2; Federal Gazette, September 4, 1817, p. 2.

[76]Israel Papers, Minutes of Society for the Relief of the Poor, 1814-1817, Methodist Episcopal Church, M.H.S.: Federal Gazette, February 4, 1817, p. 3.

[77]See, in general, Daniel Coker, Journal of Daniel Coker (Baltimore: Maryland Auxiliary, Colonization Society, 1820); Federal Gazette, June 26, 1820, p. 2; December 13, 1820, p. 2; Morning Chronicle, February 7, 1820, p. 2.

[78]Letter, Daniel Coker to James Kemp, April 20, 1821, Diocesan Archives, Episcopal Church, Maryland Historical Society.

[79]Federal Gazette February 22, 1821, p. 2; Letter Prince Saunders to Emperor of Russia, May 15, 1819, H.S.P.

[80]Letter, Samuel F. McGill to Moses Sheppard, May 16, 1854, Swarthmore College, Friends' Library, Moses Sheppard papers.

[81]See, in general, Glover Moore, The Missouri Controversy, 1819-1821 (Lexington: University of Kentucky Press, 1953); John S. Tyson, p. 105.

[82]Morning Chronicle, December 25, 1819, p. 3.

[83]Morning Chronicle, December 28, 1819, p. 2.

[84]John S. Tyson, p. 104.

[85]Federal Gazette, December 30, 1819, p. 2; December 31, 1819, p. 2; January 1, 1820, p. 2; January 4, 1820, p. 2; January 7, 1820, p. 2; American, December 29, 1819, p. 2; Morning Chronicle, January 5, 1820, p. 2; Evening Patriot, January 6, 1820, p. 2; January 8, 1820, p. 2.

[86]Federal Gazette, December 30, 1819, p. 2.

[87]Henry Wheaton, Some Account of the Life, Writing, and Speeches of William Pinkney (New York: J. W. Palmer & Co., 1824), p. 167.

[88]John S. Tyson, pp. 107, 123, 125, 131; The Friend 1828, pp. 348-349.

[89]Poulson's American, March 31, 1824; Washington Gazette, April 2, 1824, p. 3.

[90]Letter, Samuel F. McGill to Moses Sheppard, May 16, 1854, Swarthmore College, Friends' Library, Moses Sheppard papers.

[91]Joseph Sturge, A Visit to the United States in 1841 (New York: Augustus M. Kelley Publishers, 1969, c. 1842), p. 10.

Chapter III

WILLIAM WATKINS, THE TEACHER

After the death of Elisha Tyson, any number of whites acquainted with him pursued a line of abolitionist activity that was commendable. These whites, however, were not to have the significance in the black community as had Tyson; for, by then, local black leadership had grown even stronger since the days of Coker, in fact, had been encouraged by Tyson at his death to do more of the work to make all Afro-Americans free. One of the more significant black voices of these years, and for nearly thirty years, belonged to William Watkins.

Born around 1800, perhaps of a father or grandfather who fought in the Revolutionary War, Watkins distinguished himself as one of the best teachers of his day. Though unable to write, Watkins' father also named William Watkins, was a leading trustee of Sharp Street Church from at least around 1810 to the 1830s. The Watkins family probably lived on Camden Street from 1802 and was not more than about five blocks from Sharp Street Church which, in turn, was on the same block as Tyson's house.

William Watkins, the son and teacher, was a pupil of Daniel Coker's, and, supposedly took over Coker's school when Coker left for Africa in 1820, or started teaching that year. Watkins taught approximately up to 1852. He was mainly self-taught after learning the rudiments but, nevertheless, well schooled. This is evident in the range of subjects he taught in his school—History, Geography, Mathematics, English, Natural Philosophy, Greek, Latin, Music, and Rhetoric. His forte as a teacher, however, was an amazing command of the English language. Composing essays with such elegance and clarity of style, Watkins, unquestionably, abashed the detractors of the Negro, who had a habit of preferring his speech in minstrel-like ungrammatical dialect.

As a person, Watkins stood lean and tall, even, muscular, and, as should have been expected of a scholar, he wore glasses. He was economical and charitable, his carriage dignified; his manner was characterized as self-effacing. He held his emotions under control and was unable to "extemporarize" in public debate on most subjects, except on matters of vital importance to his people. The position of outspoken leadership he was to assume in the community also indicates he was a man of courage as well. The records show his life was threatened at least once, but, doubtlessly, there were more times. He evidenced a concern, not only for blacks, but mankind of other distinctions. In this regard, he urged blacks to contribute to the cause of the more destitute Indian; though it could be questioned in the 1820s, who was more in need of help--the Indian or the African.

Before Watkins obtained fame as a teacher or abolitionist newspaper correspondent, as a young man he was apprenticed as a shoemaker. Not long into practicing his profession, however, he felt led by God to preach and teach his people. Probably around 1825, Watkins married Henrietta, the daughter of Richard Russell, one of the original trustees of the Sharp Street Church. He was listed as a recognized preacher in church records as early as 1834. At about the same time, a contemporary description of his school said it consisted of between 60 and 70 pupils. Watkins' talents as teacher and preacher were vitally needed in the community, as so few blacks were highly qualified to do either.

As a young man of apparently deep faith and later as a minister, Watkins was, as should be expected, attached to Sharp Street Methodist Church for most, if not all, of his life while he lived in Baltimore. Sharp Street Church's history, in turn, was intimately bound to that of the lives of the abolitionists who had originally built the building in 1797 and which blacks purchased in 1802 and met in as a church into the 1890s. The building stood in the neighborhood of Elisha Tyson, Moses Sheppard, Elias Ellicott, and James Carey--all Quakers and all protectors of blacks in their right to freedom of worship. As a minister, Watkins, as well, circulated among the four other black pulpits belonging to the Methodist Episcopal Church, namely Centennial, John Wesley, Orchard Street, and Asbury Churches.

Watkins was taken up with the whole man as he promoted his mental, moral, and physical improvement. He somehow, besides being a minister and teacher, learned something about medicine. Having undertaken so much while young, he at this time joined with several talented contemporaries to organize a literary society dedicated to encouraging and facilitating study and mind-sharpening in formal and informal debating sessions. Among those included who joined with him in this enterprise were Lewis G. Wells, William Douglass, and William M. Lively--all former pupils of Coker.

94

Wells was a minister who appears in church records as such as early as 1826. He belonged to the Methodist Episcopal Church. In addition, he was a trained physician at the local Washington Medical College. He was trained there in order that he might go to Liberia to serve as the colony's doctor. Wells had a great wit and, as a lecturer, kept his audiences in laughter. He also authored several works, including a hymnal for his church and several poetical items. Wells did not move to Liberia and, among other things, eventually rose to the position of Grand Master of the Masons, before dying, while doing his best to curtail the effects of a cholera epidemic in 1832. He was generally remembered as an outstanding black Baltimorean, being honored as such by having any number of children and an organization named after him.

The other two associates of Watkins were to have interesting careers also. William Douglass, who at first started as Methodist minister, became the second rector of St. Thomas Episcopal Church in Philadelphia, the oldest independent black church in the North. He also wrote a history of St. Thomas and the first book of sermons to be published by a Negro. William M. Lively was a medical doctor and a classical scholar who, by 1828 was in charge of the Sharp Street School and who, in the 1830s, was living in New York City.[1]

William Watkins and his literary society associates were most likely a part of the society of blacks called into being by Tyson before his death to take up a great deal of the responsibility of securing freedom for and undergirding the entire black community. In addition, they probably were members of the growing number of benevolent societies coming into existence at this time that provided emergency aid to members in times of distress.

Doing for oneself was first nature to William Watkins. This is an impression left by the few remaining facts known about his life. Yet, in the late 1820s, after the death of Elisha Tyson, blacks still needed, to some extent, and welcomed the efforts of white emancipationists such as Benjamin Lundy, Daniel Raymond, and John Needles.

Lundy, a Quaker, moved his antislavery paper, the Genius of Universal Emancipation, from Tennessee to Baltimore in the summer of 1824. He was drawn by Tyson's legacy. He, in fact, in 1825, published Tyson's only biography. Lundy worked closely, both with Raymond, a former cohort of Tyson in the Protection Society, and John Needles, a Quaker cabinetmaker. Raymond, in the latter part of the 1820s, was Secretary of the Baltimore Emigration Society, a group promoting Haitian emigration. In 1825, Raymond ran for the General Assembly as an avowed abolitionist candidate, prepared to introduce a plan of gradual emancipation in the Maryland Legislature. The Quaker, John Needles, bought the type for Lundy's paper when it was set up in Baltimore. He remained a constant friend to blacks for approximately four more decades after 1824. Among other things he did, was to allow Prudence Gardner, a black school teacher, to hold a school in his warehouse for a long time. It was one of the more successfully run in the nineteenth century.[2]

After 1824, Lundy, Raymond, and Needles occupied significant positions on the national scene in the abolitionist movement through their presence in the American Convention of Abolition Societies, originally organized in Philadelphia in 1794, and the National Anti-Slavery Tract Society established in Baltimore in 1826. The reorganization of an abolition society affiliated with the American Convention took place in the schoolhouse of Elizabeth Needles, John's sister. The Needles family was, indeed, well represented in this organization, as brother Edward was chosen the society's secretary. In the early efforts of the American Convention in the 1790s, Tyson had been active. The organization continued to function after the 1790s but not very effectively in the South. Soon after Tyson's death, however, the Convention began to alternate its annual or general meeting between Baltimore and Philadelphia.

As for the other organization, the National Anti-Slavery Tract Society, it distributed its broadsides against slavery throughout the country. John Needles had a unique way of sending out the Society's message. He wrapped his furniture in tract material when the pieces were shipped South. On one occasion, these unwrapped anti-slavery pieces were thought so inflammatory that when brought to the attention of the governor of a Southern state, he ordered them burned.

While there were eminent white abolitionists around after Tyson's death, and as Watkins became active, there also were eminent colonizationists in the city at this time. Colonizationists wanted to send free blacks to Africa so as to lessen racial strife and interracial mixing. Perhaps, the most eminent and most active colonizationist residing in Baltimore in the mid-1820s was General Robert G. Harper. Harper was a son-in-law of Charles Carroll of Carrollton, a signer of the Declaration of Independence, and reputedly one of the largest slave owners and richest men in America. Also, Harper was responsible for the naming of Liberia. Though the General held the common view of the need for the segregation of the races because supposedly God had ordained it, to prevent the mingling of inferior races, like the blacks, with a superior one, like the whites; he was a proponent of educating blacks, but not in the sense as a William Watkins or a John Needles. Harper was for educating blacks only if they went back to Africa.

All in all, the ferment of activity in Baltimore, abolitionist and colonizationist alike, points up the fact of the city's continued central importance in matters pertaining to blacks.[3] As matters simmered and boiled, William Watkins and his associates were to be in the thick of things, as well.

Significantly, blacks, it seems, were never invited to join as members these two groups or any other abolitionist organization prior to 1833. Perhaps this was for two reasons. The most obvious being racial prejudice and etiquette involved in bringing the races together was too complicated an issue to surmount. Secondly, it seems a good deal of philanthropy before 1833 was predicated on the assumption that a social and financial elite were the natural instruments of doing and bringing about good, two criteria that almost automatically excluded in the general society's view every black from even taking part in his own betterment.

The more unwelcomed friend of the Negro, in William Watkins' view, was the one dressed in the outfit of a colonizationist. Watkins opposed vigorously the activities and attitudes of colonizationists who made allowance for slaveholding which he considered sinful in terms similar to the language used by Tyson's ancestors' protest at Germantown in 1688. Watkins opposed, as well, the patronizing attitude colonizationists had for blacks. The entrance of Watkins in public print in earnest on these two points came about as a result of what colonizationists thought was a publicity coup they engineered in late 1826.

In December 1826, after meetings held at Sharp Street and Bethel Churches, "A Memorial of the Free People of Colour" appeared in local papers and in the national organ of colonizationists, The African Repository and Colonial Journal. The memorial, claimed to be an expression of the sincerest wishes of the blacks, but was, in fact, drawn up by two whites, Charles Harper, son of Robert G. Harper, and John H. B. Latrobe, son of the famous architect, Benjamin Latrobe. Both Harper and Latrobe had been law students of Robert Harper. A few months prior to the appearance of the memorial, Charles Harper had offered himself and his plans of colonization to the public as a candidate for the General Assembly.

As the December 1826 colonizationist memorial circulated, the next month, an abolitionist memorial appeared. The abolitionist memorial supported the ending of slavery, in general, but, more importantly, in Washington, supposedly the seat of a government professing to the world its love of liberty. This assault on slavery was an outgrowth of decisions made in Baltimore in October 1826 at the American Convention's general meeting. Some enemies of the American Convention referred to the gathering as a "congress of visionaries, unwarrantably interfering in matters none of their concerns."[4] In the local elections for the General Assembly in 1826, Raymond, running on a platform of gradual emancipation, finished ahead of Harper--though neither won.

Although Baltimore colonizationists saw the abolitionist memorial as an attempt to obstruct the progress of its own memorial, interestingly enough, the abolitionist memorial hoped to win more support for their plan of gradual emancipation, by tying it with a plan of colonization. In fact, Daniel Raymond did advocate the same when he ran for the General Assembly a few months before. So in a sense, the issue dominating the scene when Watkins and his allies were to appear prominent in print, was mainly the issue of colonization, and secondly, abolition. There seemed to be an undignified rush to get blacks out of the country, as one would attempt to get an uninvited guest to leave one's house before the invited ones came to take part in planned festivities.[5]

At the colonization meeting held at Sharp Street Church on December 11, however, at which the supposed pro-colonization memorial was drawn up by blacks, there arose unsettling opposition from a gentleman named Greener, no doubt, Jacob Greener, a whitewasher, school teacher, and an associate of Watkins. Watkins and Greener did not stand alone, either, in their opposition. One estimate of an observer corresponding with Freedom's Journal said that two-thirds of the blacks at one meeting, perhaps this one at Sharp Street, were against endorsing the project. Greener thought that the objectives of the Colonization Society should be the education of black children, if it genuinely desired the amelioration of the condition of the blacks. Greener was in the thick of abolitionist sentiment in Baltimore for some time. He and his sons risked much in helping Benjamin Lundy print and distribute his paper throughout the streets of Baltimore, and, a few years later, the Greeners and Watkins did the same as they distributed William Lloyd Garrison's more inflammatory antislavery Liberator throughout the city.[6]

Ironically, Watkins and Greener were joined in their objection to the colonizationist memorial by Charles Harper, himself, who wrote Ralph R. Gurley, Secretary of the American Colonization Society, that alterations were made in the original memorial:

> ...at the suggestion of some of the leading blacks, alterations not affecting the sense at all, but removing (and very properly) some expressions in which they might seem to speak too harshly of themselves.[7]

The memorial, as it did appear in its final form, still had objectionable sections, which certainly could not have passed approval by such a person as William Watkins, remembered by his pupils as being supercritical and questioning in the manner of a good lawyer. Watkins was not necessarily against blacks going back to Africa, but was against coercion, direct or subtle, that demanded he or blacks ought to return to Africa.

Certainly the faith and self-confidence and determined attitude of promoting self-improvement Watkins exhibited throughout his life could hardly have permitted him to say of blacks, as the memorial said:

> Our difference of Colour, servitude of many and most of our brethren, and the prejudice which those circumstances have naturally occasioned, will not allow us to hope, even if we could desire, to mingle with you one day, in the benefits of citizenship. As long as we remain among you, we must and shall be content to be a distinct caste.[8]

The last statement could hardly have been hailed by Watkins as gospel truth, for he asserted his belief in the biblical verse that God had made of one blood the nations of the earth.

That Charles Harper and John Latrobe could observe the desperate plight of the blacks so unfeelingly and with apparent hatred of blacks because of their color, comes as no surprise, because these men were former students of Robert G. Harper. Robert Harper spoke likewise on such matters in 1818 in a letter that was published by the American Colonization Society. In this letter, General Harper underscored what he believed to be the idleness and viciousness of the free blacks who "were condemned to a state of hopeless inferiority and degradation by their colour." To leave no doubt as to the sweeping point he wished to make on the matter of inferiority, Harper referred specifically, by name, to Paul Cuffe, the rich black Quaker and African colonizationist from Massachusetts, the General said:

> It may safely be asserted that Paul Cuffee (sic.), respectable, intelligent, and wealthy as he is, has no expectation or chance of even being invited to dine with any gentlemen in Boston, or marrying his daughter, whatever may be her fortune or education, to one of their sons, or of seeing his son obtain a wife among their daughters.[9]

Words of such axiomatic conciseness were probably not lost on students sitting at their master's feet.

As certain as Robert G. Harper was of the hopelessly degraded situation blacks were to remain in, his two protegees were, also, as freely willing to absolve the entire American populace of any iota of complicity in the unjust position most blacks found themselves in, in the United States. The memorial, Charles Harper and John Latrobe's handiwork, said in the boldest language, purportedly speaking as blacks to white America:

> It is not to be imputed to you that we are here. How much you regret its existence among you is shown by the severe laws you enacted against the slavetrade (international) and by your employment of a naval force for its suppression.[10]

The facts belie the statement. Leaving aside the fact that the slave trade was sanctioned for twenty years by the Constitutional Convention, after which it was possible to ban it as was done in the Law of 1807, and just taking into consideration the illegal American involvement in the international slave trade after 1807, American authorities made no great effort to stop the importation of slaves, even then. Indeed, the time Elisha Tyson and others spent preventing slave smuggling belie the sweeping statement of complete absolution authored by Harper and Latrobe. It would seem that in biblical terms, a great number of Americans, until the bitter end, literally "lusted" after owning slaves. In the same vein, Harper and Latrobe, with little modesty, false or otherwise, through the memorial, spoke commendably of the well and benevolent intentions of colonizationists whose motives, plans, etc., were to be considered above reproach, even above discussion or debate, particularly among blacks.

Writing as a "Colored Baltimorean" Watkins' response in published form to the last two assumptions, and others as well as expressed in the colonizationist memorial, came in a communication he sent to Freedom's Journal. He said he believed

...a philanthropic slaveholder is as great a solecism as a sober drunkard.

Furthermore, he said he could not understand the offense given colonizationists when their program was subject to scrutiny. Watkins answered them with this query:

Why is it that they would have us yield, with implicit credulity, without the exercise of our own judgment to whatever they propose for our happiness.[11]

With regard to colonization and so much else he came across, Watkins adopted the role of a "Doubting Thomas."

The zeal and overbearing attitude with which some colonizationists pursued their aim was quite thorough and makes it understandable why Watkins was so opposed to them. Several years after the 1826 memorial, this attitude is evident in how local colonizationists handled an incident involving Rev. Charles W. Gardiner from Philadelphia while on a visit to Baltimore in the middle of the summer of 1832. Gardiner described how he was hounded out of the city because of his alleged opposition to colonization in the North. A Maryland law stated that a free black from another state could only stay in Maryland up to ten days, unless otherwise authorized. An unauthorized longer stay could result in a fine of $50.00 and imprisonment. Rev. Gardiner stayed for three weeks, his extended visit due in part to sickness.

While recuperating, Gardiner said he was informed he was in "some danger" because some people thought he had maligned the American Colonization Society. Knowing the facts to be otherwise, he did not heed the warning until a man told him the sheriff, sent by a Mr. Findley, probably Robert Findley, was about to arrest him because of accusations to this effect, supposedly made by Joseph Whittingham, a black from the Eastern Shore. Realizing that the situation was serious, though unbelievable, Gardiner said he intended to leave the following morning. This proved to be too late, however. He was aboard ship, ready to depart, but was told by the sheriff the Colonization Society had obtained a warrant for his arrest.

Fortunately, in court, Gardiner was acquitted for overstaying the ten days because he convinced authoritites he was, indeed, sick, and that he had not impugned the name of the Colonization Society; but, as Gardiner said, this was all accomplished, "no thanks to my good friend Mr. Findley, agent of the American Colonization Society." The spitefulness of the Colonization Society against its opponents, real or supposed, was quite thorough it would seem, and was of a kind with the gag rules imposed in Congress by supporters of slavery against all who would speak out against their peculiar institution.[12]

With further scrutiny of the 1826 memorial, one of the most outlandish presumptions made by colonizationists in their memorial, in Watkins' view, was that blacks in America viewed Africa as some kind of paradise, to which they eagerly wished to return, in keeping with some instinctual knowledge which, all were supposed to possess, black and white, of God's purported plans for them there. By this time, most blacks, and especially the free ones, had been born in America and, probably, felt no more need to believe that God demanded their return to Africa, than any whites felt any strong, irresistible compulsion to return to England, Germany, France, or wherever. To this colonizationist belief, Watkins said:

> ...They know...that we are not begging them to
> send us to Liberia. If we are begging them to
> do anything, it is to <u>let</u> us alone...and...
> those who would elevate us to the dignity of

men in the land of our birth, our veritable
home.[13]

Watkins realized, as most blacks must have, that they
could not trace their lineage, with any certainty, to
any specific land area, family, or tribe in Africa.
And, furthermore, they did not know who, if any, in Africa was willing to welcome a return of any American Negro.

Besides, to be told by colonizationists that Africa
was degraded, benighted, heathen, and unhealthy, and
then at the same time to expect a mass exodus to its
shores was illogical; but, this is exactly what colonizationists hoped for. Watkins noted this illogicality
and another one as well. The colonizationists could
consider the free black as the vital, indispensible tool
to civilize and Christianize Africa, and at the same
time, constantly refer to them as generally "notoriously
ignorant, degraded, and miserable, mentally diseased,
broken-spirited, scarcely reached in their debasement
by the Heavenly Light."--it would seem the African fathers would be better off without a return of their pro-
digal sons.[14]

Despite Watkins' and other argumentation, some
blacks did leave for Liberia in a short space of time
after the appearance of the December 1826 memorial.
Such eminent persons as George R. McGill and Remus Harvey went over. McGill was a minister at Sharp Street
Church, a schoolteacher there, also, businessman and
father of seven children. McGill had received his manumission papers from Gerard Tipton in May of 1809; and,
at that time, he was described as being 24 and 5'8".
Thus, in 1826, he was approximately 40 years old.

That September, previous to the appearance of the
December memorial, McGill was certain many free blacks
in Baltimore would emigrate because of recent state legislation which made certain offenses punishable by being
sold out of the state into slavery. He was the conduit
through whom the colonizers, Harper and Latrobe got a
hearing before the blacks in order to place their draft
memorial before the community. Near the end of December, McGill was seen as one of the certain ones going
out aboard the Doris. A committee of three blacks had
been established by then to accept applications. Harper
had enlisted the leading white ministers, amongst them
the Episcopal Bishop, Thomas Kemp, to take up collections for the voyage. It was about this time, however,
that McGill wavered; and, only with the encouragement

from Bishop Kemp and the inducement of setting him up as a schoolmaster in the colony, did he take the final step. McGill left for Liberia but with a smaller band than hoped for.[15]

Somewhat after the departure of the Doris, Latrobe confided in a letter to R. R. Gurley, that one reason for many not coming forth was the success of the forceful arguments of men like Watkins and Greener, and the impression in the minds of many blacks, that they were being coerced to leave; and, they being aware of their rights as free men, were not going to be so easily ordered about by others.

In addition to Latrobe's assessment of why so few had finally decided not to make history, other actions happening in the midst of all the preparation might have added into the deliberation of some at the last minute, making it easier for them to decline. For one thing, the Maryland Legislature refused to endorse the project, as had been expected. This may have undermined the confidence of some, if the endorsement was promised as a sure thing, to heighten the importance of the mission. With that failing to materialize, probably some wondered about the soundness of the project and the people being dealt with. In a similar vein, when Benjamin Lundy, a recognizable friend of blacks, was nearly beaten to death on a Baltimore street by the much larger Austin Woolfolk, the notorious slave dealer, with whom Tyson had a well-known confrontation; and, when the judge of the case and other colonizationists said, in effect, Lundy got what he deserved; this, too, could have added to the doubt and given pause to those about to leave, cause them to reflect on the kind of people they were dealing with. Furthermore, and perhaps more importantly, with the establishment of the Baltimore Society for the Protection of Free People of Color in 1826, the faith of those, like Watkins, was probably buoyed to hope that other whites in the city were really dedicated to resolving the racial problem on their side of the Atlantic.[16]

Nevertheless, colonizationists had their biggest triumph in getting McGill to go. By October 1827, it was reported he had renovated the primitive school system of the colony, organizing it on the Lancasterian system. Perhaps, McGill learned about the Lancasterian system from Joseph Lancaster, himself, when he resided in Baltimore a few years before. Later in 1827 there was another colonization triumph when Remus Harvey, another schoolteacher, went to Liberia aboard the

Nautalus. Charles Harper referred to him as "superior, perhaps to any now at the colony," whose extensive views and correctness and even elegance of his speech "would astonish some." Harvey had been secretary of the meeting at Sharp Street Church which considered the December 1826 memorial. These early successes did not, however, portend only years of success for colonizationists and the colony.

In the 1830s, Maryland colonizationists grew displeased with the way the American Colonization Society had been handling the colonization movement, and, in fact, perhaps were moved to be displeased with that organization by the constant criticism of men of Watkins' calibre. Maryland colonizationists got the Maryland Legislature to provide funds for the founding of the state's own colony in West Africa. Eventually, several other states would make efforts to found similar settlements following Maryland's example. With Moses Sheppard as Chairman, and Charles Harper and Charles Howard, the other two commissioners, efforts got underway to purchase the land for the colony. Of these three, amongst blacks, Moses Sheppard was without question the most influential. After all, he was first cousin to Elisha Tyson and seemed to indicate, in many ways, he shared his cousin's beliefs.[17]

As a colonizationist, of Sheppard it was once said, that he had more contact with the real situation in Liberia and West Africa than all of the board members of the American Colonization Society, and he was not a board member. Sheppard was an enthusiastic promoter of colonization for many years. He paid to have a glowing history and description of Liberia printed in a primer format to be placed in the black schools operating in the city. In all, three thousand copies of the Voice from Africa were printed, no doubt with some being sent to other cities. This was to be the first in a series. Latrobe was an eager partner in this promotion. It might be safe to conclude, however, that William Watkins had to think twice about allowing such an obvious piece of propaganda in his private academy. After the Voice from Africa, Sheppard thought of having General Robert G. Harper's face engraved, to be put in a second primer. Doing such would probably have made the item even less welcomed in Watkins' school, inasmuch as the General's well-defined and well-publicized views of black inferiority were probably known to Watkins.[18]

Sheppard did more than underwrite the cost of the primer to promote the colony for he seemed genuinely distraught at the persistent problems associated with African colonization. One of the major complaints against Liberia, as Watkins so often underscored, was the unhealthiness of the region; there were just too many deaths due to sickness contracted upon arrival to be uplifting in any manner. To combat this weakness in the program, Sheppard wrote to R. R. Gurley in April 1833. Indeed, Sheppard was so much moved by the problem that he had an article published, with the help of Robert Findley, in the New York Observer, a religious periodical with twelve thousand readers, giving his views with regard to the health issue. Sheppard received support in this endeavor to correct the health problem from Elliott Cresson, a Philadelphia Quaker, well-known in colonizationist circles in his own city and Baltimore as well. In 1833, complicating the overall health situation was the fact that the colonists in Liberia appeared to be on the point of starvation, according to information Sheppard had received. As for solutions to this and other problems, Sheppard advocated that the Colonization Society provide West Africa with a doctor, lawyer, and sawmill to help alleviate its maladies.

Sometime after the first article, the New York Observer printed another from Sheppard explaining his approach to solving another problem in Liberia. When emigrants arrived at the colony, they were maintained at the Society's expense for six months at receptacle stations on the coast while they became acclimated to the local sicknesses. During this period, they became idle, took part in petty bartering, and neglected to learn how to cultivate the soil. Instead of this practice continuing, Sheppard proposed that land be cleared and ready for cultivation the moment the emigrants landed. Hopefully, inculcating farming habits and self-reliance at the very outset would make the colony more prosperous. This plan was supposedly similar to one adopted by Paul Cuffe, in his pioneering efforts in African colonization. Sheppard had been, however, farmer enough himself during his stay at the Tyson property in Harford County, to know a sound agricultural base could be the foundation for wealth.[19]

From the above, it can be seen that Moses Sheppard was most vigorous in advising colonizationists before Maryland decided to acquire its own colony in 1834. Doubtlessly, Sheppard had words of a similar nature to offer to Maryland colonizationists when they did finally purchase their site. At that time, though George McGill was firmly established in Liberia, he assisted Dr.

James Hall in the acquisition of land for Maryland's settlement from the native African population.

In a letter to John H. B. Latrobe about the affair, McGill indicated his leadership and initiative. He said:

> I feel grateful to kind Providence that I have it in my power to drop you a line on the subject of the new settlement though you let me know little about it. But my interest in it was such; and seeing the situation Dr. Hall was placed in, having no permanent assistant in case of need...I therefore volunteered my services to come with him to this place (Cape Palmas) to assist him in...contract and purchase of the land; and we have so far succeeded as you will learn by Dr. Hall's letter.[20]

McGill's striving spirit, as seen in his helping Dr. Hall secure Cape Palmas, seems to have been imparted to his family members. Eventually, the family was to establish themselves in a preeminent position at Cape Palmas.

One of McGill's daughters married John B. Russwurm, one of the first blacks to graduate from an American college, who served, at its founding, as co-editor of Freedom's Journal, the first black newspaper in the United States established in New York in 1827. Russwurm emigrated to Liberia sometime after 1829 and eventually became the governor of Maryland's colony at Cape Palmas, its first black governor. George McGill's son, Samuel Ford, became, with the assistance of Baltimore's colonizationists, and especially Moses Sheppard, probably the first Western-college-trained black physician in West Africa, whose skill was such that seamen from great distances came to seek his services.

Samuel McGill carried on a considerable correspondence with Moses Sheppard, even getting advice from bachelor Sheppard about marriage and going into business Samuel, for a brief period, succeeded his brother-in-law Russwurm at his death to the governor's chair at Cape Palmas. Two of his brothers and himself became successful merchant-traders, having a fleet of vessels, one being a schooner built in Baltimore and named the Moses Sheppard of Monrovia. As of 1859, one of Samuel's brothers was the agent for Lloyds of London in Liberia; another was worth $30,000. It could be said George R.

107

McGill, for his own situation, despite the criticism of African colonization, did not make the wrong decision in going to West Africa.[21]

Regardless of the success of some, William Watkins' opposition to colonization generally remained constant and insistently negative.[22]

The opposition to colonization in Baltimore could, in general, be rather intense and well organized, in any case. In late 1831, Charles Howard spoke of the lengths blacks were willing to go to obstruct colonization. Perhaps Watkins was involved here as well. Howard wrote Gurley, Secretary of the American Colonization Society, that the reason for the small number of blacks going out to Liberia at that time, on board the Orion was because of the exertion of the leading Negroes of Baltimore and surrounding districts, who visited the persons listed as emigrating, denouncing colonizationists so that only half those prepared to go, finally did do so. Those that remained were convinced by other blacks to await news from those who left, as to the true conditions in Liberia.

The opposition was so intense even against those that did board the Orion, that blacks followed the passengers to the very wharf, constantly denouncing Liberia, with one man even boarding the ship after its departure, still preaching against the trip. While at sea, one passenger jumped overboard. He had been recently an African smuggled into the country as a slave, who secured his freedom and was allowed to go back to Africa aboard the Orion. As the ship pulled out toward the sea, he became frightened that he was again in the hands of kidnappers. The effect of the agitation of other blacks against the trip took hold of his imagination, and it literally drove him to jump ship and be sure he was out of the grasp of those that meant him no good.[23]

Watkins' brilliant stance in Freedom's Journal and elsewhere against colonization, made his name well-known to the free black community throughout the United States. His opposition to colonization arose, as he said, however, not from a "disposition to be captious." The Bostonian leader, David Walker, thought well of Watkins' positions. Walker was the author of the Appeal. In this publication, he commended Watkins' essays against colonization as being "judicious".[24]

The Appeal, published in September 1829, had an attention-getting factor all of its own when first published--quite different from Watkins' many utterances. Its novelty and significance were in its bold advocacy of violence as a means to free the slaves, if nothing else worked. The learned rebuttal of this work to the standard pseudo-historical, scientific or religious arguments against black liberation from such people, ranging from Jefferson to the numerous ministers of the gospel; along with its rather assured manner of condemnation of America as satanic, and about to be chastized by God, to its praise of things black, set this work apart from the usual items most whites were accustomed to hearing or seeing, or ever wanting to see or hear.

The consternation caused by the Appeal for white America was real. The South wanted Walker, dead or alive, to be delivered to it; and, naturally, it was a severe crime to be discovered possessing the work in one's library. Even after Walker's death in 1831, under suspicious circumstances, Elliott Cresson, a colonizationist touring England, thought the best way to indicate to the British the necessity of removing the potentially dangerous free blacks from America, was to have them read the Appeal. Cresson wrote back to America and ordered a dozen copies for distribution. He thought those few would be enough to change British sentiment strongly in favor of the American Colonization Society's programs.[25]

Walker was just one of several young blacks mobilizing in new directions to deal with the problems of blacks, with whom Watkins was acquainted. Watkins joined with the enterprising Baltimorean, Hezekiah Grice, in the formation of the National Negro Convention Movement in 1830. Grice, who once worked as a butcher in an Ellicott business, initiated the effort to bring together blacks of varying persuasions from throughout the land to meet as a nationally constituted organization to discuss matters of interest to the race. Grice involved most of the significant black leadership of his day in the convention scheme in and outside of Baltimore, such as Bishop Richard Allen of the African Methodist Episcopal Church from Philadelphia, Peter Williams, Episcopal leader in New York, and William Watkins and Lewis G. Wells from his own city. From all indications, Grice was a budding national leader.[26]

Earlier in 1829, Grice took the leading part in an effort to organize a black national trading company with stockholders from free black communities throughout the country. The company was to do business with Liberia.

Grice, in a letter to R. R. Gurley in March 1829, put his proposal for assistance from the American Colonization Society. Charles Harper previously acquainted with Grice's idea, commended the proposal in a letter to Gurley. Harper, confided to Gurley that he already had gone ahead and assured Grice of the Society's help. He said Grice told him,

> . . . that there are fifteen or twenty coloured persons here who will adventure $100 each and that several others up the Susquehanna in Philad. and N. York and at Liberia will become stockholders to a similar amount; and that he believes that several societies that exist among the blacks in this city would invest a portion of their funds in such an enterprise.[27]

In a later letter, Harper insisted that the Board in Washington inform him immediately of any action made on Grice's proposal. The attempt to form a trading company, undoubtedly, facilitated Grice's access to, and, perhaps, allowed him to see the possibility of organizing blacks nationally in the following year, in what was the beginning of the National Negro Convention Movement, a movement that periodically saw blacks assemble to plan joint strategy to their multiplicity of problems throughout the remainder of the nineteenth century.

Two other incidents indicate Grice's importance in the overall scheme of black national leadership. He acted as an agent for Freedom's Journal in Baltimore; thus he was acquainted with John Russwurm, an editor. Russwurm, about the middle of 1829, was thinking of embarking for Liberia, a very impressive catch for colonizationists, if it could be accomplished. During his deliberation over the matter, Russwurm visited Baltimore and stayed with Grice in June of that year; and, while on his visit, he was sought out by Dr. Ayers, an agent for the American Colonization Society. While in Baltimore, Russwurm also met Moses Sheppard and probably no effort was spared by Sheppard to convince him how much he was needed in Liberia. Grice probably made known his opinion on the matter as well. In one other instance, which shows Grice's significance, after the Second National Negro Convention, he organized in Baltimore a "Legal Rights Association," formed to compile a compendium of the various legal rights blacks enjoyed in the individual states. Watkins, though not joining with Grice on matters pertaining to colonization, was an active participant of this latter organization. Grice eventually moved to Haiti, sometime around 1832. From such visible early signs of success, Watkins, perhaps, regretted his doing so.

Before Grice's emigration, however, Harper disclosed in a letter to Gurley that he had tried to get Grice to tone down his criticism of the American Colonization Society, which Harper claimed was the only effective force alive in Maryland and Virginia that could bring about an end to slavery by gradual emancipation. In the same letter, however, Harper revealed the hidden side of colonization, that was really always most apparent, when he commented on the fact that most of the free blacks of Baltimore, if emigrating anywhere preferred Haiti, as Grice had done. That, said Harper, he did not mind; he did not care where they went, "we shall send them whithersoever they choose to go, as long as they go."[28]

Harper also in this letter indicated another reason why men like Grice were more inclined to go to Haiti instead of Liberia. Apparently, some of the colonists in Liberia were engaged in the slave trade, and Grice had informed Harper that he was aware of this. Harper confessed it was true, perhaps in an instance or two, but it was not a widespread practice as Grice feared. With that admitted, it is no wonder that some blacks would not want to depart from slaveholding America, to be surrounded, perhaps, by a burgeoning slavocracy in Africa. In a subsequent letter to Gurley, Harper wrote confirming the fact the Grice and some others were on their way to Haiti and not to Liberia as he wished. He thought Grice would have been an important addition to Liberia, even though Moses Sheppard, for some reason, did not think too highly of him.

Another activity arising out of the Second Convention which was more like what Watkins hoped from white America, than a boatride to Africa or Haiti, involved Baltimore's black community and Arthur Tappan, a rich New Yorker who was seeking ways to best alleviate the condition of blacks. After visiting Philadelphia during the session of the National Convention to get some ideas, Tappan came to Baltimore. While in Baltimore, it is known he saw Latrobe and Moses Sheppard. One idea Tappan promoted at the Second National Convention, and in which he may have laid before persons in Batlimore, and gotten their endorsement for, was reactivating a national abolition society of the order of the American

Convention of Abolition Societies. In this regard, he had already consulted Thomas Shipley, a Quaker in Philadelphia, and of late, perennial office-holder in the American Convention. Shipley knew Elisha Tyson, was like him in some ways, and, indeed, one of the highest tributes paid him at his death, was for him to be compared with Tyson in the manner of his commitment to abolition.[29]

Tappan wanted the new society located in Philadelphia because of the city's known traditional concern for blacks and because it would likely survive there in a free state. The society Tappan had in mind did not organize itself until December 1833, and besides Tappan, William Lloyd Garrison had a prominent part when the American Antislavery Society came into being. Watkins must have greeted this fact with pleasure. This organization had blacks in its formative stage, with Garrison being one of those speaking out in favor of active black membership. Garrison served an apprenticeship in the abolition movement and newspaper business under Benjamin Lundy in Baltimore from the summer of 1829 to the summer of 1830, and, as such, from that time onward, had an intimate relationship with blacks for the next forty years or more in which he acted as one of their staunchest allies from Boston on a level akin to the vigorous work undertaken by Tyson. It was during his stay in Baltimore that Garrison got to know Watkins, and was generally impressed and influenced by him, especially in the matter of the "right way" of thinking with regard to colonization. Watkins wrote for Garrison's paper, The Liberator, published out of Boston, for several years. This collection of essays are literary gems.

In 1831, Watkins sent several letters to Garrison. In one of his first letters, Watkins criticized his people for not realizing the importance of supporting a friendly press. He thought too many instead squandered their money on "glittering baubles." To him, the press was a "powerful engine" which he was determined not to neglect in Garrison's case, as so many had done with regard to The Genius of Universal Emancipation and Freedom's Journal. In this same letter, Watkins commented on how some of the religious editors were beginning to portray the justness of the black cause in their papers, while the average white parishioner he had come to know, and ministers as well, were:

> ... like the unfeeling priest and Levite, after viewing our condition, 'pass by on the other side,' where they now stand, with folded

hands, crying 'the subject of slavery in-
volves consideration too weighty for us to decide upon. We are not sufficiently acquainted
with local circumstances, and other peculiar-
ities in the case, to enable us to judge for
another!'[30]

Watkins called this reaction a veritable "cowering" before one of the "great evils" that prevented the "March
of the Redeemer's Kingdom." He believed the very charge
under which a minister is called was one that requires
him to spare not, otherwise the very sins of those not
warned, fell on the preacher's own head.

A subsequent letter Watkins sent to Garrison gave
the details of a meeting at which he served as secretary
and his friend, William Douglass, presided as the chairman. The people were assembled to give their yea or nay
to several resolutions that castigated in the strongest
language the American Colonization Society, termed
"founded more in selfish policy than in the principles
of benevolence." The resolutions deplored the Society's
"exaggerated statements" about the debased moral tone of
free black life, as well as the notion that Africa was
the American blacks' home, where he rightfully belonged;
and furthermore, it was regretted that "warm and sincere
friends" supported an organization so worthy of "dis-
trust".[31].

The resolutions appeared in Garrison's paper accompanied by excerpts from Watkins' letter and editorial
comment from Garrison, who praised Watkins' ability.
Garrison said, in his remarks, that the letter was from
a "highly respectable colored gentleman," and furthermore, "Is it not well written?" Garrison also compared
the situation of the blacks with that of the Cherokees
in Georgia who, against their wishes, were being forced
from their homes, to supposedly better homes, by those
professing all along that they were only making these
sacrifices for the Indians' good.

Watkins said he thought the colonizationists were
about to publish five thousand pamphlets to spread their
message. In sarcastic language, he said they were to
enlighten the public as to the true nature of their
"labors of love". In further comment, Watkins said:

Their proselytizing spirit seems unconquer-
able. In addition to all they have done, they
must publish 5,000 pamphlets! Well, I think
we should publish 5,000 in reply; we can throw

a little <u>light</u> upon the subject too. This will be necessary; for I venture to predict that after they shall have done there will be so great an <u>eclipse</u> of the truth, that a little <u>light</u> <u>from</u> the proper source will be indispensable.[32]

For some, Watkins was just the man, too, to shed the light necessary to banish the shadow of the colonizationists.

In a postscript to his letter to Garrison, Watkins informed him that during the visit of a Rev. Edwards to the city, a temperance society for blacks with 200 members had been organized. He wondered aloud at what the American Colonization Society would say to this, as temperance--abstinence from alcoholic beverages--was known to prolong life in general and this, in turn, contribute to an increase in population. He thought the Colonization Society would condemn this with words so often heard in complaint of free blacks, "but....(they) increase too fast already." Referring to the last remark and indicating his sense of humor, Watkins closed by making sport of the paternalistic, oily philanthropy of the colonizationists, "a palpable hit. O, these terrible thrusts of ingratitude."

In another letter to Garrison in 1831, Watkins responded to criticism made by "A Marylander" to the resolutions blacks adopted at their March meeting at which Watkins served as secretary. "A Marylander" urged other Marylanders to adopt measures to colonize their own free blacks inasmuch as the American Colonization Society was an anathema to them. Watkins responded, as usual, that blacks would not be driven from their homes to "the pestilential clime of Liberia." He further stated that the blacks' cause was right and inevitably would be vindicated. He also said he wanted this "precocious statesman" to understand blacks would not be "driven like cattle" against their will by these "Christian associations" to be formed, really in Watkins' view, mere mutants of the American Colonization Society's mentality.

"A Marylander" was, as Watkins had written to Garrison in an earlier letter, more concerned with the increasing number of free blacks than anything else because that supposedly threatened the existence of the whites. Watkins had some of the strongest language of rebuke for white ministers who concurred in the opinion of "A Marylander". Ministers of God who disregarded the biblical verse that stated of one blood did God make men, he called "temporizing, retrograde". Watkins, in fact, saw the collaboration of ministers of this ilk against blacks as the most powerful arm of the whole host of enemies arranged against them. He stung them, however, when referring to their lack of resolve, want of love and mercy, and featherweight significance in a moral world, when he said:

> Why the infidel with the Bible in his hands would chase a thousand and two put ten thousand to flight.[33]

Watkins concluded this article with a resolve of his own which he wanted other blacks to adopt.

> Fear not then, my colored countrymen, but press forward, with a laudable ambition, for all that heaven intended for you and your children, remembering the path, of duty is the path of safety, and that righteousness 'alone exalted a nation'.

Watkins stuck to this resolve, in Baltimore, almost to the bitter end.

Letters sent by Watkins to Garrison in 1832 still indicated his resolve to press on undaunted. In one he mused,

> I have just been thinking that if Stephen Girard had left you, your partner, and the weather-beaten veteran B. Lundy, a few thousands a piece, what an incalculable amount of good you might then be enable to accomplish; but hod carriers stand a better chance for riches than reformers.[34]

Girard was a Philadelphia philanthropist who had recently died, leaving his money for charitable purposes, some racially restricted to benefit whites only. Watkins said that for a while he fixed his mind upon the financial needs of the blacks in their struggle and was drifting into despair when he found inward solace as he took up the Bible and read, by chance, this verse:

> The Lord God is a sun and a shield, the Lord will give grace and glory; no good thing will he withhold from them that walk uprightly.[35]

After reading this, Watkins said his faith was renewed in hopes that, indeed, blacks had an even worthier ally in their struggle, if not a philanthropist.

At this juncture in 1832, Watkins, if an agent of the Liberator did not have his name listed at the top, front page with the others. Nevertheless, he continued to write. He thought that the Legislature would ban the paper anyway--a reaction to Nat Turner's insurrection in Virginia that appeared at first bloom a well-organized insurrection of the greatest extent which, nevertheless, cost more lives than whites were accustomed to experiencing from supposedly docile, happy slaves, that drastic steps were envisaged as necessary to prevent a similar breaking of rank from ever arising again. Watkins indicated, however, that though the times had placed blacks in a peculiar predicament, he believed in God's supremacy over all matters--his ability to protect and deliver the oppressed. He said, in this regard,

> We, for the most part, enjoy all the Peace of mind and confidence in Divine favor and protection, which a consciousness of innocence never fails to inspire. We know that
>
> > The God that rules on high,
> > That thunders when he please,
> > That rides upon the stormy sky,
> > And manages the seas is our
> > Father, Our Protector, our Defender. [36]

Watkins seemed prepared to consider the worst.

He thought the Legislature would enact harsh legislation to coerce free blacks to move either to Canada, Haiti, or Mexico; but, curiously enough, he did not mention Liberia. He said, if compelled to go somewhere, the blacks would sing:

> There's mercy in every place;
> And Mercy, (encouraging thought,)
> Gives even affliction a grace
> And reconciles man to his lot. [37]

There were some bright spots, however--all had not turned oppressive because of Nat Turner's uprising. The Governor of North Carolina was against the enactment of draconian laws, and a memorial from the Quakers of Virginia to their Legislature was heartening as well. Quakers, Watkins blessed because of the great amount of

good they had done blacks.   He concluded with that
thought in mind, saying:

I had almost thought that the heart of sympathy had ceased to beat for us,--that the
lips of philanthropy were totally sealed.[38]

Though more subdued than Tyson, there still were Quakers
willing to let their opposition to slavery and
oppression be known.

Whatever the restrictions the Liberator operated
under in Maryland as a result of the Nat Turner affair,
Watkins continued to send off pieces to be published.
In the first month of 1834, he took on the aggressive,
locally controlled Maryland Colonization Society.
Watkins' letter was in response to what he read in the
Address of the Board of Managers of that Society of
1834. It ridiculed Garrison. Watkins believed this
Society, as being directed as much as the American Colonization Society was, in an illiberal way, in compelling
blacks to emigrate to that "heathen land". In speaking
of colonizationists in general, he said they had arro-
gated unto themselves the enterprise of preaching the
gospel to the heathen, an enterprise which rightly belonged to true-hearted Christians who had a "humble re-
liance for success upon the goodness of the Divine
Being."-- not themselves as the colonizationists were in
the habit of doing. In this communication, Watkins was
also critical of the colonizationists' position that
proposed that blacks should receive the least bit of encouragement in the United States, so that they might, in
desparation, not forget to flee to their God-intended
homes in Africa. In another section, Watkins expressed
his exasperation because he could not understand how
some Quakers, key supporters of the Maryland Colonization Society, would assent to the arming of colonists in
Africa to protect themselves from war-like tribes while
they generally were against bearing arms, and professed
to believe all men should do likewise.[39]

Garrison's July 4, 1835, edition contained a letter
from Watkins which commiserated with George Thompson,
the English abolitionist, who suffered recently unjust
taunts and abuse through the pages of the New York
Courier and Enquirer. He said that, "Abolitionists have
little more to hope from certain colonizationists than
had our Lord from the infuriated mob who dragged him as
a felonious criminal before Pontius Pilate". Watkins
followed this with a few lines that indicate his talents
for dialogue, writing a version of the scene of Jesus

before Pilate with which to criticize a recent meeting of colonizationists at Light Street Church. In debating a serious problem before taking up the issue of colonization at Light Street, Watkins pointed out how evenly divided, or how there was a "pro" and "con" side of the debate on this matter. He said, however, as soon as the debaters turned to take up the matter of the Negro and what to do about him, that suddenly, all united, without the slightest difference of opinion on so serious a problem as forcing the blacks out of the state. Watkins compared the undignified haste to unify to do an evil thing, to the above-mentioned biblical situation. He said:

> When our Lord was about to be crucified, Pilate and Herod were made friends together.[40]

To Watkins, it seemed no one spoke up for a slow and very careful consideration of what should have been viewed as a great and drastic injustice, the forcible eviction of all free blacks from the state.

Also in this same letter, Watkins informed Garrison he would have sent him a more detailed reply he wrote to the editor the <u>Maryland Temperance Herald</u> who supported this expulsion; but, instead, he thought it better to send the reply to the editor of that magazine. He also reported that colonizationist ministers were in the habit of going about in the countryside imposing their ideas on the gullible who had respect for their office, but there was evidence surfacing that these were wearing out their welcome. He had learned some colonizationist ministers who had preached nothing but from the book of Africa were grating on the nerves of pastors of certain congregations, and were being excluded from these pulpits.

Even some slaveholders were tiring of the constant talk of Africa as the only place where blacks could be happy. These slave owners, keen to their own interests, thought this kind of talk might make their slaves discontent. Watkins said:

> I believe a vast majority of these slaves would prefer their Maryland plantations to the elysian groves of 'the land of their fathers'.[41]

Watkins reported some blacks had sense enough to be skeptical of the glowing pictures painted of Africa. In fact, even black preachers of the Methodist Episcopal Church, nominally under the control of whites, were beginning to exclude white colonizationist ministers of their denomination from their pulpits, if they insisted upon preaching about colonization and Liberia.

In 1835, Watkins wrote a letter to Garrison dealing with the recent efforts of three leading black ministers to strike a compromise--undignified in Watkins' view--with the persistent pressure of colonizationists and racists of all shades of opinion. The three were William Livington of St. James Episcopal, John Fortie of the Methodist Episcopal Church, his own Church, and Nathaniel Peck of Bethel African Methodist Episcopal Church. This Peck was the one who accompanied Coker to Liberia in 1820. Nevertheless, with a published, submissive, open letter, Watkins said the three proposed to speak for the black populace without having called one single general meeting.

Taking into account their fears, he said, "It is time enough to make disavowals, disclaimers, and pledges when we are charged with some other crime than that of our colour." Watkins knew blacks, in general, in Baltimore, rarely disrupted the peace or good order on a large scale and were not the menace people wanted to make them out to be. He related that what the three ministers did was similar to that done by five illiterate trustees of a black Methodist Episcopal Church in East Baltimore, who signed a piece of paper attacking abolitionists, when advised by their white elder that this was the only way to save the church from demolition.[42]

In this same letter, Watkins revealed how he had been threatened with a coat of tar and feathers by the three overly-fearful ministers. He received word of the threat through Robert Cowley, who had been secretary at a meeting of endorsement of the December 1826 Colonization Memorial held at Bethel Church. Presently, he was a schoolteacher at Bethel. Watkins called Cowley, for some reason, in an unclear allusion, the "negro (sic) Webb". Since he was known to be the only one published by Garrison from Baltimore, Watkins requested that his letter not be published this time. Matters were taking a serious turn; he reported he had information that a meeting was to be called shortly in Baltimore County to deal with him or, in the words of his enemies, to stop the "incindiary &c. &c." Seemingly, Watkins communicated very little, if at all, with Garrison after 1835. He may have deliberately stopped or, perhaps, vigilant postal officials stopped all letters addressed to Garrison from Baltimore, as some of South's pro-slavery postmasters thought it their duty to censor outgoing and incoming mail in their districts.

It was the next year, 1836, however, that Watkins involved himself again with the Negro Convention Movement. He appears not to have been a delegate to the various conventions from 1830 to 1835, but did, in August 1836, in Philadelphia, speak before the American Moral Reform Society, an offshoot of the Convention of 1835. Watkins spoke in a lengthy address upon the resolution: "Resolved, that a good education is the most valuable blessing that we, as a people, can bestow upon the rising generation." Throughout the speech, Watkins linked the education of mind and soul as essential. He endorsed, in essence, the biblical observation that the fear of the Lord was the beginning of wisdom.[43]

A couple of years later, Watkins was at odds with the American Reform Society, as it seriously belabored itself with trying to persuade blacks to stop using the word "colored" in referring to themselves. In a letter to a delegate of the 1838 Convention which was published, Watkins stated his displeasure about the whole matter, calling it so much hair-splitting and carping. On another point, in the same epistle, he took up a matter that some in the Society had difficulties with, that was in belonging to a body established for the sole benefit of blacks. These persons thought such a posture selfish. Watkins dealt with this by relating a personal experience he had had while traveling once somewhere on a boat.

During the ride, a black and white passenger, for some reason, fell overboard at the same time. At that moment, Watkins reported, that to his astonishment five white men quickly rushed to save the white, but, because of their ingrained hatred of blacks, the only reason that came to his mind to explain their actions, they ignored the drowning black entirely, leaving him alone to struggle to save the poor fellow. Watkins said he did so not because he was selfish or unmindful of the peril the white was in, but, because his black brother needed his help more, at the moment, than his white brother. In a word, Watkins was saying that if blacks did not readily help each other, they more than likely could expect little from the common white man.

Watkins wrote in his letter that if he were among the delegates of the American Reform Society at this

1838 sessions, he would offer the following resolution to abate any unpleasant or permanent disruption of the Society:

> Resolved, that the object of this Society is to improve the condition, mental and moral, of the colored population of our land, not because they are colored--but because being colored, they are for the most part, despised, neglected, and denied the facilities enjoyed by others, to aspire to the true dignity of rational, intelligent creatures, created in the image of God.[44]

Watkins concluded his letter by saying he had always thought the title of the Society was too broad, embracing all the people in the United States, most of whom were in a better position than most blacks to reform themselves, from the advantages they already enjoyed from simply not being black.

While in the midst of his renewed association with the American Reform Society, in 1837 Watkins wrote several articles for the Colored American. His first one provoked considerable comments from the readership. Watkins said, after timely thought, he had come to the conclusion that there was an:

> ...incompetency of the colored ministry in general, to supply the intellectual wants of the colored population of the country.[45]

He realized this was not wholly the fault of the black clergy, but their "misfortune," inasmuch as they were denied the privilege to study in theological schools as whites and generally discouraged as most blacks were against making any intellectual effort at all.

Watkins further stated, without a good grounding in a common English education, most black preachers had latched on to passages of Scripture to support the state in which they found themselves, namely their illiteracy. Such passages often quoted were these:

> The letter killeth, but the Spirit giveth life.

> Take no thought how or what ye shall speak; for it shall be given you in that same hour what ye shall speak.

> For ye see your calling, brethren, how
> that not many wise men after the flesh, not
> many mighty, not many noble, are called; but
> God hath chosen the foolish things of the
> world to confound the things which are mighty.

Watkins considered the use of these passages by the less-educated black minister akin to the kind of use a slaveholder made of Scripture to justify slavery--both misuses equally damnable.

In this opening piece, Watkins indicated his disgust of those black clergymen who, perhaps, more through envy, criticized those like himself for being able to put their sermons on paper. He related he had been held up to ridicule as an idolator for depending on preaching the "Word" from a piece of paper. What he did, he was told, was make that written sermon a "little paper god." Watkins wrote that, as a consequence of the black clergy's lack of a proper education, many of them had "acquired the art of communicating heat without light." So many, he thought, "could excite their audience, but not enlighten them."

In subsequent communications, Watkins underscored how the type of minister about whom he wrote in the first letter demeaned the pursuit of an intellectual life, and how this attitude was affecting rising generations. The average minister was not keeping pace with the intellectual opportunities opening up to the young. On this point, some three decades later, an incident in the life of Daniel A. Payne, Senior Bishop of the African Methodist Episcopal Church, who had some seminary training, proved Watkins' apprehensions to be true.

At one point in his career in the 1840s, Payne served as minister at Bethel in Philadelphia, one of the leading churches of the country, where a too-educated ministry was looked upon as too-worldly and unnecessary. Many years later, after the Civil War, Payne returned to Bethel and found the church predominantly of older people. The explanation given for this situation was the unwillingness of the young--exposed to a literate life since before and after the Civil War--to accept an ignorant or half-informed clergy as older generations had. It would seem Watkins' concerns along these lines were proper.[46]

The lack of an intimate fellowship with sufficiently educated black clergy and congregants seems to have been frustrating for Watkins. The ignorance and superstitions at times must have been unsupportable, that he seems to refer to himself when he stated that any responsible parent would almost be driven to withdraw his children from assembled worship amongst blacks. The only other choice, he wrote, would be to unite with some white church, where the literal ignorance of scripture might be less, but where one would have to suffer an unchristianlike condescension based on ingrained racial prejudice which said, in effect, "Stand thou there, I am holier than thou."

In a last communication with Samuel Cornish, editor of the Colored American, and by some accounts, a man with Baltimore roots, Watkins told of how the presiding elder of his church was "inflexibly determined to keep up the standard," recently instituted to improve the quality of black ministers in his denomination. Watkins said there was some grumbling about too high a standard being set, but he was happy to say even some older ministers were encouraging an adherence and maintenance to the more exacting requirements. Watkins ended this epistle with an appeal, particularly to Northern free blacks and white friends, to provide a place, a black college, where blacks could be trained for the ministry and become acquainted with the value of high intellectual development.

Ironically, it seems that about ten years previous to this suggestion calling for the establishment of a Negro college, the same idea had circulated in Baltimore. So said Garrison, and in his view, blacks and whites in Baltimore were near to bringing the idea to fruition, but something, left unnamed, hindered it. About two years after this first serious attempt, the idea was still popular. In the summer of 1831, Arthur, Tappan got an endorsement for erecting a college at the Second National Negro Convention. He later came to Baltimore and, no doubt, received encouragement for his idea. It is known Tappan saw Moses Sheppard and John Latrobe when he came to Baltimore that summer of 1831. These three may have seriously considered the idea of establishing a college. After Sheppard died in 1857, Latrobe revealed that Sheppard had once thought of leaving his fortune to blacks; perhaps, if he had, he intended it to found a college for them.

Nevertheless, in 1837, as Watkins reflected on matters, he believed a college would allow blacks to:

. . .be blessed with a ministry able and

123

efficient:--a ministry who shall be
zealous and untiring in promoting the
elevation of their people;--a ministry
whose souls shall glow with the holy
ambition of making those respectively
committed to their care, 'a peculiar
people zealous of good works,'--a people
who, in the day of the Lord, shall be
found, not having spot or wrinkle, or any
such thing.[47]

It would be about a decade more before the black college
idea would become a reality and, in this case, a
Watkins, William's niece, was also involved.

Some agreed with Watkins in the matter of an
incompetent ministry being the bane of the black
community. William Yates of Philadelphia, a member of
the African Methodist Eposcopal Church, was one who
readily agreed with Watkins. Yates said he hoped "the
piety and candor of the ministry, will be sufficient to
bear a thorough examination." Yates said that at his
church's conference the subject had been recently
brought up and the situation recognized as essentially
as Watkins had seen it, but Yates, too, placed more of
the blame on the whites who closed their seminaries to
Negroes.

"Augustine" from Pittsburgh also concurred with
Watkins' sentiments and rejoiced that he discussed them,
for "Augustine" was sure that Watkins could point out
how the situation could be permanently remedied. "Augustine" said the evil spoken of was nearly commensurate
with the present number of black congregations. William
Whipper, leader of the American Moral Reform Society,
also believed Watkins was performing a useful task in
bringing before his people his reflections on this important subject.

Not much is known about Watkins' life after about
1838; but, it perhaps should be assumed, he continued to
make himself heard on matters of concern to blacks.
Yet, some time and somehow in 1844, Watkins became convinced that the end of the world was near; he became a
follower of the Second Day Adventist, led by William
Miller. As the world did not end, Watkins seemed to
have lost much of his stature in the community. In the
list of appointments of the Methodist Episcopal Church,
1844 is the last year he is mentioned.

Even in Liberia, word of Watkins' taking up with the Second Adventists reached Samuel McGill, who wrote Moses Sheppard and queried if Watkins and his sons were not mad and if their erratic behavior was not genetically based.[48] McGill, in his assessment of the situation, said:

> Mr. W. . . . and his sons are individuals whom we would be happy to receive in Liberia; he is, I am led to believe, an aspiring and ambitious man, so chained down by prejudices, that he has no field for the exercise of his faculties in any high and honourable enterprise, he is therefore led to seize upon anything that presents itself, that cannot give cause to offence in order to keep his mind occupied, or to render himself forgetful of his true social and political condition in the U. States. What more natural than that he should desire the speedy approach of the millenium? Poor fellow, I pity him his only hope of relief from the chain that golds (sic) him is in expatriation or the grave. A few more years of oppression may be necessary, and W. will embark for Liberia --I cannot divest myself of this impression.[49]

Although McGill in this quote is somewhat condescending, he was not always, however, to hold the view that Watkins was to be pitied.

Sometime later, when McGill was in a reflective mood, and perhaps as he questioned his own family's response to racism by emigrating to West Africa, he referred to Watkins in symbolic fashion as to what he might have been like, tried to have accomplished in the United States, if he had remained in the lion's den of racism. He says this in a passage full of reminiscences about the time he was in the United States and his father was a preacher and teacher at Sharp Street Church.

> "The Genius of Universal Emancipation" when edited by Lundy was place in my hand when I was seven years old--previous to that and about this time I had read the History of St. Domingo, and the struggle there for liberty--I took part in dia-

> logues written by my Father, the subject
> of which was insurrection of the Blacks,
> they were performed in the old school-
> house back of the church--with the feel-
> ings I entertain on the subject of
> slavery had I grown up in the States, I
> should have been ten times more an object
> of distrust and suspicion than Wat-
> kins.[50]

Here, McGill puts in perspective the true worth and nature of William Watkins' efforts and sacrifices.

In 1851 or 1852, the climate in Baltimore was such
that Watkins left the city, ostensibly because the Baltimore & Ohio Railroad had decided to build its mammoth
Camden Station in his neighborhood; and also because he
yearned to taste the climate of a free society. Watkins
moved to Canada where his son, John, had previously
gone. There, William Watkins, as a grocer in Toronto,
occasionally wrote an article under the nom de plume, "A
Colored Canadian." Some few years later, on June 11,
1858, William Watkins died in Toronto and, presumably,
is buried in that city.[51]

William Watkins died unheralded by local newspapers in Baltimore, but his efforts had a long-lasting
effect on those he taught. The most fascinating Watkins
to come to the fore, promoting the cause of freedom
after William Watkins best years, was Frances Ellen
Watkins, his niece. Her cousin, William J. Watkins,
Junior, also did make valuable contributions; she, however, outlived him over forty years. Frances Ellen was
born in 1825 and orphaned very early, when she was
placed in her uncle's care. Her contemporary, James A.
Handy, who later was to become a bishop in the A.M.E.
Church, thought she was the best pupil of her day. When
old enough, her uncle placed her in a family to work
where she took advantage of the library in the home.
She apparently had been prepared and prepared herself
very well, for in 1847, as the African Methodist Episcopal Church was attempting to establish its first college
in Columbus, Ohio, Frances Watkins acted as an assistant
teacher to the principal, Reverend John M. Brown.

Sometime after her stint in Ohio, Frances Ellen
moved to Little York, Pennsylvania, and made her debut
as a professional lecturer. From then onward, she ably
promoted the antislavery cause as a public speaker. In
the early stage of her career, she worked for the Maine
Antislavery Society at Portland.[52]

By the late fifties, Miss Watkins gained considerable renown as an antislavery lecturer and poetess, and commentators in the antislavery press seemed eager to praise her work. At a meeting on December 30, 1855, North Bennett Street Free Will Baptist Church, Boston, her address was "much applauded . . . and in many parts was also very pathetic, calling forth the tears from many an eye." Sometime later in Hill's Airy Street Hall, Norristown, Pennsylvania, she was spoken of as being "a bright quadron," "tall and slender," and "when animated with the fervour inspired by the wrongs of her people, is graceful." Her speech was free from "denunciation and rant." This writer-observer ventured to say she was the "most eloquent women" he had seen, perhaps, beside Lucy Stone, a Quaker minister and also antislavery speaker. In Danville, Pennsylvania, on February 22, 1856, it was stated, "she preached the whole gospel of liberty and would 'let the Union slide' and the Constitution be torn into shreds, rather than that one of God's poor should be proscribed." Miss Watkins spoke six other times in the Danville region; yet, however eloquent she may have been, she shared the lot of most abolitionist speakers, collecting only small change for her labors.

William J. Watkins, Junior, about the time his cousin was gathering honors for herself, was not without some successes, either. For example, on February 4, 1853, at the Legislative Committee on the Militia in Massachusetts, he delivered an address entitled "Our Rights as Men." He said the signers of the petition demanding a charter to form a black militia company were all descendants of men who had fought in the American Revolution. Their exclusion from white militia companies was an insult to the spilt blood of their forefathers.

William J. Watkins would eventually become an associate of Frederick Douglass, one of the most eminent and widely recognized black spokesmen through both the slave years and those after the Civil War. Watkins helped Douglass to get out his antislavery paper, the North Star. Douglass was well acquainted with Baltimore, having served several years there as a slave before running away from his master in 1838. He owed much to the acquaintances and experiences he had in the city, and doubtlessly was aware of William Watkins, Senior. Ironically in his early days as an antislavery speaker, Douglass received help in his new calling from William Lloyd Garrison, the most feared white abolitionist amongst slaveholders after 1830, who had lived in

Baltimore from 1829 to 1830, and who was influenced by William Watkins, Senior, as well.

It would seem both William J. Watkins and Frances Ellen took full advantage of the influence of the senior Watkins. After several years on the lecture circuit, Frances Watkins reflected, in a letter to William Lloyd Garrison, on that time she spent in New England amongst its many abolitionists. She said, "Do you know that two of the brightest, most sunshiny (is not that tautology?) years of my life, since I have reached womanhood, were spent in New England." The comment about tautology, most assuredly points back to her uncle who, above all, it seems, was a grammarian of such precision in the way of eytmology, syntax, prosody, and so on, that one of his former pupils wrote humorously of the old leather strap Watkins used to correct grammar misuses.

In this same letter, as much as Miss Watkins praises the virtue of New England, she condemns the vices of some parts of Pennsylvania, where the spirit of abolitionism lately was not so thorough. She said that although she had been traveling nearly four years throughout the North and Canada, it was on public transportation in Pennsylvania that attempts were made to "Jim Crow" or segregate her in a colored section to which she refused to be moved. When leaving one particular train, the conductor refused to take her money which she then threw on the floor.

Attempts to hide Frances Ellen from the general public were not enough to discourage her from lecturing. In the fall of 1858, Miss Watkins toured the Michigan area in the company of William C. Nell of Boston, a community leader there and early Negro historian. Nell sent reports of their activities back to Garrison who published them in the Liberator.

The success of the meetings in Michigan were fully helped along by Mrs. Mary E. Bibb, widow of Henry Bibb, an important antislavery worker for some years. Nell and Watkins stayed with the Chandler family and were shown the writing desk of Elizabeth M. Chandler, who had contributed antislavery pieces, including poetry to The Genius of Universal Emancipation, published in Baltimore for which William Watkins wrote one or two items as well. While in Michigan, Miss Watkins and Nell also visited the grave of Elizabeth Chandler. the encounter was quite moving, especially for Frances Ellen.

As for the public meetings, Nell stated the lady

lecturer was enthusiastically received, with most gatherings demanding an encore at some later date. Throughout the tour, Watkins delivered several set lectures she had with her, variously entitled "Slavery and Its Allies," "Christianity and Slavery," "Lights and Shadows of American Institutions," "Reform and Reformers," "Human Progress, Home Culture," and "Philosophy of History."

In the eventful year of 1859, John Brown's year, Frances Watkins eyes were opened by Wendell Phillip's "Extracts from the Madison Papers," which showed the Founding Fathers' deliberate approval of slavery and the slave trade--crimes, in her words, which indicated how neglectful and forgetful these men were of the justice they owed their fellowmen. Phillip was an associate of Garrison in Boston, quite an orator, and member of a prominent Boston family. The startling attack of John Brown on Harper's Ferry, Virginia, perhaps sharpened Frances Watkins' focus on what was put in words by Phillip, that is to say, the power of the state had been and was totally deaf to what abolitionists considered the immorality in allowing slavery to exist. The aftermath of Brown's raid, which was intent upon raising a general rebellion of the slaves throughout the South, involved both Frances and her cousin, William.

After Brown's capture and jailing, Frances Ellen consoled Mrs. Brown at the house of Philadelphia underground railroad chief William Still. She wrote John Brown several letters, cheering him up by telling him God would be his refuge, as he stood certain to be hung. She also wrote a letter to Aaron D. Stevens, one of the last of Brown's men to be executed, in which she included a copy of her poem, "Bury Me In a Free Land." She was one of the first to contribute money to Mary Brown to aid her in the distressful situation of being without her husband when he was executed and martyred at the same time.

William J. Watkins, on the other hand, was accused of treason because some thought he had foreknowledge of Brown's attack. Watkins told his critics that as he was declared by the United States Government to be no citizen, he could therefore not be charged with treason, and as the courts of Virginia did not permit blacks to testify in courts in ordinary times, now was not the time, in his view, to make an exception by having him testify against Brown or himself in Virginia. At memorial services held for Brown after he was hung, William Watkins, at Wesleyan Church in Albany, New York, spoke about the coming day of liberty being a result of Brown's raid.[53]

129

All in all, the year of 1859 did see the growing influence of Frances Ellen and William J. Watkins be acknowledged in a specific manner. Both joined with Frederick Douglass and several others in endorsing the newly established magazine, The New York Weekly Anglo-African. William J. Watkins had, it seems, an even more affecting relationship with the new periodical's editor. A letter of his to the editor dated September 5, 1859, shaped editorial opinion on William Seward's speech in Rochester which had used the catchy phrase, "irrepressible conflict." The phrase referred to the ultimate death struggle that had to finally happen between a house half-slave, half-free. Watkins had said in his letter that Seward had said no more than what abolitionists had been preaching for some time. William J. Watkins probably had in mind his father as well.

Thomas Hamilton, the editor of The Weekly Anglo-African had other praise of William J. Watkins, about a year later, as he described him as being "indefatigable" in his lecturing labors undertaken in behalf of equitable suffrage laws in New York State. Watkins was an agent of the New York State Suffrage Association which wanted the property stipulation for black voters removed. Watkins was said to be as "an orator is not excelled by Frederick Douglass, himself and his telling hits were loudly applauded."[54]

As William J. Watkins' efforts were being duly noted in print, the editor of The Weekly Anglo-African also included "An Appeal from the Philadelphia Rescuers" by Frances Watkins in his paper. This was her response to the Christiana Riots, riots that broke out in the lower Pennsylvania town when slave catchers tried to take alleged runaways back into Maryland.

It was not long after this that the "irrepressible conflict" was more than mere riot and mayhem, and was a complete Civil War. During the war, Frances Watkins got married but continued to lecture. She became Frances Ellen Watkins Harper. At a meeting in Margaretta, Ohio, she was introduced by the secretary of the meeting as one of the "most worthy and efficient anti-slavery lecturers who have visited the western country." Among the resolves of the meeting were the usual ones, including a condemnation of slavery, the Fugitive Slave Law, prejudice and the like. Mrs. Harper was solemnly thanked in the last resolve, as having helped to increase the zeal and determination of those who were about to join Union forces on the battlefield.[55]

In the Liberator, in the midst of the war, a poem by Mrs. Harper appeared, entitled "To the Cleveland Union-Savers." The poem condemned the return of a fugitive slave woman to her owners by persons living in Ohio--a state supposedly in the Northern column. This, however, was just illustrative of the true extent and reach of the slavocracy and prejudice in the United States, just as the Northern draft riots and refusal to allow, at first, blacks as soldiers were illustrative, of the same point. In addition, the frank avowal by so many throughout most of the war that the war was one to save the Union and not abolish slavery, indicates how little people wanted blacks to intrude into this situation. Nevertheless, several poignant lines of Frances Harper's poem were:

> Ye may bind your trembling victims,
> Like the heathen priests of God:
> And may barter manly honor
> For the Union and for gold: --
> But ye cannot stay the whirlwind,
> When the storm begins to break,
> And our God doth rise in judgment
> For the poor and needy's sake
> And your guilty, sin-cursed Union
> Should be shaken to it's base,
> Till ye learn that simple justice
> Is the right of every race.[56]

The stringent moralism with regard to abolition as preached by her uncle comes through these lines.

The stern talk of doing one's duty which William Watkins preached as being paramount, was what the Union could have used in the first months of the war. Eventually, however, as the Union turned near disaster into success, and began winning the war after 1863, the border states, and especially Maryland, took it upon themselves to consider abolishing slavery within their own borders, as Lincoln's Emancipation Proclamation issued in September 1863 affected only those slaves held by states in rebellion. The people in Maryland reached a decision to free its slaves with the ratification of its state constitution in October 1864. With that accomplished, the emancipation of Maryland's slaves was celebrated in New York at the Cooper Institute on November 28, 1864. Henry Highland Garnet, a runaway slave from Maryland's Eastern Shore and Frances Harper took part in these festivities. Harper's address kept the audience "breathless" as she explained the lessons that should be taken to heart from so much war and destruction being visited upon the country. She spoke of the conflict as being sown in the arrival of the first Dutch slave ships in the early 1600s. On a personal note, she spoke of the delight she felt in being able to return to Baltimore without fear of arrest, or something even worse happening.[57]

Frances Harper did return to Baltimore in the first days of January 1865, about a couple of months after Frederick Douglass, a former choir member of Sharp Street, first made his way back. Douglass came in November 1864 where he spoke at Bethel Church on the 17th of that month. Inside the church he addressed an audience that included his sister who had been freed by the state's abolition provision in the newly ratified constitution. Douglass had not seen her in nearly thirty years. On the 22nd of November, at a sword presentation by blacks to Colonel Bowman of the 81st Pennsylvania Volunteer, Douglass made another speech with the Lieutenant Governor, members of the Maryland Legislature, military officers, City Councilmen, and clergymen present. Bowman was Union recruiting officer for blacks in Maryland and the 81st was assembled and trained at Camp Birney on Madison Avenue. The Colored Ladies Union, headed by Mary Gibbs, wanted Douglass to speak at their Thanksgiving dinner given for the black troops at McKim Museum Hospital, but Douglass was otherwise engaged. Nevertheless, Douglass spoke an additional four times in the city.[58]

The occasion of Maryland's emancipation of its slaves and the free unhampered return of such important critics of that slavery as Frances Harper and Frederick Douglass was a situation that vindicated the spirit of those like Elisha Tyson, Daniel Coker, and William Watkins who had persevered in earlier years while condemning slavery. Now that Baltimore proved to be safe, William E. Matthews, a former student of Watkins who had informed William Lloyd Garrison of the return of Douglass and Harper, requested that Garrison and his long-time associate Wendell Phillips also come to the city and observe it as a freer and more open place.

In addition, as another indication of the rapidly changing times, Matthews sent Garrison a circular of the Baltimore Association for the Moral and Educational Improvement of the Colored People in Maryland which was described as "an association of gentlemen of generous impulses and philanthropic" in nature who were trying to establish a free educational system for blacks. Matthews wanted Garrison to promote the new association as a new phase of the work old abolitionists could join in. Indeed, the members of the association included the old abolitionist John Needles as a leader, with whom Garrison was acquainted, and a Tyson as treasurer. For a while, the group met at No. 3 & 4 Tyson Building. Matthews served as an agent for the association, as he did for a similar group sponsored by the African Methodist Episcopal Church which was under the overall direction of Bishop Daniel Payne. Rev. John M. Brown, who served as pastor of Bethel, was the more active leader of the latter group, known as the Parent Home and Foreign Missionary Society.

William E. Matthews was just one of several of Watkins' pupils in the city to become more visible during and after the Civil War. Matthews was born in Baltimore in 1843 and was a member of the Galbreth Lyceum, which probably existed from around 1855. It was named in honor of Rev. George Galbreth, a pioneer Zion African Methodist in Baltimore. At its height, the Galbreth Lyceum had one of the finest libraries of any black organization in the city, and published the Lyceum Observer, said to have been the first black newspaper published below the Mason-Dixon Line. The Lyceum was of similar quality to the one William Watkins and his friends formed in their youth.[59]

The Galbreth Lyceum was truly a remarkable institution which, at one point, had as members besides William E. Matthews who later became a lawyer, Federal Government official, the first black investment banker, an associate of Frederick Douglass and reviver of the Afro-American League idea for self-defense in the 1890s when violent racism was rampant; two other members of note who were students of William Watkins, John H. Butler and Reverend James H. A. Johnson. Butler was a life-long member of Zion Methodist and one of Baltimore's wealthiest blacks who was, it appears, perennial President of the Lyceum. Butler actively supported programs to improve the educational opportunities for blacks after the Civil War. Johnson was an accomplished orator and newspaper editor.

There were several other outstanding members of the Galbreth Lyceum. Reverend Hiram R. Revels was a member while an A.M.E. pastor in Baltimore in the late 1850s, who eventually became the first black man to sit in the United States Senate in 1870, representing Mississippi. Similarly, supposedly J. Willis Menard, a poet and first black elected to the House, representing Louisiana, but not allowed to take his seat, was a member. Another prominent member of local distinction but highly honored in Episcopal church circles throughout the country was Reverend Harrison H. Webb, rector of St. James, who at one point served as cashier of the Freedmen's Bank branch in Baltimore, and who was one of the first blacks to sit on a United States court jury in Baltimore. Webb joined in the Watkins-led opposition against colonization in the early days of that struggle. Solomon G. Brown was a corresponding member who lived in Washington. Brown worked at the Smithsonian Institute for 54 years and helped S. F. B. Morse build the telegraph line between Washington and Baltimore.

Finally, it seems likely that George T. Watkins, William Watkins third oldest son was a member of the Galbreth Lyceum. At a lecture given to the body in early 1860, George T. spoke on "The Varieties of the Human Race" and was described by an observer as a "powerful" lecturer whose "arguments were clear." With their being such a strong William Watkins infuence in the Galbreth Lyceum, it is no wonder it had a strong and lasting reputation.[60]

The reputation of William Watkins continued as well a long time in the city because of the activities of his sons as teachers in Baltimore. George T. Watkins lived a long life, even into the twentieth century. He was thought to be the second black in the United States to have received a doctorate of divinity, and also one of the first to have received a doctorate in systematic theology.

George T. Watkins had a distinguished career as an African Methodist Episcopal minister and was known throughout the churches of this connection in Baltimore, at one time or another, for working miracles of sorts, in getting them out of debt. He was also quite an active person in the fraternal circles--the secret societies and the like. As a teacher, George Watkins could list among his illustrious pupils: John H. Murphy, builder of the Afro-American newspaper business, one of the most succesful in the nation; and Henry McNeil Turner, at various times first black chaplain in the United States Army, Reconstruction politician in Georgia, Senior Bishop of the A.M.E. Church and supporter of back-to-Africa movements from the late 1890s into the early twentieth century.

George T. Watkins died at the house of his son, J. L. H. Watkins in April or May 1915 in Berwyn, Pennsylvania. He was 87. This son had a doctorate of divinity and was on the board of directorate of the community house in York, Pennsylvania. Another son, John S., once resided in Grand Rapids, Michigan, in the 1890s. So, in a sense, the Watkins seed seems to have multiplied and spread all over the country.

William Watkins' second son, Richard, most resembled his father by being a minister, teacher, physician, and concerned citizen. One worthy example of his public concern was his participation in a move in 1852 to erect a monument to John Russwarm, first black Governor of Maryland's colony in West Africa; and Benjamin Banneker, first black scientist in the United States. Richard died at an early age.

Another son, John, before leaving for Canada conducted his own school as well in the city, which his brother, George, joined with his own school after John's leaving.

William Watkins is known to have had at least one other outstanding female student beside his niece Frances Ellen, but no doubt there were more. Adele Jackson, as this female student, eventually became a teacher at Sharp Street Church School and was considered one of the best teachers in the city. She afterwards conducted a private school on West Biddle Street which was taken over by her daughter, staying in existence well into the twentieth century. Adele Jackson exhibited a social consciousness, say for example, concerned for the aged, that would have been heart-warming to her former teacher and minister. Mrs. Jackson (nee Martin) was aided in her endeavors by her husband, James Jackson, who, as one of the wealthier blacks and as well a leading politician after Negroes acquired the right to vote in 1870, could ably undergird her activities.

Two other persons, George W. Lester and William T. Carr, gladly acknowledged the influence of William Watkins in their lives as a teacher. Lester became a wealthy poultry dealer operating in the Lexington, Hanover, and Old Marsh Markets, and was a member of John Wesley for 54 years. Most of that time he was an officer and, at times, served as president of the Board of Trustees of the church. According to contemporary accounts, he had a wide range of knowledge. At his death in 1915, the Reverend William T. Carr was considered the oldest black Presbyterian minister in the country. Having received his own educational training from the master, Carr established himself as a teacher early in his life at Port Deposit, Maryland. His son, Dr. W. T. Carr, Junior, was involved in founding the most successful black medical institution in Baltimore—Provident Hospital.[61]

As surely as Watkins in pursuing worthwhile endeavors can be given part of the credit for instilling in the minds of his pupils the desire for valuing the same, he can, with the same logic, be seen as a spiritual ancestor to the establishment in Baltimore of the Douglass Institute, a cross-cultural institute which promoted the kind of excellence in mental and moral nurturing advocated and exemplified in Watkins' entire life. Besides, here, too, former Watkins' pupils had a leading hand when the Douglass Institute opened with dedicatory service on September 29, 1865. Frederick Douglass, whose name graced the building, was the speaker for the occasion.

The Institute was, without question, for nearly twenty-five years, the most important black institution in all of Baltimore, being a cultural center including within its walls at some point, all of the following: various-sized meeting rooms for secret societies, a music department, exhibition space, high school, library and newspaper. The high school was one of two operated for blacks in the state for quite a while.

The Institute was housed in a building formerly Newton University, which had served, during the war, as a Union Hospital. In the Spring of 1865, a group of thirty or forty blacks purchased the building for $16,000. The company also made investments in houses, with the rents secured from these going to help defray the expenses of the Institute. Five thousand dollars was spent in renovating the 34 x 70 feet, four-story structure. John H. Butler was chairman of the Board of Trustees.

Those besides Butler to have a prominent hand in the success and operation of the Douglass Institute included George Alexander Hackett, son of Charles Hackett, an important person in the founding of Bethel Church. George Hackett was unquestionably the most important black in Baltimore after William Watkins lost much of his stature after his involvement with the Millerites. Another key figure at the Institute was Rev. James H. A. Johnson, a pupil of Watkins who was early in his career a barber, but then a minister, and referred to as "one of the brainiest men in the African Methodist Church." Johnson, at some point in his life, studied theology at Princeton. He was editor of the True Communicator which had its offices in the Institute. A securely owned black paper edited by one of his own would surely have delighted William Watkins, if he had lived to see it.[62]

As for the dedicatory exercises themselves, with a full-length portrait of Lincoln hanging down in the

136

center of the stage of the main auditorium, the opening commenced with a prayer from Bishop Alexander W. Wayman, a friend of Douglass. Next, William H. Woods, Secretary of the Institute, once a teacher in his own private school, read letters of regret from the likes of General Winfield Scott Hancock, Bishop Daniel A. Payne, and some others. Woods married Annetta Watkins, perhaps some relative of William Watkins.

In his speech, Douglass said:

> The establishment of an institution bearing my name by the colored people in the city of my boyhood, so soon after the act of emancipation in this state, looms before me as a first grand indication of progress.

Douglass went on to liken the establishment of the institution as having nationwide and epoch-making significance. Apparently, the Douglass Institute was the first or one of the first such venture of its kind amongst blacks in the country. Douglass said further:

> . . . a people hitherto pronounced by American Learning as uncapable of anything higher than the dull round of merely animal life--held to be originally and permanently inferior. . .
> .63

had by erecting the Douglass Institute, shown themselves to be capable of fostering among themselves the refined aspects of civilization. Yet, surely if whites had ever taken note of what really went on inside the Watkins' schools in the city, they would have concluded as much from what they would have seen being taught.

In a section of his speech, Douglass dealt with great men of learning and achievement in the race, such as Benjamin Banneker, whose accomplishments, he observed ironically, had no great effect on lessening the stigma of racial inferiority attached to blacks by white Americans, as say the accomplishments of Benjamin Franklin could do in the early days of America, when the land was considered barren, even barbaric by Europeans.

After Douglass' lecture, several others addressed the audience. When introduced to the crowd, the Reverend James Lynch, a Baltimorean by birth, his father probably being Benjamin Lynch, a Methodist Episcopal minister, was described as a missionary to Georgia and South Carolina. He was further identified by the newspaper as

137

the one who electrified the Nashville Colored Convention recently with his oratory. Lynch had been a former student of Daniel Payne from the age of 13 to the time he was sent to Dartmouth College in New Hamphsire--truly an educated clergyman as Watkins and Payne had long ago called for.

After Lynch's remarks, the president of the Institute, John Butler, introduced John Needles as a friend of the race for the last forty years, and with that, Butler said he "felt much honored by the presence of this noble old man as they would have been by that of the President" of the United States. Much applause followed this observation. After Butler, several others spoke, rousing the audience to the issues ahead, now that slavery was ended, such as securing the right to vote for blacks. Douglass, himself, returned to the podium to speak on the merits of the suffrage issue.

Indeed, as the Douglass Institute concluding ceremonies indicated, with the end of the Civil War, blacks everywhere were invigorated to preserve and extend their right to freedom. Frances Ellen Watkins Harper continued to lecture with this in mind and confined a good deal of her time to the Southern States. Reconstruction, in her words, should not be built upon the "shifting sands of policy and expediency, but upon the granite of eternal justice. When the colored man drops the bullet, he must have placed in his hands the ballot." Mrs. Harper was in agreement with Congressional plans about entrenching Union men, black or white, in Southern States, if these states were to be allowed back into the Union, reconstructed to the point that rebellion would not again raise its head. Mrs. Harper advocated rather wistfully that if the poor white and black of the South were together in an alliance, both having been exploited by what she called "scum" rebel leaders, then, perhaps, a more equitable society could arise out of the ashes of the Civil War.[64]

While lecturing in Portland, Maine, a place where early in her career she started professionally to lecture, Frances Harper spoke on "The Mission of the War and the Demand of the Colored Race in the Work of Reconstruction." She was well received; one listener said she was probably the most accomplished woman lecturer in the country. Mrs. Harper said, among other things, "people might call her 'nigger' till their tongues were tired, she would not care so long as the laws would not allow them to treat her as a 'nigger.'"

138

In speaking of social equality in ironical tones and responding to the often-repeated objection of whites, who simplified the issue to mean that blacks wanted laws enacted to allow them to force themselves into a close, intimate relationship with whites, regardless of distinction as relates to manners and breeding, by saying this was not the intent of what was meant by social equality.

Mrs. Harper said what most blacks wanted social equality to mean was the right to be able to enjoy equally public accommodations, such as in hotels, in restaurants and in trains. She responded to the whites' oversimplification of the issue, however, with an emotional response of her own; she said that as hard as it may seem to say and for others to comprehend or believe, she would consider it a great encumbrance "to have a law that would compel her to associate with some white people she had known."

Finally, in summarizing the whole situation as so many refused to see it, she "referred to a class of Rip Van Winkles, who, during four years of war, had forgotten nothing and learned nothing, and who seemed not to have heard that Judge Taney is dead." Taney was Chief Justice of the Supreme Court of the United States during the Dred Scott decision which announced that no black had a right that a white man was bound to respect.[65]

On one of her tours in the South, apparently by paying her own expenses, Harper lectured several times in Louisiana. In the Spring of 1871, the editor of the Louisianian prepared his readers for her lecture before the State Legislature in the Senate chamber on "The Work Before Us," a lecture she had been giving since at least around early 1868, by reprinting comments on her previous performance. They were very commendable. In her lecture, Harper reviewed the history of the struggle for human freedom in America, then turned her attention to the future and things blacks could do to help themselves in time "acoming," by "alluding to the means in their power," and the prime elements at the command of blacks to make things better. She developed this theme by a course of "clear, close, logical reasoning and a force of illustrations which so commended themselves as to draw repeated applause." The reporter who witnessed Mrs. Harper's performance said he had heard numerous women lecturers before, but not one had "the command of language, the graceful and easy flow of words, the power of reasoning united with an ability to infuse burning satire and cutting sarcasm" as Frances Ellen Watkins Harper.

Several days later, Harper lectured again in New Orleans, this time at Straight University. She thought compulsory education for all would better equip the race, which had not yet sufficiently appreciated the boon of education capable of "establishing home life, . . . the elevation of woman, and to (laying) a ban on sin." Harper defended women's right to the surprise of some who thought she was not of that mold.

The reporter observing the lecture given at Straight University had some criticism in the manner in which it was given. He said, in sum, there was not a word of encouragement or praise for the work already done and the willingness shown by blacks to improve themselves since the end of the war. Having said this, no higher compliment of sorts could have been paid this relative and pupil of William Watkins who, by what had been left to judge him, did not seek to praise men, but instead to prick them to strive to a higher and nobler life, itself. Another matter regretted by the reviewer was the belief that Mrs. Harper held the belief that blacks, because of their envy of each other's advancement, hindered the rise of each other to positions of eminence. Again, no higher compliments, could have been made to William Watkins, through his niece, who, like him, was like unto the prophets of old and, perhaps, rightly so, saw that one never did enough to assist his brother.

Whatever the manner of criticism, Frances E. W. Harper suffered in 1871 at the hands of the Louisianian; in the following year, she was singled out for distinctive citation in the same paper. In an article entitled "Literature Among Colored People," the writer lamented the fact that there were too few literary efforts amongst blacks. He said, historically speaking, there had lived two entitled to the name of poet, namely Phyllis Wheatley and James M. Whitfield, and just two presently worth the name of poet--Mrs. Harper and Richard T. Greener.

Interestingly enough, Greener was the grandson of an old associate of William Watkins in Baltimore in the struggle against colonizationists, namely Jacob Greener. Richard T. Greener was the first black graduate of Harvard College. The acknowledgment of Harper's and Greener's achievements seem to justify their elders protest against colonizationists some forty years before, who wanted to drive blacks out of the country because of their supposed eternal damnation to remain inferior if they remained.[66]

Frances E. W. Harper was to continue to use her talents as a writer and lecturer for uplifting her people and in doing so, made real, the contribution of William Watkins to his people's progress. At her death in 1911, a <u>Crisis</u> editorial by William E. B. DuBois, a leading black intellectual with Harvard and European educational experience, recognized Harper's contribution. DuBois said although she was not a "great writer," she was above all sincere "and all the young could profit from her dedication under the circumstances and time in which she lived," for even in 1911, DuBois said one could count on one's hands the black writers making her kind of sacrifice for the sake of a worthy literature based on the race's history and culture. In conclusion, he urged the young "to follow the hallowed footsteps of Frances Watkins Harper!"

It is amazing, however, that as DuBois acknowledged the fact of her association with the great and talented persons of the race over the last sixty years of her life, he obviously excluded the fact, or did not realize the facts surrounding her birth: That she was born into and grew up around greatness, namely, her uncle William Watkins. The contributions of William Watkins to the elevation of his race were, to say he least, of even greater proportion than most have yet realized.[67]

NOTES

Chapter III

[1]William H. Morris, "William Watkins," _A.M.E. Review_, 3 (1886): 5-12; Betty J. Gardener, "William Watkins: Antebellum Black Teacher and Anti-Slavery Writer," _Negro History Bulletin_ (September/October 1976) pp. 623-25; E. A. Andrews, _Slavery and the Domestic Slave Trade in the United States_ (Boston: Light & Stearns, 1836), p. 56; Merton L. Dillon, _Benjamin Lundy and the Struggle for Negro Freedom_ (Urbana, Ill.: University of Illinois Press, 1966), p. 89; _American_, September 16, 1894, p. 20; Baltimore County Land Records, W. G. 115, p. 625 (John Sinclair Deed of Trust to Jacob Gilliard and others, May 13, 1811; _Anglo-African Magazine_, October 1859.

[2]See, in general, Merton L. Dillon, _Benjamin Lundy_; E. M. Wright, "John Needles (1786-1878): An Autobiography," _Quaker History_, 58 (Spring 1969), pp. 4, 13, 16, 17.

[3]Jared Sparks, "Emigration to Africa and Hayti," _North American Review_, 20 (January 1825): 194-200; Robert G. Harper, Sketch of an Address to the People of Baltimore in 1824, M.H.S., Harper-Pennington papers.

[4]_African Repository_, December 1826, p. 296, _Genius of Universal Emancipation_, September 16, 1876, p. 1; September 23, 1826, p. 12; Letter, Charles C. Harper to R. R. Gurley, December 13, 1826, A.C.S.

[5]_Genius of Universal Emancipation_, November 4, 1826, p. 53; November 11, 1826, p. 61; _Federal Gazette_, January 6, 1827, p. 1.

[6]_Freedom's Journal_, May 18, 1827, p. 38.

[7]Letter, Charles C. Harper to R. R. Gurley, January 3, 1827, A.C.S.

[8]_African Repository_, December 1826.

[9]Robert G. Harper, _A letter from Gen. Harper of Maryland to Elias B. Caldwell_ (Baltimore: American Colonization Society, 1818), pp. 6-7.

[10]_African Repository_, December 1826.

[11]_Freedom's Journal_, July 6, 1827, p. 66.

142

[12]Liberator, August 18, 1832, p. 131.

[13]Liberator, April 2, 1831, p. 54.

[14]Liberator, January 25, 1834, p. 14.

[15]Letter, Charles C. Harper to R. R. Gurley, January 3, 1827, A.C.S.: Register of Certificate Granted by Clerk of Baltimore County to Negroes Freed by Manumission in Virtue of an Act of Assembly Passed November Session 1805, Commencing of First of June 1806, p. 159, Department of Legislative Reference, Bureau of Archives.

[16]Letter, John H. B. Latrobe to R. R. Gurley, January 5, 1827, A.C.S.; Letter, Charles C. Harper to R. R. Gurley, January 19, 1827; Christian Advocate, October 5, 1827, p. 1; Thomas Earle, The Life, Travels and Opinions of Benjamin Lundy (Philadelphia: William D. Parrish, 1847), pp. 29, 206-209.

[17]Letter, Charles C. Harper to R. R. Gurley, November 20, 1827, A.C.S.; See, in general, Penelope Campbell, Maryland in Africa: The Maryland State Colonization Society, 1831-1857 (Chicago: University of Illinois Press, 1971); William Lloyd Garrison, Thoughts on African Colonization (New York: Arno Press, 1968) p. 53; Christian Advocate, October 5, 1827, p. 1.

[18]Letter, John H. B. Latrobe to R. R. Gurley, April 5, 1828, A.C.S.

[19]African Repository, 1833, p. 222; Letter, Robert Findley to John H. B. Latrobe, November 2, 1833, M.H.S.; Letter, Elliott Cresson to Walter Lowrie, January 30, 1854, A.C.S.

[20]Letter, George R. McGill to John H. B. Latrobe, February 15, 1834, M.H.S.

[21]American, November 2, 1859, p. 1

[22]Liberator, January 10, 1835, p. 7.

[23]Letter, Charles Howard to R. R. Gurley, November 18, 1831, A.C.S.

[24]_Liberator_, January 25, 1834, p. 14; David Walker, _Appeal_ (New York: Hill and Wang, 1969, C. 1829), pp. 4-5.

[25]Letter, Elliott Cresson to R. R. Gurley, June 6, 1831, A.C.S.

[26]_Anglo-African Magazine_, October 1859.

[27]Letter, Charles C. Harper to R. R. Gurley, April 9, 1829, A.C.S.

[28]Letter, John B. Russwurm to R. R. Gurley, June 16, 1829, A.C.S.; Letter, Charles C. Harper to R. R. Gurley, May 30, 1832, A.C.S.

[29]Letter, H. B. Latrobe to Moses Sheppard, June 13, 1831, M.H.S., Latrobe-Sheppard papers; Letter, Arthur Tappan to Thomas Shipley, August 6, 1831, Haverford College, Quaker Collection.

[30]_Liberator_, February 19, 1831, p. 1.

[31]_Liberator_, April 2, 1831, p. 54.

[32]_Liberator_, April 2, 1831, p. 54.

[33]_Liberator_, June 4, 1831, p. 66

[34]_Liberator_, August 18, 1832, p. 131.

[35]_Liberator_, January 21, 1832, p. 1.

[36]_Liberator_, January 21, 1832, p. 1.

[37]_Liberator_, January 21, 1832, p. 1.

[38]_Liberator_, January 21, 1832, p. 1.

[39]_Liberator_, January 25, 1834, p. 1.

[40]_Liberator_, July 4, 1835, p. 106.

[41]_Liberator_, July 4, 1835, p. 106.

[42]Letter, William Watkins to William L. Garrison, September 31, 1835, Boston Public Library, Manuscripts Division, William L. Garrison papers.

[43]See Dorothy Porter, _Negro Protest Pamphlets_, p. 155.

[44]Colored American, September 15, 1838, p. 18.

[45]Colored American, June 17, 1837, p. 2.

[46]Colored American, June 24, 1837, p. 2; July 1, 1837, pp. 2-3; July 15, 1837, p. 22.

[47]Colored American, July 1, 1837, p. 2.

[48]William H. Morris, p. 9; Plan of Appointment for Baltimore City Station, 1843-1844, Lovely Lane Museum, Baltimore, Maryland.

[49]Letter, Samuel F. McGill to Moses Sheppard, March 11, 1845, Swarthmore College, Friends' Library, Moses Sheppard papers.

[50]Letter, Samuel F. McGill to Moses Sheppard, April 25, 1849, Swarthmore College, Friends' Library, Moses Sheppard papers.

[51]Morris, pp. 9-10; William Watkins' Will, Ontario Archives, Toronto, Canada.

[52]Daniel A. Payne, The Semi-Centenary and the Retrospective of the African Methodist Episcopal Church (Freeport, N.Y.: books for Libraries Press, 1972, c. 1866), p. 76; Indianapolis Freeman, January 5, 1889, p. 5.

[53]Liberator, January 11, 1856, p. 7; National Anti-Slavery Standard, July 4, 1857, p. 2; February 27, 1858, p. 3; Liberator, April 23, 1858, p. 67; November 12, 1858, p. 184; National Anti-Slavery Standard, April 9, 1859, p. 3; November 26, 1859, p. 3; Weekly Anglo-African, September 3, 1859, p. 4; Liberator, February 24, 1860, p. 3; March 8, 1861, p. 4; National Anti-Slavery Standard, January 14, 1860; Benjamin Quarles, Allies for Freedom: Blacks and John Brown (New York: Oxford University Press, 1974), p. 69.

[54]Weekly Anglo-African, September 24, 1859, p. 1; October 22, 1859, p. 22.

[55]Weekly Anglo-African, June 30, 1860, p. 1; June 23, 1860, p. 1.

[56]Liberator, March 8, 1861, p. 40.

[57]Liberator, December 9, 1864, p. 198.

[58]Liberator, January 27, 1865, p. 116.

[59]American, September 16, 1894, p. 20; Washington Bee, April 11, 1885, p. 2.

[60]American, September 16, 1894, p. 20; Afro-American, July 1906, p. 4.

[61]Afro-American, December 5, 1914, p. 4; February 24, 1911, p. 3; April 3, 1915, p. 1.

[62]American, September 29, 1865, p. 4; September 30, 1865, p. 4; Sun, September 29, 1865, p. 1; September 30, 1865, p. 1; The Colored Tennessean, August 12, 1865, p. 1; October 4, 1865, p. 3.

[63]Philip S. Foner, The Life and Writings of Frederick Douglass (New York: International Publishers, 19), Vol. 4, pp. 174-182.

[64]Liberator, March 3, 1865.

[65]Liberator, August 11, 1865, p. 128; December 29, 1865, p. 208.

[66]Louisianian, April 9, 1871, p. 2; April 16, 1871; April 20, 1871, p. 2; June 18, 1872; p. 2.

[67]Crisis, April 1911, p. 21.

CHAPTER IV

GEORGE ALEXANDER HACKETT, THE LEADER

As much as William Watkins' life, from early youth onward, is best viewed from the perspective of Sharp Street Methodist Church, so is the life of his successor, George A. Hackett, as the leading black of Baltimore, best viewed from his youth onward from Bethel African Methodist Episcopal Church. Bethel Church in Baltimore has a remarkable history; in part, it grew out of Sharp Street Church. In 1815, the Bethel congregation acquired from William Carman, an associate of Tyson in the Protection Society, the old church property of Zion Lutheran Church located on Saratoga Street near Gay.

The evidence indicates Bethel was organized and established from the very beginning without ever having been a part of the General Conference of the Methodist Church, something which few, if any, other substantial black Methodist churches of this time could claim. This fact is the more significant because a great many blacks throughout the country favored the Methodist persuasion in the early years of the 1800s. Baltimore Bethel's beginning prevented arising the legal hassles which the black Methodists in Philadelphia and New York experienced when they sought to come out from under the control of white Methodists as racial discrimination within the very walls of the church became too burdensome.

The significant early support of Elisha Tyson in the church's establishment and acquisition of this Saratoga Street property helped ease the acceptance of this kind of independence by blacks which some others viewed as quite threatening.[1] In order to help pay off the debt incurred in buying the property in July 1815, the Trustees of Bethel appealed through the newspapers for aid from whites, saying:

> The Trustees rest satisfied, that the motives
> by which they are influenced will be correctly
> estimated by all those that believe the most
> inconsiderable individual shares the bounty
> and interest of God.[2]

Any number of white friends of blacks, including Tyson, attached their names to this appeal.

Bethel grew from this shaky beginning to become from at least the 1840s to the first few years of the

147

twentieth century, the most influential and, perhaps, the wealthiest black congregation in Baltimore. Along the way, Baltimore's Bethel and its leading members were, in turn, prominent participants when the first national organization of Negroes, the African Methodist Episcopal Church, was formed in April 1816, drawing together black Methodists from Baltimore, Philadelphia, Wilmington, Delaware, and a few other places.

Bethel Church, in 1840, was an enthusiastic church. In fact, one observer complained that the church's worship service was done too enthusiastically, that is to say, too boisterously. In his letter to the editor, this critic described the services as sounding more like a "corn-husk" than anything devotional--with cries, groans, wails, laughs, measured stamping of feet, and songs done loudly enough to disturb the entire neighborhood (perhaps he wanted to say the devil), including the police station close by.

He remarked further,

Many and many a harmless street stroller has been dragged off to the watchhouse for singing a song or bawling in the streets at unseasonable hours--while here are hundreds of negroes (sic) assembled together for purpose of 'worship' making night hideous with their howls, dancing to the <u>merry</u> song of some double-lunged fellow, who glories the more his <u>congregation</u> yells.[3]

The writer concluded by saying,

Is an entire neighborhood to be disturbed day after day and night after night by these <u>rioters</u>-- because some well meaning persons choose to say they are free to worship?

Apparently, there were still some in the community who considered the Constitution as applying to blacks, as well, who should be guaranteed the right of freedom of worship.

George A. Hackett was one of the most remarkable of several laymen of Bethel who proved to be the basis for the continuing strength and determination of the church that made it a veritable beacon for worthy efforts of race uplift after 1840. George Hackett was the son of Charles Hackett, who held positions of responsibility in the church government on the local and national levels for over fifty years. Charles Hackett is one of the ones given credit for securing the services of Daniel Coker as the first black teacher in Baltimore at Sharp Street around 1808. He later, with Daniel Coker and some others, established Bethel during the War of 1812.

According to one source, George A. Hackett was born on Christmas Day, 1806, on the island of Jamaica, Spanish Town, St. Catherine's Parish. The census of 1860, however, states he was born in Maryland. He married a daughter of Nicholas Gilliard in October 1828 and was, therefore, a relative by marriage of Coker who had married a daughter of Jacob Gilliard, Junior. Nicholas Gilliard, his father-in-law, had also acted with Charles Hackett to bring Coker to the city as a teacher and was important in forming the African Methodist Episcopal Church. Very early in Hackett's life, and up to the late 1830s, as a seaman, he had seen most of the world by the time his seafaring days ended. A high point in his days at sea came when he served as steward aboard the ship <u>Constitution</u>, a frigate built by the United States Government during Revolutionary times. Determined on being an independent businessman from the 1830s onward, Hackett owned a livery stable. Later in his life he operated a coal yard with his office at the Douglass Institute.

In 1838, Hackett's son George D. C., died, the only son he seems to have had; and, perhaps not having a grown son made it easier for him to develop a father/son relationship with so many of the young men of the community as he became the recognized black leader in the city. The Hacketts had two other children to reach adulthood; however, Eliza Ann, who married Charles W. Tilghman in 1852, and Catherine Henrietta.

George A. Hackett was a man of tremendous courage and seems to have commanded deep loyalties from people as he undertook matters in behalf of blacks. He was surrounded by several outstanding associates and co-workers. Among the more important in the early years, after retiring from the sea, was Rev. Daniel A. Payne.[4]

Daniel Alexander Payne arrived in Baltimore in mid-1844 to assume pastoral duties at Bethel Church; he was one of the first blacks with seminary training. Just before coming to Baltimore, he had previously served at Bethel in Philadelphia. A native of South Carolina, Payne was driven out of the state while a schoolteacher when he offended slaveholders for teaching blacks to read and write. At the time of his arrival in Balti-

149

more, Bethel's membership was about 1,200. He headed a strong church said to take care of all its poor, something, supposedly, no other church in Baltimore did.

From the beginning of his arrival, Payne, though very small in physical stature, delved into the most significant community activities. Though the record is silent as to the particulars, Payne doubtlessly received the cooperation of Hackett, a man noted for his wide range of interests, considered well-read and quite blessed with oratorical skills to lend his voice to any cause he chose to promote. Payne joined in efforts very soon after his arrival to keep alive the memory of Benjamin Banneker, the first black man of science who was largely self-taught. On one level, Payne's interest in Banneker is understandable; he had established an enviable record for himself in South Carolina as an amateur naturalist. The efforts to honor Banneker occurred around the time of the spring 1845 publication of John H. B. Latrobe's short memoir of Banneker which was mainly based upon reminiscences of the Ellicott family.

For its part, the black community organized the Banneker Monument Committee with John Fortie as president and Harrison H. Webb, the secretary. Fortie was a Methodist Episcopal minister, schoolteacher, businessman; Webb was a teacher and active Episcopalian. The committee of blacks proposed to build a monument to Banneker and place it over his grave, if found. Payne was most active in this phase. Robert Carey Long, Junior, whose services were secured through John H. B. Latrobe, designed the monument. While this was happening in Baltimore, blacks in Washington were attempting to do something similar. Perhaps, both cities took up the project to raise the monument jointly.[5]

Although no monument to Banneker was erected in 1845, Payne continued to be in the midst of important activities. In 1846, in concert with others, including once again John Fortie, Payne presented to Rev. Robert J. Breckenridge, a Presbyterian minister, a gold snuff box in appreciation for things he had done to better the condition of blacks. Breckenridge was, as well, president of Jefferson College in Pennsylvania. He did not attend the ceremony to accept the gift, but had a friend pick it up for him. In a letter published in the Lutheran Observer, Breckenridge apologized for not being present and thanked the givers for the gift.

In his letter, Breckenridge did not fail to use the opportunity to offer his thoughts on the black man's

destiny as he saw God had decreed it. It had the familiar sound of a colonizationist sermon. He said that American blacks were the only means by which a "civilized
state within the Tropics" could be formed. He stated
further he was not advising individuals or masses of
blacks to emigrate to Africa, but he did want to testify
against

> . . . that general and concerted hostility to
> African colonization, which in various parts
> of the country, whether amongst yourselves or
> amongst us, had had no better effect, than to
> delude and embitter the minds of the free
> blacks, and exasperate those of the whites,
> and embarrass the noblest and most fruitful
> movement of the present century.[6]

Despite opening disclaimers to the contrary, Breckenridge hoped more blacks would emigrate to Christianize
the regions of Africa.
                                                    .

Daniel Payne did not seem to oppose with such tenacity as William Watkins did, the efforts of the American Colonization Society. There is, similarly, no record of Bethel men, Hackett included, being so deadly
adverse to colonization as Watkins. Indeed, in October
1847, Payne conducted religious services aboard a ship
about to depart for Liberia, something unthinkable to
Watkins. In this vein, Payne was no different than the
first Bishop of the African Methodist Episcopal Church,
Richard Allen, who vigorously opposed the American Colonization Society in 1817 when it appeared merely a tool
of slaveholders to rid America of the free blacks, but
who by 1823 had changed his mind about colonization and
conducted religious services aboard a ship in Baltimore
harbor bound for Liberia.[7] Breckenridge would have welcomed more involvement from Bethel men in colonization.

Breckenridge sought the agreement of blacks on another front. In another part of his published letter,
he said that the further extension of freedom to blacks
depended upon the benevolence of the slaveholders as had
been the case in the past; and, for this reason, "gratitude and every dictate of prudence and wisdom," demanded
blacks already free in the slave states remain "quiet,
loyal, peaceable, and docile." This attitude was not
accepted by all, including Hackett and Payne. In fact,
Payne was an acquaintance of Charles Torrey of Massachusetts who had helped several hundred slaves escape to
the North. Perhaps, Payne even assisted Torrey.

Payne did warn Torrey in 1844, by letter, not to come to Baltimore just before he did so and was subsequently arrested in the city, eventually dying a martyr in a Baltimore prison in 1846. Torrey's imprisonment was a cause celebre among abolitionists which involved the efforts of many to get his release, including John Quincy Adams, the former President, but then a member of the House of Representatives. While in prison, Torrey, as an admirer of Elisha Tyson, reflected upon the changed atmosphere in Baltimore; there seemed to remain no man of Tyson's stature, as a dauntless and unswerving advocate of freedom for the neglected, oppressed black. Such a position was gradually being filled however by George A. Hackett, with a solid and innovative Bethel behind him.[8]

Payne was an enthusiastic churchman, as were the Hacketts. A few years after his arrival, he took the innovative step to introduce instrumental music in the African Methodist Episcopal Church. In July 1848, a new Bethel was dedicated, built on the location of the old Bethel. Building started in June of the previous year. Robert Carey Long, Junior, who had drawn the Banneker Monument plans and who was the leading architect in Baltimore, designed the church structure. It cost $17,000 and seated 1,500. It was a combination Gothic and Romanesque structure with drab-pastel brickfront. The building had a second-story main auditorium, with galleries, while the basement floor was divided to accommodate a school, library, pastor's office, and other meeting rooms. Payne taught in the school and was at times ably assisted by Mary A. Prout, who, no doubt, handled the young ladies.

At the dedication of the new Bethel, which was to remain the largest for a long while and the model for A.M.E. churches built in this country, the opening services were presided over by Bishop William P. Quinn. Next, Elder William Moore of the African Israel Church in Washington, the first A.M.E. church in that city, established primarily by Reverend David Smith, a Baltimorean, read a consecration hymn composed by Payne. Reverend Matthew Clark based the dedicatory sermon on II Chronicles 6:7, "But will God, in verity dwell with men on earth? Behold Heaven, and the Heaven of Heavens will not contain thee. How much less this house which I have built."

Although, from the scant records existing, Hackett is not mentioned as figuring prominently in building the 1848 Bethel, he must have had a decisive hand in the enterprise. In 1859, Hackett was singled out for being a part of the building committee that supervised the extensive renovation done on the church because of the swaying and shaking of the building, brought about because of the way the floor was laid in 1848.[9]

Payne left Baltimore after the completion of the new church in 1848, but he continued to be connected in a close way with the city, as he rose to the position of Bishop, the first A.M.E. historian, first black president of a successfully established college, Wilberforce, in Ohio, and lastly Senior Bishop in his connection. The evidence shows, however, that no matter where Payne was, he cooperated with local leadership, including Hackett; and, Baltimore, in turn, supported him. After Payne's death in 1893, his body was buried in Baltimore. In this way, he signified his attachment to the city which had developed from those hectic days of the mid-1840s.[10]

As the 1840s became the 1850s and 1860s, others at Bethel joined and shared in Hackett's activities. Some of these included Thomas Bradford who held positions of authority at Bethel for several decades, and his son, James T., who became one of the wealthiest and most visible blacks after the Civil War. John W. Locks, another to hold a prominent place at Bethel, assisted Hackett. Once a caulker, then a supervisor in the shipyards, Locks used his earnings to become a well-off hack operator and funeral director. Others of means who held positions of authority at Bethel as well, and who supported Hackett in some measure, were Solomon McCabe, John A. Fernandis, and Isaac Myers. Alfred Ward Handy and William H. Spriggs were members of the church with less means, perhaps, than the others, but who provided invaluable assistance, especially in their connection with the Civil War veterans.

There are not many facts known about George Hackett's life prior to 1865. It is known, however, that he took a demonstrative part in an effort to commemorate the life of John B. Russwurm, Governor of Maryland in West Africa. Russwurm, one of the first blacks to graduate from an American college and coeditor of the first black newspaper, _Freedom's Journal_, went to Liberia sometime after 1830 and married a daughter of George R. McGill, once a minister at Sharp Street Church, who was also a teacher and businessman. In February 1852, a group of citizens gathered at the house of Reverend Darius Stokes, pastor of Bethel. At the meeting, Hackett supported a motion that Stokes draw up a list of

153

resolutions to be considered by the group at-large.

Among other things, the group agreed to a proposition offered by John H. B. Latrobe that he be allowed to give an eulogy on the recently departed Russwurm at an assembly of the black community at Madison Avenue Presbyterian Church on Wednesday evening, the tenth of March. Apparently, another service conducted by blacks, for blacks, in remembrance of Russwurm took place on Monday, the eighth, at the same church. At the March 10 meeting, nevertheless, Hackett thought it best someone give a rejoinder to Latrobe's eulogy. Significantly, those present at Stoke's house were cooperating with others to help the Laurel Cemetery Association set aside lots to erect monuments to both Russwurm and Benjamin Banneker. Laurel Cemetery was gradually becoming the place where more and more of the leading blacks were buried.[11]

Some seven years later, Hackett came into greater prominence as he, at first almost singly, undertook to defeat the Jacobs' Bill of 1859, an attempt to re-enslave or expel Maryland's free black populace which stood at nearly one-fifth of the total free black population in the United States, around 90,000. Jacobs' Bill was, in fact, a package of measures introduced by Col. C. W. Jacobs, a House of Delegates member from the Eastern Shore. Hackett's persuasiveness against Jacobs' proposed legislation was such that he supposedly converted numerous slaveholders to his side.

The story of the wrestle with Jacobs was reported to The Weekly Anglo-African by a regular correspondent from Baltimore. The fight lasted from the latter half of 1859 to the end of spring 1860. The whole affair's beginning could be said to be a reaction from the slaveocracy in Maryland to John Brown's raid on Harper's Ferry in October 1859. With his raid, Brown sought to raise a general rebellion of slaves throughout the entire Southland. Starting in this small town, it was hoped a success here would permit Brown to proclaim a different kind of freedom and democracy than had been inaugurated some fourscore and three years before by the Founding Fathers.[12]

Writing under the name "Delphic," someone in February 1860 sent a copy of the Jacobs measures to the editor of The Weekly Anglo-African to show the barbarity of the proposals. In his accompanying letter, the writer included the happy news that no editor of a city paper had endorsed them. All the leading barbershops in the community had solicited their customers to sign a petition against the bills. In addition to this, "Delphic" said that 200 of the city's "best" white women sent their own petition to the State Legislature which contained the following words:

> As wives and mothers, we implore that the curse of the Creator of all men be not called down upon our beloved state by the adoption of such unrighteous bills. As Christians, we plead in the name of God and of religion that we be not ranked with the heathen nations by the passage of laws which trample underfoot every precept of the Gospel, and outrage the religious sentiments of all Christendom.[13]

A similar petition headed by such names as Reverdy Johnson and George M. Brown, top lawyers in the community, was forwarded to Annapolis as well, causing a bit of uneasiness in some circles.

The blacks themselves were holding weekly meetings for their own "consultation," so as to decide each of their steps in opposition. On February 9, the blacks assembled at Bethel Church at 3:00 a.m. to observe a whole day of prayer and fasting against the evil decrees. At this early service, Harrison H. Webb was the key spokesman, he being the oldest minister with a long record of opposition to the opponents of good. At an evening service that day, Rev. Henry McNeil Turner denounced the bills. After each preaching session, a praying session followed.

Other ministers who had a hand in the affairs of the day included Reverends William H. Waters, Hiram R. Revels, Noah Davis, and Moses Clayton. The message blacks wanted all to know, was that they had the utmost confidence in God being able to deliver them. This belief had the familiar ring of William Watkins' similar profession of faith, when colonizationists of his day attempted on various occasions to rid the state of free blacks.

In subsequent letters to the editor of The Weekly Anglo-African, "Delphic" provided more details about the opposition to Jacobs. He said that at a meeting held at Sharp Street Church, which was crammed full, George A. Hackett, and a Mr. Bishop, probably William H. Bishop, a leading barber, spoke to the gathering which had been called under the aegis of the Protection Association, the league set up to counter Jacobs. These two spoke to the audience having just returned from Annapolis.

Baltimore's Delphic oracle said, in unambiguous tones:

> Mr. Hackett (sic) is a working man--he loves, he lives, and works for his race. He alone obtained over 1,000 signatures to a petition. . . . He was the first man to call a public meeting to organize the "Protection Association."[14]

After Hackett's report, Bishop and some others took turns at the podium. "Delphic" reported some successes: one of the bills relating to selling blacks into slavery if they failed to pay their debts had been defeated. On the negative side, however, the State Senate had passed a bill authorizing the incorporation of the "Southern Slaveholders Insurance Company of Maryland," a piece of legislation intended to insure and indemnify slaveholders against their more rambunctious property. "Delphic" also reported that the wealthy, white ladies who had been responsible for circulating a petition, went in person to present it to the Legislature. Included in the delegation were Mrs. Swann, wife of the Mayor, and Mrs. Reverdy Johnson.

In the midst of all of the commotion and excitement "Delphic" reported some thought it better to leave the city. Thirty had already gone up North, some as far away as Canada. One old man said he thought it was one's Christian duty not to submit to such outrages any longer. A few of the younger men in the city organized an Emigrant Association to assist those who wanted to leave. Those at the head of this movement included James A. Handy, from Bethel, J. F. Jackson, Tristy Richfield, and Peter Hill. They called a public meeting with the hope others would help them form a more permanent organization to assist the emigration.

Many responded to the call. One resolution put forth at the meeting urged every black to save one cent per week and in a short time $20,000 would be at hand, the amount seen as needed to carry on the work required. At the meeting, the desire was to go to Haiti, if one had to leave at all. There was no strong sentiment to move to Liberia, though certainly matters had improved at the place, now an independent country, since the days of William Watkins' strenuous protests. Yet, not even the newly built <u>Mary Caroline Stevens</u>, a very large and handsome ship, expresssly built for the local Colonization Society, seemed to impress blacks enough to make them want to settle in Liberia.

With all the agony Jacobs was causing blacks by the introduction of his package of legislation, "Delphic" said Jacobs is supposed to have openly professed that he loved black folk, to which the general reply from blacks was, "Nonsense!" Most of the churches had taken up collections for the Protection Association, with Bethel having raised a large part of the total.

In his March 31 communication, "Delphic" reported on an interview held between Hackett and Jacobs. While on a visit to Baltimore, Jacobs thought a personal confrontation with the prominent blacks of the city who were in opposition to his bills would help them see the virtue in his proposal. Besides Hackett, Bethel's pastor, John M. Brown, more than likely the person behind the "Delphic" articles, was also known to have attended this meeting. The interview took place at the Banner Hotel.

As the parties met, and as the introductions were made, Jacobs, upon hearing Brown's name, asked if he were a relative of John Brown of Harper's Ferry fame. (Perhaps an inept attempt at "breaking the ice," relieving the tension.) Rev. Brown replied in the negative, to which Jacobs responded, his answer showing he had some knowledge of blacks. He said he had heard any number of blacks whom John Brown had helped get to Canada some years before had named their children after him.

Jacobs then asked Rev. Brown if he could read and write, to which the pastor said "Yes." And, then, as if to put Rev. Brown on notice that he, Jacobs, could read and write also, and with comprehension, Jacobs said, "You read the Bible, I suppose? I have read it through three times." After that boast, Rev. Brown answered—"I do and have read it through many more times than that."

In the next breath, Jacobs professed to be a minister like Brown, and spoke to his brother of the cloth in these words:

> You ought to try to do your colored friends all the good you can. Instill into their minds the spirit of the gospel (sic), which among other things, teaches that servants must be obedient to their masters, faithful and true in all things; and that masters must

give unto their servants that which is just and equal, knowing that they also have a master in heaven.

After this banter which seemed to be a studied disregard for George Hackett's presence, whom Jacobs had wanted to see moreso than Rev. Brown, the real interview commenced. Jacobs opened by saying he had always heard so much about Hackett, he being referred to so often as an "intelligent" black, and thus wanted to meet him, to ask him some questions. Hackett only said he had some questions of his own.

First of all, Jacobs wanted to know if Hackett were a free man. Hackett said he was, and that he bought his freedom before he was twenty-one years of age. This is not exactly clear as to meaning, for one other source claims Hackett was born to free parents. Nevertheless, in his interview with Jacobs, Hackett gave other particulars of his life. He spoke of the two and one-half years he spent aboard the frigate Constitution, as steward with Commander Claxton; then, of his starting a livery stable business in Baltimore, where he employed some whites, particularly a white bookkeeper whom he paid $25.00 per month, and who presently was a leading citizen, holding a government position and "highly respected."

Although Jacobs was impressed, perhaps embarrassed, with Hackett's personal accomplishments, he thought that if blacks were slaves again, which his bills hoped to achieve, things would be better for them. Jacobs said he had slaves and thought it equally right for all blacks to be slaves; and, of course, his notion was based on Scripture, which he had already assured the others he had read three times from cover to cover. When Hackett replied to this, he "evinced much shrewdness and ingenuity which, according to "Delphic," nettled Jacobs. Hackett pointedly challenged Jacobs to point out anywhere in the Bible where God made slaves, his point being, God may have sanctioned or overlooked slavery, allowed it to stand, but He did not, Himself, say he made slaves, made man to be a slave, and especially only black men to be slaves.

To support the latter, Hackett let it be known that their existed slaves in Russia, they being white. Perhaps this unsettled Jacobs a bit, though, perhaps again not much, because the slave holders were using as an argument as why they should be allowed to keep blacks in slavery, the one that they treated their blacks better

158

than Europe and the rest of the world treated its peasants.

Hackett concluded his remarks by saying he stepped forward to defend the free blacks because it seemed as if no one else would, and he considered himself just a "specimen" of the free blacks in the state and what they had accomplished in the face of a great deal of "lordly" discouragement from the majority of the people. Jacobs, for his part, ended the discussions by hinting at wanting to be invited to give a lecture before a black audience about his most "liberal" sentiments, no doubt an idea that received no reply from Hackett or Brown, except contempt and a smile. The correspondent to The Weekly Anglo-African referred to Hackett at this meeting as being "very polite, shrewd, and intelligent." This may not have been all the truth, however, with regard to Hackett's handling of Jacobs.

According to another source, at a meeting between Hackett and Jacobs, the two men brawled on the State House grounds when Hackett dared to present a petition against the bills. Jacobs felt this a particular, impudent insult coming from a Negro. Hackett supposedly severely caned Jacobs in this encounter. In all events, Hackett was an especially courageous and active advocate of the rights of blacks at this time, whether with his hands or his mind.[15]

While in the midst of fighting Jacobs, in April 1860, Hackett's wife, Mary Jane, nee Gilliard, died. her obituary said, in tribute to her active life on behalf of her people, simply that she was well-known, but that her husband was "well known (sic) everywhere!"--a testimony to George Hackett's undisputed position as leader of the Baltimore and Maryland black communities. In March 1861, Hackett married his second wife, Mary Ann Davis, a native of Washington, Louisiana, who was a widow and mother of a new-born baby, Henrietta. If the documents are right, Mary Ann was around 15, Hackett 55. Perhaps this was as much a marriage made for love, as out of compassion. Eventually, Jacobs' bills were defeated, and, during the commotion to get them passed, Jacobs died suddenly.[16]

The significance of Hackett's long and distinguished life cannot be fully appreciated with the few facts known about him prior to 1865, when much of black activities were unrecorded, or seldom mentioned in the press, white press, that is, there being very few black newspapers. According to no less an authority than Bishop Daniel A. Payne, however, the last thirty years of his life, Hackett was looked upon by both black and white as the undisputed leader of the Baltimore black community. After the Civil War, more information is available to judge the Bishop's assertion, as the white local press included more material originating from the black community in its pages.

Some dominant characters or features of his life are these: Hackett practiced the virtue of charity; he actively concerned himself with the plight of widows and orphans. He belonged to numerous organizations, benevolent and secret, such as the Masons, Odd Fellows, Good Samaritans, Sons of Temperance, Order of Nazarites, and so on. He was a founding member of two bodies, Rising Star of Daniel A. Payne Lodge of the Good Samaritans and the Good Intent Building Association. The fraternal and secret societies had a history of pooling the meager resources among blacks which, in turn, allowed members to receive some aid in times of sickness, death, mortgage foreclosing, and other misfortunes. It was, as one newspaper said:

> The prominent position he (Hackett) held in those orders, and the active part taken by him in all matters connected with the colored race (that) gave him not only great influence in the colored community, but also attracted to him the attention of many others of our citizens, so that he was well known in this city and state.[17]

Indeed, the intensity and courage of Hackett's leadership was such that it was said that nearly a dozen assassination attempts had been made upon his life.

With regard to the latter, at the very outset of the Civil War, a Union soldier found himself in Baltimore, which was somewhat hostile territory at that time as Lincoln's skulking through the city in disguise and the riots against Massachusetts' 54th Regiment indicate. As an indication of the degree of courage he possessed, however, Hackett housed the officer and later escorted him out of the city when it was, yet, still dangerous to do so.

After blacks had received official sanction to serve in the Union Army in January 1864, Hackett recruited blacks from an office he opened on Holliday Street near Saratoga. He is given particular credit for filling in the ranks of the 30th and 31st Regiments of

U.S. Colored Troops. Baltimore was, in fact, a center for free black recruitment during the war. As Hackett had recruited the troops, he could be found, at times, assisting them, and their relatives received bounties and benefits due the men.

Sometime during the war, Hackett was brevetted a captain by Col. Edward F. M. Faehtz of Maryland's 8th Regiment. Hackett's appointment was one of the highest held by a black, inasmuch as the highest position normally was sergeant.

As another indication of the depth of his commitment, before the emancipation of Maryland's slaves was accomplished by the adoption of a new constitution in 1864, Hackett issued, unilaterally, a sort of emancipation proclamation of his own. According to one account, it was his habit to:

> . . .hire a wagon, go on a plantation, fill it with slaves, and with a six-barrelled revolver in each hand, defy the master to prevent it.[18]

It seems that no matter what the outcome of the Civil War, the blacks of Baltimore and Hackett, in particular, were not going to accept any return to business as usual once peace came.

After the war, Hackett and others showed their appreciation to the blacks who fought, such as when the Fourth United States Colored Troops, First Regiment which was raised in the city, one of its black oficers being A. Ward Handy, a Bethelite, returned to be discharged in May 1866. Hackett acted as chairman of the committee of welcome. The troops were met at Camden Station and conducted under escort by the Lincoln Zouaves, a black volunteer militia company, to Zion Church in South Baltimore, where Samuel Chase gave a welcoming address. That evening, the 460 survivors of the one thousand recruited were entertained at the Douglass Institute.[19]

Even just barely after hostilities between the states had ended and before the discharge of most of the fighting men, Hackett was energetic in winning a peace and new place for blacks in the city. He was a key person in the organization of the Douglass Institute, a comprehensive cultural center named after Frederick Douglass who spoke at the dedication of the building on the 29th of September 1865, after having spent the night

before at Hackett's house. Hackett was a part of the
Committee of Arrangements for the opening and, along
with Walter Sorrell, he was described as "indefatigable"
in making preparations for the affair. Over his signature, invitations to the City Council were sent, which
apparantly were not well received. Hackett served as a
member of the Executive Committee of the Institute.[20]

Ironically, in the same week that blacks had ventured to open the Douglass Institute, the white caulkers
were bidding to exclude black caulkers from the shipyards in this latest example of the perennial conflict
between white and black labor. Hackett had a hand in
the solution decided upon for this problem as well.
Blacks organized their own shipyard, the Chesapeake and
Marine Railway and Drydock Company.

Other leading partners in this venture were members
of Bethel, including Isaac Myers, who generally is given
the most credit for bringing the idea to fruition in the
community at large. He got his business experience as a
clerk-porter in what was the largest grocery business in
the South. William F. Taylor, a caulker like Myers,
was given almost equal credit with Myers for helping
promote the idea, especially among the caulkers themselves. Another Bethelite eventually became president
of the concern and was reportedly the largest stockholder. This was John W. Locks, a former caulker and
childhood playmate of Frederick Douglass. Causeman
Gaines, son of a minister, also of Bethel, at one point
was treasurer.

When the Chesapeake and Marine Railway and Drydock
Company was firmly established a couple of years later,
it was held up as an example to blacks throughout the
country to form joint stock companies for their own benefit. With so many Bethelites in prominence in the organization, it must also be concluded Hackett had more
than a little interest in seeing the company take hold
and prosper.[21]

Doubtlessly, Hackett wished to see the Douglass Institute thrive. Indeed, the Institute very clearly assumed the position for which it was intended, that of
being a central meeting place for blacks throughout the
city and state where problems could be discussed and decided upon. In the first week of December 1865, a city
convention of black delegates, selected by wards, met at
the Institute. The convention memorialized the state to
repeal its "black code" or those laws dealing with va-
grancy and apprenticeship that virtually reinstated

slavery in some areas of the state, especially on the Eastern Shore. The blacks got very sympathetic and immediate action upon this subject from Judge Hugh L. Bond of Baltimore Criminal Court, who issued writs of habeas corpus for several children illegally held on the Eastern Shore. Bond had been instrumental in forming the Baltimore Association for the Moral and Educational Improvement of the Colored People. He was at least, in the 1860s and perhaps before, very sympathetic toward blacks.[22]

Indeed, as a friend of the blacks a little after the December convention in January 1866, Bond was partly responsible for assembling the white lay members of the Methodist Episcopal Church, to interest them to be even more concerned about blacks. Bond and his family had been prominent communicants of the church for a long while. Such illustrious national luminaries as Chief Justice of the Supreme Court Salmon P. Chase, General O. O. Howard, head of the Freedmen's Bureau, and Senator-elect Evans of Colorado were on the platform. After an opening hymn and prayer, Bond stated the purpose of the gathering was to recommend to "the Methodists of the state (to) give their strongest efforts to break down this prejudice against the colored man whom, under the doctrines of Christianity, we are bound to regard as a member of God's family."

Afterwards, General Howard, as head of an organization concerned with supervising many activities dealing with the emancipated slave, spoke to the sound of appreciative applause. He spoke of the 100,000 children in the school systems in the South, established during and after war, under his jurisdiction, which needed great assistance from the religious denominations if the schools were to be successful. Howard wanted the Methodists to join with other denominations in helping to undergird the education the emancipated slaves were receiving. In the end, resolutions were offered calling for support in state aid for black education, the passage of civil rights legislation, the expurgation of laws of caste, and a general purging of prejudice from amongst the people at large. All were unanimously adopted.[23]

In addition to the city gathering at the Douglass Institute in early December 1865, the first state convention of blacks held after the Civil War assembled in the same month as Bishop Alexander W. Wayman of the African Methodist Episcopal Church presided. As a result of this meeting, Lewis, the son of Frederick Douglass, and William E. Matthews, were sent to Congress to lobby on behalf of the black cause in Maryland. Possibly the two delegates were also sent as Maryland's representatives to the National Negro Convention held in Washington for the first part of January 1866, which had Henry Highland Garnet as presiding officer. Another decision made at the state convention was to ask the Missionary Society of New York for aid in rebuilding several churches which had been burned down in Maryland rural areas by white supremists.[24]

On the 23rd of January 1866, a follow-up meeting was called by those responsible for the December state convention. The principal objective of this meeting was to perfect the state organization created by the December convention, known as the Maryland Colored Leagues. The meeting was opened and closed with prayer by Bishop Daniel A. Payne who urged those in attendance to "labor for the elevation of their race in all that pertains to true manhood and Christian principles." Robert M. Deaver, a prominent member of Madison Avenue Presbyterian Church, got adopted a resolution directing the delegates in Washington, namely Lewis Douglass and William E. Matthews, to prepare sufficient data pertaining to the state of the condition of blacks in Maryland in order to adequately influence the Congress.

In addition to the delegation sent to Washington, another had been sent to memorialize the State Legislature; and, at this gathering of the Maryland Colored League, it made its report. Among the resolves adopted by the League was one praising the efforts of the recently deceased Maryland Congressman, Henry Winter Davis, who had labored favorably for blacks as an important national politician during the years of the Civil War Crisis.[25]

As much as the Douglass Institute could be used as a setting for conventioneering, it also provided a place where blacks could invite and entertain their true and tried friends in a congenial atmosphere. General O. O. Howard was one of the first to be invited in this setting in this manner. Howard spoke on March 27, 1866, at an integrated affair with numerous whites of distinction present. He related how he first learned of the principles of liberty and equality in a concrete manner during his school days when one of his companions was a Negro. On a concluding note, General Howard advised blacks to put their eyes on something above government as a source of their inspiration and strength, namely, to put their trust in God.

Following Howard a couple of months later, on May 16, Senator Henry Wilson of Massachusetts lectured at the Institute. He spoke out in favor of a civil rights bill recently, vetoed by President Andrew Johnson. He also endorsed social equality. Wilson was presented with a gold-headed cane by the blacks in appreciation for the services he had rendered their cause.[26]

At about the time of the appearance of Senator Wilson, two court suits were instituted to bring about some of the social equality the Senator had endorsed. Aaron Bradley, a black lawyer from Boston instituted a suit against the City Passenger Railroad because of its segregated seating policy. The suit had been filed in Federal Court but the judge disclaimed jurisdiction, and the matter was then brought before the Criminal Court of Baltimore. Apparently Bradley's seemingly unilateral action irritated some local blacks, especially Isaac Myers, who, supposedly, at a meeting of blacks, told Bradley to mind his business.

Possibly Myers' concern was that an outsider's interference would unnecessarily ruffle the feathers of the local establishment, in reflex fashion, allowing little chance for a consideration of the issue at hand. Indeed, a few weeks later, the City Passenger Railroad was sued by several ladies, amongst them the wife of Henry Jakes, a wealthy, well-known black caterer. This test case was handled by Archibald Sterling, Jr., son of the President of the Savings Bank of Baltimore, an institution which supposedly held most black savings; and, if true, is understanbly so, since this institution came of age in Elisha Tyson's time, even having Moses Sheppard, Elisha's first cousin, as president for a brief period. The outcome of these two civil rights cases are not known.[27]

Integrating public transportation was just one effort supported by Baltimoreans to continue battering the walls of prejudice until they came tumbling down. At a meeting called for the Douglass Institute on June 26, 1867, on behalf of the National Reform Educational Association, Reverend Harrison H. Webb called the meeting to order, while George A. Hackett introduced Mr. C. L. Yancey of New Albany, Indiana, business manager for the Association, whose aim was to erect an integrated college at New Albany. The Association also intended to establish schools in the South with the idea in mind of making them economically self-reliant. On a motion from Hackett, the meeting endorsed the objectives of the National Reform Educational Association, and it was further proposed that a subsequent meeting be called, at which General Edward M. Gregory, Freedmen's Bureau head in Maryland, Judge Bond, and William Howard Day, black agent for the Freedmen's Bureau, could speak on the subject of how to provide education for the blacks of the state.[28]

Hackett seems to have had a good rapport with General Gregory and made use of this relationship to establish the Gregory Aged Women's Home in July 1867. Brigadier Gregory evidenced an evangelical zeal in seeing that educational as well as other opportunities were provided blacks in his command area. He once said, in a statement that would have pleased William Watkins, at a meeting of both black and white, that he had heard a great deal from others about preparing blacks to go to their native land, Africa, but he thought this, the United States, was their native land, and that blacks were entitled to enjoy the full rights and benefits of the country as other citizens. At this occasion, Gregory stated the heroism of the black soldier in the Civil War, particularly at such places as Port Hudson, a vicious battle in the War where the Mississippi came under the control of the Union, rather entitled them to full citizen rights. Consequently, he thought blacks should be given the vote. It is no wonder, then, that the Aged Women's Home was named after General Gregory.

The grounds on which the Gregory Aged Women's Home stood was given by Mayor Chapman to the Trustees, who were termed "colored philanthropists" by one newspaper. The grounds had previously been the location of Hicks Army Hospital, which had been one of the largest in the country during the war, with a capacity of 1,000 to 1,200 beds; but, no doubt, just one or several of the wooden halls were turned over to the blacks. The dimensions of a hall were 24 feet front, by 87 feet, one story high. Even before being used by the Army, the area contained the city's almshouse. The grounds were in the northwest end of the city, on a piece of land consisting of 42 acres, situated on a rising plateau, in the way of constant breezes, thought to be very conducive to a healthy recuperation.

At the dedication service officially opening the Home held on July 21, 1867, Bishop Wayman preached the sermon, "The needy shall not always be forgotten, the expectation of the poor shall not perish forever." General O. O. Howard, Gregory's supervisor, and Judge Bond also spoke. Mary Ann Prout was president of the Association in charge of the Home. She was a teacher at

Bethel who also had organized the Order of St. Luke in 1856, a beneficial society then gaining affiliates throughout the Atlantic Seaboard region. Mrs. Adele Jackson was secretary, a former Watkins' pupil who taught at Sharp Street School, and George A. Hackett was superintendent.

The Gregory Aged Women's Home seemed to last but several years and was struggling to survive then. In 1872, as the Home, at a new location, was struggling to survive, the Gregory Aged Women's Home Aid Association was formed to assist the trustees. John A. Fernandis was president, a barber and member of Bethel, and John H. Butler was vice president. Other members, all substantial citizens, were Adam Warfield; Burwell Banks, a provision merchant, William H. Waters, a dray business operator; Solomon McCabe, a barber; George Myers, a Federal employee; James T. Bradford, a provision merchant; and William H. Bishop, Senior, a former barber. The trustees of the institution itself were integrated, including such Quakers as James Baynes, R. M. Janney, and Samuel Townsend, while the two black trustees were John W. Locks and Mary Ann Prout.

As much as Hackett was concerned with education, financial and health matters, he as well took part in the voluntary militia companies being organized after the Civil War, when blacks were not allowed in the State Militia. In the summer of 1867, the first parade of the Henry Winter Davis Guard, under the command of Senior Captain Greenbury Burgess or Greenbury D. Morton, took place. George Hackett, Cyrus M. Diggs, and Thomas Fisher were the other captains in the body. The Guard had about 1,000 men, most of whom were veterans with headquarters at the Douglass Institute. On the route of their first march, fire was returned when the Guard was attacked by some reactionary whites.

The Henry Winter Davis Guard was just one of the two most successful militia units at the time. The Lincoln Zouaves, the other unit, was organized by Colonel E. F. M. Faehtz. Faehtz, a European refugee of the 1848 struggle from Austria commanded Maryland's 8th Regiment during the Civil War. It seems likely that William U. Saunders, a black veteran who served in Florida, should be given part of the credit for organizing the Zouaves.

In September 1867, the Lincoln Zouaves held a picnic on the Gregory Aged Women's Home grounds that lasted several days, and the Henry Winter Davis Guard participated in the festivities and were again fired upon when

167

parading to the grounds. Needless to say, they responded in like manner.[29]

Boldly taking part in militia activities was just one of the more unusual activities in which blacks participated after the war. In the last three years of his life, but not to the exclusion of everything else, Hackett and the men of Bethel and their allies also struggled to harness the political powers within their grasp, as it seemed eventually blacks would soon be accorded the vote.

Most blacks in Maryland, as elsewhere, in their hearts were Republicans because they believed Republicans to be the party of Lincoln, liberty, and the Union victory. In Maryland they were not given the vote, legally, until the adoption of the Fifteenth Amendment in 1870; but, in the states of the former Confederacy, they were allowed to vote after the war. Despite the legal prohibition in Maryland, it seems the case that some were voting as early as 1867, or prior to that year in some places in Baltimore. Perhaps, though not legally entitled to vote, local blacks did participate in the Border State Convention of Republicans held in Baltimore on September 13, 1867; and, thereby, did gain invaluable experience in the political arena as they were making themselves ready when the vote would be officially granted.

The Border State Convention met at Front Street Theater and assembled under a call issued by Maryland Republicans. An aim of the convention was to support the equality of all citizens in civil and political rights. The other delegates hosted by Maryland included those from the states of Delaware, West Virginia, Kentucky, Tennessee, and Missouri. Dr. H. J. Brown, a Baltimore black, was appointed to the Committe on Permanent Organization. Other prominent local blacks to participate in the Border State Convention included George Myers, caulker and grocery store owner, and William E. Matthews.

As business on the agenda began to be methodically dispatched, repeated calls were made throughout for the President of the Convention to introduce Brown who had recently been employed to canvass the Southern States, as had another Baltimore black, William U. Saunders, on behalf of Congressional candidates for the Republican Party. When the President relented and invited Brown forward to speak of his experiences in the South, Brown said that he literallly went about his work with his

168

life in his hands. Previously, in 1865, Brown had been secretary of the North Carolina Freedom Convention, so he was acquainted with the anger of defeated rebelldom.

Brown said, among other things, that as far as he was concerned, social equality, a key issue of the day, was not an issue to be viewed only from the vantage point of blacks wanting to crash into white social arrangements; because, in his words, there were some whites "he would not let marry his daughter or come into his house," either. Social equality had to be viewed, he thought, in terms of granting blacks full rights to participate, insofar as their manners and money would allow, all that existed in the country.

In his impromptu talk, Brown also recounted an encounter he had had with Montgomery Blair, Lincoln's Postmaster General, who believed blacks lacked intelligence to participate in the political sphere. As for what he thought of Blair's belief, Brown said he could point out an example of "pure" black intelligence which would be capable of participating in politics at any level. He was referring to Henry Highland Garnet who ran away from Maryland's Eastern Shore when a slave and thereafter became distinguished as an abolitionist, being as well, at times, an editor, lecturer, minister, and first black to speak before Congress.

In concluding his remarks before the Border State Convention, Brown said, "The one thing that was needed in the State of Maryland was a radical leader who wasn't afraid of anybody." With that said, as if on cue, cries went up for "Bond, Bond"--Judge Hugh L. Bond.[30]

After the Republican Border State Convention in October 1867, George Hackett presided over a political meeting that discussed, among other things, the issue of radicalism in the Republican Party. Those selected to share the place of honor on the platform included Isaac Myers, I. D. Oliver, William H. Woods, and Richard A. Mason. After the usual opening with prayer led by Reverend John H. Brice, Hackett denounced the Governor and police as opposed to black progress. He said that the Governor did nothing to see the militia integrated and the Police Board had banned permission for the black militia to march. With the Democrats plainly seen as enemies, a resolution was presented and endorsed, backing Judge Bond as the Republican candidate for governor. Also, a committee was appointed to investigate a Federal Hill murder of a black and to ascertain whether or not blacks had adequate protection from such incidents under the Civil Rights Bill recently passed by Congress. As chairman, Hackett concluded the meeting by appointing a committee to consider calling a state convention to discuss all problems affecting blacks. Those appointed to this committee included Isaac Myers and Samuel W. Chase, both of Bethel; Reverends John M. Brown and Robert Squirrel, also both of Bethel; Robert Deaver, John H. Butler, Aaron Russell, Dr. J. F. Brown, and Arthur Smith.[31]

It was easy enough to find reasons to denounce Democrats, seen as former rebels, but some several months later, black Baltimore politicians were put in a disagreeable position with regard to Republicans. Apparently the egalitarian sentiments manifested by Maryland Republicans in the fall of 1867 faded away by the spring of 1868. That spring, the black Republican Party adherents, the radical wing, Bond supporters, met at Douglass Institute. At this meeting, Dr. H. J. Brown let it be known to the Republican Party that at the party meeting to be held on May 6, blacks wanted to be admitted to the proceedings as full-fledged members, not consulting parties or observers. The next week, after the party meeting on May 14, a mass meeting of five hundred black Republicans took place at Douglass Institute, again to discuss the future relationship of black people to the Republican Party. The meeting was called to order at 8:00 p.m. by Robert B. Sorrell, a stevedore. Isidore Oliver was elected president.[32]

Although Oliver led off calling for blacks present to support those in Congress, the Radical Republicans, who were doing so much for the blacks, the main reason for the meeting, as stated by H. J. Brown was that the State Central Committee of the party reversed itself in denying the admittance of slates of delegates to the State Republican Convention elected with black votes. Brown said that in 1867, blacks were allowed to participate more fully in all party activities, including the primary, even though, technically, they could not vote in the general election. Brown's charges were denied by the editor of the American, C. C. Fulton, a leading Republican Party official, who said that those delegates not admitted were refused entrance because they had not been elected according to the rules of the party, not because they were elected with black support. Brown remarked, however, that the "colored people wanted to know more of the working of party machinery, they ought to be admitted into the Republican Party for the sake of political education."

At this gathering, there were other sentiments expressed, as the Committee on Resolutions deliberated. William F. Taylor, a Bethelite said:

> . . . the steps of the colored people should be well measured, and they should avoid precipitation.[33]

With regard, in general, to the factionalism within the party, Taylor said:

> The best position of the colored people of the State of Maryland, and particularly of the city of Baltimore, should be an independent one, and they should stand aloof.

This statement received respectable applause. Taylor's concluding remarks, however, received even greater applause.

> I am just as much for advancement as any gentleman who may speak here tonight. I have worked for the elevation of our race, and assisted in liberating hundreds of other children of freedmen who were bound to and reenslaved by their former masters. We are not voting yet, and we are talking and going along as if we had the full right to vote. The chasm between us and the right of suffrage is too wide for us to step over. If things should go wrong a few miles from here this question (universal suffrage) would be put back a long way. So measure your words and measure your steps.[34]

As to who would be right, as far as whether to move slowly or rapidly on this issue, only time would tell.

After Taylor's remarks, the Resolution Committee reported, with Dr. H. J. Brown reading the resolves. They, in effect, pleaded for a return to the situation and precedent established by the May 1867 convention which permitted blacks more fully to participate in party machinery. One resolution praised Judge Bond, wishing him success as leader of the radical faction of Maryland, in his fight to be accredited a delegate at the National Republican Convention soon to be held in Chicago.

171

Afterwards, discussion ensued as to whether the resolution should be adopted. Isaac Myers, W. F. Taylor, and Robert M. Deaver were opposed to blacks demanding what seemed like putting the cart before the horse, that is, demanding the right to participate in a political party's machinery yet not having the right to vote. Furthermore, these men were against being identified with one clique, the Bond wing. On this point, Deaver said that he knew when Bond was not "with them." If he had been more "pro-black" at the 1864 State Constitutional Convention and acted with congressman John Creswell, C. C. Fulton, and some others, blacks might now have the right to vote, so Deaver thought.

The resolutions were laid on the table by a large majority and a committee of seven appointed to draw up "a platform of the principles of the colored men of the State." Those appointed included George A. Hackett, Rev. John M. Brown, Dr. H. J. Brown, Isaac Myers, E. T. Crew, Robert Deaver, and Charles Dutton. Subsequently, five of the above sent a resolution to Chicago supporting the radical faction within Maryland's Republican Party. This action, however, was denounced by an anonymous writer to the _American_ who claimed the group exceeded its authority.

As blacks stood on the threshold battling for full-fledged political participation in the political system, they protested another kind of discrimination which tended to exclude them from full participation in what Baltimore offered its white citizenry. At a mass meeting held at the Douglass Institute on June 31, the School Board's refusal to use colored teachers was discussed. Blacks had never figured prominently in the mind of white elected officials as far as being educated out of the public treasury was concerned. At this time, what the City Council was willing to do was endorse verbally the kind of separate education being provided by the Baltimore Association for the Moral and Educational Improvement of the Colored People, commonly known as "Timbuctoo" and founded in late 1864. Several years later, when the Association eventually turned its schools over to the School Board, the Board refused to hire black teachers even though, when the Association looked after the educational needs of blacks, it hired some black teachers, even though most of its personnel were white. In an East Baltimore school of the Association, the black T. W. Cardoza was principal, with most of his staff probably black[35]

At this June 31 protest meeting, A. Ward Handy, a Civil War veteran and also a member of Bethel, was made president. George Myers was appointed secretary. A committee of five on resolutions was constituted, consisting of George A. Hackett, H. J. Brown, Robert M. Deaver, Samuel W. Chase, and Robert B. Sorrell. William F. Taylor, as seemed his manner, asked that actions, when decided, be moderate. With this in mind, the resolutions only respectfully protested against the exclusion of blacks from teaching positions. Ater the adoption of the resolutions, a committee consisting of Hackett, A. Ward Handy, Samuel W. Chase, Robert M. Deaver, and H. J. Brown were appointed to present the resolutions to the School Board at its next meeting. Handy seemed well qualified to serve the overall effort to improve black educational opportunities because, before enlisting in the Army during the Civil War, he was an editor, perhaps of the <u>Galbreth Lyceum</u>. He was also known throughout the city for his debating and literary skills.

Politics was never far from the minds of the leadership, even when other matters were taken up. On August 4, 1868, a Colored Border States Convention met in Baltimore. The call for the convention issued in June, bore the signatures of George A. Hackett, Dr. H. J. Brown, and Walter Sorrell, among others. There were delegates from Kentucky, West Virginia, Delaware, Missouri, Pennsylvania, New Jersey and New York. At the opening of the convention at the Douglass Institute at 12:00 Noon, George Hackett called the gathering to order, no doubt an indication of his large responsibility for setting the idea in motion; and he nominated Dr. H. J. Brown temporary chairman. Rev. James Lynch, a former Baltimorean, was elected chaplain.

William Nesbit, Vice President of the National Equal Rights League, and most likely a participant in National Negro Conventions before the Civil War, spoke shortly after the opening, saying he was:

> . . . proud to see a Convention of colored men in the City of Baltimore alive to the interests of the colored race, and whose proceedings, it was hoped, would be marked with the adoption of some plan for the united action of the colored people of the country.[36]

Nesbit pointed out the irony of recent emigrants being allowed to vote, but not native-born blacks. He said even in the North the situation of the Negro had not improved since the days when the reach of the slaveocracy extended to that region as well, in the forms of the south's powerful examples of refined prejudice the North took note of, and the business deals slaveholders could make with the Yankee, thereby tempering the North's criticism of the "peculiar institution." Nesbit wondered what would be the reaction if the blacks organized themselves into a terrorist organization like the Irish Fenians, a group of American-Irishmen who used violence to promote their aims of an independent Ireland.

After Nesbit, William E. Matthews next addressed the audience. He spoke of the dismal situation in Maryland and indicated his willingness to leave the state had not so many of his ancestors been buried in her soil. Then, sounding like the William Watkins pupil he was, he said:

> But there is a good time coming. Revolutions never go backward. There is a spirit of freedom and of liberty in the land which has not only thrown off the shackles of millions of slaves, but it is giving hope to Hungary, Crete, or wherever there is a slave pining in his chains, the inspiring sound of liberty gives him renewed strength to struggle against the oppressor and to vindicate his manhood. Once in a time in the history of men and nations comes a crisis in their history, and that crisis has come in Maryland. It will either go down with Sodom and Gomorrah, or else will rise a radiant thing of beauty in the glorious sunshine of manhood suffrage. . . the colored people understood their wrongs, but were bearing them for a season; soon they would vindicate their manhood; and liberty shall shine over a redeemed commonwealth.[37]

Matthews would stay in the state only a few more years, however.

Following these few speeches, the Committee on Organization reported and their choices were unanimously elected. William Nesbit of Pennsylvania was elected president. Reverend James H. A. Johnson, from Baltimore and a Bethelite, was an assistant secretary. Hackett was on the all-important Business Committee. A moment after the assumption of office by the permanent officers, an address to the blacks in the South was read lamenting the inability of Northern Negroes to support the Republican Party on the most part, but urging blacks in the South, now able to vote because of policy set by the President and Congress as a result of the war, to vote solidly Republican in the approaching election.

At the evening session, a letter from Judge Bond was read to the Convention. He replied to an invitation extended him to speak before the gathering. Bond responded by saying that the blacks present were competent to conduct their own affairs which should be done at this time because:

. . . colored people should write their own resolutions, make their own speeches, and conduct the proceedings of the convention themselves, because any interference of their friends would lead their opponent to suppose that everything done by them in Convention was at the dictation of the white men.[38]

Taking into account recent happenings in Maryland, Bond ended his letter by deploying the exclusion of blacks from the primary meetings of the Republican Party in several states.

Though Bond thought it better not to appear that night, William H. Day of the Freedmen's Bureau, Reverend James Lynch, and Frances Ellen Watkins Harper--all black, provided ample enough speeches to hold the attention of the delegates. Mrs. Harper said the prejudice existing against the colored race existed because the color of their faces pointed backward to a time of slavery and degradation, so that here was a confession of weakness on the part of the white man "in not being able to manifest the Christian virtue of forgiveness and forgetting."

Mrs. Harper urged blacks to fight on for the sake of their children "even if their bones were to bleach in the wilderness of American prejudice, they would leave the condition of the race better than they found it." She wished also that "colored men and colored women (would be) represented in every branch of art, science, business, and literature. They must learn to outgrow their old condition and get a new class of associates for themselves. Although slavery had ceased to exist as an institution, its spirit still lived."

On the second day of the Convention, some time during the proceedings of the morning session, President Nesbit revealed he received a letter, purportedly written by an Irish Fenian, threatening his life. The let-

175

ter was made a part of the record, at which point George Hackett said they were "prepared to protect their President, and he might come to his home and live with him if he pleased. This affair only showed the ignorance and meanness of their opponents." Hackett's remarks received cheers and applause.

Several resolutions were taken up in this morning session. William H. Sprigg, a former sergeant in the 4th U.S. Colored Troops and a Bethelite, offered one which denounced in the strongest language, blacks who voted Democratic. Dr. H. J. Brown's resolution urging the formation of Colored State Central Committees was referred back to the Business Committee for further discussion inasmuch as not everyone had seen it.

The concluding serious business of the Convention took place at the afternoon session on the second day. At this time, various other resolutions were adopted supporting the erection of a monument to Lincoln, calling for a National Convention in Washington to meet in January, and condemning the American Colonization Society.

At the final evening session of the Convention, William Howard Day presented a chrome lithograph to the Convention of Schuyler Colfax, Republican Vice Presidential candidate and Radical Republican, with whose humble origins he thought blacks could most easily identify. William E. Matthews in his presentation recounted the names of many distinguished black Marylanders who graphically indicated the blacks' ability to be free. Also, at this last session, Mrs. Harper made a few remarks and recited an original poem.[39]

In response to the decision of the Border States Convention to hold a National Convention in Washington, which was assented to by blacks from other parts of the country, James H. Hill, Chairman of the Colored City Executive Republican Committee, advertised that a meeting would be held on November 14 to elect delegates to this national gathering. This meeting, held at the Douglass Institute, was not well attended because of the lack of proper publicity. Another meeting on the 24th of November was better attended, and on a motion of Dr. H. J. Brown, seven were appointed to select ten persons to go as delegates. The seven on the selection committee included Isaac Myers, George Hackett, John C. Fortie, a shoemaker and former sergeant in the 30th U.S. Colored Troops, Joseph Thomas, a rich boss stevedore, and Isidore D. Oliver, at times employed at the B & O, and Internal Revenue Service. Those eventually chosen to represent Baltimore at Washington included Hackett, James H. Hill, Isaac Myers, his neighbor A. Ward Handy, I. D. Oliver, John C. Fortie, and Robert M. Deaver.[40]

Taking advantage of the assembled group, other business conducted at this meeting included the adoption of resolutions congratulating the Grant and Colfax team for being elected and encouraging the efforts of the Radical Republicans in Congress to start the process of amending the Constitution with the proposed Fifteenth Amendment which would guarantee universal suffrage for all. One resolution expressed outrage with the situation revealed in letters received from Louisiana and Georgia, where blacks were intimidated by the thousands from voting in these states. In addition, a resolution offered by Isaac Myers was adopted over the objection of H. J. Brown, requesting the appointment of a committee to go before the City Council to seek funds for a black high school, as the city was only giving support to primary schools for blacks. Some of those appointed to present the request to the City Council included Isaac Myers, John W. Locks, George Myers, William F. Taylor and Robert M. Deaver.

At subsequent meetings, Baltimoreans took concrete steps to support their delegation to the Washington Convention. At this December 8 meeting, the choices made at the November meeting were ratified. Hackett spoke in favor of the ratifications. Later that month, another meeting was held at the Douglass Institute, where Reverend Henry McNeil Turner, a former resident of the city during the time of the Jacobs Bill crisis, but then a member of the Georgia State Legislature, spoke as funds were raised to defray expenses of the delegates. C. C. Fulton, as Chairman of the Republican State Executive Committee, gave fifty dollars.[41]

At the National Convention itself, the usual discussion arose about universal suffrage, Republicanism and so forth and were properly dispatched. Interestingly enough, one incident occurred during the proceedings which underscored the national eminence of Marylanders--indeed the importance of the state, and especially the city--had held in the struggle for freedom since the days of Elisha Tyson. Frederick Douglass, a native Marylander who spent years of his childhood in Baltimore, was elected president and upon leaving the Convention one day, he appointed Henry H. Garnet, another native Marylander and a vice president, to take the chair during his absence. Instead of this happening, however, another vice president, F. G. Barbadoes of Massachusetts, took the chair, since his name appeared first on the list of vice presidents. At this point, George Hackett arose to find out why Garnet was not in the chair as Douglass had requested, after which, as the report says, Garnet took the chair. Judging from what is known of Hackett's rather commanding personality when insisting on a particular point, many, and perhaps most, found him too much to trifle with in such a situation—not to mention the fact he seemed to be more right and judicious in most of his actions.[42]

It seems that as a result of Baltimoreans having organized the Black Border States Convention and also having advocated the National convention, these successes prompted Isaac Myers at the victory of the Republican presidential team in November 1868 to send a letter to president Grant, requesting him to acknowledge the part played by black Republicans in his victory and give them their share of the spoils. Myers suggested that this could be accomplished by placing blacks in the diplomatic posts of Liberia, Haiti, and several countries in Central and South America. These suggestions were supposedly at the behest of the Baltimore City Executive Republican Committee; and, besides recommending Myers for one of the positions, others listed from Maryland as capable appointments were A. Ward Handy and John H. Butler. Those from outside the state thought worthy of consideration for appointment included Douglass from New York; William Howard Day from Philadelphia; J. Sella Martin and William Nesbit, Pennsylvania; George S. Downing, New York; Frederick G. Barbadoes, Massachusetts; John M. Langston, Ohio; Henry M. Turner, Georgia; William U. Saunders, Florida; and A. H. Galaway, North Carolina.[43]

Whatever may have been the exhilaration black Baltimoreans may have experienced as their counsel in national circles was looked up to, this did not lessen the worst of reality of how racial matters stood in the city itself. Baltimore blacks still had to consider the matter of not enough local governmental support for the education of their children. Yet another meeting in 1869 was held at the Douglass Institute to take up this continuing problem. George Myers called the gathering to order and Isaac Myers was elected president. Among the vice presidents were George Hackett, Bishop A. W. Wayman, John H. Butler, William F. Taylor, James Jackson, and Joseph Thomas. Isaac Myers addressed the crowd on the matter of memorializing the Mayor and City Council to give the blacks funding for a high school. Myers deplored the dismissal of colored teachers when the School Board took over management of the black schools from the Baltimore Association for the Moral and Educational Improvement of the Colored People.[44]

In making his point that blacks were not shiftless, ne'er-do-wells, begging for funds, Myers said one should look at the tremendous advances made by blacks even before the Civil War--that alone indicated blacks merited better public support for what they were made to do because of prejudice's hold on the public treasury. He said that during slavery seven literary and debating societies were kept in operation by the black community's slender means, which were even more slender now with so many of the newly emancipated slaves coming to the city. He further stated that the church property of blacks in Baltimore was more extensive and valuable than that of any other black community. This property was valued at half a million dollars, which was annually supported by one hundred thousand dollars in tithes and contributions. Myers said, "This looks like we recognize there is a God and that we take an interest in His cause."

Myers asserted that besides the thousands of dollars already owned in property acquired through the building associations supported by weekly savings of the people, $75,000 worth of property annually was being bought in addition. The public hall property was considerable. There were seventy-nine beneficial societies for the relief of the sick and poor with an average membership of eighty and the average contributions per month being forty cents per member. Continuing his accounting of the community, Myers said:

> . . . we have the most extensive corporation that can be found with colored men in any part of this globe, and it has added to the influence and wealth of the State as much as any corporation of the same dimension in the State. We mean the Chesapeake Marine Railway and Dry Dock Company.[45]

Concluding his remarks, Myers then offered for adoption a memorial to the City Council praying for a high school and readmittance of black teachers in the school system. In some sense, one wonders what this cataloguing of success would really do to affect positively the minds of an avowed Negro-hater, to loosen the purse strings. Such kind would probably wonder if this was already achieved without public support, why could not even more be done?

A series of resolutions offered by Dr. H. J. Brown but, according to one source, "intemperate in language" were tabled. The president appointed a committee which included, among others, Hackett, Bishop Wayman, Reverends Webb and William Williams, John H. Butler, James Jackson, and Isaac Myers, to prepare the memorial and present it to the City Council. The meeting, before adjourning, adopted a resolution thanking the efforts of Mrs. J. S. Norris, a granddaughter of Elisha Tyson, and some others, for establishing an Orphan Asylum for Negro Children.

While the school situation was a continuing concern, it was not soon after this latest protest against black school conditions that the political situation engaged the community's attention again. On March 25, 1869, a mass meeting of black Republicans at the Douglass Institute met in accordance with a call signed by John W. Locks, James T. Jackson, Lemuel Griffith, and H. J. Brown. George Hackett was elected president of this gathering which included some whites. Dr. Brown stated the object of the gathering and, in doing so, apparently offended C. C. Fulton, head of the Republican Party in the city, inasmuch as Brown ventured to make a suggestion to the Republican leadership as to whom should get the position of collector of the port.

Conventioneering, seemingly, was a never-ending process; accordingly, that May 11, 1869, the City Convention of Black Republicans was called to elect delegates to a state convention. About two hundred Negroes attended with twenty whites present. Isaac Myers, as Chairman of the Colored City Executive committee, called the Convention to order. Dr. H. J. Brown objected to his doing so, however, and for some time confusion lasted with even pistols being drawn when a white man made an "offensive" remark, not reported, as Myers attempted to explain why he was entitled to preside at the meeting. Within a quarter of an hour, with some effort, however, John H. Butler successfully got some semblance of order restored.

As for the dispute between Brown and Myers, Brown's contention was that the Colored City Executive Committee, which supported Myers, had no right to represent the people since it was "irregularly organized." Myers responded that Brown was one of the principle organizers of the Committee which had, in the past, cooperated with him on two occasions in some matters, but not in a third case; and, because of that, Brown, according to Myers, became recalcitrant and obstructionistic and was eventually expelled from the Committee. After this, Myers said, "Brown had gone about town denouncing it"--the Committee. Brown's attempt to regain the floor was amid great confusion when again weapons were drawn.

Seeing matters getting out of hand, at this point George A. Hackett obtained the floor, and as the newspaper stated, "by dint of steady shouting, managed to make himself heard." After order had been restored, he then moved that a committee be appointed to bring in resolutions to the convention. He declared his motion adopted, apparently unilaterally, and proceeded to appoint the following to the committee: Dr. H. J. Brown, Isaac Myers, J. H. Hill, William H. Spriggs, and Walter Sorrell.

While the Committee was out, A. Ward Handy, James Jackson, William F. Taylor, and William U. Saunders made speeches urging harmony and commitment to the principles of the Republican Party and not to any faction, white or black.

It was rather ironic that Saunders should be one of those to urge harmony. He served in Florida during the War in the 7th U. S. Colored Troops and afterwards, he used his considerable ability, oratorical included, to champion the radical faction in that state's politics. He was considered a serious threat to a harmonious restoration of any semblance of order in Florida after the war because of his radicalism. While in the region of Florida in December 1866, Saunders had served briefly as a consular agent at Green Turtle Cay, Bahamas.

When the committee on resolutions returned, it reported John H. Butler was its choice for permanent president. This was adopted. The convention also adopted resolutions of the committee instructing the wards of the city to elect five delegates to a state convention for June 1. Furthermore, the committee acknowledged the Colored City Executive Committee as irregularly formed, but authorized its existence until August 4, 1869. The meeting then adjourned, according to the newspaper account "in perfect harmony, uniting on the great principles of progressive Republicanism and equal political rights for all American citizens."[46]

About a couple of weeks after this potentially disrupting convention and before the June 1 State Convention, a Reunion Dinner of fifty of the leading Colored Republicans from throughout the state took place at Hudson's City Hotel, owned by the black physician, Dr. D.

181

H. Hudson. At this meeting, in contrast to two weeks before, John H. Butler presided over this gathering where, from start to finish, "good feeling existed." The purpose of the meeting was to cement colored Republicans of the State upon the broader principles of Republicanism.

During the dinner, a number of planned toasts were offered and elaborated upon by certain persons. Several were "The Reunion of the Colored Republicans of Maryland--May it be as lasting as the Eternal Hills."--responded to by William F. Taylor; "Impartial Suffrage--The temperate exercise of whose privileges, and proper appreciation of whose blessings, will bring peace and security"--responded to by Isaac Myers; "The Grand Army of the Republic--The heroes who snatched victory from the jaws of defeat; preserved the country's liberties and placed black sentinels upon the watchtowers of the Republic"--responded to by A. Ward Handy; "The State of Maryland--The birthplace of our great men; may her soil be prolific of more Douglasses, Garnetts, Wards and Bannekers"--responded to by J. H. Butler; and finally, "The Ladies--As mothers they shape our future destinies; as wives, purify and elevate our sentiments; may they not become strong minded and unsex themselves"-- spoken on by George A. Hackett.[47]

One other significant gathering took place before the June 1st political gathering. Decoration Day, held on May 31, was a time for commemorating the sacrifices of men in the armed forces. Blacks conducted their own separate celebrations at Laurel Cemetery. George A. Hackett was marshall of the citizens' escort of the paraders, with those assisting including William Oldham, a barber with a shop near Gay Street bridge; Isaac Myers, William F. Taylor, and John W. Locks--all fellow Bethelites.[48] Some orphans of men who died in the war accompanied the procession. The military proceedings were nominally handled by Post No. 7 of G.A.R. whose headquarters were in the Samaritan Hall adjoining Bethel Church. The leader of the post was the 6'2" A. Ward Handy, a former sergeant in the Union Army. He gave the oration for the day. In speaking of the many thousands of blacks who fought in the Civil War, Handy said, in poetic fashion, they

Marshalled themselves for battle beneath yon banner, And the nation's bondsmen prayed to

'Draw one free breath,
Though on the lips of death.'

182

Continuing in more prosaic words, Handy said:

> Then those noble hearts that be yonder still
> in death--those noble types of a suffering
> people--blotted from remembrance the bitter-
> ness of the past, and, instigated only by lib-
> erty, loyalty and union, burying the wrongs of
> two and a half centuries standing, and clasped
> hands with the nation across the grave.[49]

Others to speak at this affair included J. H. Butler, I.
D. Oliver, and William U. Saunders.

After Decoration Day, the following day, the June
state-wide Black Republican Convention convened at
Douglass Institute with policemen at the entrance,
admitting only those with tickets. John H. Butler
called the Convention to order, but before he could
finish his speech of welcome, the meeting became a mass
of confusion. H. J. Brown arose and pushed for the
temporary presidency, a man to his liking. Brown
declared his man elected with considerable vocal support, but without, seemingly, an actual election taking
place. After the election of Brown's man for temporary
president, motions about the size of the Committee of
Credentials and Permanent Organization were contested
by H. J. Brown and Isaac Myers. Apparently the two had
not forgotten their quarrel of some few weeks before.
Perhaps, because there were no weapons drawn in this
dispute, and if he were there, Hackett might have been
prepared to let his younger associates feud to their
hearts delight.[50]

In a real sense, power at this convention, or a
good deal of it, was constituted in the Business Committee and on this one, Hackett was a member, along with
Isaac Myers and J. H. Butler. The Business Committee
reported resolves complimenting and encouraging Republicanism as represented in such persons as Grant, Hugh
L. Bond, and J. A. J. Creswell, and in such actions
taken as drawing up the Fifteenth Amendment to the Constitution, guaranteeing blacks the right to vote, and on
appointing blacks to Federal Government positions.
There also was a resolution asking for the extension of
public education throughout the state and one thanking
the Baltimore Association for the Moral and Educational
Improvement of the Colored People for all it had done to
educate blacks in the state. Segregated railroad cars,
segregated local public conveyances, as well as the Police Commissioner for forbidding volunteer militia
companies among blacks were appropriately denounced and
adopted in resolutions.

After the Convention's concluding gavel, the process of the election of officers at the gathering aroused protests from city Republicans who considered certain irregularities too gross to be ignored. Just a few days after the June 1 meeting, some Republicans met at Mt. Vernon Hall to denounce the Convention for attempting, among other things, to impose a gag law with the assistance of "Democratic policemen." Furthermore, because the State Central Committee formed as a result of the Convention actions was elected without proper guidance from all members of the Convention and outside the rules of common equity and gave most representation to certain sections of the city, the Convention was again condemned.

The meeting at Mt. Vernon Hall was not attended by Isaac Myers, but he sent a letter to the president and members of the Third Congressional District Republican Association who sponsored the gathering. Myers said four-fifths of the delegates to the June 1 Convention were "hirelings of a faction that is acting in the interests of the Democratic Party of the State. They, like so much merchandise, were consigned to a certain importer labeled 'duty free,' travelling expenses, hotel and whiskey bill gratis, and five hundred dollars in the hands of one man for soup, whiskey, lunch, sheep tongue, cigars, lager and lodging to make the country believe that all the colored men of the State were on a conventional drunk."

Myers termed the way the temporary chairman was elected as illegal; and furthermore, when the temporary chairman let it be known the Convention was to be a Bond Convention, Myers thought this contrary to the declaration of the May 10 Baltimore City Convention which "proposed (not) to carry Judge Bond or any other man on their shoulders." Myers also spoke of the needs of standing by principle and exercising good judgment, he said he:

. . . would have all men, white or black, to understand that all conventions or meetings of any character or name gotten up in the interest of any individual before they are nominated by a regular nominating convention and the colored men have the right to vote and support said nomination at the ballot-box, is an insult and an injury to the colored men of the State of Maryland.[51]

Apparently Myers was still willing to carry on the feud with Brown.

There were other denunciations of the June 1 Convention. Again, Isaac Myers took part in one of them. This time he addressed a gathering held at Eastern Hall; George Myers called the meeting to order. In another instance, James H. Hill, Chairman of the Colored Republican City Executive Committee, sent a letter to George Myers protesting what he believed to be irregularities at the Convention. Hill said:

> As I entered the hall and found a man in the chair as Temporary President, who could not put a motion when made, and who did not know what an amendment was, and who never heard of such a thing as 'previous question,' then, I say, I knew that things were being "worked through" in the interest of a certain party, through a secret organization, the members of which are pledged to a certain man who supplies their leader with money and whiskey to keep up a dissension in the ranks of the colored Republicans.[52]

Hill said he was told that the rather ignorant Temporary Chairman was pushed before the conventioneers, out of "courtesy for the counties." Hill thought that there were more intelligent ones in the counties who would have both added more credit to the counties and overall performance of the Convention as well.

Hill also stated that the whole affair was rigged, that two hours before the Credentials Committee had made its report, the Nominating Committee had its slate prepared. Indeed, only one man's name was put in nomination, Dr. H. J.Brown, and no others allowed. Hill added:

> Not being content with such absurdities, they go further, and nominate a future candidate for Governor for the State of Maryland in advance of the Republican Party, and before, we have the privilege of voting for him. Now who will elect him?[53]

Hill concluded by saying blacks should bind themselves to no man, but to the principles of the Republican Party. Unfortunately, there is no opinion of what George A. Hackett had of the whole June 1 Convention and its aftermath.

185

Hackett's ally, Isaac Myers, was busy on a different front, however. As a part of the effort to further prepare blacks for eventual full citizenship, Isaac Myers had been instrumental on July 19, 1869, in assembling together mechanics and tradesmen in the city and from throughout the state to form a more permanent organization to look after black skilled labor's particular interests. After Isaac Myers spoke to the gathering, George Myers said, ". . . opening of the meeting with prayer was the right way--the invoking of Divine assistance in the great work in view could not but result in that assistance being given, with which they must be successful." George Myers also said that the organization was needed in order to influence the State Legislature to do away with discriminating class legislation.

On a motion by Isaac Myers, a committee of five on permanent organization was appointed. This committee subsequently nominated Isaac Myers for president, and he was elected. On a motion from George Myers, an executive committee was appointed, consisting of one person each from the various trades.[54]

The following week, the black mechanics and tradesmen under their new organization met at Douglass Institute--the object being to attempt to better organize black workers. Isaac Myers called the meeting to order. George Myers, Chairman of the Executive Committee, offered resolutions which condemned the discriminatory action of white labor organizations and urged the formation throughout the country of black unions. In a practical way, one resolution urged all black labor associations to study Wayland's Political Economy, believing, perhaps a little too naively, "that when the relationship between capital and labor is more generally understood, a better feeling will exist between the employer and the employed and the vexed questions of wages be adjusted without resort to strikes." One resolution urged every member acting in association with them, be a regular depositor of a savings bank, a member of a building association, and holder of a life insurance policy,.

One participant of this Convention, Lemuel Griffith, called injudicious the language in the preamble of the Constitution of the group which criticized white mechanics for preventing blacks from obtaining a living. Both George and Isaac Myers responded to the contrary, however. Isaac Myers said:

White men know that when the Fifteenth Amendment is adopted the colored men will be allowed to enter the workshops of the country. They had assembled for the purpose of laying down a great principle. By combining and organizing, the colored men would be enabled to present a respectable front, and it was only in this way that their full strength could be ascertained.[55]

The preamble as read was adopted.

Other measures were proposed and accepted. One proposed that all trades should meet on August 6, 1869, and organize themselves individually, more effectively. Another called for a more adequately prepared state convention to be held in Baltimore on the 28th of September. Finally, there ws a proposal made calling for a national convention of black labor to meet in Washington on the first Monday of December 1869. This resolution was adopted with the proviso that admittance to this National Convention be so, regardless of race or color. In a similar vein, five delegates, including Isaac Myers, were selected to the National Labor Convention, mainly a white gathering of labor to be held in Philadelphia on August 16. Finally, another measure put forth by J. C. Forte inviting Frederick Douglass to speak to the new state labor organization was also approved.

Douglass appeared several weeks later at Sharp Street Church on a Friday evening to speak on the subject of "The Equal Rights of All Men to Labor." He counted his abolitionist years as being, in fact, a visible argument for the right of all men to own themselves and enjoy the fruits of their labor. He also dealt upon the physical and moral laws governing man. His performance frequently provoked laughter. He said, "Time was when the man who could lift the barrel of cider and drink from the bung was the greatest man, but . . . now the greatest was the man who could make the barrel of cider lift itself." Douglass appealed to black ministers to be more liberal in their views concerning education and not to discourage intellectual advancement. He was against closing the doors to Oriental emigration and doubted if the promotion of their emigration here was to harm laboring men or blacks in general. He closed his speech by advising people to save up for the proverbial rainy day.[56]

Isaac Myers' star of ascendency was rising during
this time period, before Hackett's life was to end in a
few months. Besides all that he was accomplishing in
concert with other black leaders and on his own, if one
is to believe an opposition Democratic paper, he was being groomed by the American, to run for the Third Congressional District seat in the city, the apparent
reason for his recent appointment to the Custom House.
This opposition paper made sport of the whole affair,
referring to Myers and William U. Saunders, as "dark-
ies," and by saying Myers' growing progress in the party
and his growing impudence, too, could be measured by the
fact he had taken to correcting the Collector of the
Port's use of English--telling him he should say, "I did
it," instead of "I done it." To be sure there was more
to recommend Myers for a political job than his correct
use of the English language.[57]

At the time of the mammoth celebration and commemoration of Maryland's emancipation of its own slaves
in 1864, Hackett's life and leadership in Baltimore were
indeed drawing to a close. The emancipation festivities
were held on November 4, 1869, which turned out to be a
bright sunny day. Hackett, on a spotless white horse,
was chief marshall for this celebration, witnessed by
25,000 participants, some coming from the counties and
Washington. The houses of the blacks, as well as some
whites, were decorated with flags. Most of the black
associations and organizations were represented. The
parade moved from downtown to the Homestead area in the
northeastern outskirts of the city, final destination of
the march.[58]

On the Homestead grounds, the opening prayer was
offered by Dr. E. P. Smith of Washington. Then Dr. H.
J. Brown read Lincoln's Emancipation Proclamation.
Next, General O. O. Howard was introduced as orator for
the occasion. Howard recalled marching through the
streets of Baltimore after some citizens rioted against
the Massachusetts 54th Regiment and was glad to note the
change in the situation of Baltimore's black population
since the war. He noted, however, all was not yet fully
accomplished and, with that, he heartily looked forward
to seeing blacks with the vote. After his half-hour
speech, Dr. H. J. Brown offered resolutions which were
unanimously adopted, resolutions accrediting God for
what partial rights and privileges blacks then enjoyed
in Maryland; praising Republicanism, and endorsing
Myers' National Labor Convention. Perhaps Brown and
Myers had mended their difficulties and realized they
both needed each other.

After the adoption of the resolutions, Richard T. Greener, grandson of an associate of William Watkins, Benjamin Lundy, and William Lloyd Garrison, and a resident of Washington, spoke. In commenting on the apparent visible progress made in race relations in the last several years, Greener spoke with amazement that even the Democratic Party seemed part of this progressive spirit which was no more than a "vindication of the truth and righteousness of God" to triumph. Greener could only wish that with the enactment of the Fifteenth Amendment, its acceptance would be in such a spirit as "the spirit and good faith" exhibited by both black and white on the present occasion.

Greener drew to a close by complimenting the state for producing such paragons of fighters for freedom as Henry Winter Davis, J. A. J. Creswell, and Hugh L. Bond among the whites, and Frederick Douglass, Henry H. Garnet, William Watkins, and, of course, George A. Hackett among the blacks. With that done, the essentials of the day's services were concluded, only a night concert at Douglass Institute remained to be held. Overall, in the opinion of one newspaper account, the successfulness of the day was due mainly to the efforts of George A. Hackett and James Jackson whose common seafaring experiences made, perhaps, the problem associated with this affair rather smooth sailing.

Being chief marshall for the Emancipation Day celebrations was indeed an honor bestowed on Hackett. Yet, about a month later, the blacks of Baltimore were even more explicit in their admission of admiration for the Captain. At the Douglass Institute on December 13, the St. John's Lodge No. 2 of the National Compact of Ancient York Masons presented to Hackett an ornamental silver pitcher with salver and two goblets in appreciation of his "service in behalf of the colored race." The ceremony was well attended by other lodges of the order as well as representatives from other societies. The master of ceremonies was Henry P. Fortie. Ample singing was provided by Bethel's choir with one song being "Sound the Loud Timbrel," and solo selections from Madame Fleetwood, Madame Tilghman, his daughter, and the Ockemay Family.

Isaac Myers made the major address of the occasion, after which Miss Sophie J. Cole presented the above gift on behalf of the ladies "as a token of the true and never-dying esteem they bear toward you for the noble manner in which you conducted the ever-memorable procession in honor of the Emancipation Proclamation. . . and

when your work in the elevation of your race shall have
ended, may you enter the sacred abode of eternal bliss,
there to remain forever with the blessed."

Captain Hackett's response to this, virtually the
only literary remains of his life of any substance yet
discovered, is quoted in full:

Ladies and gentlemen--I lack language to express to you how much I appreciate this evidence of your friendship. I value this beautiful and costly gift more than I would a
hundred times its weight in gold. It will be
handed down in my family from generation to
generation as a precious heirloom. My friend
who has just taken his seat entirely overesti-
mates the little that I have done for our
people. Though my heart is too full for ut-
terance, yet I cannot refrain from saying a
few words to you. Thank God, I have lived to
see slavery abolished in the United States.
The colored man now stands on the same platform in this country with the white man. He
now has an equal chance in the race of life,
and it will be his own fault if he does not
show the world that he is entitled to all that
our friends claim for us. Let us labor, then
to show ourselves in every way worthy of all
that has been done for us by the philanthropists of this country.

The colored man who at present disgraces
us by committing a crime is an enemy to his
race, and we should unite in assisting in
bringing him to justice. Now that the chains
of slavery have been struck from our hands,
let us not give those who are opposed to our
advancement an excuse for stigmatizing us as
an inferior race. Let every one of us do all
in his power to better our condition, and a
bright future is near at hand. Under the intellectual and moral training which our
children are receiving, we have everything to
expect from them. It is intellectual and moral worth, and not the color, that make the
difference between man and man. Be truthful
and strictly honest in all of your dealings,
and you will soon be more respected than the
less honorable man, though he be as white as
snow.[59]

After Hackett's remarks, the band played "Hail to the Chief," then came intermission.

There were several other addresses by A. Ward Handy, William U. Saunders, William H. Brown, and William Howard Day. Interestingly enough, during one part of the ceremonies, an essay entitled "Benevolence," read by Miss Isabella Houston, was quite fitting for this occasion honoring Hackett, and most certainly could have been just as fittingly used on any occasions called to remember Elisha Tyson or William Watkins. After the more solemn ceremonies, there was a grand promenade.

With the remaining months of his life, Hackett attended a few more public meetings of a political nature, several to plan for the celebration of the adoption of the Fifteenth Amendment. At one of these held at the Douglass Institute in late March, Hackett called the assembly to order and stated the purpose of the gathering, at which time it was unanimously adopted to celebrate the ratification of the Fifteenth Amendment at a proper time and place with "a grand demonstration and civic process." Hackett then offered a resolution that five delegates from each society, ward association, or organizatin be chosen by said group to make necessary arrangements and to report back on or before April 11.

At the April 11th meeting, Hackett held no position of elected responsibility. William U. Saunders, Dr. H. J. Brown, and John H. Butler made speeches with reference to the new threshold blacks would enter upon with the official adoption of the Fifteenth Amendment. Yet, Butler noted that much had to be done, inasmuch as still in the City of Baltimore, qualified black teachers were not allowed to teach and civilized blacks were not allowed to ride public transportation, as the forcible removal of blacks from the City Passenger Railway cars, just that very week, indicated. Hackett spoke on this occasion.

Hackett boosted Republicanism, and said he had been an adherent to that philosophy since the days he served aboard the old frigate Constitution. He discounted talk by some opposed to blacks entering into politics because their votes could be bought by a bottle of whiskey. He said, perhaps in some exaggeration, he had not met the first black who would allow that, though he knew whites who had been purchased as cheaply. Education would be the key in the future, as it had been in the past. Hackett said he was prepared to meet any white and discuss the issues of the day, either in English, Spanish, or

French, and in a short time, he hoped to be able to "poke facts at them in Latin as well."[60]

In his speech at the April 11th meeting, A. Ward Handy exhorted everyone to go to the polls like Captain Hackett, vote and not linger to be abused by whites; in other words, go with firm resolve. The alacrity with which Hackett was to vote before or on the heels of the ratification of the Fifteenth Amendment was, again, indicative of his courage. With this said, there remained perhaps one other unfinished business—the election of officers for the day of the celebration. Hackett only received a few votes for this honor, perhaps he did not want to appear greedy for honors, and, then, too, perhaps he and the assembly were aware he was sick. Indeed, only a few days later, he died.

At his death, notices appeared in the local papers which attached a request asking the newspapers in Washington, Philadelphia, New York and Boston to copy the obituary. Hackett had a national reputation, though his work was mainly done in Baltimore and Maryland. Bishop Alexander Wayman, a friend of Hackett and an acquaintance of many of the nation's leading blacks, testified to that fact some years later in a book. He wrote of Hackett that "No man of color was better known than he, and no man did more for his race. He was fearless in helping his people when they were in trouble . . . no man is more missed in Baltimore City than George A. Hackett." The Bishop was parenthetically implying as well, that perhaps no man was more missed in the nation also.[61]

At Hackett's funeral, those to pay their respects included the masses, and the famous as well. Amongst the latter were Bishop Daniel Payne, and Senator Hiram Revels, first black to sit in the United States Senate. the funeral procession to the grave site was said to be a mile long, with six to eight abreast, with many other people standing along the route of march.

As the various celebrations for the Fifteenth Amendment took place in May, Hackett was not forgotten at these occasions either. During this period at a meeting held at Zion A.M.E., a resolution was offered praising Hackett as "one of the brightest ornaments, an able worker, and an honorable and dignified worker for his race." And, during the massive city-wide Fifteenth Amendment celebrations, the largest and most important in the country, with Frederick Douglass and others of eminence in attendance, a banner was carried by a group near the front of the parade that contained a portrait of George A. Hackett. The honor seemed worthy of the man.[62]

NOTES

Chapter IV

[1]Federal Gazette, July 25, 1815, p. 2; James A. Handy, Scraps of A.M.E. History, pp. 14, 16, 23.

[2]Federal Gazette, July 25, 1815, p. 2.

[3]Baltimore Clipper, June 17, 1840, p. 2.

[4]See, entry on George A. Hackett, Daniel Murray: "Murray's Historical and Biographical Encyclopedia," The State Historical Society of Wisconsin, Daniel Murray papers; American, April 25, 1870, p. 4; Sun, April 22, 1870, p. 1; April 25, 1870; Baltimore City Directory, 1866; Baltimore City Wills, Vol. 36, p. 192; Thomas L. Hollowak, Comp. Index to Marriages and Deaths in the (Baltimore) Sun, 1837-1850 (Baltimore: Genealogical Publishing Co., Inc, 1978, p. 241; Hollowak, 1851-1860, p. 202.

[5]Daniel A. Payne, Recollections of Seventy Years (Nashville: Publishing House of the A.M.E. Sunday School Union, 1888), pp. 98, 100, 224; Letter, Harrison H. Webb to J. H. B. Latrobe, August 26, 1845, M.H.S.; Maryland Colonization Society papers; Afro-American, November 16, 1901, p. 8; Sun, August 12, 1845, p. 2.

[6]National Anti-Slavery Standard, April 16, 1846, p. 1.

[7]American, April 14, 1823, p. 2; Sun, October 2, 1847, p. 1.

[8]Charles T. Torrey, Memoir of Rev. Charles T. Torrey (Boston: John P. Jewell & Co., 1847), p. 130.

[9]American, July 7, 1848, p. 3; Sun, July 11, 1848, p. 2.

[10]Sun, May 22, 1894, p. 7.

[11]National Era, April 1, 1852, p. 3.

[12]Weekly Anglo-African, February 18, 1860, p. 1; February 25, 1860, p. 3; March 3, 1860, p. 2; March 10, 1860, p. 3; March 24, 1860, p. 1; March 31, 1860, p. 1; American, January 19, 1860, p. 2.

[13]Weekly Anglo-African, March 3, 1860, p. 2.

[14] _Weekly Anglo-African_, March 10, 1860, p. 3.

[15] Daniel Murray, George A. Hackett entry.

[16] Mary A. Hackett, RG56, Entry 210. General Records Department of Treasury. Applications and Recommendations For Positions in the Washington, D.C. Office, 1830-1910.

[17] _American_, April 25, 1870, p. 4.

[18] _New National Era_, April 28, 1870, p. 2.

[19] _Baltimore Daily Commercial_, May 10, 1866, p. 1; November 5, 1866, p. 1.

[20] _Sun_, September 30, 1865, p. 1; _Baltimore Gazette_, September 29, 1869, p. 1.

[21] Betty C. Thomas, "Nineteenth Century Black Operated Shipyard, 1866-1884," _Journal of Negro History_ (January 1974):1-12; _Sun_, (Supplement), January 27, 1891, p. 4; _American_, January 27, 1891, p. 5.

[22] _Sun_, December 7, 1865, p. 1.

[23] _American_, January 25, 1866, p. 4.

[24] _Sun_, December 30, 1865, p. 1.

[25] _American_, January 25, 1866, p. 4.

[26] _American_, March 29, 1866, p. 4; _Baltimore Daily Commercial Advertiser_, May 17, 1866, p. 1.

[27] _Baltimore Daily Commercial Advertiser_, May 23, 1866, p. 1; May 26, 1866, p. 1; _Baltimore Gazette_, July 9, 1866, p.1; _Sun_, June 22, 1866, p. 1.

[28] _American_, June 28, 1867, p. 4.

[29] _American_, July 22, 1867; August 5, 1867, p. 4; August 26, 1867, p. 4; September 2, 1867, p 4; September 3, 1867, p. 4; September 5, 1867, p. 4; April 31, 1872, p. 4; _Baltimore Clipper_, July 31, 1865, p. 1; _Sun_, January 22, 1867, p. 2; July 22, 1867, p. 1.

[30] _American_, September 13, 1867, p. 4.

[31] _Sun_, October 9, 1867, p. 1.

[32]American, May 7, 1868, p. 4; May 15, 1868, p. 4; May 21, 1868, p. 4.

[33]American, May 15, 1868, p. 4.

[34]American, May 15, 1868, p. 4.

[35]American, July 1, 1868, p. 4.

[36]American, August 5, 1868, p. 4.

[37]American, August 5, 1868, p. 4.

[38]American, August 5, 1868, p. 4.

[39]American, August 6, 1868, p. 4.

[40]Sun, November 14, 1868, p. 1; November 25, 1868, p. 1; American, November 25, 1868, p. 4.

[41]American, December 9, 1868, p. 4.

[42]American, January 16, 1869, p. 4.

[43]See, Isaac Myers, Letters, Applications and Recommendations of U.S. Grant 1869-1877, M968, National Archives.

[44]American, February 16, 1869, p. 4.

[45]American, February 16, 1869, p. 4.

[46]Sun, May 11, 1869, p. 1; American, May 11, 1869.

[47]American, May 22, 1869, p. 4.

[48]American, May 31, 1869, p. 4; June 1, 1869, p. 4.

[49]American, June 1, 1869, p. 4.

[50]American, June 2, 1869, p. 4.

[51]American, June 11, 1869, p. 4.

[52]American, June 15, 1869, p. 4.

[53]American, June 18, 1869, p. 4.
[54]American, July 2, 1869, p. 4; July 20, 1869, p. 4; Sun, July 20, 1869, p. 1.

[55]American, July 27, 1869, p. 4.

[56]Sun, August 23, 1869, p. 1.

[57]Baltimore Weekly Commercial, August 28, 1969, p. 4.

[58]American, November 5, 1869, p. 4; San Francisco Elevator, December 3, 1869, p. 2.

[59]American, December 14, 1869, p. 4; Sun, December 11, 1869, p. 1.

[60]American, March 29, 1870; April 12, 1870, p. 4; Sun, March 30, 1870, p. 1.

[61]Alexander W. Wayman, Cyclopedia of African Methodism (Baltimore: Methodist Episcopal Book Depository, 1882), p. 70.

[62]Sun, April 26, 1870, p. 1; American, May 19, 1870, p. 1.

Chapter V

ISAAC MYERS AND ASSOCIATES:

COLLECTIVE LEADERSHIP

With the death of George A. Hackett in April 1870, Baltimore's black community was left partially leaderless. Yet, despite his passing, those remaining, such as Isaac Myers, John H. Butler, John W. Locks, Dr. H. J. Brown, and a few others, continued to persevere in his spirit, if not with his command. In addition to local leadership, with Frederick Douglass' move to Washington, to a degree, he affected matters in Baltimore just forty miles away. Since his childhood days as a slave in Baltimore, Douglass seemed to have looked favorably on Baltimore as his spiritual birthplace, if not in fact his real one. The fight for a Republicanism that truly respected the equality of men and the battle to gain acceptance of public funding for black schools with black teachers were two matters left unresolved at Hackett's death. Indeed, though just a few days before his death, Hackett told a friend that he could thank God that he saw blacks finally get the vote, in some regard the vote was not to improve drastically the overall condition of most blacks for long, as one might have expected.

Isaac Myers was, after Hackett's death, the man to evidence a range of concerns as wide as that of the Captain's. Myers was an active leader of Bethel, as was Hackett. For many years, as superintendent of Bethel's Sunday School, he was praised by the national head of the Sunday School section of the African Methodist Episcopal Church as being in charge of the best Sunday School in the world. It was said to be the largest black Sunday School in the state, if not the world's best.

Myers' long-term service in this, one of the most important aspects of Bethel or any church's activities, entitles him to be seen as a minister without collar, one kept active in his own denomination and before others in the community-at-large. Yet, as might be expected, Myers' management of Bethel's Sunday School was just one burden he bore as a kind of minister without collar.

As early as 1869, Isaac Myers was involved in formation of the African Methodist Sunday School Union. He, along with H. J. Brown and A. Ward Handy, spoke forcefully as to the purpose of the Union at its organizational meeting. Bethelite Handy was eventually elected president of the body. It seems the Sunday School Union did not last or functioned little at all; because, in 1875, James A. Handy, also of Bethel, was a prominent part in organizing another association. The Sunday Schools united in that year became a more permanent institution, and here, too, the name of Isaac Myers is to be found in the fore of its business. By November 1877, Myers was presiding over a meeting of this body. The Union contained about forty schools from different denominations throughout the state. Harvey Johnson, a leading Baptist and pastor at North Street Baptist, was a participant in 1877.

By 1878, a National Convention of Sunday Schools had been convened at Bethel. Local persons to take part in its operations included J. C. Fortie and J. H. B. Dungee. There were two hundred representatives from Maryland, Virginia, Delaware, North Carolina, Pennsylvania, and Washington, D.C. Frances E. W. Harper registered for the Convention and was subsequently elected vice president-at-large. One serious question debated at this convention was whether the word "colored" should be struck out of the official minutes.

The next year a local Convention of Colored Sunday Schools of Baltimore City and County which cut across denominational lines opened in May at North Street Baptist Church. Isaac Myers was elected president. Some of the vice presidents were Harvey Johnson, R. M. Deaver of Madison Avenue Presbyterian, J. B. Sanks of Sharp Street and John H. Butler of Zion A.M.E. Church. G. S. Griffith, President of the mainly white Maryland Sunday School Union, made an address. Also present was the black delegate-at-large of the latter organization, Rev. W. H. Weaver.

An issue arising here above the usual business at such conventions involved a desire to see afternoon Sunday worship services turned over to the Sunday Schools. It seemed, however, that some ministers opposed the idea for fear of losing members to churches that might not adopt the measure. At this, Myers suggested that all ministers meet and all agree upon doing away with afternoon Sunday preaching services, before such an idea be instituted by any single church.

At an evening session, Myers introduced F. E. W. Harper, who spoke on a favorite topic, temperance, and upon the recent death of William Lloyd Garrison. The group resolved to hold its next convention in Philadelphia, perhaps an indication of Baltimoreans' desire to maintain the impetus for a National Sunday School Convention Movement they had initiated in 1878.

As much as Myers was active in interdenominational Sunday School convention work, he remained attentive to his own denomination and Bethel's activities. In 1881, at a convention of African Methodist Sunday Schools held at Bethel, Myers was to be seen and heard from. At the convention, he proposed that rooms be rented to hold libraries so Sunday School workers and poor Sunday Schools of the convention could have access to pertinent and valuable literature. Later, in April, no doubt as a part of celebrations commemorating the founding of the A.M.E. Church, Bishop Henry McNeil Turner and Mrs. Harper were invited to special Bethel Sunday School exercises, seeing Myers in action. In October 1882, Children's Day was for one of the first times set apart and sanctioned by the Bishops of the African Methodist Church's Sunday School Union. Bishop Daniel A. Payne was president of the Union and Isaac Myers its treasurer.

In other capacities at Bethel Church, besides the most intimately connected with the Sunday School, Myers shared in a leading role. In 1870, though Reverend James A. Handy was chairman of a group in charge of holding a National Camp Meeting to be held on August 4, 1870, at Wilton Grove, Harford County, with all branches of black Methodism to be present, Handy most probably relied upon Myers' organizing skills to assist him to bring the endeavor to fruition. At other times, Myers indicated his breadth of activity at Bethel. In February 1879, he introduced Richard H. Cain, an African Methodist Episcopal clergyman and former member of Congress at a Bethel meeting where Cain spoke on the "Future of the Colored Race." The lecture was to benefit a literary association which was across the street from the church. This was most likely the Monumental Literary Association located at 13 Saratoga Street, just opposite Bethel, and which had opened in August 1878 with George T. Watkins delivering the dedicatory address. Probably Myers and the men of Bethel had a great deal to do with the opening of this society.

Myers was involved in yet other A.M.E. activities. In July 1879, Bethel gave Bishop J. P. Campbell a send-off to participate in the General Conference of the Methodist Church of England, the first time an A.M.E.

representative had been sent. This Conference's agenda took up the question of the possible union of the various adherents of Methodism throughout the world. James A. Handy was the orator for the occasion and Isaac Myers superintended the refreshments. A couple of years later, and at a similar affair in December 1881, a reception was held for Bishop Daniel A. Payne with Baltimore Republican Party leader Postmaster Adreon, presiding. Many important persons attended such as Myers, William E. Matthews, John W. Locks, the black ex-United States Senator, Blanche K. Bruce, and Richard T. Greener. Frederick Douglass, however, sent his regrets.

While a strong A.M.E. man, Myers seemed to have had an easy association with the black clergy of the city of all denominations. In February 1869, Bishop Alexander Wayman invited the black pastors to form a union which had its lay element. Myers was a member of Bethel's delegation. This pastor's union took upon itself to discuss all problems affecting blacks, including such issues as drunkenness and idleness and the possibility of establishing a YMCA to handle the situation. Myers was apparently elected by the pastors' union to be a part of a committee to study the YMCA proposal. Those who assisted him included Myers' fellow Bethelite Sunday School worker, John A. Fernandis. Isaac Myers as a minister without collar got along well with those with collars.[1]

Although Myers was a vital enduring aspect to the continued success of Bethel after Hackett's death and, indeed, in church-related activities in all of Baltimore, his endeavors in this regard, as well as with regard to other matters, undoubtedly were magnified in meaning by the able and worthy efforts of associates at Bethel, who had been partners in Hackett's main undertakings as well. These men included the likes of John W. Locks, Solomon McCabe, Thomas Bradford, his son James T., and John A. Fernandis.

John W. Locks was born on the Eastern Shore of Maryland to free parents. Later, when he came to Baltimore, he was apprenticed as a caulker and worked in the shipyards of Baltimore. There, sometime in the 1830s, he met Frederick Douglass. Indeed, Douglass, himself, spoke in his autobiography, published in 1845, that the school boys of Bethel helped him to learn to write; perhaps, Locks had been of this number. Eventually, Locks rose to the position of foreman in one of the ship yards. From the savings accumulated over the years, and with the managerial experience he had acquired, Locks started a hack and funeral business. A couple of years later, he put these same skills to use as he was active in the formation of the Chesapeake and Marine Railway and Drydock Company and at his death was president and said to be the largest stockholder.

After the Union victory opened up the field of politics to blacks, Locks took part here as well; but, according to one source, he did so reluctantly. His stature in the community was recognized by the whites, as he was one of the first blacks to serve on a Baltimore jury, that being a Federal jury. He helped the needy, whether black or white, in a quiet way throughout his life.

Locks died in 1884, and his funeral held at his house, 65 South Wolfe Street, was one of the largest held since that of Hackett's. The Bethel choir sang his favorite hymn, "Christ in the Dying Hour." His active pallbearers, as he requested, were his four hack drivers and Solomon McCabe, wealthy black barber and fellow Bethelite. Honorary pallbearers included officials of the Chesapeake Drydock Company, and Isaac Myers. Frederick Douglass, his life-long friend, and one of his sons were present. Lock's estate was valued at $30,000, by no means equivalent to the massive sums left by white entrepreneurs; but in the black community, large enough to indicate he was one of its richest members. All of his children were by his first wife, the sister of the leading barber, John A. Fernandis.

Solomon McCabe, pallbearer at Lock's funeral, also died in 1884 at around 65. According to one account, he was born in Baltimore; according to another, in Elkton, but moved to Baltimore very young. By his will, he left his house at 125 St. Paul to be established as the Solomon McCabe Home for Indigent Old Colored Men and Women. The home was to be in the care of Bethel and Trinity A.M.E. and along with his other property, was valued at $40,000. McCabe, as a barber, worked for at least ten years at the Mission House from where he retired from business in 1878 because of failing health.

Thomas Bradford, another son of Bethel, and undoubtedly an associate of Myers, was well respected in the general community. As evidence of this, in December 1884, Bradford was president of an association of male and female beneficial societies, consisting of some forty organizations which held their annual celebrations that year at Wilson Hall. The aggregate membership of the group at that time was about 2,500; and a reckoning

with the books of the societies over the years indicated, in toto, they had paid out to members $125,000 in
sick benefits, $27,045 in widow benefits, $45,000 in
funerals, $40,000 in dividends, $10,700 in house rents,
$11,441 in accidentals, and had on hand $22,000 in the
banks.

Not much is known of Bradford's ancestry, but he
might have been a son of or relative of Paraway Bradford
who was one of the trustees who bought the old African
Academy from James Carey in 1802 to establish Sharp
Street Church. Thomas Bradford, for a long time, served
as body servant to Thomas Swann, who was a governor and
congressman. At his death in 1886, Bradford was said to
have been a member of Bethel for over fifty years and an
official for several decades. He was 72 at his death.

The son of Thomas Bradford, James T., was to evidence the same kind of qualities as his father. For over forty years he was a successful green grocery
merchant in Baltimore. He was on the Board of the
Maryland Home for Friendless Colored Children, located
at 404 Courtland Street. He maintained both a residence
in Baltimore and Washington, and as leader of one of the
two black Republican political factions in 1901, was
prominently mentioned as a likely candidate for Recorder
of Deeds in Washington, a traditional appointment for a
black of national political prominence.

John A. Fernandis was another who gave long service
to Bethel and who supported and magnified the efforts of
general community leaders like Hackett and Myers. He
was a brother-in-law to John W. Locks. He was known as
an efficient Sunday School worker. He was also a
wealthy barber who took charge of a shop established
prior to 1820 by his Brazilian father. Fernandis took
over the business in 1845. The Barbers' Beneficial
Association, of which Fernandis was a founder and
lifelong member, was one of the more enterprising black
groups of the time, and, evidently, barbering was a
source of dependable income, even riches for some
blacks. Yet the black barbers were not just interested
in money.

In 1874, the black barbers formed part of a general
movement whose aim was to close barber shops on Sunday,
no doubt both out of desire for a day off and respect
for the Sabbath. At a meeting held at Jackson Hall on
Saratoga Street to consider the Sunday closing, all the
shops in which blacks were employed were represented.
After prayer and the reading of a chapter of Scripture,

John Chamber took the chair and Edward Sythe was appointed secretary. H. D. Ruffin moved that a committee of seven be appointed to draft resolutions. They were: John A. Fernandis, H. D. Ruffin, John W. Nichols, Beverly Lowe, J. C. Hamer, Isaiah Drone, William Ellison, and Theodore Saunders.

The blacks eventually endorsed a resolution to close the shops to back-up the initiative started by whites. A committee of three appointed to represent the group before the Maryland Legislature included John Fernandis who, at first, declined to be a part of the committee but was persuaded to take the charge, inasmuch as he was one of the very few barbers, black or white, to have closed his shop on Sundays, having kept it closed out of respect for the Sabbath for at least ten years. Fernandis died in February 1890.[2]

To say the least, as he assumed a leading position in the community-at-large, Isaac Myers was surrounded by invaluable help at Bethel, men of means, yet men with, it seems, a spiritual side as well. Myers always showed a keen interest in the material progress of the race. He had a concern for the laboring black man and small black businesman who almost always was a laborer, himself, and this concern was most evident, as previously mentioned, as he initiated the national labor movement among blacks in 1869.

Myers' interest in the black laborer and small businessman did not slacken years later, either. In 1881, the People's Advocate published a letter of his which stated Myers' alarm at the increasingly fewer and fewer numbers of blacks holding jobs in the skilled trades. Myers recalled how, in the 1840s, in Baltimore, blacks were found in all the trades, even being foremen over whites. The influx of foreigners, especially the Irish, however, led to blacks being pushed out of the trades after the 1840s. He said blacks could have contended with the Irish and regained entrance into the trades but, because of a "lack of energy, and want of confidence and pluck," opportunities were not taken advantage of." In this letter, Myers gave two examples to illustrate his reasoning along these lines--one was about black tradesmen refusing to work for less than whites on construction jobs, even though they were paying 2-1/2 to 3 times as much as unskilled labor. Myers thought a little pride-swallowing could have secured these blacks above a poverty level. Another example he gave was of a man moving from the South to Baltimore who became a successful contractor, even having enough work to employ whites; but, because of desultory living, he lost everything. Here the preacher in Myers is evident. Myers did more than reminisce about the golden days of black labor and small businessmen; he proposed to do something about their plight in the late 1880s.

Myers was president of the first Colored Industrial Fair of Maryland held in October 1888 to praise and encourage black labor and skills. Those who assisted him in this endeavor included Jacob A. Seaton, Thomas I. Hall, Malachi Gibson, Joseph Warren, and Samuel E. Young. The Fair, held at the Monumental Assembly Room at St. Paul and Centre Streets had seven hundred exhibitions and three thousand articles on display. At the outset of bringing the project to realization, Myers enlisted support of official Baltimore, getting endorsements for the venture from Mayor Ferdinand C. Latrobe, Cardinal Gibbons, and some others. The father of the mayor, John H. B. Latrobe, a long-time supporter of African colonization schemes, visited the fair. The Baltimore American and the Morning Herald generously praised the effort of the fair, probably the first one or one of the first undertakings of the sort by blacks in the country.

A couple of months later, continuing his interest in furthering the industrial competence of blacks, in December 1888, a committee consisting of Myers, E. J. Waring, Dr. W. H. Weaver, Hiram Watty, and J. H. A. Johnson visited Mayor Latrobe to get his assistance in establishing a manual training school. By May of the next year, although no action had been taken on the proposal then before the City Council, the committee itself, had $1,000 of the $2,500 needed to purchase a building to house the school.

Simultaneous with the efforts to start an industrial school, in 1889, February, the few colored businessmen in the community organized at Samaritan Temple. Myers was made president of this as well; he was a successful coal yard owner. Indeed, this effort was apparently a more successful attempt by similar forces who wanted to organize a businessmen's association back in April 1888. At that earlier organizing effort, James T. Bradford had been seen the likely head of the group if it had succeeded.[3]

At Hackett's death, and even a little before, Myers was, as has already been shown, a man of great importance on the local scene; yet he was developing, as the Captain, a national constituency as well. Indeed, an obituary duly noted this dual importance of Myers in 1891. The African Methodist Episcopal Review said:

Few men amongst us have occupied so important a place in local and national affairs as did he. His work was done without much flourish of trumpets . . . . One desire dominated his every effort, and that was a desire to succeed.[4]

Myers was a leading national Republican politician, and, as such, received Federal Government appointments. He served in the Post Office as a postal inspector-at-large for the whole country, where he distinguished himself for his detective skills. His appointment in the postal service was one uniquely created for him; there was one other like it, and it belonged to another Baltimorean, a former barber and veteran, William U. Saunders, who did important political work in the south, especially Florida after the war. Myers also spent time in Baltimore's custom house.

As a national politician, Myers was involved in the important campaign of 1871. In January of 1871, he was president of the national gathering of blacks which urged upon black communities throughout the nation the creation of state organizations to keep black voters within the Republican ranks and prevent the efforts of some, especially white labor organizations, who were that year busily trying to wean blacks away from the Party. In March of the same year, Myers reported before the Colored Labor and Educational Convention at the Douglass Institute relative to his observations of the situation in the South which he had witnessed for the past six months while touring there. The blacks in Baltimore, since and after the Civil War, had taken a proprietary interest in the situation in the South.

Later in 1871, Myers defended Grant before a gathering of white organized labor in Philadelphia, and was almost assaulted for his remarks. With such varied and important responsibilities in 1871 and other years, it is no wonder that Myers was considered, at the end of his life, some twenty years later as a man who had both a local and a national constituency, like, perhaps, no other man of the race.

There were problems after Hackett's death; not all were easily managed, but with the support and backing of the men of Bethel and some others, Myers and these men

undertook two strenuous struggles. These two were demands for equal treatment by the Republican Party of
blacks, and, indeed, a demand for equality in the overall political process; and better educational opportunities for black children and black teachers.

Besides Myers and the men of Bethel, another
leading exponent of promoting educational opportunities
for blacks after Hackett's death, was John Henry Butler.
By January 1870, Butler was an appointed traveling
superintendent of the public schools of the Freedman's
Bureau in Maryland. He was viewed as a friend and
adviser of Judge Hugh L. Bond, a key figure in
establishing the Baltimore Association for the Moral and
Educational Improvement of the Colored People. Then,
too, apparently Butler spent out of his own pocket to
support black education. One newspaper, speaking of
Butler's expertise in educational matters said, "Mr.
Butler's experiences in this department had made him
especially earnest and impressive in all he says in
relation to educational matter." With the above having
been said about a former William Watkins' student, this
certainly would have pleased the old master teacher, if
he had heard it.[5]

In March 1870, the issue of the appointment of
black teachers in the local public schools was raised
again. The school system, as much else in Baltimore,
was viewed as a patronage pantry by the Democratic machine, which, on two counts, resisted giving appointments to blacks: one because they were black, the other
because they were Republican. A memorial demanding that
black teachers be hired circulated at this time with the
signers including among others, John W. Locks, Causeman
H. Gaines, and John A. Fernandis, all of Bethel; and
Daniel Keith and Enoch Cummings, two members of Dallas
Street Methodist Church Trustee Board--Frederick Douglass' old church. The memorialists did not want the
dismissals of whites from positions in black schools but
thought blacks should fill vacancies as they occurred.

Several years later, in June 1873, a similar group
addressed another memorial to the Mayor and City Council. This one was formed after the investigation of a
committee of "an organization devoted to the general
advancement of the colored people." Some members of
this committee included Willaim H. Bishop, Causeman H.
Gaines, John W. Locks, and Augusta Roberts; the group
was mainly interested in getting a high school and additional grade schools. The committee said:

For over a half century, indeed, ever since the establishment of the public school system, have we been consciously paying into the treasury of our city government, annual assessments upon real and personal property for the support of the same, as well as performing all other duties and responsibilities applicable to other citizens, and that too, without receiving the slightest benefits accruing there from, until within a very recent date, when colored primary schools were established.[6]

The petitioners acknowledged that at times it seemed hopeless to petition, inasmuch as in fifty years, no good came of their petitioning. They stated, however, that the recent measures of those in power, probably the authorization of a grammar school for blacks in the central city, had buoyed their faith in their fellow man, and made them think, hope, favorable consideration would be given to this petition.

The reason for needing a colored high school was the increasing humber of qualified graduates of the Howard Normal School, presided over by Professor Durand, and those being educated at the Douglass Institute's High School, presided over by Professor Robert Rowan. In addition, there were still some being graduated from the private schools maintained by blacks. The Howard Normal School, founded by philanthropic whites around 1867 had an integrated Board, with John W. Locks, Harrison H. Webb, and John H. Butler as the black trustees.

A few days after the submission of this June 1873 petition, several blacks were recommended for the proposed new black grammar school principalship. They were John R. Roche, Maggie J. Sorrel, and William U. Saunders. Saunders was supported for the position by several important city whites, including General Ferdinand C. Latrobe and Isaac Freeman Rasin, Clerk of the Court of Common Pleas and Democratic political boss of the city. No results came of those efforts, however.[7]

Again in January 1875, a petition was presented to the City Council asking for a high school to be established in the community. This one was signed and presented by, among others, J. H. A. Johnson, Henry Jacques, and Henry Bradford. The committee suggested that a suitable site would be the premises on St. Paul

Street, then occupied by City College, but soon to be vacated. No success attended this effort either.[8]

Several years later the demands for a deeper commitment from the powers in the city to black education came again, as on April 9, 1879, a mass meeting took place at 32 North Calvert Street, the meeting place of the St. Paul Lyceum, an important literary society. George Myers was elected president of the meeting. Dr. H. J. Brown made a major speech urging moderation, saying the subject should be approached with care and that it surprised him to see a city of culture like Baltimore, constantly putting barriers in the way of the race's progress. In several cities--New York, Washington, Richmond, Philadelphia, Boston, and St. Louis--blacks were already allowed in the public school system as teachers. Brown said the democratically controlled Department of Education spoke of being friends of the blacks; but they, in truth, were not, because they would not give competent black teachers a chance to teach in the black schools. In addition, he said white teachers in these schools would not mingle with the parents of pupils.

Brown said, furthermore, on investigating all but one of the colored schools, he found certain conditions which would disgrace any civilized city, but which could not be related at the meeting because ladies were in the audience. He continued by saying:

I have known white teachers to correct scholars for using perfectly correct language, because it may have sounded a little pedantic; for instance, a child was corrected for saying 'eleven' instead of 'leven,' as 'niggers' spoke.[9]

Brown concluded that if there were no competent blacks, as the School Commissioners said, why not allow them to take the competitive examinations to prove the point?

After the speaking, resolutions were brought in and discussion ensued. Here again, Brown took an active part. Brown related how he had gone before certain School Commissioners several times in the past with the applications of colored teachers, but was replied to on one occasion that "Your race is going ahead too fast." Isaac Myers, noting the fact that no law prohibited black teachers, suggested a "test case" be made to force the issue before the public. Brown responded, how could you expect the Commissioners to grant your request "when they would not let you in the same room with them." He said petitions had to be sent by mail. Myers insisted that someone be sent competent to take the examination. Brown countered "They will not listen to your applicant. I have been, a dozen times, and they would not hear me." In this regard, Brown may have made some trips on behalf of his two daughters, then teaching in the counties.

Myers insisted that someone competent be sent, for example, like William Williams, who obtained a Ph.D. at Rome from De Propaganda Fide and could speak, in Myers' words, "as many languages as any white man in the city." Myers said if he is not accepted, then they would know why. Myers' position was supported by S. Q. Sanks, but Brown's attitude was, "What's the use." Sanks said he would like to see the "try, try again" style amongst blacks, and not so much seeming giving in to the seeming hopelessness of the situation. The meeting lasted until midnight and was well run, as President George Myers kept a tight hand on things with the use of proper parliamentary procedure. The Chair finally appointed a committee of three: Dr. H. J. Brown, S. Q. Sanks, and G. W. Nicholson, to obtain the cooperation of a black to apply before the School Commissioners as a test case and report back the outcome.

Several days later, the committee appointed to bring about a test case, with one additional member, Dr. R. M. Hall, a graduate of Howard University's Medical School, met at the residence of Dr. H. J. Brown, after which a statement issued to the public asserted that blacks desired no radical change, but the right of their own to compete in the examination for teaching positions, and that those found competent be allowed to fill vacancies as they occurred in the black schools.[10]

Also about this point in time, Rev. James H. A. Johnson, a member of Bethel and graduate of Princeton's Theological Seminary, published a letter in the Morning Herald on April 22, 1879, in which he said denying blacks the right to teach was injustice, plain and simple. He said:

> No matter how the case may be turned over, it will show but one spirit: that is, injustice to the Negro. It is this spirit to-day (sic) which the American People, like Pharoah, will not confess and eliminate from their hearts, that is now endangering the very existence of the Nation. It runs like a poisonous stream through all transactions which concern black and white men in every relationship and is the

cause in connection with the terrible injustice to the Indian that is to throw the American government into anarchy, and destroy the
peace, beauty, harmony, and prospects of a Republic that might otherwise be the ruling power of the world. America has drawn her sword
against the Almighty.[11]

Johnson concluded his epistle by making further compari-
sons between what was happening then, with what was happening in the time of Pharoah. He took a meteor's drop-
ping on Chicago after it voted Democratic as a sign of
God's displeasure and the yellow fever and potato bug
infestation of the year, as even more ominous signs of
that displeasure.

The Morning Herald, on June 6, 1879, published another letter from Rev. Johnson. In this one he answered
the specific charge of incompetency against black teachers. In essence, he said, the argument was insincere
because whites, generally, never showed any great concern for promoting black interest or employment in anything, not in its fire department, police department,
transit system, so why should one believe whites were
now teaching black children because they were looking
after the interest of future generations of blacks--be-
cause the positions paid well was the only reason for
whites being there, so he believed.[12]

Later in the year, about the time of opening for
schools, at the first of a series of meetings held at
Bethel, the subject of black teachers for black schools
was again aired. The meeting was called to order by
Rev. J. W. Beckett, pastor of the church. At this
meeting, Rev. J. H. A. Johnson also spoke:

. . . everyone knows that the day schools or
public school is necessary to the proper development of Christianity, and it is, therefore, not a political but a moral duty we have
undertaken. I think we have no doubt of our
right to teach our children, and I think there
is no reason that we should get on our knees
and beg for the right, like mendicants, but
should stand up and respectfully but firmly
demand it.[13]

He further stated this bit of wisdom:

If the white teachers who have been teaching
our children all this time and have not been

able to turn out one teacher amongst them all,
what kind of teachers must they be?

Johnson, as presiding elder of the A.M.E. Church of the
Hagerstown district, spoke from first-hand knowledge
when he said, during his speech, areas in Western Maryland had competent black teachers and even school commissioners. He said when Republicans controlled things
in the City of Baltimore, there were black teachers, but
when the Democrats came in nearly all the funds and attention were devoted to educating whites. Interestingly
enough, Johnson's whole family seemed imbued with a spirit that believed in the importance of education; his
brother John M. was a dentist and his sister married Dr.
R. M. Hall, a medical physician.[14]

After Johnson's delivery, several others came forward to occupy the podium. Reverend C. B. Perry, white
rector of St. Mary's Episcopal Church, testified to the
numerous other cities which had qualified black teachers. Dr. H. J. Brown reemphasized the sentiments of
Rev. Perry. He, too, underscored the difference between
Washington and Baltimore. In Washington, blacks were in
charge of all their schools. George T. Cook, who used
to be editor of a newspaper published out of the Douglass Institute when it first opened in 1865, was superintendent. After Brown's speech full of facts and figures had ended, suitable resolutions were adopted as before on other occasions condemning the manner of things
in Baltimore and demanding a change in the situation,
asking all the ministers in the city to hold meetings to
indicate the depth of feeling throughout the community
that demanded an end to discrimination against the black
teacher.

At the end of 1879, Baltimore's black community
again assembled at Bethel in December to take up the
school issue and pursue it futher. Reverend J. H. A.
Johnson presided as Frederick Douglass and William E.
Matthews spoke to lend their support to the matter at
hand. Johnson said the right of blacks to be admitted
as teachers to the school system was the most pressing
issue of the day and seems insurmountable while Democrats controlled the city. Johnson distributed petitions; he wanted those present to get both white and
black signatures. As an indication of the worsening
situation in race relations, as Johnson saw it, he related how a black in the city recently was shot to death
in cold blood by a white man when the black acknowledged
that he was a Republican. The deed done was shameful in

itself, but it was made even more appalling as a Democratic United States Senator, in Johnson's words, left "the height he occupies to defend a coldblooded murder."[15]

Matthews preceded Douglass to the speaker's post. In his remarks, he said that blacks have always been citizens of this land, inasmuch as they fought in this country's wars, beginning with the American Revolution, and it is about time they enjoyed some of the privileges of citizenship, namely be allowed to teach in the school systems. He said just the other day the heroism of the Buffalo soldiers, black cavalry troops, was applauded as they rescued white soldiers from Indians on the frontier. Matthews compared the present white teachers with those whom he had known from personal experience as they came down from the North just after the war to set up schoolhouses for blacks. The devotion and sacrifices of these ladies were most evident, while those now teaching have no such devotion and "whose chief interest, in their work," he deemed, "is centered in the signing of the payroll."

Furthermore, this present-day white teacher will have no social contact with the pupil and his environment. Matthews said he believed teachers need to know a pupil's environment in order to know how to help him, both intellectually as well as morally. Black teachers would arouse black pupils to emulate their teachers' own success stories. Picking up a theme Johnson had earlier in the year illuminated, Matthews announced the white teachers stood as self-confessed failures if they could not point to one of their former pupils as capable of teaching. Then, echoing an often-repeated statement of Douglass, Matthews further stated, without agitation no effort would succeed.

In concluding his remarks, Matthews stated that the fault lay with blacks who did not organize immediately after obtaining the franchise to take advantage of an opportunity which would have born fruit by now, in blacks being represented in all forms of public service. Matthews said he welcomed the approach of a planned state convention for which ways would be sought to remedy the present plight of black Marylanders, in general.

After Matthews' speech, Frederick Douglass stood in the podium to give his views. Douglass started by commenting on the sagacity of Matthews' speech. He said he had not come to make a speech and, especially having

213

heard the preceding one, he only wanted instead to let people know his old "gray head" was "still on the side of freedom and equality; on the side of justice and fair play." He further stated, "We are only following the line marked out for us by Bethel Church more than fifty years ago—the principle of the assertion and dignity of manhood, and Bethel Church can be in no better service than it exercises this evening." Douglass also said he was glad to be a part of a meeting whose purpose was to assent to the principle of a man being able to rise to a position for which his talents merit. "I am very glad of the cautious yet bold assertion of the purpose of the meeting by the speakers. No tirade against white teachers because of their race or color is to be permitted. This matter of colored men and women being admitted to colored schools supported by taxes contributed by white and colored alike is not a question of color, but of prejudice."

Douglass counselled those present not to despair by relating incidents out of his own life which proved, so he thought, the unalterable march forward of progress for the race. He said he could remember witnessing with his own eyes the visible amelioration of the condition of blacks in the city, when at first and at the worst of times, they were with impunity, driven through the streets in chains like swine to be sold and shipped South or taken to the County Wharf to be whipped for disobedience, to that day when slave dealers were forced to carry their trade in covered wagons out of respect for the growing hostility of others to their business, and to that time when the County Wharf whipping post was permitted to rot and Sunday Schools were opened to blacks, and finally to that day when blacks were not allowed to be sold to New Orleans.

Having made these personally poignant observations, Douglass said:

Some among us have the spirit of Isaiah; they cry aloud and spare not. There is a meaner thing than a slave and that is a contented slave.[16]

Drawing to a close in his speech, Douglass also remarked: the pretext of the repulsive nature of a black man's skin being used as an excuse by opponents to keep the administration of schools in white hands, the excuse used to discriminate against blacks in so many ways, was just an excuse. During the Civil War, blacks fought side by side with whites to save the Union, without too

214

many disruptions because of color prejudice. In a word, Douglass was saying there was no basis for keeping blacks from working side by side with whites in the school system. The School Commissioners, Douglass also thought, should have been at the meeting if they had any interest in the welfare of the blacks; and, this fact he wanted the newspaper reporters present to include and underscore in their dispatches.

Douglass closed by saying color prejudice was almost exclusively a possession of the United States. He said, however:

> We will not be kept down, but we must struggle
> for and demand our rights. There is nothing
> valuable under the sky but a struggle must be
> made for it. There are rights in reserve for
> us, but we must contend for them. No nation
> that enjoys liberty can wear it so sublimely
> as one that has wrenched it from the reluctant
> hand of some tyrant. We put the colored
> schools on the defense before Christianity
> and humanity of the community and ask the
> colored teachers to be placed before the tri-
> bunal of the people. Our cause is just, and
> must triumph; but you must continue to agitate
> it until you secure your rights.[17]

Douglass knew the value of agitation, having been active in advocating justice as such in various situations, some pleasant, some frought with danger, and some on foreign soil, for the past thirty years.

While in Baltimore to lend his support for the fight against discrimination in the school system, Douglass spoke at his old church, Centennial, formerly Dallas Street Methodist Church which he attended while a slave in Baltimore, off and on from 1825 to 1838. He spoke on the occasion of the 49th anniversary of the Sunday School, which he said was founded by William Wallace, John Fortie, Joseph P. Wilson, William Douglass, Joseph Young, and some others. To prevent ill-deserved suspicion being drawn to the Sunday School, Douglass said a white man was made superintendent. Douglass said he attended the first anniversary of the school held back in 1831 and at one point, taught in the Church's Sunday School.

At the first anniversary of the Sunday School exercises, Douglass recalled that Dr. Lewis G. Wells made

an address. It was the first time Douglass said that he
saw a black man with a manuscript before him. He said:

> It did him good to see a black man--for Dr.
> Wells was a real black man--display so much
> learning, and he went away with a higher opin-
> ion of the possibilities for and capacity of
> his race than he ever had before. It gave him
> confidence and hope for the future.[18]

This memory, no doubt, gave added incentive for Douglass
to support black teachers in the school system. In addition, he was a Sunday Schoolteacher, himself, as a
slave though, and surely matters had advanced since
those days.

The agitation for black teachers apparently led the
Catholic Reverend J. R. Slattery, pastor of St. Francis
Xavier Catholic Church, to put colored teachers in
charge of the free schools or parish schools in his
church. The teachers were Oblate Sisters, the first
black order of nuns established in the 1820s, who had
run successfully since that time, their own schools for
blacks that attracted pupils from throughout the country.[19]

The beginning of 1880 saw no diminution in black
protest of the school situation; a meeting was held at
Madison Avenue Presbyterian Church on February 5, at
which Dr. H. J. Brown acted as secretary. Reverend J.
H. A. Johnson took the chair. Letters of support were
read from Frederick Douglass, Richard T. Greener, and
John W. Cromwell, publisher of Washington's People's
Advocate. J. D. Kennedy of New Orleans as the first
speaker was just twenty-five but recently ran for Secretary of State on the Republican ticket in Louisiana.
Among other things, Kennedy spoke of how he was discouraged not to run by whites who believed the supremacy
of white intellect entitled them to this position automatically. Kennedy was saying, in effect, the fight
against racism was one that cut deeply across all facets
of society.

Kennedy's remarks were followed by some observations from William E. Matthews. Matthews stated blacks
had done their part in agitating the question but were
"waiting for some philanthropist in his study, or minister from his pulpit or great educator through his
paper to come to their rescue," some white, as was done
recently in Philadelphia by a Rev. Turner in taking an
active part in the desegregation of the streetcars of

that city. Matthews alluded to an article in the North American Review by Gladstone, the English politician, which predicted a great position of power for the United States, but no true greatness until justice had been done to all its citizens.

Douglass was to have addressed the audience but instead sent a letter with Matthews in which he wrote that he was in favor of black teachers who would more "lovingly" teach their charges than whites. He also stated the wisdom of continued agitation because soon public sentiment would cause those in control to yield to righteousness. A letter from J. W. Cromwell declared:

> Separate schools are established to accomodate the prejudice of the whites of this country . . . . The colored people of Baltimore would be unworthy of that freedom of political action guaranteed them and the Constitution, if they allowed this discrimination to continue without manly protest.[20]

Professor Greener also wrote in his letter of the "disgraceful anomaly" of caste schools in a republic and desired no end to the agitation until blacks teach whites as was the case in Chicago.

After this, a committee was appointed to present a petition to the School Board. The committee included Reverends J. H. A. Johnson, J. H. Reddick, J. W. Beckett, W. M. Hargrove, and Messrs. H. J. Brown, John W. Locks, and Dr. Philip T. Gross. If possible, the group also intended to speak at the Board meeting when the petition would be presented. Reddick, the Centennial Church popular pastor, appeared several times before the Board in behalf of this latest drive to integrate the teaching corps.

By March 1880, the colored teacher question had reached a stage where, after a black committee had confronted the School Board, it was conceded by the Board to allow colored teachers in two new schools in planning. The next month, however, a slight qualification had been added. The colored teachers would be employed, it was decided, if more than the three who had already passed the examination could be secured.[21]

A general meeting was held on September 21 with Dr. H. J. Brown in the chair and Isaac Myers as secretary to hear the report of the committee sent to meet with the

School Board in April. The Saturday before the September 21 meeting took place, Reverend J. H. Reddick, along with a Reverend J. C. Waters, principal of a public school in Jacksonville, Florida, visited the black schools to survey the reaction of white teachers to blacks teaching in schools with them. They got only one negative response. Waters addressed the September 21 meeting. John W. Locks, H. J. Brown, and William Vessels reported they had called upon John T. Morris of the School Board to follow up on the pledges to make changes agreed upon by the Board earlier in the year, but no action had been taken since. Supposedly, the Board was still seeking to rent two schools to which black teachers could be assigned.[22]

As the year 1880 drew to an end, there was still need for agitation. On Christmas Eve 1880, Frederick Douglass spoke at Centennial on the subject of John Brown. The meeting, however, led off with a discussion of the school question, with the Reverend J. H. Reddick reading an address to be delivered at a mass meeting to be held the following week at Bethel which condemned, in the strongest language, the apparent reneging on the agreement by the Board. The language was harsh. Reddick, speaking to the Board of School Commissioners, said:

> We approached them with the full consciousness that they were a board of gentlemen and who dare say that they are not? even though they have mistreated us and have said one thing and finally done another? Is not every one a gentleman, even though one should call educated colored ladies and gentlemen 'nigger teachers.'[23]

Reddick praised the efforts of some of the Board, however, such as those efforts of members: Morris, Poe, Denny, Lee and Conway, to better the situation.

The black community's written reply to the reneging School Board concluded, as follows:

> The honorable press of our glorious city said the request was just. The people of our race felt that it was just. We know that it is just; and we are as earnest to-day (sic) in making that appeal as we were when we first made it. We have asked for colored teachers in our colored schools, and we intend to agitate the question until we have them there,

218

though we may have to step from the ordinary
method of petition and enlist on our side all
the power of the altar. We will work and
pray, and pray and work, until, by God's assistance, we shall be delivered from this most
shameful injustice. Henceforth it is to be
understood that the bar at which we shall
plead shall be that of public opinion. The
executive power upon which we will depend
shall be that Almighty power that breaks up
all forms of injustice and oppressions.[24]

The address was signed by Reverends J. H. Reddick, J. H.
A. Johnson, J. W. Beckett, and William H. Hargrove; and
Drs. Philip T. Gross and H. J. Brown, and John W. Locks.

After the reading of this reply to the School
Board, Bishop Wayman introduced Douglass to the Assem-
bly. Though Douglass had ostensibly come to lecture on
John Brown, he interrupted his lecture to say:

Colored people should not ask too little, for
that breeds contempt for them, and is an acknowledgment of lowilness (sic). We should not
ask too much, to persecute others or seem forward, nor too soon, nor too late. But I think
we have not asked too much when we asked for
our children that have been taught and qualified to teach younger colored children--that
they should be appointed to the position of
teacher.[25]

Douglass, to make the transition back to the topic of
his speech, observed that where there is some injustice,
then there would arise some John Brown to end it or pro-
voke its end.

The indignation meeting announced by Reddick at
Douglass' Christmas Eve lecture did take place on January 6, 1881, at Bethel Church. The meeting went on record protesting the refusal of the Board of School Commissioners to go through with a pledge to have black
schoolteachers by the first of the year. Rev. Reddick
called the meeting to order and other officers for that
night included Bishop Alexander Wayman, president, with
the list vice-presidents including: John W. Locks, Joseph W. Thomas, William H. Bishop, Sr., James Jackson,
John H. Butler, George Myers, and Samuel W. Chase.

After the singing of a hymn, Bishop Wayman led the
meeting in prayer. Next followed Reverend James A.

Handy who spoke of the need of constant agitation until they get teachers who do not feel it a disgrace to teach blacks and who will speak to them on the streets. The audience was given the School Board's reason for not following through on its promise--lack of funds was cited as the reason. Yet it was noted by Handy, that funds were found to rent halls for two new schools for blacks where seven new white teachers were hired to fill the positions. Handy concluded his remarks requesting a vote of thanks be given the Baltimore American because of its support for their cause.

Reverend James H. A. Johnson spoke after Handy and was presented by Bishop Wayman to the audience in the humerous way. The Bishop asked Reverend Reddick what "squatter" meant, a term applied by School Board members to the supposed influx of black teachers to come to the city if the Board were to allow for black teachers, inasmuch as it was their opinion that Baltimore blacks could not supply the needed qualified persons. The Bishop, getting his answer of what "squatter" meant said he did not want to introduce Johnson if he met the definition of being so repugnant a person.

Johnson's text was the violated promise of the Commissioners to allow the black teachers. He said:

When the School Board promised they would give us teachers in our public schools the eyes of the press and the people were upon them, and when they violated their promise they fell beneath the odium of the community. Having violated their promises in this thing, they are not to be trusted, and we do not propose to go to them again. We are pleading before a higher court--the community itself, the white people of the land. I would not draw a pen to go again before that School Board.[26]

Though Johnson revealed his bitterness and disgust at the perfidy of the School Board in his speech, he was known to have a sense of humor of his own, as the Bishop's introductory remarks indicate; and it was, perhaps here, that he released some of the audience's and his own tension with this anecdotal story, he was known to tell arising out of the attempt to integrate the teaching corps in Baltimore. The story is that a white lady in meeting a black lady teacher on a narrow street said to the black, "I don't step aside for Niggers," whereupon the black teacher replied, "Well, I do."

The resolutions offered at the meeting denounced the turn-around in the Board's decision and the practice of whites in the black schools of insisting that the front door to the black schools be used by whites only. The children were forced, in some cases, to use alley entrances which were filthy and unsafe because of the loitering in the area of unsavory characters. Dr. Brown, in support of the resolutions, said he heard one white principal use language before the children that could not be repeated to the audience. Brown said this principal was "unfit morally to teach a dog."

Rev. J. H. A. Johnson concluded the situation in the schools was so bad that the children should be withdrawn and an educational system be established by the blacks. John H. Butler remarked that this was financially impractical: in his view, the churches were just barely supporting themselves. The people could not support a school system of its own and help pay in taxes for the whites, too.

The demand for better educational opportunities was kept up on February 21, 1882, at a meeting held at Bethel with Isaac Myers presiding; a committee consisting of Myers, George Myers, Causeman H. Gaines, William F. Taylor, and John H. Camper was delegated to petition the General Assembly for authorization of funds for more black schools. Another committee was also constituted, consisting of Isaac Myers, George Myers, C. H. Gaines, and John H. Camper to lobby before Congress for the passage of the Blair Education Bill. The petition to the General Assembly recited a statistic that 134,000 blacks over age ten in the state were unable to read or write. It was not possible for blacks alone to remedy the situation; they had not the means to establish that many private schools. The Legislature was praised for its past liberality in encouraging the city to remedy the inadequate Baltimore School System. It was also stated in the petition to the Legislature that the blacks, in their efforts to promote a change in the city, could count on the sizeable support of an "enlightened Christian public sentiment." This latter group, however, did not seem too vocal.[27]

The issue of black teachers for black schools was again before the public in November 1882; a committee to protest the fact of no teachers included among others H. J. Brown, Joseph E. Briscoe (well-known Custom House employee), and George Myers. In December of that year, the black teachers of Baltimore organized at a meeting held at Howard Normal School. Charles K. Uncles who would become the first American-trained and ordained Catholic priest was chosen president.[28]

The next year, July 1883, peitions were submitted to the School Board for black teachers with many whites on the lists, including such blacks of prominence as James T. Bradford and Samuel W. Chase.[29]

Several years later, toward the end of the 1880s a sustained vigorous protest emerged. In 1886, a decided push developed to end the exclusion of black teachers. A delegation with such notables as Rev. W. H. Weaver, pastor of Madison Avenue Presbyterian Church; H. J. Brown, Robert M. Deaver, and George Myers met with Mayor Hodges about the matter, In April, the effort seemed successful but, eventually, this, too, proved to be another hope smashed. In July 1886, a permanent state teachers body amongst blacks was organized at the Normal School and called the Maryland State Teachers Progressive Association, with Garrison D. Trusty as president and Anna P. Reed as vice president.

In April 1887, more meetings were organized and another organization, The Maryland Educational Union, was formed to accomplish the object of getting black teachers and, in addition, a black high school. some participants were Revs. P. H. A. Braxton and William Alexander, and John H. Butler. The Union threatened to appeal through the courts to make their point before the School Board about the right of blacks to be teachers. At the same time, the Union requested that the private Howard Normal School replace the head who recently died with a black principal. The school had been founded by whites, mainly Quakers, around 1867, to provide a high school education for blacks and provide for the training of black teachers.

At last by May 1888, success attended the many efforts of some twenty years of unrelieved pressure on the forces in control in the city to better black education. By the fall term of 1888, a high school was made ready and the Mayor, having signed an ordinance authorizing black teachers, saw Roberta Sheridan as the first black teacher at Waverly Colored Public School. With the acceptance of black teachers and a publicly funded high school, the blacks of Baltimore could breathe a sigh of relief after such a long and difficult struggle.[30]

The other important fight to remain throughout the rest of the nineteenth century, after Hackett's death, was the fight to make the Republican Party what it pro-

222

fessed to be, a party of liberty and equality. The unity of leadership for which Hackett stood and for which he worked throughout his life, was fast coming apart a few years after his death as indicated in a June 1873 political meeting at the Douglass Institute. Blacks divided on two sides of the question, whether or not the Republican Party was giving them the rightful number of spoils. Here Myers was rather active, as well as several others visible during the schoolteacher issue.

At this particular meeting, John W. Locks, from the Third Ward, was nominated as permanent chairman of the convention. The nomination of Locks meant, according to one source, that the majority of the delegates wanted a "harmonious" relationship with the Republican Party. It was said by Nelson C. M. Grooms, that the blacks of Maryland cast 40,000 votes for the party, but got 21 jobs, Federal appointments, and most of those were no better than laborers' jobs such as cleaning spittoons. To contrast the twenty-one jobs given blacks, the 1,000 Republican voters of the Seventh Ward, Groom said, were given the same number of appointments and better positions, of course. With this exact depiction of a tale of two cities, so to speak, Groom's remarks were loudly applauded. Isaac Myers responded to Groom by saying "getting office" was an individual concern. The welfare of the colored people depended more on their getting chances to learn trades than on any partisanship.

With regard to patronage problems in local government, a couple of weeks later, this same group met under the chairmanship of John Locks at Davis Hall on Saratoga Street. It was decided that a delegation consisting of one person from each ward would lobby before the various department heads of the city government for blacks getting a better and bigger share of the jobs given out by the city. Blacks wanted jobs at all governmental levels.[31]

Throughout 1873, however, the dissatisfaction with the Republican Party in Baltimore continued with one of the chief complainers continuing to be N. C. M. Grooms. Indeed, apparently all over the country, blacks were willing to express their dissatisfaction with the Republican Party. In December 1873, Baltimore blacks made preparations to elect delegates to a National Civil Rights Convention called by Pennsylvanians to meet in Washington to put pressure on Republican congressmen to support Charles Sumner's civil rights platform.

Those attending a delegate selection convention at

Douglass Institute for the National Convention were apprised that "the colored men of Maryland, if they had brains could control the convention" in Washington. The sentiment represented in this expression, crudely stated, indicated a desire, perhaps, to extract more patronage, as well as support for the civil rights legislation from Republicans. William U. Saunders, who, according to one source, had recently turned Democratic, said the convention should be used as a forum to advance the interests of blacks regardless of party or clique.

On Saunders' recommendation, seven men were appointed by the chair as a committee of resolutions, including Saunders, Dr. R. M. Hall, William H. Spriggs, John W. Locks, and Walter Sorrell. As the Committee of Resolutions deliberated, Grooms spoke of the continued injustice perpetrated on blacks in Maryland, such as their exclusion from juries. When the resolutions were returned, they gave fulsome praise to Charles Sumner and his Civil Rights Bill. In addition, there were resolutions deploring the continued slavery with all its brutality in the Spanish possessions in the Caribbean. Furthermore, the resolutions wanted the U.S. Government to support the Cubans in their proclamation of universal freedom. Those elected as delegates to the National Convention in Washington included J. W. Locks, William U. Saunders, Jacob A. Seaton, Casius A. Mason, N. C. M. Grooms, Dr. R. M. Hall, A. J. Kelly, James H. Hill, Augusta Roberts, Walter Sorrell, and George Washington Perkins.

In conjunction with this latest attempt to influence the Republican-controlled Congress, Isaac Myers thought that some effort should be made to petition the Democratic-controlled Maryland Legislature to grant full civil rights to blacks in the state. To effectuate this purpose, during the above meeting, a resolution was offered by Myers and seconded by Saunders, that urged delegates to the National Convention draft a memorial to be presented to the Maryland Legislature, as well.

In Saunders' seconding speech, a curious thing for him to do, if he were a Democrat, he warmly praised C. C. Fulton, owner of the <u>Baltimore American</u>, as a staunch Republican which "aroused the audience to a high pitch of enthusiasm." Saunders said those "who turn their backs on the staunchest Republican, and who had tried to run the Republican Party of Maryland without C. C. Fulton. . . had so ingnominiously failed." Although seconding Myers' resolution, Saunders accused Myers and others of coming to the meeting to control it, that is

Saunders seemed to imply that Myers was trying to keep the convention favorable to the Republican Party and denunciatory of all Democrats. Myers' resoluton was carried, however.[32]

Apparently the above meeting was not the only meeting called to elect delegates to the National Civil Rights Convention, because seven days later, another gathering, somewhat different in make-up, met at Douglass Institute. George Myers called the group to order. Afterward, George W. Perkins was unanimously elected temporary chairman. Here, John C. Fortie and John H. Butler made important speeches. Fortie said of the Republican Party:

> After praying for years for the year of deliverance, he was not going to turn his back on the party. Whatever disadvantages the colored man labored under, he could not get anything from any party but that.[33]

Fortie said those Republicans who, for the last eighteen months, had been criticizing the Republican Party could still not get blacks appointed to the police or school system from the Democrats in command. He stated further:

> If you can't get an office stick to principle. Let colored people have patience, and their rights will be recognized. The party of enlightenment, the party of truth, the party of God, was the one from which progress was to be hoped.

William F. Taylor also spoke affirming what he thought was the correctness in Fortie's statements.

The list of permanent officers at this meeting included Robert B. Sorrell as president and numerous vice presidents amongst them, John W. Locks; George Myers was one of the secretaries. John C. Fortie and William F. Taylor escorted the President to the chair. On a motion by Fortie, a committee of nine, including himself, J. H. Butler, George Myers, Augusta Roberts, Joseph W. Watkins, and Dr. Hudson, was appointed to prepare resolutions for the meeting. Also, a committee, one member from each ward, offered in a resolution by J. H. Butler, was appointed to select nine members who would, in turn, select delegates to the Washington National Civil Rights Convention. Some of those elected to go to Washington from this gathering included J. C. Fortie, William Matthews, Jacob A. Seaton, John H. Butler, and George Myers as a delegate-at-large.

Not long after the Washington Civil Rights Convention, Charles Sumner died. His death was duly noted and commemorated by blacks at the Douglass Institute on March 13, 1874. Bishop A. W. Wayman was called to the chair to preside, while Dr. R. M. Hall was made secretary; and N. C. M. Grooms elaborated on the subject of the meeting. On a motion by Bishop Wayman, a committee was appointed to draw up resolutions to be presented at a commemorative service to be held on the following Monday. Those drawing up the resolutions included Dr. R. M. Hall, Rev. William Alexander, Robert B. Sorrell, Professor Robert Rowan, and Solomon W. McCabe. The committee also urged black congregations to hold commemorative services for Sumner. Bishop Wayman spoke of Sumner as "a man that stood up for human liberty so long that his name could never be forgotten--at all events, not by the colored people." Wayman said Sumner's last words were "Take care of my Civil Rights Bill." "That expression should never be forgotten by the colored people of America," said the Bishop.[34]

At the subsequent memorial meeting, held at Bethel Church on March 16, 1874, Dr. H. J. Brown spoke. Apparently, Brown felt his efforts inadequate and, on a resolution by him, it was requested that Bishop Wayman deliver a memorial sermon on Sumner on the first Sunday in April. Also, a committee was appointed to cooperate with a committee in Massachusetts which was established to erect a monument to Sumner's memory. Members of this committee included Charles Deaver, Isaac Myers' father-in-law, Isaac Myers, Dr. H. J. Brown, N. C. M. Grooms, Augusta Roberts, Robert B. Sorrell, John C. Fortie, and Dr. R. M. Hall.[35]

The praise for Republicanism expressed at the Sumner memorial services did not lessen or negate black criticism of other Republicans; however, for in July 1874, the first seven wards of the city organized themselves into the Equal Rights Association of the Third Congressional District to extract whatever additional benefits from the Republican Party it could get and thought itself entitled to. The organziation had as one of its most important supporters, William F. Taylor, but this effort was opposed by Isaac Myers. Taylor defended the actions of the new organization as within the right of the people to elect their own ward leaders and without the interference of the "ring" in the Custom House which attempted to control the party in the state.

The dissidents were amazed that they would get the sobriquet of traitor, while Democrats, even former Confed-
erates, and similar types, got the jobs.[36]

The Republican Party came in for its share of criticism on another front in 1874. Here, Isaac Myers was
in the thick of things as well. The Freedmen's Bank, a
company chartered by the Congress shortly after the Civil War to be a place where blacks were encouraged to
save, collapsed in 1874; and, to the amazement of many,
it was discovered that this institution was not as sound
a guarantee as people thought, whatever its past connection with a Republican-controlled Congress was supposed to mean. Indeed, in this state of bankruptcy and
fraud of the little black depositor, Frederick Douglass
was president though he was not a party to any of the
disreputable aspects of the collapse.

Baltimore had a branch office of the bank which the
Rev. Harrison H. Webb headed as Assistant Cashier and
his assistant being William H. Bishop, Jr. Robert B.
Sorrell was made chairman of a meeting to discuss the
closing of Baltimore's branch which was held at Ebenezer
A.M.E. Church. The Rev. J. H. A. Johnson and G. Washington Perkins were for going to Washington to confront
the Bank Commissioners recently given charge of the institution, to demand the honoring of the account books
of the depositors. The bank, throughout most of its existence, had been dominated by white officers who made
"bad" loans. Isaac Myers was for waiting, believing
that the commissioners would make good on the deposits.
The consensus of the meeting proved to be for sending a
delegation to Washington. Rev. James H. A. Johnson,
George Washington Perkins, and Robert B. Sorrell were
appointed to take the complaints of Baltimore's depositors to Washington.[37]

About a month later, the delegation made its report
to about 400 of the Freedmen's Bank depositors at a
meeting held at Ebenezer. Robert Sorrell opened the
meeting and commented on reports circulating in the community about his rather angry confrontation with the
Bank Commissioners. He said if the community "considered his language at the meeting very uncouth and Cal-
vinistic, he had not intended to impeach the honor of
the Commissioners, and in his speech he had only referred to the villians that had defrauded the depositors
of the bank." In answering the most important query the
delegation was sent to Washington to find the answer to,
it was reported that the bank was broke, at least for
the present; but when all matters had been properly set-

tled, there might be money to pay off 96 percent of a depositor's account. They did not know, however, exactly when this would take place.

When the report ended, the delegation submitted a resolution to the depositors requesting that a permanent society, known as the Freedmen's Right Association be formed and that efforts be made to establish branches of this society wherever there were Freedmen Bank branches, so that a corporate drive could be mounted to expedite the fulfillment of the bank's obligation to its depositors. Isaac Myers objected to the resolution. He thought it would take five to six years for the bank's affairs to be straightened out, and during that time, considerable money would be needed to run a permanent organization representing depositors. Reverend Harvey Johnson of North Street Baptist supported Myers, even though his church lost considerable money it was going to use to build a new church. Those in favor of the organization included J. H. A. Johnson, George W. Perkins, and Dr. H. J. Brown; they carried the day. Baltimore, supposedly, had 3,500 individual depositors with about $281,000 on deposit. The beneficial and building societies had deposited an additional $50,000. The bank held a $10,000 mortgage on the Douglass Institute and a $2,000 one on Dallas Street Church.[38]

Again, Myers' penchant for being in the thick of controversy, other than purely political matters, arose in 1876 when the Chesapeake and Marine Railway and Drydock Company experienced a stockholders' fight over control of the company, at a meeting held at Douglass Institute on October 30. The charge was mismanagement and unaccountability, as some thought that much money wasted by those in charge, who then did not allow the books to be examined by an auditing committee. Myers was accused of coming to break up the meeting in the interest of the present management. John H. Butler apparently was for a change and he and Myers were opposed to each other's intentions.

Butler claimed that for the past six years no dividend had been declared. Myers, on the other hand, defended the management of the company under the lead of John W. Locks, a fellow Bethelite. Butler's side won out and a new Board of Directors was installed that included, among others, George W. Perkins, Solomon McCabe, Alexander Allen, James Green, Aquila Johnson, and John A. Gold. This election did not hold for long, however, for by January 9, 1877, all those directors installed in October, except Solomon McCabe, were defeated in a new test of strength. Locks and his associates were back in control.[39]

In the midst of the controversy over the Chesapeake Drydock Company, the approaching presidential election in 1876 saw Myers and other staunch Republicans welcome the return of Frederick Douglass to the city on September 21, 1876, to boost the Party's chances. The meeting, held at Douglass Institute, was called to order by Dr. H. J. Brown, while the Reverend James A. Handy was elected president; other officers were Jacob A. Seaton, James Jackson, Samuel W. Chase, James H. Hill, and William F. Taylor. Taylor read the resolutions which were adopted. The resolutions commended Rutherford B. Hayes and William A. Wheeler to the voters and noted the pleasure which the people had in having Frederick Douglass, the co-laborer of William Lloyd Garrison, Wendell Phillips, and Gerritt Smith among them.

Taking the rostrum and keeping in mind the demands for changes in Federal Government leadership, mainly because the Republicans had been in power too long, Douglass said:

> I am a party man, a Republican party man, a black Republican party man, dyed out in the wool, not for the sake of party, but as a patriot for the sake of country, and yet I am free to confess that I should be very glad to hand this great Government of ours, with its possibilities, its powers and opportunities for good to the Democratic Party, if I thought that party could take care of it. But I doubt the fitness of that party for the task of protecting the nation's honor, its credit and its liberty under the principles of our reconstructed Constitution.[40]

To further stress his point, Douglass brought up a comment of Montgomery Blair, prominent Maryland Democrat, who recently spoke to a reporter about "niggers" and how they had sold their votes and never did anything to lift themselves up to deserve freedom.

Douglass countered by saying Negroes, when released from slavery, were in the worst condition of any nation that had been in bondage; even the Israelites left the Egyptians with spoils, the Russian serfs were given land; but, ever since their release, blacks had improved their position, mainly through self-exertion. As for never doing anything to gain their freedom, Douglass said Blair should know better than to make such a charge inasmuch as he was Lincoln's Postmaster General, and when the Union was about to crumble, blacks were drafted in the thousands into the army, intended only for guard duty.

> . . . but history has left it on record that wherever a rampart was to be carried, wherever a wall was to be scaled, wherever courage of the highest nature was required and danger of the sternest sort stared them in the face, the black troops were there and turned the tide of victory.

Others also testified to the bravery of black troops during the War.

The restrictiveness of the political process, but viewed from a different perspective than the above, was in the thoughts of Douglass as he returned to Baltimore in late October 1877 to lecture at Centennial Methodist Episcopal Church; his subject was "William, the Silent." Douglass recalled he became a member of the church in November 1830 due to the preaching of Joseph P. Wilson, Joseph Young, and some others. He said it was from that church that he got his direction to follow in the world, and to it he owed all he had accomplished.

Douglass, introduced by Dr. H. J. Brown, drew many analogies from the war of independence fought in the Netherlands between the Dutch, led by William, the Silent, and their Spanish overlords, and the Civil War in the United States. Douglass said, on the Dutch side, women fought side by side with the men. The reason thrown out by those opposed to women's suffrage at the present was that women did not fight or would not fight in a war situation. Douglass countered by saying, "Men don't vote because they fight, but because they have brains."[41]

In about two years in 1879, Douglass revisited the city and again urged the people to keep the faith in the Republican Party, despite its shortcomings. Yet, at a meeting called in early Spring to discuss whether blacks should celebrate the Fifteenth Amendment in 1879, a mixed attitude prevailed. Joseph P. Baker was called to the chair and J. H. Butler was made one of the vice presidents. Dr. H. J. Brown spoke out against commemorating the occasion of the ratification of the Amendment until blacks in the South truly had their rights. Brown said he would rather celebrate the birthdates of

Douglass and Benjamin Banneker. A resolution placed before the consideration of the gathering at the commencement of the meeting wanted the pastors of the various churches to deliver sermons on the Fifteenth Amendment, but objections were made to this because of its political tone. Some, in effect, were against glorifying past Republican deeds as a way of papering over present failures.

Indeed, some noted that Republicans, because of their ineptitude had lost control of Congress. The question on many minds was, why hitch one's wagon to a dying institution? Others made speeches to the effect, however, that supported the celebration of the adoption of the Fifteenth Amendment, to show the race not lacking in gratitude to the Republican Party. Somehow, someone saw the celebration as likened to the Irish celebration of St. Patrick's Day.

Others questioned the propriety of not celebrating because some of the rights had been denied blacks. One claimed it was only idle talk of an entire abandonment and overturning of the rights blacks had, not a fact of law. Isaac Myers, however, did not relish the disregard of rights blacks were beginning to experience. He said that when he went into the criminal courts in Baltimore and saw colored men on trial, he wondered why there were no colored men in the jury stand. He also wondered why there were no qualified lawyers allowed to practice in the local courts. He ventured further to say that the people in the South were as much slaves as before enfranchisement. He thought that blacks should migrate from the South, and that they would not enjoy equal rights with whites until they were mechanics and merchants. He said, summing up the last statement, "then will men put their prejudices in their pockets."

Finally, the Committee on Resolutions brought in a different compromise to the earlier suggestion that the pastors hold celebrations in their churches, each giving a sermon related to the amendment. Instead, it was requested that all churches hold services on Sunday, April 13, at which time the Fifteenth Amendment would be mentioned but perhaps not glorified and, on the 15th of April, that the national flag would be displayed from houses of those who think it advisable. Because the winter was a severe one, the Committee thought a more expensive public display not worth the cost. Finally, Lemuel Griffin said, "it was fitting that they should have a celebration of their resurrection from the political grave two days after Easter." The suggestions were adopted with one dissenting vote, which John H. Butler characterized as the "Lone Star," at which point the audience broke out in laughter. The plan to organize a permanent organization to further black aims, in general, was also adopted.

At the above meeting, a significant part of Isaac Myers speech opposed the stance taken by Douglass lately that, in essence, was against the blacks moving from the South, moving out of reconstructed-klansman-ridden-Democratic-Dixie, to settle in Kansas or other places, especially in the West, where they could hope for a freer, safer existence. What Myers was hinting at, was Douglass' seeming more apparent concern for maintaining Republican power in the South, by keeping its black voters in large concentrations in the region, than for supporting the desire of many to seek a better life.

In fact, a few days later, another meeting was convened, perhaps under the auspices of the organization formed at the last meeting which considered how to handle the Fifteenth Amendment celebrations, at which delegates were elected to attend the Nashville National Convention where the Kansas Exodus was to be prominent on the agenda. Several of those chosen to go to Nashville were James A. Handy, Samuel W. Chase, Dr. H. J. Brown, Dr. R. M. Hall, George Myers, and John W. Locks.[42]

The Exodus question remained constantly before the public in 1879 as some blacks celebrated in a more elaborate style on April 15 the adoption of the Fifteenth Amendment. The black Odd Fellows had charge of such festivities and convened at the Maryland Institute with Isaac Myers as master of ceremonies and J. W. Cromwell, editor of the People's Advocate in Washington, urging people to contribute to those who left the South for the North or West, but found themselves stranded along the way. Richard T. Greener of Howard University also urged the same compassion from the listeners as he spoke at this occasion.[43]

Frederick Douglass came to Baltimore on May 4, spoke in Centennial Church, and talked on several points including the Exodus question. Douglass thought that throughout the entire history of blacks in the United States, "more harm" had been done black businesses and enterprises by schemes of emigration than from any other cause. He said emigration schemes deceived the people when portraying someplace as a paradise for blacks, whether it was Haiti, Canada, Jamaica, Nicaragua, or

Liberia--all of which were not remotely like and para-dise. He said to leave land and homes already owned was unwise, especially if those coming north expected it easy; because now they would have to compete with the many poor emigrants from Europe for jobs.[44]

A few weeks later, before the Convention of Colored Sunday Schools in Baltimore County, the matter of the Exodus came up in this forum as well. Isaac Myers was president of the Convention. Some of the vice presi-dents were Rev. Harvey Johnson, Robert M. Deaver, and John H. Butler. Frances E. W. Harper was one of the national figures in attendance. Having conducted its usual business, the already-set-adjournment was delayed when General Thomas W. Conway of New Jersey arrived in town. He was introduced as the living William Lloyd Garrison; Garrison had recently died.

Just recently Conway had spent considerable time in furthering the migration of blacks from the South to Kansas or other parts of the West. Before the conven-tion of Sunday School workers, he spoke of having just left seeing the President of the United States about getting Federal assistance for the Exodus, and the situ-ation as he observed it in St. Louis, where some 8,000 blacks on the Mississippi were camped out in the worst condition. He said the planter class put pressure on the river boat captains to deny passage to those blacks wishing to leave. Conway revealed his preparedness to lease some boats to take the blacks where they wanted to go and President Hayes's encouragement of his plan.

Conway cut his speech short, being aware of the Sunday School Convention's wish to adjourn and announced he would hold a meeting in the near future to discuss this matter exclusively. He said he thought it proper to hold a meeting in Baltimore because "here in Balti-more the first blood was shed in 1861" at the commence-ment of the Civl War "and here in Baltimore the first push to the boat that goes after the negro (sic) emi-grants should be given."[45]

General Conway's Exodus meeting took place on May 28 at Bethel Church. There inside the church criti-cism of Frederick Douglass and his opposition to emigra-tion was made. General Conway and a Rev. John Turner, Treasurer of Colored Refugee Relief Board of St. Louis, gave out pamphlets depicting the operations of those supporting the emigration. Also present was a Reverend Emory from Kansas. Conway spoke of blacks leaving to provide a better future for their children.

The planter class in the recently held Vicksburg Convention promised a better future for black laborers, but the blacks were not listening. Acknowledging that the fight had truly just begun, Conway said:

> Bigger conventions won't be able to stop it, and it will take a bigger man than Fred. Douglas (sic) to stop it. God watched the exodus of the children of Israel from their oppressors in Egypt, and the same God rules now.[46]

Conway said, on the whole, those wanting transportation were not paupers, bad debtors, as the planters said, but had sold their homes and land and had money to pay their way. He said some captains and owners of boats told him of the planters' threats against them if they transported the blacks.

Conway also stated it was his belief that there was a fundamental question at stake here: whether or not this government would protect the right of all citizens to move about as they so desired. Conway said President Hayes assured him armed protection would be given the boats if found necessary.

Conway ended, but Reverend Emory from Kansas continued in a similar vein. He said:

> There is not a man in the country who does not know that the colored people in the South are persecuted and oppressed, and if he does not know it, he is either a fool or a knave. (Applause) Reverdy Johnson who was sent South to defend the Ku-Klux, saw that their deeds were shocking, and denounced them.

Reverdy Johnson was a Baltimore lawyer who had at various times from the 1820s associated with the blacks and their problems, especially with regard to colonizaion.

Emory's humorous and picturesque reply to those who charged the blacks leaving were really bad debtors, by saying:

> General Chalmers (a former Confederate) objects to the exodus, and thinks something must be done to stop it because the planters have been feeding the negros (sic) all winter. The truth is, however, that the negroes (sic) have been feeding the planters for the last fifty years. (Applause and laughter.)

At the conclusion of the remarks by the speakers, Isaac Myers offered a resolution which was adopted and which urged blacks to support efforts of those raising funds to secure steamboats to transport the blacks out of the South who wanted to leave. Those appointed to raise funds in Baltimore, hopefully $1,000, included John W. Locks, Samuel W. Chase, H. J. Brown, George Myers, Harvey Johnson, Simon Smith, J. H. Butler, and Causeman Gaines. By the first of June, the Maryland Emigration Aid Society had been organized with John W. Locks as president; it distributed a printed appeal to city residents to aid its effort.

The decoration of the graves of black soldiers on May 31 provided yet another occasion for further exegesis of the Exodus question. As a speaker, Rev. James A. Handy, who had known Douglass since they worked together in Baltimore shipyards in the mid-1830s, said of those who fought in the Civil War, did so that:

. . . the country might be free, that black men and white men might be free to go and settle anywhere in this broad land, Mr. Frederick Douglass and the Mississippi planters and storekeepers to the contrary notwithstanding. You cannot stop the Exodus any more than you can bail the Chesapeake with a seine or reheave the Alleganies with a single puff of your breath.[47]

Handy said one million blacks should leave the South to break the grip of the resurrected slaveocrats, generally Democrats, and better themselves in the virgin West.[48]

Frederick Douglass appeared in the city later in the year, in September, to deliver a paper before the Social Science Association. His paper also dealt with Negro emigration from the South. Douglass reiterated his previous announced position; he said that the move was not politically timely and was enormously expensive. He also stated that all those who go around advising the blacks to leave because of the supposed inability of the Federal Government, its executive branch of Republican leadership, to protect them, play into the hands of the enemy of the Negro who say blacks should never have been freed in the first place. As to how this was so, he did not elaborate.

Douglass also said these same harbingers of doom will tell of the numerous destitute, but not those many more times their number who remained, determined to make a life for themselves in the South. He said the signs indicated the authorities were about to put themselves to the task of protecting the life and property of blacks and that it was too soon to pick up and leave when the black man's labor was a necessity and in demand in the South, which was not the case in other parts of the country. Douglass concluded his speech on a note probably more to the liking of his Baltimore audience than was his beginning when he said he was for black men staying in the South, but he was against coercion from any quarter to keep them there.[49]

The issue of the Exodus was so strong that the sympathetic Baltimore American opened its columns to a special piece from John M. Langston, former Ambassador to Haiti, in reply to Douglass' position. His main thought was that the emigration movement was justified on the ground that since seventeen years of emancipation, the Negro haters, with violence when necessary, had kept blacks from realizing their independence from the class that kept them in slavery before the War. To break this utter dependency upon the planter and assert themselves, blacks should leave the South, so said Langston. Langston's contention was that so much in the South impressed blacks with their former servility, that a change of scenery, in and of itself, would do wonders to bring out self-assertiveness.[50]

In the same month, another nationally known black contended with Douglass before a Baltimore audience. Henry H. Garnet, a leading abolitionist before the Civil War and Presbyterian minister, lectured at Madison Avenue Presbyterian Church on the Exodus. He said blacks should leave where they are not allowed to exercise the franchise. He scoffed at Douglass' purported notion that a Negro could not survive in a colder climate, by making reference to the numerous blacks who ran away from slavery to Canada. Garnet thought that as blacks thinned out, whites would demand the labor of those remaining and give them just compensation for it.[51]

Toward the end of 1879, the blacks of Baltimore themselves, experienced an example of the ruthlessness on the part of the Democratic Party whose more Southern branches were responsible for doing much worse and precipitating the Exodus. Several thousands of blacks were removed from the voter lists, according to some whim of the Democratic machine, without the blacks being informed until the polls opened on October 22. The Democrats feared the blacks would vote for Republican mayoral candidate William J. Hooper, publisher of the Morn-

ing Herald, possibly the most liberal white paper in the
city. It was reported some of the blacks who had been
dropped from the rolls had been voting for up to twenty
years, but were "peremptorily" told at the polls they
could not vote any longer.

A meeting was held at Douglass Institute to protest this maneuver with such persons as Dr. H. J.
Brown, George Myers, and John C. Fortie present. The
disenfranchised blacks were urged to go to Superior
Court and get papers, certificates of registration,
forcibly putting their names back on the registration
books.[52]

Despite their eager willingness to carry the Republican banner, blacks had as much to protest against
their party as against the opposition in late 1879. A
little after the fall elections, at a meeting at the St.
Paul Lyceum, blacks met to protest the continued lack of
recognition from the Republican Party and the dismissal
of Dr. H. J. Brown from the Custom House by Collector
John L. Thomas who added insult to injury in appointing
a man from Alabama to a political office that a black
should have filled. The blacks said it was time the
local party gave due recognition to two-thirds of its
members--its black voters--as the Democrats recognized
its regular Irish and German voters. The lack of black
participation in the machinery, none on the City Executive Committee, and only three on the State Central Committee, was another complaint. Reluctantly, blacks
acknowledged they had been used by white Republicans to
get themselves elected or appointed to office.[53]

Another meeting soon followed, seeking the same
end, how to get more from the Republican Party. It,
too, was held at St. Paul Lyceum with John H. Murphy
presiding. Murphy, from a free black family with roots
in Bethel Church, had served in the Civil War as a sergeant. Dr. Brown spoke at this gathering and said lack
of unity amongst blacks was responsible for the deplorable lack of jobs held by the group in the Federal agen-
cies. He also said he had agitated the question
throughout the state, even on the Eastern Shore recently, and found favorable support for demanding the rightful share of the rewards of party regularity.

A result of this meeting was the instituting of a
primary among the blacks to elect delegates to a city
convention to organize a permanent organization, similar to the old Colored Republican Central Committee, to
look after the interests of the Negro. The convention

was set for January 1880. In the meanwhile, it was decided to hold weekly meetings to keep the issue before
the public; and Dr. Brown said he would visit the counties again to secure their support.[54]

The black Republicans held their convention at
Douglass Institute, not in January but on February 10,
1880, with such people in attendance as Causeman H.
Gaines, George Myers, Charles H. Hackett, David D.
Dickson, James Jackson, Joseph E. Briscoe, and John C.
Fortie who was chosen temporary president. The conven-
tion called itself the Equal Rights League Convention.
Addresses were made by Isaac Myers, Rev. James A.
Handy, William F. Taylor, and N. C. M. Grooms. The
permanent officers selected were Rev. James A. Handy,
President; Isaac Myers, a Secretary; and C. H. Gaines,
Treasurer; clearly the meeting was influenced by the
Bethel men.[55]

In addition to its purpose of getting more patronage slots from the Republican leadership, the Equal
Rights League got involved in the black teacher question
and in a move to get blacks included in city juries.
John H. Murphy seemed a particular leader in the latter
effort. It is likely that Murphy was peculiarly sensi-
tive to this issue as he may have been the John H. Murphy attacked in the Exchange Building some 13 years before; and afterwards involved in a vigorous dispute that
developed over who had jurisdiction over his case,
whether Federal or local courts. It seemed that the
dispute at that time over jurisdiction basically was one
about the right of blacks to serve on juries--the Federal Courts were more lenient in this regard, city
courts not so. Some of the first blacks to serve on
Federal juries included Rev. Harrison H. Webb, William
H. Bishop, and John W. Locks. The Equal Rights League
was encouraged in this effort to integrate the jury selection process by the result of the United States Supreme Court ruling that granted the right of blacks in
Virginia to serve on state courts of that state.[56]

It seems meetings of the Equal Rights League took
place at American Hall opposite Bethel Church on Saratoga Street. At one gathering in its efforts to integrate the jury system, the League decided to press the
issue in a test case by retaining Charles J. Bonaparte
as a lawyer for a black accused of killing his lover.
Bonaparte, though a Republican, was selected because of
what was described as his being less likely to draw objections because of his political ties. Bonaparte, on
his maternal side, was a descendant of a first family of

Baltimore, the Pattersons, and was a relative of the Bonapartes of Europe. Interestingly enough, the man accused of the murder supposedly did not want to be tried by colored jurors. He was, doubtlessly, well aware on the whole whites would not take his crime of killing another black as seriously as blacks would.

Despite this, however, by March 21, the League's efforts were successful as blacks were recognized as having the right to serve on juries by the Supreme Bench of the City. Two of those first selected were James A. Harris, well-known wealthy caterer, and William L. Vessells, ex-State Senator in Virginia. These were two selected from a list that included such others as William H. Bishop, William Brown, John Myers, John H. Smith, James Williams, Walter W. Lewis, Levi Kelly, Simon Smith, and James T. Bradford.

Though recognized as equals on the jury selection list, blacks were not being placed in equitable terms on the Republican Party's patronage lists. Matters were growing progressively worse, as far as black participation in an overall sense on a footing of equality within the Republican Party. On May 17, 1880, an indignation meeting was held at Courtland Street Hall, with Rev. William Alexander in the chair, to protest the recent state convention held in Frederick which did not select any of the race to attend the national convention, though John W. Locks had been promised a seat by the so-called liberal Grant-wing of the party. What made the matter more appalling was that apparently Locks was defeated and betrayed, in part, by whites from his own district. By July, however, the disagreement amongst blacks about the party had grown so intolerable that two groups, one headed by Isaac Myers, the other by Dr. H. J. Brown, had formed on either side of the patronage question. Myers' group was more conciliatory toward party shortcomings; where Brown was more impatient with the party's paltry gifts to its black phalanx.[57]

Not all blacks were prepared to withdraw their support from the party's national choices, so at least one ratification meeting for the national ticket was held, presided over by Isaac Myers and Rev. William Alexander. Blacks were encouraged to register, and the pastors were encouraged to lead their unregistered to sign up to be able to vote. Richard T. Greener was welcomed to the city in September, as he spoke on behalf of the national Republican ticket. He told Baltimore's blacks not to be deluded into voting for the Democrats because they nominated General Hancock, a Union veteran; they should disregard this nominee as they once had disregarded the Democratic nomination of the abolitionist Horace Greely. The people should vote Republican, Greener said, because of the party's principles which showed a long-standing commitment to freedom and equality. The commitment may have been long-standing, in some minds, but of late, it must have seemed to some persons that Republican elephants did indeed forget.

It is significant that Dr. H. J. Brown was attracting attention in the community, not only because of his demand that the Republican party acknowledge its debt to blacks; but also because he was willing to test the party's faith in a vivid manner as he entered the contest for the Republican nomination for Congress in the Fourth District. The party central organization eventually nominated Enoch Pratt who won out over Brown, 32 to 8. Pratt was a successful businessman, philanthropist of the abolitionist tradition represented in the likes of Elisha Tyson. Later in the year, blacks meeting at Samaritan Temple with Rev. James A. Handy presiding, William F. Taylor as secretary, and John H. Murphy as treasurer, the party was asked to consider Dr. Brown for the position of surveyor of the port. The group was determined to even request this appointment in person in Washington. So wide had become the difference between local blacks and their allegiance to the local party.[58]

It was a different story, however, with regard to the national party. At an integrated meeting held at Douglass Institute in November, just after the elevation of Garfield and Arthur, blacks suppressed their differences with the party to celebrate over what was conceived in the beginning of the presidential campaigning as possibly the year of the Democrats. Frederick Douglass and William E. Matthews were to be a part of the scheduled festivities, but for several reasons Douglass did not attend. Dr. H. J. Brown was elected president of the meeting. A resolution read by William F. Taylor acknowledging the victory as a portent for continued adherence of the Federal executive to the principles of Christianity and freedom, was adopted and forwarded to the newly elected team.

Following Taylor, at William E. Matthews' introduction, he received applause and cheers that lasted several minutes. Matthews said the election of General Hancock, the Democratic presidential candidate, would surely have led to the Fourteenth and Fifteenth Amendments being declared unconstitutional by a Supreme Court in sympathy with Hancock's views. Matthews also said

Douglass told him he would had been "compelled" to go to Canada if the Democrats had been elected. Matthews thought that with the election of the Republicans, blacks in the deep South would be protected in their rights as well as any white man in Massachusetts. He concluded his remarks by praising the Republican press, especially the <u>Baltimore American</u> for underlining to the people throughout the campaign the seriousness in consequences to ensue in electing a Democratic president.

After concluding his speech, Matthews read a letter of regret from Frederick Douglass who was unable to attend because of duties at home and some ailment he had. In his letter, Douglass seconded Matthews' sentiments about the dire consequences of a Democratic victory. Douglass, in speaking of the anticipated tenor of the meeting to be held, said:

> I hope that nothing will be said calculated to make race and color prominent as an element in political Rejoicing, but rejoice as men, as citizens and as Republicans. The Republican Party is not only the party of justice for the black man and to the North, but it is such to the white race and to the South.[59]

Apparently many Democrats did not believe this to be so.

It was not so long after the new presidential team's inauguration, however, that blacks were to find something else to be less optimistic about. On March 25, 1881, a State Convention of Colored Republicans met, again at Douglass Institute, to register their protest against insufficient recognition for Federal patronage appointments. Joseph E. Briscoe called the assembly to order. Permanent officer for president was Rev. Daniel P. Seaton of Frederick; for vice president, James Jackson; and secretary, Oliver O. Deaver. A Committee of Resolutions was appointed with Isaac Myers, as chairman. After some statistical remarks by J. L. H. Smith about the crucial nature of the black vote in the last presidential election, Dr. H. J. Brown attempted to speak, but was so strongly opposed by many who thought him not "solid" Republican enough that he was not able to speak long.

William F. Taylor counselled harmony and said that any visible opposition to Brown probably would deny him the position of surveyor of the port. Indeed, about a month after this wrangle, some black Republicans of the Fourth Congressional District, headed by James Jackson,

241

passed resolutions opposing Brown as surveyor of the port and, instead, supported G. W. Brooks for that position. To quiet the crowd down at this Frederick Convention, Taylor enlisted the aid of someone to sing "The Star Spangled Banner."

When Isaac Myers brought in the majority report of the Committee on Resolutions, he was opposed with a minority report and, for some time, he was unable to give his report because of the disruptive tactics of his opponents. Myers' resolutions praised Garfield and suggested that a committee be sent to the President urging him to appoint no man to a Federal position who would not reward the tremendous effort blacks made in the Republican election in Maryland. The minority report, offered by J. W. Adams, was much harsher, demanding removal from office of those who showed an unwillingness to appoint blacks.

A motion was then offered that both sets of resolutions be adopted; this was opposed by Myers, who said:

> The majority of the committee has no personal interests to subserve. They are in the interest of no man or faction. They represent the feelings of the colored voters of the state. Their report covers all the ground of the minority report, but it is presented in language more respectful and suggests the remedy for the evil complained of. President Garfield will not misunderstand it when he sees it.[60]

J. L. H. Smith was for the majority report; J. E. Briscoe, Chairman of the Advisory Council, something like a black Republican City Central Committee, was for the minority report. Eventually, the majority report was adopted by a large margin; after which the Chair appointed a committee to take that report to the President. Those selected included Isaac Myers, O. O. Deaver, Joseph F. Briscoe, John C. Fortie, James Jackson and D. P. Seaton.

Apparently, neither efforts of conciliation or denunciation would do much to improve the situation in the remainder of 1881 as the Republican postmaster felt free to dismiss J. L. H. Smith, a newspaper sorter from his position, one of the few remaining positions held by blacks in his department. Two delegations went to see the Postmaster to get him to reinstate Smith and retain John E. Grace, a janitor who had not yet received the ax. These delegations included such people as Reverend J. H. Reddick, J. A. Seaton, Dr. H. J. Brown, John W. Locks, and William H. Bishop.

In June, the dissatisfaction with the lack of Republican leadership attention to black patronage demands led to still another try to form a splinter black Republican organization. This was thwarted, however, by James Jackson and O. O. Deaver and matters in October got worse despite all signs to the overwhelming loyalty by most blacks to the party. Joseph E. Briscoe, in October, declined a nomination by a group of dissatisfied black Republicans to the first branch of the City Council, after getting pressure from white Henry M. Stockbridge, Chairman of the Republican State Central Committee.

In addition to the niggardliness of Republicans, the Democrats were not helping matters. They were denounced at a mass meeting at Douglass Institute on November 4, because, again, black Republicans were being arbitrarily stricken from the voting rolls. It would seem that at the end of 1881, both Republicans and Democrats would rule the roost without regard to right or the black race.[61]

At this time in the early 1880s, as this tug-of-war continued between the established leadership of black and white factions in the Republican Party, a relatively new person was making himself heard. In April 1882, the Reverend Harvey Johnson became more visible as a leader, intent upon tackling the race problem. At a meeting held at Ebenezer that month, calls to form The Order of Regulators, whose purpose would be to demand equal rights and privileges for blacks, such as the right to practice law before Maryland courts, were made. In May, Johnson presided over a meeting at Douglass Institute where, again, the theme was equal rights for colored people. In September, at a convention of black ministers to discuss general race problems, the address of welcome was given by Harvey Johnson, while Bishop Wayman presided. The meeting was held at Grace Presbyterian. These efforts by Johnson and others led the Supreme Bench of Baltimore City to recognize in principle, in March 1885, the right of black lawyers to practice before it. Edward J. Waring, in October of the same year, was the first black actually admitted to practice before the Supreme Bench. In the mid-1880s, Johnson led the way in the organization of the Brotherhood of Liberty, a later-day form of The Order of Regulators, he wanted to establish in 1882. At the initial grand meeting of the brotherhood, Frederick Douglass spoke on the self-made man.[62]

The pastors, like Johnson, in the struggle to extract proportional patronage or privileges for the votes given, had always been an important factor in success; and, even political organization demanding the same at this time, such as the Colored Advisory Council headed by Joseph E. Briscoe and O. O. Deaver, relied-upon pastors, to rally people to the polls.[63]

Though much effort was applied by blacks to reform the Republican Party, not all were prepared to allow only this kind of reform to define themselves. In 1882, the blacks seemed to have made a major decision to support a slate of candidates for local office in the court system, running on an independent ticket. Leaders in this drive, on the black side, were Isaac Myers, J. C. Fortie, William F. Taylor, J. L. H. Smith, John H. Murphy, and O. O. Deaver. That year, apparently as a reward for the black community's support of a successful campaign, William F. Taylor was made a bailiff in Criminal Court.[64]

By 1883, the Colored Advisory Council, with its headquarters at 16 Courtland Street, and with Joseph E. Briscoe at the helm, seems to have taken over the function of organizing the bulk of political activities in the community. The Council also seemed intent upon advising blacks in their best interests without regard to party ties, and, as such, called a meeting to select delegates to the National Convention of blacks to be held in Louisville, Kentucky, on September 24, 1883. John H. Murphy was an active associate of Briscoe.

Indeed, Murphy was becoming more active and aggressive in the early 1880s, as were Harvey Johnson and Briscoe. He had political experience from the time of the Black Border States' Convention in 1868. Murphy could be found at many meetings and taking a leading part in the discussion of matters; whether they dealt with politics or the schoolteacher situation. Murphy chaired a meeting of independent colored voters in September 1883, at which T. Thomas Fortune, a nationally prominent black newspaper editor from New York, spoke.[65]

Being independent-minded seemed an increasing phenomenon in the community. In October 1883, the Citizens' Reform Committee nominated a candidate for Mayor, J. Monroe Heishell, Fire Marshall. Many leading blacks supported him as an act of independence from the Republican Party; even Ferdinand Latrobe, the Democratic candidate was supposedly assisted by Rev. Charles W. Fitzhugh, pastor of Ebenezer A.M.E. Church. Fitzhugh's maverick behavior or kind of independence was not tolerated, however. His activities were considered serious enough to be investigated by the Morning Herald which found the Reverend implicated in a bribery scheme. Fitzhugh supposedly offered $100 to men to work the wards for Latrobe. Fitzhugh went to lengths to deny, in writing, his part in any bribery scheme; but Isaac Myers, as editor of the Colored Citizen, apparently had valuable documents indicting the veracity of Reverend Fitzhugh. Eventually, Myers' use of his paper forced Fitzhugh to admit his guilt.66

About two years later, in another reform attempt, blacks evidenced their independence. Many supported George William Brown for mayor, not the regular Republican Party choice. Bishop Wayman was on the nominating committee of this movement which selected persons to run for other municipal and state offices. Charles J. Bonaparte was one of the most prominent whites involved and spoke before an assembly of black voters at Raine's Hall on October 23, 1885. Reverend J. H. Reddick, popular black minister, was there at this meeting. Also on Sunday, October 25, many of the black clergy supported this reform effort in their sermons. Reverend J. H. Collett of Trinity A.M.E. spoke of this as the "Golden Opportunity" for all those "who would be freemen indeed (sic) and citizens in fact."67

That November, Douglass made an appearance at Centennial where he touched on the subject of independence in voting which was becoming a way of life for many in Baltimore. Douglass' topic was supposed to be "The Philosophy of Reform," but one paper said his remarks "soon took a political complexion." Douglass said:

Some of his race . . . were complaining of the evil of being out of office (Laughter) but being out of office was easier to bear than being in slavery. (Applause) He was sorry to see there was a feeling of ingratitude growing out of this not getting office. It was a common thing to hear men of his race say they were under no obligation to the republican (sic) party. If not under obligation to that party, then in Heaven's name to whom were they? If not to the strong arm which rent their chains and set them at liberty, then to whom? Speaking of those who advise the colored men to set up for themselves in politics, he said he would rather be a small piece of something than a large piece of nothing.

Whatever the striving may have been for independence and a desire to break away from the Republican Party in the 1880s, it would be decades before blacks en masse, became completly disillusioned with the party.[68]

Equally, the political fortunes of blacks did not fair better as the "gay" 90s approached and as Democrats in the city with impunity struck blacks from the voting rolls, and the division within the community itself as to the worth of Republicanism, was making smaller those who attempted to speak for the black electorate on the Republican Party's behalf. Harvey Johnson, a considerable influence in the city went over to the Prohibition Party. Then, too, the persistent calls by the leaders for blacks to register is evidence of apathy to the whole process.

The most telling picture of the mess in which things were was the deep division among black leaders in 1889, about the advisability of holding another state convention. Some like David D. Dickson and Joseph E. Briscoe wanted it supposedly to discuss the whole range of problems affecting blacks, while such old heads as Isaac Myers, H. J. Brown opposed it because they thought it was just another move by the ambitious to seek to push themselves forward as acceptable for the few jobs being granted by white officeholders.

That same year, a national effort to affect the lives of blacks by making use of the ministers was attempted. The new organization, called Home Guard, hoped that one thousand ministers would enlist in the body. In Baltimore, the new group was being pushed by Dr. T. G. Stewart of Bethel, President of the local chapter. He received assistance from Philip H. A. Braxton and Harvey Johnson.[69]

With the election of Harry S. Cummings to the City Council in 1890, the result in part of Democrats attempting to strategically place themselves ahead and beside disgruntled black Republicans; in a word, control and exercise as much influence in black political operations for its own benefits, blacks finally achieved the election of one of their own to office, something no amount of allegiance to the Republican Party ever allowed them to accomplish.

Ironically, within a year of Cummings' election, Isaac Myers was dead and so, basically was a kind of heroic leadership in Baltimore that spanned the days from Elisha Tyson to William Watkins, through George A. Hackett and then to Myers, himself, which made the City of Baltimore the most vibrant black community throughout most of the nineteenth century. These men and some others tried to achieve with a high regard to principle and ethical action, an abolition of slavery and prejudice, and the establishment of equitable and just relations between the races, in this, the nation's unofficial black capital. A great many successes attended their efforts.

Chapter V

[1]American, January 7, 1865, p. 4; August 15, 1878, p. 4; August 16, 1878, p. 4; October 18, 1881, p. 4; October 30, 1882, p. 4; Sun, February 11, 1869, p. 4; February 16, 1869, p. 1; February 24, 1869, p. 4; June 10, 1870, p. 1; December 17, 1875, p. 1; November 13, 1877, p. 1; August 16, 1878, p. 1; February 4, 1879, p. 4; Morning Herald, October 21, 1881, p. 1; December 16, 1881, p. 4; May 28, 1882, p. 4; People's Advocate, July 12, 1879, p. 1; April 23, 1881, p. 2.

[2]American, March 8, 1884, p. 4; March 11, 1884, p. 4; The Grit, March 15, 1884, p. 2; Sun, March 8, 1884, p. 4; August 14, 1884, p. 4; December 10, 1884, p. 4; New York Age, February 19, 1887, p. 4; Morning Herald, December 10, 1884, p. 3; February 13, 1887, p. 3; Afro-American, November 11, 1899, p. 2; December 28, 1901, p. 1; January 2, 1902, p. 4; Sun, February 25, 1890, p. 4; February 18, 1874, p. 4.

[3]People's Advocate, September 24, 1881, p. 2; American, October 3, 1884, p. 4; October 5, 1888, p. 4; October 9, 1888, p. 8; December 22, 1888, p. 6; May 7, 1889, p. 8; Morning Herald, January 26, 1888, p. 4; December 3, 1889, p. 1; December 28, 1889, p. 1; Sun, February 6, 1889, p. 4; New York Age, April 28, 1888, p. 1.

[4]A.M.E. Review, 1891, p. 351; Sun (Supplement), January 27, 1891, p. 4; American, January 27, 1891, p. 5.

[5]American, January 29, 1870, p. 4; March 2, 1870, p. 4; April 7, 1870, p. 4; Richard P. Fuke, Black Marylanders, 1864-1868 (University of Chicago, Ph.D., 1973), p. 57.

[6]American, June 13, 1873, p. 4.

[7]American, June 18, 1873, p. 4; Sun, June 19, 1873.

[8]Sun, January 19, 1875, p. 1.

[9]Sun, April 10, 1879, p. 1.

[10]American, April 12, 1879.

[11]Morning Herald, April 22, 1979., p. 4.

[12] _Morning Herald_, June 6, 1879, p. 3.

[13] _American_, September 12, 1879, p. 4.

[14] _Sun_, September 12, 1879, p. 4.

[15] _American_, December 5, 1879, p. 4; _Sun_, December 5, 1879, p. 1; December 8, 1879, p. 1.

[16] _American_, December 5, 1879, p. 1.

[17] _American_, December 5, 1879, p. 1.

[18] _Sun_, December 8, 1879, p. 1.

[19] _Sun_, January 7, 1880, p. 4.

[20] _Sun_, February 6, 1880, p. 4.

[21] _Sun_, April 6, 1880, p. 1.

[22] _Sun_, September 17, 1880, p. 4; _Morning Herald_, September 20, 1880, p. 4.

[23] _American_, December 25, 1880, p. 4.

[24] _American_, December 25, 1880, p. 4; _Sun_, December 25, 1880, p. 4.

[25] _American_, December 25, 1880, p. 4.

[26] _American_, January 7, 1881, p. 4.

[27] _American_, February 21, 1882, p. 4; _Morning Herald_, February 21, 1882, p. 4.

[28] _American_, November 18, 1882, p. 4.

[29] _American_, July 10, 1883, p. 4.

[30] _American_, July 10, 1883, p. 4; February 24, 1886, p. 4; April 6, 1887; _Sun_, October 5, 1888, p. 4.

[31] _American_, June 11, 1873, p. 4; June 14, 1873, p. 4; _Sun_, June 28, 1873, p. 11.

[32] _American_, December 2, 1873, p. 4.

[33] _American_, December 9, 1873, p. 4.

[34] _American_, March 14, 1874, p. 4.

[35]American, March 17, 1874, p. 4.

[36]American, July 3, 1874, p. 4.

[37]American, August 11, 1874, p. 4.

[38]American, September 15, 1874, p. 4.

[39]American, October 31, 1876, p. 4; Sun, January 9, 1877, p. 4.

[40]American, September 22, 1876, p. 4.

[41]American, October 30, 1877, p. 4; Sun, October 30, 1877, p. 1.

[42]Sun, March 27, 1879, p. 4.

[43]American, April 16, 1879, p. 4.

[44]American, May 5, 1879, p. 4.

[45]American, May 27, 1879, p. 4; Sun, May 27, 1879, p. 4.

[46]Sun, May 29, 1879, p. 1.

[47]American, May 31, 1879, p. 4.

[48]American, June 15, 1879, p. 4; Sun, June 14, 1879, p. 1.

[49]American, September 14, 1879, p. 4.

[50]American, October 8, 1879, p. 4.

[51]American, October 22, 1879, p. 4.

[52]American, October 28, 1879, p. 4.

[53]Sun, November 13, 1879, p. 1; American, November 1879, p. 4.

[54]American, December 4, 1879, p. 4; December 17, 1879, p. 4.

[55]American, February 10, 1880, p. 4; February 11, 1880, p. 4; Sun, February 10, 1880, p. 1; February 11, 1880, p. 4.

[56]American, March 8, 1880, p. 4; March 10, 1880, p. 1; Sun, February 26, 1880, p. 4; March 11, 1880, p. 1; Morning Herald, March 30, 1880, p. 4.

[57]American, May 17, 1880, p. 4.

[58]Morning Herald, July 16, 1880, p. 4; September 11, 1880, p. 4.

[59]American, November 9, 1880, p. 4;

[60]Morning Herald, April 20, 1881, p. 4; May 21, 1881, p. 4; American, May 21, 1881, p. 4; June 1, 1881, p. 4; October 22, 1881, p. 4;

[61]American, November 5, 1881, p. 4.

[62]American, April 25, 1882, p. 4; August 28, 1882.

[63]Morning Herald, June 19, 1882, p. 4.

[64]American, October 23, 1882, p. 4; October 30, 1882, p. 2.

[65]American, August 1, 1883, p. 4; November 2, 1883, p. 2; Sun, September 14, 1883, p. 4.

[66]Morning Herald, October 10, 1883; October 20, 1883, p. 1; October 22, 1883, p. 1; October 29, 1883, p. 4.

[67]Morning Herald, October 24, 1885, p. 1; October 26, 1885, p. 1.

[68]American, April 9, 1884, p. 4.

[69]American, February 14, 1889, p. 6.

Chapter VI

BALTIMORE AS THE CHIEF BLACK METROPOLIS

Numerically, before and after the Civil War, the blacks of Baltimore constituted one of the largest black populations of the nineteenth century; and thus, this fact along would make it a significant place in black life in this time period. Indeed, at the time of the Civil War, the city had 26 thousand free blacks and the state altogether had about one-fifth of the approximate 450 thousand free blacks in the country--the largest concentration of free blacks--additional facts that speak to the overall. importance of the Baltimore and Maryland communities. Yet, just as important as these realities, there lived and were connected with the city, men and activities of outstanding and unique merit which focused even more attention upon Baltimore, and thus made it a vital center of things. Something of the foregoing histories of the lives of such men as Elisha Tyson, William Watkins, George A. Hackett, and Isaac Myers, hopefully, underscore this point. In essence, then Baltimore was the chief black metropolis of the nineteenth century.

Baltimore stood at the crossroads to many diversified activities that enlivened it. Secret orders were founded in the city and, of course, had their annual meetings there. Baltimore had notable literary societies and the achievements of its sons and daughters in the field of letters were important. The city, with its churches, generally noted to be the largest and finest group amongst a black population; and, of course, the Douglass Institute allowed for many an important visitor or affair to use its platforms to promote some matter or idea to the country-at-large. Another measure of the solidness of the community can be seen, perhaps, in the generally held belief up to the early 1900s, that the city had more black home owners than any other metropolis. In addition to all this, the blacks of Baltimore seemed most conscious of the significant aspects of black history and its connection with their town and state. Baltimore was indeed a city of lights on the Potomac.

Not much can be gleaned from sources of the dynamism of free black Baltimore society, its day-to-day existence, the foundation of the city's pride of place in black history, prior to the 1860s. These free blacks became noteworthy in the press and documents of the time before the Civil War, only in relation to the slavery issue. But the free blacks lived lives to a degree independent of the benumbing topic of slavery--it surely was not a 24-hour a day obsession. Though it colored much of the activities in the community.

On the eve of the 1860s, however, there is an overall picture of black Baltimore free life in action which can be culled from the reporting of a Baltimore correspondent to The Weekly Anglo-African, a New York publication.

In mid-year 1859, Baltimore's correspondent, under the pen name, "Mifflin," most likely the Rev. John Mifflin Brown of Bethel Church, started this series of letters to the Anglo-African. In his introductory letter dated July 28, "Mifflin" stated he had been reading black newspapers from since the time of the founding of the Colored American in the late 1830s. Of Baltimore, he said "No city where I have been can boast of better churches amongst our people--other cities may have more of them, but our people displayed taste and judgment in the structure of theirs." He listed the total number of churches as being six A.M.E., five M.E., one A.M.E. Zion, three Baptist, and one each of the Presbyterian and Episcopal persuasions. There were also present 15 schools in operation from early fall to the "warm season," which were at this time in July in the midst of their annual exhibitions--a closing display of what a year's work had produced. Recently, Mrs. Mary A. Handy of Water's A.M.E. chapel, a granddaughter of the late Bishop William Water, held a "grand" exhibition. Mrs. Maria Stewart at Madison Avenue Presbyterian had had a similar affair.[1]

The Maria Stewart that "Mifflin" mentioned had an interesting history which doubtlessly enlivened or gave a particularly fine edge to her teaching. Born in Hartford, Connecticut, in 1803, she was orphaned at five, brought up by a minister, married at twenty, widowed in 1829. After which, she soon joined the church. Not long after that, she showed William L. Garrison, who had recently established his newspaper in Boston, a manuscript she had been laboring on which she eventually published with his encouragement, under the title Meditations. Soon after that, she moved to New York, met young Alexander Crummell, a black Episcopalian minister who further encouraged and directed her in her efforts to obtain an education. She subsequently became a teacher and finally ended up in Baltimore by 1853.

In his first letter, "Mifflin" had other news to report as well. He reported on William T. Dixon closing his school in order to return to New York to try out for the ministry at his father's church, Abyssinia Baptist. His father, George Dixon, was a clerk of the church. "Mifflin" also lamented the fact that though Miss Lake of Annapolis' entry of needlework, a portrait of George Washington, at the National Fair was vocally proclaimed the best item in that category, she was not awarded a prize because, in the words of the judges, she was a "nigger."

As for his letter written August 8, "Mifflin" told of the large number of Baltimore blacks who journeyed to Harrisburg, Pennsylvania, to join in the First of August celebrations, a commemoration of the emancipation of slaves in Jamaica by the British in 1833. "Mifflin" recalled how when quite young, he had attended similar services at Zion Church in New York, where the white Reverend Leroy Sunderland spoke and where he gazed upon Christopher Rush, an organizer of that branch of black Methodism.

The correspondent journeyed to Harrisburg and heard Rev. Henry H. Garnet speak. He wrote, "Mr. G. excelled himself." Garnet was a runaway slave from Maryland, who later became a forceful abolitionist, newspaper editor, minister, and well-regarded overall black leader throughout the North. "Mifflin" further characterized Garnet by saying, "He has the power to fire up his auditors in such a way as to make every man feel like daring to do." "Mifflin" pointed out that Rev. Garnet was just one of the illustrious sons of Maryland to become famous after running away; the other famous ones being Frederick Douglass Samuel Ringgold Ward, a cousin of Garnet, and James W. C. Pennington.

The Rev. Charles W. Gardiner followed Garnet and was thought to be in his eighties, but whose "eloquence" had not diminished, especially as it attacked his home state Pennsylvania's own special kinds of proscriptions against blacks. After leaving Harrisburg, "Mifflin" stopped off in York, Pennsylvania, on his way back to Baltimore. He described what he found in that city—the people were most industrious and thrifty. He singled out, especially for these enconiums, Mr. G. J. Goodridge.

During the time of the celebrations of the First of August Day, back in Baltimore, the Odd Fellows, a secret society, had a picnic, just one of several to take place in the city. The Odd Fellows picnic and parade was admirably led by George A. Hackett, who generally received the sobriquet of "Col. Geor" and who, according to "Mifflin," directed things "with much credit to himself and satisfaction to his friends." At the Odd Fellows celebration, Past Grand Master Joseph T. Jackson was presented with a set of fine china.

There were other outings, such as the Bethel Ladies' Sewing Circle, which was more selective in its invitations to the community than the Odd Fellows. The Barbers Association had 1,000 present at its affair, while that of the Family picnic surpassed that number; and William H. Woods, a schoolteacher, organized a picnic just for the children. It seems the first week of August could be called city-wide picnic week, as far as blacks were concerned. Such being the case, "Mifflin" related his opposition to such an extravagant use of money out of poor pockets, made the poorer. The total spent in railroad fares to the destination of these outings was, in "Mifflin's" eyes astronomical and should be put to better use.

In this same August 8 letter, "Mifflin" reported on the August 4 anniversary service of the Moral Mental Improvement Society of Bethel, one of the leading literary and debating societies in the city. The audience in attendance, however, was much reduced by the rain and heat. The Rev. John M. Brown was president and he made the opening remarks; William T. Dixon, secretary. In the annual report, it was stated that one young man was at Oberlin College in Ohio, studying for the ministry out of funds provided by the Society.

After business came essays by John Wesley Cepheus on Ancient History, by Miss Annetta Jordan on Modern Literature; but, due to the lateness of the hour, Rev. Harrison H. Webb, who was supposed to make the annual address, was not able to do so, nor was the prize-winning essay on "Health" heard. The Moral Mental Improvement Society met the first Sunday of each month at Bethel and, in this regard, the theme for the October 1 program was to center around missionary work.

In closing this August 8 letter, "Mifflin" described the recent visit of Rev. William Russell from Cumberland, Maryland, to the city and the creditable showing he made before several audiences.[2]

The letter dated August 29 drew a vivid picture of "Mifflin's" recent sojourn at the country estate of

Thomas L. Sterrit, 20 miles outside the city. Judging from the lengthy description of the abundant flowers at Sterrit's home, it might be safe to assume that "Mifflin" was a true nature lover. In the same letter, he said every second Tuesday of each month, those who had an interest in the success of Sabbath Schools in the city met. The organization, The Colored Sabbath School Union of Baltimore, founded many years before 1859 had Rev. John Fortie as its first president, who was still foremost in its activities.[3]

A good bit of "Mifflin's" message for September dealt with the lyceum or debating societies. Six were of particular note. One of the best, the Galbreth, was under John H. Butler's presidency, who was described as "one of the nature's noblemen." In the Galbreth's opening lecture for the season, Rev. Harrison H. Webb spoke of "The Antagonistic Properties of Nature." The Society was named in honor of Rev. George Galbreth of Zion African Methodist to which Butler belonged. The membership was relatively young. Besides giving lectures, debates were staged which discussed the issues of the day. It had a good library and an adequate meeting place. Every week the members sat through instructions on grammar, rhetoric, logic, declamation or composition given by one of the membership. Some of the ladies had recently presented the Lyceum with a set of the Britannica Encyclopedia.

In other matters related in his September newsletter, "Mifflin" reported that G. J. Goodridge of York, Pennsylvania, was preparing to take over William T. Dixon's school in the city, Dixon having finally gone to New York to study for the ministry there. In the last week of September, "Mifflin" sadly reported the death of his friend, Thomas Sterrit, whose country quarters he had recently visited and of whose beautiful layout he had reported to the readers. Sterrit was in the lumber business and, by implication in the letter, he left quite a small fortune for his survivors.

In this same article, "Mifflin" let it be known that Baltimoreans were willing and noted for taking care of its less fortunate. Along these lines, he reported how George A. Hackett, Augustus Roberts, J. P. Adams, and Alexander A. Roberts and some others sponsored a benefit concert for Mrs. Maria Stewart who had been recently widowed. Those who performed included Harrison H. Webb, Jr., described as excellent at the pianoforte and the young Miss A. Fleetwood, a vocalist, who also had a large following in the city. The benefit was quite successful.[4]

In the meanwhile, "Mifflin" also wrote of having seen Rev. Noah Davis' autobiography which he was trying to sell to pay for the freedom of some of his family still in slavery. Reverend Davis was pastor of the Baptist Church on Saratoga Street, that had been erected only a few years before.

With the passing of Rev. John Fortie, one of the city's oldest and most respected ministers, the Colored Sabbath School Union passed a resolution calling for a commemoration of his life at a special service to take place at Zion Church, with the Baptist minister William Williams and Rev. Harrison H. Webb of St. James Episcopal Church, in charge of the services. From Fortie's son, Henry, "Mifflin" got a few facts about the deceased. John Fortie was born in 1783, "got" religion in 1800, and was licensed to preach July 1, 1816, having as his first sermon Hebrews 2:3. He was ordained a deacon by Bishop Robert R. Roberts on April 22, 1822. His ordination as an elder was by Bishop Beverly Waugh on March 25, 1838.

Throughout his ministry, Fortie had preached 1,916 sermons, and baptized 1,096; the figure for the marriages he performed was lost. He taught school for nearly fifty years. In "Mifflin's" words, he was "not a man of varied learning, what he knew he knew well," however. He was considered one of the best black arithmeticians in the city.

While he had a lifelong attachment to the Methodist Episcopal Church in his last years, he favored the African Methodist Episcopal Church, and had actually started advising the young of his acquaintance to enter that denomination instead of his own, doubtlessly because of the racial discrimination in his own sect. Harrison Webb fortified this statement by recalling at the memorial services, Fortie's own words to the effect that if he had been younger, he would have gone over to the A.M.E. connection himself. This was a testimony, of sorts, to the success of Bethel Church.[5]

In his letter of early December, "Mifflin" stated he had been to Wilberforce, Ohio, where the black community and its recently founded college for the A.M.E. Church was thriving.[6]

Sometime in December also, someone under the penname "Praesidium" wrote to The Weekly Anglo-African decrying the fact of there being only two bishops in the A.M.E. Church and thought those two should be augmented because of the vast territory and numbers they had to supervise. This Baltimorean thought that there were five likely candidates for the new bishop's seat, if one were created. They were J. P. Campbell of Philadelphia, W. R. Revels of Chicago, J. M. Brown of Baltimore, A. W. Wayman of Washington, and G. Green of Ohio.

At around General Conference time of the A.M.E. Church in early 1860, "Praesidium's" earlier suggestions were viewed as interfering in an unhelpful manner in the affairs of the Church. Indeed, in response to one of his statements that Bishop Paul Quinn had told him he had thoughts about retiring; the Bishop called his assertion a lie. For suggesting younger men for the bishopric, if a new one had been created, "Praesidium" apparently caused many an older minister, with long service, to soundly denounce the idea as subversive. In a subsequent letter, "Praesidium" recanted his views and let it be known he was not interested in imitating Martin Luther.[7]

After "Praesidium's" brief stint as correspondent, "Mifflin" returned to do the letter writing to New York. During the Christmas season, much of what Baltimore was like for its black residents at this season was revealed in a letter dated the day after Christmas. Because Christmas was on a Sunday that year, there was not the usual level and amount of noise, with boys and their firecrackers. Indeed, the mayor had ordered the Sabbath be strictly observed with regard to the matter of raucus behavior not being permitted. "Mifflin" added, that having been in most large cities, he had not witnessed so strict an observance of the Sabbath as took place in Baltimore.[8]

Also in this Christmas letter, having had time to reflect on John Brown's raid on Harper's Ferry, his trial and subsequent hanging, "Mifflin" commented on the reactionary response to the whole affair in language with which he was most familiar. He said "The frogs, mice, and flies of Egypt did not haunt Pharoah's palace more than the Negro haunts, perplexes, and maddens the councils of the people of this country." He related to his Northern audience, in effect, preparing them for the consequences, if certain state legislatures such as in Mississippi, Tennessee, Kentucky, Missouri, and Arkansas then giving "grave" consideration to the notion of expelling free blacks from their borders, carried out their threats. The misery and consequences could be like those experienced when Indiana and Illinois once expelled its free blacks, terming them a nuisance.

"Mifflin" did not dwell only on John Brown and its after-effects, he reported on other matters as well. He had high praise for the Ladies' Sewing Circle of Bethel Church that had recently had its "grand demonstration" on Thanksgiving and were addressed by Rev. Harrison H. Webb, Rev. John M. Brown, James H. A. Johnson, Raymond Carter, and James Buchanan. The Circle aided the poor by giving them clothing, food, and fuel. It had helped two hundred in the past winter, had bought nearly one hundred cords of wood.

The lyceums were also active with their winter series of lectures. The Galbreth Lyceum had one featuring Rev. Hiram R. Revels which, according to "Mifflin," "all speak of it in praise." The Lone Star Lyceum had recently dedicated a beautiful room and acquired an admirable library. The Mental and Moral Improvement Society of Bethel had its semi-annual gathering. The order of the affair went something like this: Rev. John M. Brown, President, made an opening address; Mr. William H. Woods, a teacher, read an essay, "The School Master." Miss Josephine Wells read one entitled "Prayer." Miss Mary A. Jacques' was on "Botany." Mr. G. J. Goodridge spoke on "Memory." And then Rev. Harrison H. Webb gave an address on "Advantages of Mental Culture."

A debating period ensued which took up the question, "Which had benefited the community more, the pulpit or the press?" John H. Butler, J. H. A. Johnson, A. Ward Handy, and Raymond Carter were the discussants-- all former William Watkins' pupils, except, perhaps Handy. The press was the victor in this dispute. A part of the occasion was the presentation of a bookcase by the ladies, which was immediately filled with $75.00 worth of books.

An early spring letter contained more information on the activities of Bethel's Ladies' Sewing Circle. Mrs. Eliza A. Tilghman, Hackett's daughter, on behalf of the ladies, presented $600 to the Trustees, and at a "grand" dinner given by the Trustees of Bethel for the congregation, there were 309 at the first table alone. There was plenty of good singing and music from Benjamin Murphy and Joseph Wheeler. The Ladies' Sewing Circle had been given five hundred loaves of bread by certain men to distribute to the poor, with the understanding that they were to do so in conjunction with a

259

celebration of George Washington's birthdate. These loaves seemed to have been distributed at this Trustees' dinner. To say the least, however, it was rather ironic that the bread should be given under such circumstances, when blacks were not in many official circumstances considered citizens and were being urged and told by many to leave certain parts of the United States, or all of it altogether. The president of the Circle, Mrs. Annetta Jordan, was in charge of dividing the loaves.[9]

The 31st of March letter was sent off by someone signing his name, "Delphic." Much in this letter was written about the plight of Enoch Stewart, a preacher at Ebenezer A.M.E. Church and apparently a slave, who was put in a slave-holding pen at Campbell's Jail to be sold if his wife could not raise the necessary money needed, $500. She had already in hand $300. To raise the rest, there was a dinner held at Mrs. Stewart's at which such speakers as Henry McNeil Turner, Rev. William H. Waters, and Rev. Scott spoke. "Delphic" himself also said a few words. The Ebenezer choir also participated.[10]

In the meantime, other matters had taken place. At an affair given by the St. James Episcopal Sabbath School on the 13th of March, Rev. H. H. Webb, the pastor of the church, spoke. At Bethel, there was a revival going on. Bishop D. A. Payne arrived in the city for the 14th, sufficiently recovered from a late illness. He brought with him Rev. James Lynch, son of local M.E. preacher Benjamin Lynch, whom Payne had been training for the ministry since he was 13 years old. Sometime afterward, Lynch went to Dartmouth College and was at the present stationed at Galena, Illinois. "Delphic" volunteered that Bishop Payne had done more to encourage the industrious, but idle young men, to enter the minisry than any other person.

The Weekly Anglo-African reportage continued until the middle of 1860 and gives a look at the dynamics of black Baltimore society as seen in its most important weekly, daily, and monthly activities. Another measure of the vibrancy of the community can be seen with regard to its prominent families having sway throughout most of the nineteenth century. These leading women and men, not necessarily in the limelight as orators, or writers, say as a Watkins, Hackett, or Myers, had distinctions which should not be overlooked. They seemed a part of the foundation. Family ties of the prominent are dis-cernible in some cases and can be characterized as probable or problematic in others. Clearly, however, some of the more outstanding families were the Gilliard,

Fortie, and Deaver families.

Jacob Gilliard was a man set free from slavery at age 45, who apparently labored to pay for his two sons' freedom as well, as he is the person granting them their freedom or manumission papers, filed in court documents in 1808. Jacob, Jr., was at this time 38, and Nicholas, 24. Jacob Gilliard, Sr. was surely one of the most remarkable black men in Baltimore, of whom little is known. Though unable to write, his name appeared on several significant deeds. He was a trustee, along with his son Jacob, when in 1802 the old abolitionist building was purchased from James Carey and became known as Sharp Street Church and School.[11]

When blacks became dissatisfied with being under the control of whites, as Sharp Street was under the control of the Methodist General Conference, some members withdrew and help found Bethel Church. Both Jacob Gilliards, Senior and Junior, were trustees, according to the deed of purchase of this congregation's first sanctuary as well.

Certainly it must be concluded that Jacob Gilliard, Senior, had some influence or place of honor in his community. Some little more information of his life can be seen in an advertisement he was forced to put in the newspapers against his own son, Jacob, in 1805. The advertisement, titled "Base Ingratitude," offered a reward of $40.00 for the return of his son whom he claimed was addicted to gambling. The old man said he was about to be forced to pay a sum of $510.00 which he had given as bonded security, apparently to the master of his son, for allowing him to roam as a free man. Jacob, Senior, said:

> I leave it to a generous public to judge, whether such base ingratitude in a young man towards an aged father can pass unnoticed.-- who, in his declining days, is obliged to pay a sum of money which he is unable to raise, without selling part of that property which he labored hard to produce against old age come on. My lot was such that I was not at liberty to do anything for myself till after the age of 45 years, and now I am obliged to part with that which my old age requires for my support and comfort. This is the sole cause of my offering the above reward.[12]

Gilliard had posted for sale in the papers of the same

date some of his property. The final particulars of this episode are not known.

Jacob Gilliard, Senior's significance in the lives of both Sharp Street and Bethel Churches, was important from another angle, besides the monetary one. Daniel Coker, the very literate leader of, at one time either Sharp Street or Bethel, married Maria, the daughter of Jacob, Junior. Similarly, George A. Hackett, generally considered the most important leader in Baltimore from the 1840s to his death in 1870, married Mary Jane, daughter of Rev. Nicholas Gilliard. Indeed, it seems the Hackett family was further united with the Gilliards, as Hackett had a nephew named George A. Hackett Gilliard. So, in a sense, to the extent it can be said that Coker and Hackett had essential roles in the development of black Baltimore and black history, in general, it can be said that Jacob Gilliard, Senior, is part and parcel of their lives.[13]

Yet this does not end the seeming influence of the Gilliards or their association with that which is noteworthy. In 1872, a J. E. M. Gilliard returned to Baltimore, having spent several years on the West Coast, in San Francisco, where he was part owner of The Elevator and quite an orator and regional leader, judging from the news accounts. He was often the main speaker on auspicious occasions. J. E. M. Gilliard, while in Baltimore, sent a letter back to California and the internal evidence suggest his socially elite position in black society throughout the United States, something surely sensibly his, if he were an offshoot of Jacob Gilliard, Senior, which seems likely.

Gilliard said he arrived in Baltimore just in time to speak during the election excitement of that year. He observed:

How the times, the manners, and the men have changed! Nineteen years ago, aye! twenty-one years ago I used to run up Calvert Street to Monument Square when fifes were playing and drums beating and I heard Gen. F. Pierce of New Hampshire--then the President nominee of the Democratic party. I wondered then why no colored man ever stood up there in that square and pleaded against what I conceive to be the best interests of man. Little did I think that the time would come when from that very standpoint where the greatest minds who have stood, that I should occupy a position to the right of the Chairman of the L. C. Committee, and speak in company with the Vice-President elect, Hon. H. Wilson, Postmaster Gen. J. A. J. Creswell, Professor W. H. Day, and other distinguished gentlemen who addressed that vast concourse of enthusiastic Republicans.[14]

The Gilliard Family was, without question, well entrenched in what constituted the best of black life in the nineteenth century.

Similarly, the Fortie name belonged to a remarkable group of men of the nineteenth century, of whom Jacob Fortie was father of John Fortie and John Fortie was father of John C. Fortie and Henry P. Fortie. An observer of Baltimore in the 1830s said that Jacob Fortie was "regarded by the colored members of that church (Methodist Episcopal) as a venerable patriarch among their preachers."

Jacob Fortie's veneration also may relate, in part, to his being an early member of efforts to form an independent black Methodist meeting in Baltimore in the 1780s. He remained a part of the independent black church movement long enough to be represented when a building was purchased by Bethel and set apart for worship. However, by 1826, Jacob Fortie left the independent black church movement and returned to the Methodist Episcopal Church, administering to such black congregations in the denomination as Sharp Street, Dallas Street, Asbury, and John Wesley Churches. The elder Fortie was an active minister until the early 1840s when it was written in church records at that time that he was too infirm to preach.

Jacob Fortie's son, John, was to become a minister in the Methodist Episcopal Churches, serving the same congregations as his father. He also conducted a school east of the Jones Falls for fifty years which was nearly as significant an influence among East Baltimoreans as William Watkins' school was among West Baltimoreans. John Fortie apparently was in some phase of the shipping business before the Civil War. His name could be found in several instances which indicated his high standing in the community, such as being president of the Banneker Monument Committee, a group that intended to raise a monument to the accomplishments of supposedly the country's first black scientist. He also was a founder and longtime president of the Sunday School Union established in the city.

Fortie's name was also found on a petition from the black congregations of the Methodist Episcopal Church asking the General Conference in 1848 that something be done to remedy the denial of seats and votes to blacks in official meetings of the church. The petitioners said they did not want to join the African Methodist Episcopal connection, but wanted all black clergy of the Methodist Episcopal Church in the United States organized into an annual conference under the supervision of the Baltimore Annual Conference. Although rejected at this time, the contents of this proposal were accepted in 1864, some five years after the death of John Fortie.

John Fortie died on July 6, 1859, aged 76. He was nearly a lifetime resident of the city. His obituary was one of the few of blacks found in newspapers of the period before the Civil War. It said that he had amassed considerable property. Incidentally, his wife died a few weeks before he did. It was further stated in this obituary that "by his uniform Christian deportment and correct life attached to himself a large circle of friends, not only among those of his own color, but among the white population."

John C. Fortie was born in September, 1835 and was apprenticed to the shoemaking trade. During the war he served as a sergeant in the 30th U.S. Colored Troops. After the war, he was a man of considerable importance, often called upon to speak, preside, or act as secretary at various gatherings. He was also an associate of Isaac Myers in his labor organizing efforts. In fact, Isaac Myers was a pupil of his father.[15]

Apparently John C. Fortie had a genial spirit like his grandfather and father, and was not given to undue ambition. He spoke before the Colored Fourteenth Ward Republican Association in May 1869, just about the time when the Fifteenth Amendment which would guarantee blacks the right to vote, appeared certain to pass. Several blacks were vying for positions of leadership of a group so as to be able to bargain with the white bosses in the party for patronage.

Fortie said, speaking about this scramble for leadership:

There is a great talk about a leader, and that question has been agitated for the last three months, until we cannot meet one another on the street but that we hear what party do you belong to? Have you taken the Oath? Have you been sworn? and all such foolishness, that sleepeth but in the bosoms of fools, who, for personal ambition and selfish motives arouse these dissensions now and then among the people.[16]

About twelve years later when it seemed possible that a violent fight would take place between him and another person for the presidency of a State Republican Convention, he immediately withdrew his name to preserve harmony. Fortie generally stated his support of the Republican Party was because of the party's principles, not its men.

In addition to political work, Fortie, as a veteran, was also a visible worker and leader of the local G.A.R. post, Lincoln Post No. 7, having a conspicuous part at its Memorial Day celebrations.

In 1895, the Afro praised John C. Fortie's lifelong interest in racial advancement and let the public know his latest interest was to get the ladies involved in the women's department of the Northwest Family Supply Company, a cooperative grocery business. Of John's brother Henry, not much is known, except that he was an important Mason. As with the Gilliards, then, to say the least, the Forties were an integral part of the continuity of life in black Baltimore throughout the nineteenth century, of which more should be known.[17]

Another family name that stands out throughout the nineteenth century happens to belong to the Deavers. A James Deaver looms as important as early as 1826; he served as chairman of a meeting held at Sharp Street Church when blacks considered a proposal of endorsing an American Colonization Memorial. About six months later, James Deaver presided at a July 4 dinner meeting at the house of James Walker of the Friendship Society, probably Friendship Lodge, the first masonic lodge in Maryland, to commemorate the abolition of slavery in New York. At this meeting, various toasts were offered in praise of freedom, John Jay, Freedom's Journal, Elisha Tyson, and so forth. One toast was "The members of Friendship Society--may they be distinguished for their integrity, love of harmony and anxiety for improvement."

There was also a toast to Deaver, "The President of the day--may he continue to be distinguished by his moral conduct." After this toast, Deaver arose, made a short speech, and offered his own toast, "May justice as well as law be a guide to the Judge of Baltimore City

Court--Woolfolk improved." Deaver's toast was in reference to the trial of Benjamin Lundy, Quaker abolitionist and publisher of The Genius of Universal Emancipation, who brought suit against Austin Woolfolk, a slave trader who nearly killed him on the street because he disagreed with Lundy's anti-slavery activities.

James Deaver was also an associate of Hezekiah Grice. Grice, the initiator of the National Negro Convention Movement in 1830, brought together black leaders from throughout the United States to devise plans to better the lot of the race in the country. Deaver was a delegate from Maryland to the first convention held in September 1830 in Philadelphia. Deaver also was a member of the Grice's Legal Rights Association, an organization also formed around 1830, to determine the legal status of blacks in the various states, so that the better one would be able to defend them in their rights.

The death of James Deaver is not known, nor is it known for certain who were his descendants, but they may have been Charles and Smith Nicholas Deaver, both of whom were born about 1820. Both of whom died in the same year, 1884.

Both Charles and Smith Nicholas Deaver were remarkable in having worked nearly fifty years for one employer. Smith Nicholas was apprenticed with a Dr. Aiken, a druggist. After his apprenticeship, Smith Deaver became an employee of R. H. Coleman & Company. His obituary said he was very competent and was generally known as Dr. Deaver.

On the other hand, Charles Deaver was apprenticed as a butcher and became an employee of Sterling Thomas & Sons. He worked many years out of Belair Market. He was very amiable and known as "Uncle Charley" by his many friends. He was the father-in-law of Isaac Myers; Myers' having married his daughter Sarah E. as his second wife. Isaac Myers, of course, was one of the leading blacks in Baltimore, even the country, after 1865 until his death in 1891. He helped to establish the Chesapeake and Marine Railway and Drydock Company, held up as an example to follow by black businessmen elsewhere. He also helped establish the first savings and loan among Baltimore's blacks. Myers' marriage into the Deaver Family added luster to his own life, because the Deaver name was one singled out in an 1878 account as being leading socialites in the community.

Possibly Robert M. Deaver was another relative of

266

James Deaver. He was a well-off, long-time superintendent of the Sunday School at Madison Avenue Presbyterian Church. Robert Deaver, among his many assignments from the community, was made president of the Colored Protestant Sunday School Association at its tenth anniversary in 1885. Incidentally, John C. Fortie was secretary for that year. Robert Deaver's name also appeared prominently in many attempts by blacks to improve their public schools. It seems that he could be counted on to link his name with many activities in which Isaac Myers took an interest.

Indeed, another Deaver, O. O. Deaver, appeared to work in tandem with the Myerses, especially in Republican Party matters. The Banneker Social Club was organized in 1879 with O. O. Deaver as secretary and George A. Myers, Isaac Myers' son as treasurer. The club contained 300 members and, supposedly, held one of the largest and most successful private picnics in the state in 1879.

The social event of July 1891, according to some accounts, was the marriage of Robert Deaver's daughter to Reverend C. Lee Jefferson, pastor of the Second Presbyterian Church, West Chester, Pennsylvania. At the wedding, Mrs. Isaac Myers, Sarah Deaver, appeared. To be sure, Deaver was a name of considerable prominence in black Baltimore whose eminence lasted throughout the nineteenth century, and whose likely progenitor seems to have been James Deaver.[18]

The evidence seems to support the fact that the Gilliard, Fortie, and Deaver families were quite remarkable ones for the variety of their concerns. There were other families, however, singled out in an 1878 article as having standing in a social sense. These families were the Quomeys, Briscoes, Masons, Wheatleys, Rogers, Emersons, Seatons, Johnsons, Browns, and Kelleys. It was said that the name of any of these families attached to "the circular of a ball or sociable, a picnic or entertainment is a certain evidence of its gentility." It was also stated of black Baltimore society, as opposed to what was happening in some other places, that skin color did not prove a hindrance or an advantage in most cases to those entering into the various social circles. One observer, the dentist, Philip T. Gross, who was trained in Springfield, Massachusetts, and who had traveled extensively throughout the United States and Europe, said that black society in Baltimore was far superior to any he had seen anywhere else.[19]

Presumably Dr. H. J. Brown was of the Browns referred to above. He was prominently mentioned throughout the last third of the nineteenth century. His marriage had great social significance as well. He and Richard T. Greener married the daughters of James H. Fleet. Fleet was from Washington and had been vice president of the National Negro Convention in 1835. Greener's grandfather was one of the earliest teachers in Baltimore, and Richard, himself, was the first black graduate of Harvard College.

H. J. Brown had secured his education in the North. He was self-taught in the fields of phrenology, physiology, physiognomy, hypopathy, and electricity, as they relate to medicine. He acquired all this knowledge, apparently, in Philadelphia and lectured throughout the country. Once, while in New Haven, Connecticut, at the Temple Street Church, his performance was described to have surpassed others well-known in his field. It was said of him at this time that, "He devoted himself to the arduous task of climbing the hill of science amid the constant struggle for daily bread in one of the humble occupations of life."

Brown was quite an entertainer. At one of his parties at his residence, 141 West Biddle, in honor of Frederick Douglass and United States Senator Blanche K. Bruce, guests included the socially elite from throughout the country. At the marriage of his daughter, Ione Eiveta, the services were performed by C. B. Perry, white rector of St. Mary's Episcopal Church. The daughters of such persons as Frederick Douglass, William E. Matthews, John H. Butler, James T. Bradford, Richard Mason, Bishop Wayman, James Jackson were in attendance, perhaps as bridal maids.[20]

Another Episcopalian with social eminence as Brown was Richard Mason, presumably of the Masons mentioned in the 1878 article already cited. Mason was a leading shoemaker and old communicant of St. James. His store was on Baltimore Street and his work had been exhibited at the Maryland Institute. He was a founding member of St. James Beneficial Society, one of the strongest mutual aid societies. One son, Casius M. C. Mason became an Episcopal priest and was the moving force in the founding of St. Mary's Chapel in Baltimore and All Saints in St. Louis. Casius Mason, a shoemaker before becoming a priest, had Daniel Hale Williams apprenticed to him when he came to live in Baltimore with the Bishop family. Williams later became an outstanding physician and was the first doctor to operate successfully on the heart.[21]

There was a third important Episcopal family, the Bishops. The name of Bishop with any prominence attached to it was first connected with Hannibal Bishop, who opened a school in 1810. Perhaps Hannibal Bishop was father, grandfather to William H. Bishop. William H. Bishop ran a barber shop on the corner of Pratt and Charles Streets for a number of years. For fifty-five years he was a vestryman at St. James Episcopal Church, and as a man of wealth, his name could easily be found attached to any worthy cause. One of his sons, William H., Junior, was to hold a clerkship in the Federal Government, especially in the Internal Revenue Service for over thirty-five years. He also worked in Baltimore's branch of Freedmen's Bank. His minister, Harrison H. Webb, was his boss. William Bishop, Jr., also assisted Casius Mason with the founding of St. Mary's. For a long time, William Bishop, Jr., was President of the Baltimore Assembly, said to be the most exclusive black organization in the city. Another son of William, Senior, Hutchins C., was the first black graduate of the Episcopal Church's General Theological Seminary in New York, and for over thirty years was rector of St. Phillip's in New York, the second oldest black Episcopal church in the country, and in the early twentieth century, called the wealthiest black church in the land. A third son, John, was a successful undertaker in Baltimore.[22]

As much as certain families and their social activities highlighting Baltimore society would attract the notice of the outsider or observer as being the "best" of black Baltimore, the city also had individuals, men of wealth, and noted as such, who also caught the eye of the observer for this fact and the activities they engaged in. Some were readily seen helping out the less fortunate. Perhaps the most noteworthy of this group was Simon Smith who was a director and the largest stockholder of Douglass Institute when he died in 1885. In the 1870s, he was thought to be the only black living off his rents and interests. He was described as quite generous and lenient toward his tenants. He was a member of the Board of Trustees of Centenary Biblical Institute, now known as Morgan State University. He also was one of its incorporators. Smith attended Orchard Street Methodist Church.[23]

As wealth and what one did with it conferred prestige, at times prestige came to some in the community, like Jack or John Murray, Trueman Pratt, and George Murray, because of their worthy contributions to the community over a long period of time. John Murray was born somewhere at the headwaters of the Northwest Branch of the Patapsco in 1751. When he die in 1861, he was 110 years old. During his youth, Baltimore was just a village, but at his death, a metropolis. Murray's recollection and constitution were quite strong when he died. He worked up to within a few months of his death. As a repository of the living memory of the community, Murray was apparently quite a storyteller. He would, at times, recall the times when he helped gather apples from an immense orchard that covered the entire eastern section of the city. Murray worked for some of the first shipbuilders in various capacities, including such builders as William Price who had a yard on Fells Street. He claimed he was the first black caulker in Baltimore.

Murray said that during the American Revolution he served on several occasions as a servant to General Washington and other American officers. He claimed to be present at the battles of Bunker Hill, Lexington, and the surrender of Cornwallis at Yorktown. Sometime around the late 1780s he was given his freedom. He was known as "Fiddler Jack" in East Baltimore, where apparently he lived most of his life. With his fiddle, he had a prominent part in the dances and "shindigs."

At his death, Murray left numerous descendants. A possible descendant of his may have been J. Murray Ralph, a long-time resident of East Baltimore, a friend of Frederick Douglass who encouraged Douglass to buy, in 1892, Old Dallas Street Church, the church in which Douglass was converted, which was itself an old East Baltimore institution. Douglass turned the structure into houses which still stand. He used some of the same structures of the old building which was, and is the oldest remains of a Methodist church in Baltimore. The church was constructed in 1776.

J. Murray Ralph also led a group that annually commemorated Douglass' birthdate in Baltimore in the early years of the twentieth century, the only city to do so, seemingly, on a grand, regular basis at this time. Ralph, in addition, had a memorial window placed in Centennial Church, the new name of the Dallas Street congregation, in memory of Frederick Douglass.[24]

Trueman Pratt, another centenarian at his death, was founder of Orchard Street Methodist Episcopal Church. He was born on March 27, 1775 on West River in Anne Arundel County, a slave of Colonel John Eager

Howard, wealthy Baltimorean, famous for his exploits at the Battle of Cowpens in Revolutionary times. Howard sold Pratt after the War of 1812, but he ran away from his new owner. With the help of a Mr. Brice, Pratt purchased his freedom and became a carter. In 1825, he began to hold regular prayer meetings and gave the first $20.00 to a building fund out of which came the first Orchard Street Church, supposedly dedicated in 1837. Trueman Pratt's son, Lewis, became an active Republican and was father of Harry T. Pratt, first black to enter the Maryland Institute as an art student. Later, Harry T. Pratt became principal of Douglass High School and co-founder of one of the most successful businesses in Baltimore, the Druid Hill Laundry.[25]

The other centenarian, George Murray, died in August 1890 at 115 years of age. It is not known if he was a relative of Jack Murray. Originally from Chestertown, Kent County, he came to the city after being freed by William Hopper who had inherited him by marriage. Murray was a founder of Bethel Church and participated in bringing Daniel Coker, the first black teacher to the city around 1808. At his death, Murray's only surviving son, Daniel, was Assistant Librarian at the Library of Congress where he was an ardent black bibliophile and would receive an honorary degree from Wilberforce University in 1916, cited as a world authority on the Negro. In 1920, Daniel Murray contemplated writing a "Historical and Biographical Encyclopedia of the Colored Race Throughout the World."

Daniel Murray was also a leading member of St. Luke's Episcopal Church in Washington. In 1879 he married Anna Jane Evans, a niece of two of John Brown's five black recruits at Harper's Ferry. His high esteem in Washington society can readily be seen as he was usually most significant to the success of inaugural affairs in Washington amongst blacks when a President began his term. He was one of the wealthiest blacks in Washington and was an accomplished violinist. Along with this, he was involved in other ways in the community such as being on the School Board. His brother, at one time, was manager of the United States Senate Restaurant.[26]

A family's orientation and its success, as cited in the examples mentioned above, were due mainly to the strength of its male members. There were, however, some successful families of which women seemed the predominant reason for the successes. Marie Matthews, at her death in July 1889, was described as well-known and ven-

271

erable. She was living with one of her sons, John C., at 611 West Hoffman Street at her death. Her church was Grace Presbyterian. William E., her most accomplished son, born in 1843, had been a pupil of William Watkins. William E. Matthews was a stellar black orator in Baltimore before leaving and taking up a similar place in Washington society.

Indeed, in Washington, Matthews became the first black investment banker. The Matthews, though seemingly not with much financial means of their own, were relatives of the wealthy black barber, Edward Sythe, who was involved in such ventures as the Chesapeake and Marine Railway and Drydock Company. William E. Matthews, as an investment banker, handled money belonging to such nationally prominent blacks as Frederick Douglass, Bishop Daniel A. Payne, and John Mercer Langston.

Another of Mrs. Matthews' sons, George M., was Captain of the Baltimore Rifles, a militia company which performed at ceremonial functions, and which acted as a unit of the State militia. Her fourth son, Samuel S., lived in New York. A measure of Marie Matthews' importance in the community can be attested to by the fact that her pallbearers included among others, Isaac Myers, H. J. Brown, and William H. Bishop.[27]

Another venerable matriarch, Mrs. Catherine Mossell, who was 94 years old when she died in 1891, had been a life-long member of Sharp Street for seventy years. Her parents had been free blacks. She had a host of descendants, including Dr. N. F. Mossell in Philadelphia, founder of the Frederick Douglass Hospital there; Aaron A. Mossell, a lawyer in Philadelphia as well; and Rev. Charles W. Mossell, at the time of his mother's death, pastor of St. John's A.M.E. in Baltimore.

Charles Mossell and his wife, Mary E., also a native of Baltimore, were missionaries to Haiti. The account of their stay in Haiti was recorded by Mary Mossell, which entitled her to be considered a significant black woman of letters. She had been a teacher in Baltimore before going to Haiti. When she died in 1886, her life was commemorated in memorial services at Trinity A.M.E. by no less a person than John M. Langston, former Ambassador to Haiti. No doubt her mother-in-law, Mrs. Catherine Mossell, if in the audience, had feelings mixed with pride and sadness.[28]

Yet another matriarch, Fannie McGuinn, spent only

fourteen years in Baltimore, having been born in Fredericksburg, Virginia, in 1820. She came to Baltimore in 1875 and her children from two marriages were to have considerable influence in the city. Her two husbands, Thomas Alexander and Jared McGuinn, were substantial persons in the Richmond community. Three children were fathered by Alexander--William, a minister of Sharon Baptist in Baltimore; J. A., caterer in Richmond; and Mrs. Dr. John M. Johnson of Baltimore. Three sons were fathered by McGuinn--Joseph, seemingly proprietor of Brighton Hotel in Atlantic City, New Jersey; Warner T., Yale law graduate and eventually one of the few blacks to serve on the Baltimore City Council before 1960; and another son. The business outlook of Mrs. McGuinn's family was, indeed, highly evident. In fact, besides her husbands being in business before the Civil War, two of her brothers went to Canada and established themselves in business there. Her son, William Alexander, was partly responsible for the phenomenal growth of black Baptists in Baltimore after 1870, but also carried on the family business instinct. He, in fact, founded the Afro-American newspaper which he eventually sold to John H. Murphy. He also was a founder of Southern Life Insurance Society, perhaps the largest such concern in Baltimore during his day.[29]

Several other women, though not mothering a brood of successful children as the above three women, did contribute mightily in mothering of a different kind. When Clara Anna Williams died in July 1883, it was reported she had been one of the most respected persons in the community, male or female. She was a native of Norfolk, Virginia, and was about seventy years old at her passing. Her husband, George Williams, was steward of Sharp Street Church. Mrs. Williams was a member of eleven beneficial societies and president of nine of these and, in thirty years time, her associations had raised $60,000 in aid. Mrs. Williams was also a member of the secret orders and had a special interest in the Daughters of Jerusalem which originated in 1848.[30]

Mrs. Adele Jackson, another communicant of Sharp Street Church, was apparently involved in supporting benevolent institutions like the Gregory Aged Women's Home, a home that mainly grew out of Bethel, through the efforts of George Hackett and Mary Ann Prout. Fairs were held annually to support this community project and others. Mrs. Jackson, whose husband was one of the more wealthy blacks in the city, seemed to take a leading hand in these fairs.[31]

Success or eminence has been looked at from the predominating male or female side in the foregoing, it is interesting, however, to look at it from yet another angle. Possibly the most interesting married couple in nineteenth century Baltimore, noteworthy for the accomplishments of each partner of the marriage, happended to be Captain and Mrs. Alex Haley. Alex Haley, in his October 1885 obituary was believed to have been probably "the only colored man who ever commanded a vessel in the ocean trade out of the United States." Haley was born in 1799, in Salisbury, Maryland; his mother was free, his father a slave. At fourteen years of age, he went to sea, and in 1815, he came to Baltimore. He learned navigation on the bark <u>Corinthian</u> from Captain Richard Bennett. While on a voyage from the East Indies, Captain Bennett and the officers fell ill, and Haley was the only one left to bring the ship home.

At times, afterward, he served as mate under Captain John Goddison and at one point was Captain of the schooner, the <u>George R. McGill</u>, owned by Dr. James Hall, a member of the Maryland Colonization Society. At first, however, the underwriters refused to insure the <u>George R. McGill</u> until Captain Haley was thoroughly examined. He later served on two other ships, the <u>Mary Caroline Stevens</u> and the <u>Golconda</u>, both owned by the Maryland Colonization Society. At the Captain's death, he was survived by his wife and two daughters, both of whom were schoolteachers. Mrs. A. R. H. Miller, who once taught at Douglass Institute, was principal of the Eastern Female Colored School, and the other, Mrs. Lizzie J. R. Stewart, was a schoolteacher in Queen Anne's County. John Fernandis, leading black barber, and Captain E. J. Wheatley, owner of the only black-owned resort in Maryland, located on the West River, acted as pallbearers at Haley's funeral.[32]

Captain Haley's wife, Elizabeth, at her death in August 1888, was the oldest black teacher in Baltimore who had been teaching for about sixty years. In her youth she received a liberal education, after which she opened a private school on Eastern Avenue. About ten years later, she built a schoolhouse on to her home on Dallas Street, at that time being married to Captain Haley, who encouraged her in her work. She was teaching school until the time of the death of her husband. In her obituary, it stated that she taught some of the leading black men and women, not only of the city, but from throughout the country. She joined the church, presumably Bethel, at 14, and was described as being an earnest, consistent, and exemplary Christian. Two of her pallbearers were John Fernandis and William F. Taylor, both members of Bethel and possibly two of her students.[33]

If it is proper to view a specific family or various families as distinctly helping make Baltimore black society what it was, it also is proper from a broader perspective, to view the numerous secret and benevolent societies and their outlook as having a fundamental impact on society as well, as well as upon the individuals who joined together to identify with such groups. Baltimore was a place known nationally for its secret societies. The city having the largest free black population in the United States before the Civil War, did have an ample population to supply the membership lists of such varied groups as the Good Samaritans, Nazarites, Galileans, all founded in the city, and others like the Odd Fellows and Masons.

There existed also numerous other beneficial and more locally oriented groups that provided relief for members when misfortune struck. Some of the more impressive of these kind were the St. James Charitable Relief Society; the Brothers Immediate Society, which provided help on the first day of need, not a week later, as was the practice; the Colored Caulkers' Association, very strong throughout the nineteenth century; Queen Esther Society; Daughters of Jerusalem; Knights of Jerusalem; Cadets of Knights of Jerusalem; Adoptive Rite of the Eastern Star; Junior Grand Division Sons & Daughters of Temperance; Grand United Order Sons & Daughters of Nun; and last, but not least, The United Consolidated Order of the Sons & Daughters of the Knights of Four Men of Baltimore City.

It was not unusual for these organizations to have uniforms and from the very earliest years of the nineteenth century, many--whites included--enjoyed their outings and parades, especially at the death of a member, when nothing seemed spared to send a brother off to that larger fraternal organization in Heaven. These groups were also usually included in the most dignified of affairs sponsored by the community. When a statue of Lincoln was unveiled in Washington on April 14, 1876, with such persons as Frederick Douglass in attendance, so were the Knights Templar of St. John from Baltimore there.

So exclusive of white interference or domination were these groups and so important were they to black morale for that very reason, that the enemies of the

275

community were always ready to try to undo them. A serious effort along these lines was attempted in 1843, with the State Legislative Committee on Colored Populations responding to a presentment of the Grand Jury and two judges in Baltimore on the independent nature of these organizations. Fortunately none of this came to pass, however, as the white friends of blacks came to their defense. These organizations remained free and prosperous.[34]

The first instance of mass black assertiveness after the Civil War was the meeting of the Independent Order of Odd Fellows in October 1865 in Monument Square. The Odd Fellows were one of the more popular in the city. All the lodges in the state were represented at that Octoberfest; some representatives from neighboring states as well came. Ostensibly, the gathering had assembled to commemorate the anniversary of the issuance of the Emancipation Proclamation.

At first, the brothers gathered around Mount Vernon Square and from there marched all over the eastern regions of the city before arriving at Monument Square, where a stage awaited the dignitaries and a banner arching the podium contained the words "Friendship, Love and Truth." The assemblage was immense, attracting nearly every black in the city as well as those within fifty miles of its bounds; because, as one newspaper put it, the whole affair had been "profusely" talked about by the orginators for several months.

This happening, it should be noted, occurred within a week of the opening of the Douglass Institute and, undoubtedly contributed to the high spirits which remained amongst blacks for some time. At this outdoor rally, William H. Brown, past Noble Father, was honored. Others mentioned as having a prominent part in the activities were the Revs. Samuel W. Chase and James H. Jordan, and Patrick H. Reason of New York.

By 1873, the Odd Fellows were operating out of a hall on Lexington Street, near Calvert, the very vicinity of the Douglass Institute. It had, at this time, 10,000 members in the state; its first lodge, Eden, had been established on June 13, 1848. The Odd Fellow lodges in Baltimore before the Civil War were the only ones below the Mason-Dixon line. In Maryland, in this period before the Civil War, there were eleven, while in Pennsylvania there were fifteen. At this 1873 Convention, Isaac Myers spoke at the evening session held at the Douglass Institute.

Toward the end of the 1870s, the Odd Fellows were even more visible. In 1878, a highlight of fraternal affairs was the incorporation papers of the Frederick Douglass Lodge No. 715 being filed with the Clerk of Superior Court in the city. A few days later in October, the Order held a demonstration at the Douglass Institute to raise money because of the ravages of a yellow fever epidemic in the South. They were addressed by Rev. George T. Watkins, a member; music was provided by the Virginia Julibee singers.[35] Watkins, like so many of the black leadership, was quite active amongst several groups and after his participation in Odd Fellow affairs in October, proceeded right away to help the Grand Lodge of Maryland, Independent Order of Good Templars, celebrate their affair.

In April 1879, the Odd Fellows were the first black organization to gather at the Maryland Institute. At this Convention, in one evening, speeches by Joseph Rainey and Richard H. Cain, former members of Congress; John W. Cromwell, publisher of the People's Advocate, a Washington paper; and Richard T. Greener, Dean of Howard University's Law School, were made.

Before the evening festivities, however, a parade in full regalia of black suit, silk top hat, white gloves, and the various lodge banners moved through the streets of Baltimore on a day not made for parading--it rained steadily. The Morning Herald observer said, however:

> Each member of each lodge looked well, dressed well, marched well, and what cannot always be said of the parades of other organizations, kept sober. Indeed (the care) colored people take in displays of this character, is so well-known as scarcely to need comment. It seemed as if each person felt that the dignity of the entire affair rested upon his shoulders, consequently, realizing the importance of bearing a good reputation individually, it was sustained collectively.[36]

The music was provided by the Odd Fellows Monumental Band, founded by John A. Bridges, who also was responsible for founding the John A. Bridge Lodge in the organization.

At the eight o'clock evening session, which lasted until between one and two in the morning, Isaac Myers served as master of ceremonies. Other local persons to speak included H. J. Brown, George Myers, John W. Locks, and Thomas I. Hall. The statistical accounting for the year, as read by Myers, were 4,700 members, $10,000 in property, $14,000 in sick, widow and orphan benefits paid out, and $65,000 in the banks.

Joseph H. Rainey's speech was about the progress blacks had already made on the "plane of civilization" and how whites would be forced to give blacks positions, honors, and respect in coming years, because the group, more and more were meriting them. An editorial in the Morning Herald commented upon the statements made by speakers at that session and echoed Rainey's words of praise for their efforts, under extremely discouraging conditions, at which many blacks had gotten a formal education since emanicipation. The editor said unremitting prejudice had burdened blacks to the point that it was well nigh debilitating; but, somehow, through it all, many had risen to positions of eminence as doctors, lawyers, and so on--with this the editor said, "Let no individual despair."[37]

Most of the black leadership belong to several societies, and when in August 1879, the Good Samaritans of the state had their annual meeting, Myers was there as well. Indeed, the first Samaritan Temple was attached to Bethel Church, Myers' church. The Good Samaritan order was founded in 1848, in part by such as Rev. Daniel A. Payne, James A. Handy and Hemsley Nicholas. By 1877, the order had moved out of its meeting quarters at Douglass Institute and into the purchased site of the Old Baptist Church at Calvert and Saratoga Streets.

That August 1879, visitors of the order coming from Western Maryland were met at Camden Station by other members which signaled the commencement of the festivities. The usual parade brought about 400 marchers into the streets, in full dress. At an evening session, Isaac Myers served as master of ceremonies. There were 78 lodges and 3,000 members in this temperance beneficial society, called by the Morning Herald, the most charitable society among blacks. Only the year before, it was reported there were just 2,400 members in 71 lodges, so it was growing also. The celebrations did not break up until one o'clock the next morning. No doubt in response to its origins, as late as 1886, the Grand Council of Good Samaritans, the national organization, was dominated by Marylanders such as Jacob A. Seaton and John W. Martin.[38]

Another organization in which the men of Bethel and

churchmen in general and especially Isaac Myers had an interest was the Masons. For quite a while, about thirty years, two Grand Lodges existed in Maryland; but, in 1876, September 12, a combined total of 39 lodges of the two sections of masonry, met at the Douglass Institute and united under the leadership of Reverend James A. Handy, the pastor of Bethel. Handy was Grand Master and Causeman H. Gaines, a Bethelite, and director of his church's choir, was elected Deputy Grand Master. Isaac Myers, along with such others as George T. Watkins, Grand Chaplain, George Myers, Jacob A. Seaton, and Hiram Watty, had been part of the commission set up by the two bodies to bring about the union.

During the ceremonies on this occasion, James A. Handy brought forth a gavel once used by Dr. Lewis G. Wells at Friendship Lodge over forty years before, and gave it to James Morris, Past Grand Master of St. John's Lodge No. 2, which he founded thirty-five years before. Throughout the occasion, Isaac Myers acted as master of ceremonies, while music was provided by John H. Murphy.[39]

Several other organizations founded in Baltimore branched out beyond its borders. The Nazarites were organized in 1854, in a cabin of a boat off Bowley's Wharf. The founders were James A. Handy, David B. Nelson, Noah Butler, and Noah Carey. This order held an annual passover levee on Whit-Monday. In 1876, the Nazarites were flourishing and expanding toward Norfolk, Virginia, and Frederick, Maryland. In 1895, at the 42nd Annual Grand Pasture, 3,200 members were on the books. In the early part of the twentieth century, it had the largest and one of the most widely-used halls owned by blacks in Baltimore.[40]

The Galilean Fishermen came into being in 1856 through the efforts of Hemsley Nichols, who had been one of the founders of the Good Samaritans. Nichols was a class leader at John Wesley Methodist Church, and, as such, that church's members shared greatly in the success of the Galilean Fishermen. Nichols was so devoted to this society that he left provisions in his will that, after the death of his wife, his property was to go to the order. Thomas I. Hall, a leader at John Wesley as well, succeeded Nichols as head of the Galileans. He served as head of the organization for nineteen years.

By the end of the 1880s, the membership was a little over 30,000, with lodges established up and down the

East Coast and as far away as Chicago. This group had a particularly large juvenile division. A new hall was erected at 43 South Liberty Street in 1882 on the site of the society's previous home. At the laying of the cornerstone, such items as the Ark of Covenant, Bible, banners, minutes of the national organization from 1858 to 1881, constitution, and hymnals were placed in the stone. At the dedication of the new five-story structure, which cost $9,000, Bishop Wayman made some remarks. As a culmination of the 1882 round of dedications, the Galileans went to the black owned Wheatley's Grove on West River, where Thomas I. Hall addressed the gathering. This order had an annual fish passover and performed the usual beneficial services as providing expenses for the sick, widows, and funerals.

No doubt a highlight in the history of the Galileans came in December 1886, when Rev. George T. Watkins, pastor of Trinity A.M.E., located on Linden and Biddle Streets, preached a special sermon on secret societies, showing their antiquity and accomplishments, at which conclusion he presented Thomas I. Hall with a twig taken from a tree near Galilee, originally given to him by Rev. Daniel P. Seaton who had made a trip to the Holy Land several years before. Seaton was prominent in the Good Samaritans, and apparently the Samaritans and Galileans shared a friendly relationship. At the annual celebrations in September 1886, as the Galileans in full regalia marched to Calverton Stock Yards to purchase an ox for a roast to be held at Irving Park, the Good Samaritans accepted an invitation to participate in the festivities.[41]

Two other orders were significant. The Order of St. Lukes founded in 1856 by Mary A. Prout, a member of Bethel, became national as well. The Knights of Phythias of the Eastern and Western Hemispheres was organized in the city in 1889; it, too, was a nationally recognized body.[42]

Though many supported the secret societies, it must be said, however, that secret orders were not enthusiastically supported by everyone. And a minister of such prominence as Rev. Harvey Johnson spoke out against them; but this was toward the end of the century when, perhaps, from sheer longevity of existence, they were not what they were initially conceived to be. Nevertheless, even then, this condemnation of this popular form of association provoked considerable reaction against Johnson's criticisms.[43]

Somewhat of a spirit and akin to the secret societies, but not having the success as the secret societies, were the military groups that sprange up after the
Civil War and the kinds of activities they sponsored.
The city had provided a considerable share of the free
men who fought in the Civil War, and after the conflict,
these men formed the militia companies or organized
themselves into veterans groups.

The Lincoln Zouaves were organized with the help of
Col. Edward F. M. Faehtz in 1865 because Governor
Swann's militia generals refused to recognize blacks in
uniforms, allow them in the state organizations. Col.
Edward Faehtz, an Austrian refugee of the 1848 Revolu-
tion, had had considerable european military experience
before he headed the Maryland 8th Regiment during the
Civil War and had brevetted George A. Hackett a captain
during that conflict. The leading black members of the
Zouaves were Albert G. Carroll, C. L. J. Lee, Richard
Green, A. J. Kelly, William H. Scroggins, and William
U. Saunders. Saunders served as Lt. Colonel under Col.
Faehtz. Indeed, Saunders, who had served as a sergeant
in the 7th Regiment U.S. Colored Troops in Florida, and
who became an important radical politician in this state
after the war was, perhaps, more responsible for promoting the idea of the Zouaves than anyone.

The Lincoln Zouaves was not the only military com-
pany. In 1867, another important militia company, the
Henry Winter Davis Guard was formed and headquartered at
Douglass Institute. It owed it existence, in part, to
George A. Hackett. As the Guard was being completed,
two other units were being organized—the Creswell
Zouaves in South Baltimore, and Denison Guards in East
Baltimore. In addition to this, there were plans afoot
within this space of time to form two batteries of ar-
tillery, and one regiment of cavalry to be known as the
Bond Loyal Guards.

Despite these other groups, it seems the Lincoln
Zouaves was the more lasting and substantial militia
company. On the grounds of the Gregory Aged Women's
Home, in September 1867, the Lincoln Zouaves held an extensive picnic which lasted several days. At this time
the Zouaves had nine hundred men, four hundred of whom
had paid for their guns and equipment. The men's uniforms were modeled after the Maryland Guard who flour-
ished in the city before the outbreak of the war. The
regimental flag had a painting of Lincoln on it. By
1873, the Zouaves had evolved into a beneficial society
as well and its armory was on Mulberry Street. The per-

formance of the group was such that it was the only military company to represent Maryland at Grant's second inauguration, having already appeared at his first. By March 1876, police regulations were hindering blacks from forming militia companies, a violation of their civil rights, which A. J. Kelley, a captain in the Zouaves, and some others protested.[44]

In line with the affairs of the militia companies, Decoration Day of soldiers' and sailors' graves at Laurel Cemetery was an annual thing for a long time. In 1873, preparation for the day was made at a meeting held at Douglass Institute on May 6, by the Lincoln Post No. 7 of the G.A.R., Grand Army of the Republic.[45] John H. Murphy was called to the chair, and John C. Fortie acted as secretary. Again in the following two years, preparations for Decoration Day were under the care of John H. Murphy and John C. Fortie.

Fortie was chief marshall in 1875. That year, a crowd of ten thousand took part in the services. Rev. James Handy, a native Baltimorean, acted as orator for the day. The Sun said:

> Mr. Handy is a forcible and intelligent speaker and his words, which are big with common sense, should find a place in the memory of every black man and woman in Maryland. If all the teachers of the race would give them as good and solid food as in the greater part of Mr. Handy's address, there would soon be a marked changed in their general enlightment, which is the first step towards prosperity and peace.[46]

Several years later, in 1879, Handy spoke again at Decoration Day services where it seems more than honoring the dead had grown to be a part of the topic of the main speaker. This time Handy supported the Exodus of blacks from the South where the Klan reigned. As for other advice, he said: "Vote, but cease to be politicians." Handy thought it inexcusable to spend $30,000 annually on excursions and concluded by saying, "We must forget the dark past, live in the present, and remember that we are American citizens."[47]

The Decoration Day services were under the charge of the Lincoln Post, as earlier stated, and it seemed it was a very vibrant group. In 1877, the Lincoln Post No. 7 attracted the nationally renowned John Mercer Langston to its services. At memorial services held for the dead in 1878, Professor Richard T. Greener, also from Washington, spoke. John H. Butler was master of ceremonies for this occasion held at the Douglass Institute. Bethel's choir, led by Causeman Gaines, sang. Also in 1878, a reorganization of the post occurred.

Several years later, in 1881, the services for Decoration Day paid special attention to decorating the graves of Greenbury Morten, A. Ward Handy, and George A. Hackett. In this same year, the Lincoln Post took it upon itself to try to erect a monument to black soldiers and sailors who fought in the war. W. H. Sheppard was president of a subscription list group which conducted a statewide drive to collect funds to build the monument, costing $2,852, to be made of Italian marble, in accordance with a design by D. Maxwell & Company of Baltimore. The basic design was of a soldier in a kneeling position bearing the colors.[48]

Though activities honoring the military for the most part sought to celebrate the deeds of the dead, the living veterans were not forgotten during this period either. One of the more enduring military traditions of the city was the annual gathering of the 7th Regiment, U.S. Colored Troops. In 1889, about 100 survivors of the unit gathered at St. John's A.M.E. Church to hear a sermon preached by Rev. Charles W. Mossell acknowledging the debt owed to the 7th Regiment from ordinary citizens.[49]

Yet the need of blacks to celebrate the deeds of its military heroes or organize itself in militia companies was a result of white official racial discrimination. Apparently as late as 1881, the white militia authorities had not made up their minds as to what to do with black militia companies, comprised of veterans whom blacks wanted not forgotten. At one moment, State authorities promised the companies arms, then they changed their minds. But, by February 1882, the State mustered in the First Separate Company, which had sixty-five men. Bringing into existence the First Separate Company did not stop the formation of private militia companies, however. In 1883, the two most prominent units were the Monumental City Guards and the Baltimore Rifles, both having been organized within that past year.

In 1883, these two companies celebrated Washington's Birthday at the armory of the Monumental City Guards located on a corner of Eager Street, between Charles and Cathedral. At an evening session, with Bishop Wayman presiding, such notables as Isaac Myers, Henry Jacques, George Myers, William F. Taylor, J. H. Butler, and H. J. Brown took part. In the fall of 1885, the City Guards had an affair at the Douglass Institute at which Congressional Medal of Honor winner Christopher Fleetwood, a native Baltimorean, was present.[50]

The City of Baltimore, because of its being in virtue of fact, the black capital throughout the greater part of the nineteenth century, having associated with it the names of greatness, the blacks of Baltimore knew how to celebrate the distinctive events in black history. The city served as a convenient and much welcomed stop for the renowned lecturer or distinguished visitor. The most impressive celebration put on by black Baltimoreans occurred during the community's rejoicing over the enactment of the Fifteenth Amendment on May 19, 1870.

The Executive Committee of blacks preparing for the celebration had worked closely in cooperation with the Maryland Republican State Central Committee consisting of, among others, C. C. Fulton, editor of the American. Those selected to head up the marching included William U. Saunders as chief marshall; his aides being Hiram Watty and Captain R. Piper. About two hundred mounted aides and numerous others generally assisted in the day's activities. Of course, contingents of bands were present to set the tempo of march. Some of the bands came from the counties and Washington.

With a salute of one hundred guns being fired from Fort McHenry, at eight in the morning, the marchers located at various sections of the city began to move toward the point of general assembly, the Battle Monument Square. At the Battle Monument Square, two large stands were erected facing Calvert Street, south. To accommodate the expected large turnout, speaking and activities took place in four different areas.

Dr. H. J. Brown, Chairman of the Committee of Invitations, invited numerous whites of prominence to the celebration, including Postmaster General Creswell, a Marylander; Senator Wilson of Massachusetts, a close associate of Senator Charles Sumner; and William Lloyd Garrison. Garrison sent a letter of regret, but acknowledged in the letter that he got his start in the abolition business in Baltimore, more than forty years before.

Many of the secret orders and various societies such as the Odd Fellows and caulkers, brickmakers, took

284

part in the celebrations, each with its own float and bearing such items as a picture of Senator Revels greeting the goddess of liberty, a temple of liberty, or a portrait of George A. Hackett. One mobile unit was a wagon with a printing press, striking off handbills headed "The New Vote. Isaac Myers, Editor." There were also banners prominently displayed which advertised the Freedman's Savings Bank, or made a pledge that every colored vote in Maryland would be for the Radical Republicans.

When the procession finally arrived at Monument Square, Master of Ceremonies Dr. H. J. Brown moved for the election of a list of already-selected officers. Isaac Myers was duly elected president without a hitch. Myers thanked the crowd, saying that he was presiding over "the greatest, grandest and most important gathering of colored men in Maryland or in the whole country." He read the letters of regret, especially the ones from Charles Sumner and Garrison. Afterward, suitable resolutions were passed thanking God, Republicans, President Grant, pledging loyalty to the Republican Party, endorsing the idea of better education for blacks, and promising that blacks would contribute their might to uplifting state and country. William E. Matthews performed his functions as secretary for the day admirably.

Afterwards, Dr. H. J. Brown introduced John M. Langston, orator for the day. Langston said among other things that "they met to celebrate the triumph of universal democracy as affirmed by the fathers of the Revolution in the Declaration of Independence, and subsequently defined in an amendment to the Constitution." Others to speak included Postmaster General J. A. J. Creswell, and Frederick Douglass.

Dr. Brown, when he introduced Douglass, acknowledged that though he lived in New York, they, the people of Baltimore, intended to have him come to Baltimore when he was needed and such proved to be the case later on. Douglass, for his part, recounted his life in Baltimore, and he duly noted and welcomed the change from slavery to freedom which the day's celebration recognized. Douglass, during his talk, asked the crowd if they remembered which party had emancipated them--the response unanimously yelled out in anti-Democratic terms was, "The Republican Party," which surely must have broadened the already wide grin of every Republican politician, or would-be politician in the audience, as he reckoned the votes.

After the speeches that night, a ball was held at the Douglass Institute, with supper in a lower saloon of the building, and with the festivities going on well into the next morning.[51]

Though the 1870 Fifteenth Amendment celebrations were the definitive highlight of all gatherings held after the Civil War, at which blacks and whites could come together at their ease, there were many other significant assemblies worth mentioning. John M. Langston also spoke at Bethel in August 1867. He was a lawyer from Ohio and, at that point, general inspector of the Bureau of Refugees, Freedmen and Abandoned Lands. At Langston's arrival at Bethel, the church was already crowded, as well as the streets adjacent. A black militia company, most likely the Henry Winter Davis Guard, with muskets at the ready, assisted in maintaining order. Some important white friends of the Negro present to hear Langston's speech on the educational needs of the race included General O. O. Howard and General E. M. Gregory, both of the Freedmen's Bureau.[52]

The death of Thaddeus Stevens, Radical Republican leader in Congress from Pennsylvania, and friend of the blacks in the early days of Reconstruction, occasioned the commemoration of his life at Douglass Institute with John C. Fortie presiding at this August 1868 day of mourning.[53]

Henry Highland Garnet, who surely must have come to Baltimore more times than the newspaper accounts showed, at one time in 1873, was slated to speak at the meeting of the Cuban Anti-Slavery Committee at Madison Avenue Presbyterian. Garnet was detained elsewhere, however, and when the meeting was called to order by I. D. Oliver, A. J. Kelley was elected president and S. R. Scottran, Chairman of the Cuban Anti-Slavery Committee, did speak, telling the audience of the Cubans' fight against their Spanish oppressors.[54]

In the same year, 1873, when the Jubilee Singers came to town and refused to sing before a segregated audience, because of their refusal, blacks were eventually admitted to sit anywhere in the local playhouse. It could be said that throughout the latter third of the nineteenth century, the very best kind of black entertainer came to Baltimore, including the likes of such as Madame Selinka, a famous singer.[55]

In March 1874, the famous black woman abolitionist, Sojourner Truth, came to town; she spoke before a large audience at the Friends' Meeting House on Lombard

Street. The American spoke highly of her, saying she had a little house in Wisconsin but had mortgaged it to raise money to travel about and investigate the situation amongst blacks and promote improvement where needed. She carried a petition to be presented to Congress, asking that body to enact legislation setting apart a section of the Western lands for blacks. Sojourner Truth hoped buildings would be erected for the aged and infirmed on this land. In her speech, she spoke of the destitution and poverty she saw on her travels; she wanted the blacks of Baltimore to contribute to uplifting the less fortunate of their brothers.

After her remarks, John Needles, an old abolitionist, well into his eighties, said Sojourner Truth paid her expenses by selling photographs of herself and, immediately a number of people left their seats to buy copies. Sojourner Truth, in taking note of her own age, denied that she ever nursed General Washington and said she "has done quit telling people how old she was." To explain her activity at such an advanced age, she said, "Sometimes folks just quit growing and stop as they is, and I specs that I had jis quit growing old and keeps on de same all de time."[56]

Baltimore audiences were not only available for the renowned outsider, they were also available for local talent and its development as well. In 1874, the Lincoln Dramatic Association made its debut. The Association's home was on a second-story landing in a hall on Union Street. The group started out as a literary society in a South Baltimore church, but was reorganized into a dramatic association. The manager was a Mr. Samuels whose regular trade was barbering but who, for two years, was connected with a minstrel show.

By November 1874, the association planned to stage a performance at Douglass Institute. The orchestra consisted of a violin. The contents of a show reviewed by a reported included a song and dance from David Sorrell, a banjo solo and song by Charles Thompson, and a kind of Punch-and-Judy slapstick piece. There were songs by a quartet and a comedic delivery of a stump speech by another performer, after which came intermission. Next, a two-act production of Richard, the Third, followed. The audience of young men appreciated nothing of the higher values in the Shakespearean work, but what the groundlings loved in Shakespeare's time, namely the blood and guts.[57]

The approaching centennial of the founding of the United States in 1876 led some black Baltimoreans to help form the Centennial Jubilee Singers. Four men and four women made up the group as they made their debut at the Maryland Institute. The group was actually formed by somebody in the North and included Baltimoreans Charles, James, and Isaac Butler, Henry Wilson, and Susan Cornish.[58]

As for centennial celebrations themselves, Jacob C. Hazeley, a reporter for The African Times, a London publication, came to the city to cover the happenings. Hazeley lectured in Baltimore on several occasions. On one of these, he lectured on the Greboes, a tribe in Liberia. Hazeley's grandfather was one of the group of black supporters of the English during the Revolution who had been settled in Canada after the peace. Hazeley's grandfather left Nova Scotia for Sierre Leone in 1792--a colony founded by British abolitionists with Granville Sharp having a leading role, to serve as a haven for the oppressed blacks, as Liberia was some thirty years later to be founded by Americans for similar reasons.[59]

In June 1877, blacks in Baltimore had a genuine reason to rejoice, though on many levels and throughout the country a retreat from Reconstruction was in full swing. Charles Taylor, a black lawyer from Boston, was admitted to practice before the United States Circuit Court in Baltimore by Judge Giles. The motion to admit Taylor came from Archibald Stirling, Jr. district attorney, son of the President of the Savings Bank of Baltimore. The admission of Taylor to the Bar was cause for envisioning a better day, so thought James A. Handy, as he spoke before the black masons celebrating the feast of St. John in that year.[60]

That same year, the Douglass Institute, which had admirably served as a place to hold meetings and celebrate had undergone extensive renovations and was reopened after a two-month closing in October 1877. The improvements had been under the supervision of John H. Butler and Simon Smith, two of the largest stockholders.[61]

Over the next several years, the steady flow of important lectures continued. Josiah Henson, a former Marylander, lectured at the Maryland Institute in January 1878. Henson was on his way to see his mother's grave. He was the man upon whom Harriett Beecher Stowe based her character, Uncle Tom, in that important novel, Uncle Tom's Cabin.[62]

288

Richard T. Greener was as frequent a visitor and lecturer to Baltimore as Frederick Douglass. On February 25, 1879, he spoke at Centennial Church on the black astronomer, Benjamin Banneker. A few months later, he appeared at a memorial service on June 19, at Douglass Institute for William Lloyd Garrison, with Reverend James A. Handy presiding. The opening hymn was a favorite of Garrison, "Awake, My Soul," while the opening prayer was by the Episcopalian Reverend C. B. Perry. Greener's euology was described as "eloquent," parts of which "aroused the highest pitch of enthusiasm in the audience."

Greener spoke of the late 1820s and about the abolition movement when his grandfather, father, and uncles assisted both Benjamin Lundy and Garrison in the publication of The Genius of Universal Emancipation. He said, at that time, Lundy's policy of gradual emancipation proved better, while Garrison's policy of immediate emancipation was later to be viciously opposed by the "minions of strong slave power". Yet, when Garrison founded the Liberator in 1831 in Boston, "even that early the colored people were not hidden in a corner indifferent of their rights." Greener said his grandfather and Samuel W. Chase were agents of the Liberator who "stealthily distributed it throughout the city" in Baltimore.

Greener also recounted some of the high points of Garrison's career, his nearly being killed by a mob in Boston, opposed to his advocacy of freedom for the Negro, his gaining the support of Wendell Phillips and his eventual witness of the defeat of the Confederacy when he was invited to speak in South Carolina at Fort Sumter after the Civil War ended. Interestingly enough, at the death of Wendell Phillips in February 1884, black Baltimoreans honored him also in a public service with James A. Handy the principal speaker.

On this occasion honoring Garrison, however, Greener thought that if there were to be another Garrison to complete the work of freedom, he would have to come from among the blacks. Greener concluded his remarks by referring to the last time he saw Garrison, just a few days before his death, when Garrison wrote a letter deploring the situation in the South as thousands of blacks fled the region in order to enjoy in the West some of the fruits of freedom, away from oppression.[63]

After Greener's speech, Dr. H. J. Brown offered resolutions praising the work of Garrison and regretting his death. The resolutions were assented to by a standing vote. Then followed a short speech by Professor J. E. Rounds who stated that Garrison was a man who had great confidence in God. He said Garrison:

> . . . was a fanatic in the sense that John the Baptist was, but no one ever made a greater mistake than to suppose that he appealed to the feelings rather than the understanding. At first the church was antagonistic to him, and yet in the end it was perhaps the mightiest single influence through which the final success was achieved.[64]

After Rounds's speech, the Doxology was sung and the meeting adjourned.

On two other noteworthy occasions, Greener came back to the city and spoke. In March 1882, he spoke at Centennial Church at a reunion of colored soldiers, and in December 1883, he gave a talk at First Baptist Church on "The Civil Rights Decision and Its Effect on the American Negro," which dealt with the Supreme Court's recent decision declaring unconstitutional the Civil Rights Bill of 1875. Greener probably came to the city on plain social reasons as well, for his wife's sister had married Dr. H. J. Brown.[65]

The blacks of Baltimore not only held memorial services for the nationally famous, they also commemorated the lives of local friends as well. On April 16, 1879, memorial services for William J. Albert were held at St. Paul's Lyceum, 32 North Calvert Street, with John H. Butler in the chair. Albert's service to the race was characterized as invaluable. He took a prominent part in the founding of the Baltimore Association for the Moral and Educational Improvement of the Colored People. At his memorial service, Bishop Wayman and Isaac Myers also spoke.[66]

In the 1880s, many an important speaker came to the city, following in the footsteps of those who visited in the 1860s and 1870s. On January 3, 1881, Bishop Henry McNeil Turner returned to the city, in which he was licensed to preach, to lecture at Ebenezer A.M.E. Church. His topic was "Has the Nation Done Its Duty to the Colored Race?" In no uncertain terms, Turner, soon to become one of the leading "Back-to-Africa" exponents, answered his own question with an emphatic "No.". In hindsight, Turner thought the Federal Government should have provided more for the education of the newly emancipated slave than it did and should have set aside public land to assure this was carried out. He said:

The colored people are not ungrateful, at the same time they earnestly desire something more than reminders of their indebtedness to those who were instrumental under God in securing to them the blessing of liberty.[67]

A reporter commenting on the Bishop's style, said that he spoke without notes, fluently, and apparently knew his subject thoroughly. The audience was well attended by the ministers of the city.

Bishop Turner had been a former George T. Watkins pupil, and, in 1881, two other things happened to indicate the continuing link of past abolitionist workers with the present. On April 16, 1881, the Shelter for Aged and Infirmed Colored Persons was incorporated and had as a guiding hand in the project, Isabella Tyson, once in charge of an orphanage for the children of black Union soldiers. Miss Tyson was a granddaughter of Elisha Tyson. Then, too, in the summer and fall of 1881, Frances Ellen Watkins Harper was a temperance worker in Maryland for the Maryland State Temperance Alliance. Mrs. Harper was a niece and student of William Watkins, the teacher.[68]

At the end of 1881, Bishop Daniel A. Payne, former pastor of Bethel, then Senior Bishop of the A.M.E. Church, was given a reception on his return from Europe, after attending a conference on Methodist Ecumenism. That following year, in April 1882, Bishop Payne's thirtieth year in the bishopric was celebrated in the city with Bishop Wayman in charge of the arrangements.

A little before this triumphant celebration took place, however, Baltimoreans had to hold an indignation meeting at Bethel, with Bishop Levi Coppin presiding, Isaac Myers as secretary, and assorted vice presidents including Harvey Johnson, J. H. Butler, and George Myers, to protest the expulsion of Bishop Payne from a first-class railroad car in Florida. The retreat from Reconstruction was at full gallop. At this meeting, Richard T. Greener, Martin Delany, a nationally prominent anti-slavery worker in the days before the Civil War, Isaac Myers, and Bishop Alexander Wayman spoke. At a subsequent meeting, Bishop Payne gave his first-hand account of his first-class expulsion.[69]

Martin Delany spent several weeks in Baltimore during the spring of 1882; as noted above, he spoke at the indignation meeting held with regard to Payne's expulsion from the Florida train. While in Baltimore, Delany lent his support to establishing an organization to be known as The Order of Regulators, a self-defense body. The organizers wanted The Order of Regulators to be a national body and political in its intent, educating its members to looking at men, not party labels. Speeches made at the organizing gathering included, besides Delany's, ones by Reverend Harvey Johnson and Reverend J. H. Reddick.

Significantly, some three years later, the Brotherhood of Liberty was established in Baltimore, seemingly modelled after the Regulators. Revs. Harvey Johnson and William Alexander took an active hand in its formation.

Delany remained in Baltimore in the spring of 1882 and gave several lectures on Africa during this time. In one effort, he corrected notions that the Sahara was just a barren desert and spoke of its lushness in certain areas. At another time, he replied to a contention by Henry Ward Beecher, famous Protestant clergyman and brother of Harriet Beecher Stowe, that if Africa were to sink into the ocean, the world would lose nothing of value. Delany's reply came in the form of a lecture he entitled "The Black Race as a Factor in Civilization."

A few days after the meeting involving the formation of The Order of Regulators, a fitting complement to the political independence and looking inward shown at that meeting was made, as the bishops of the African Methodist Episcopal Church and Colored Methodist Episcopal Church, held a meeting at Bethel to try to bring about a union amongst themselves. Bishop Wayman acted as secretary of a public meeting of the bishops and introduced Bishop Henry M. Turner for a speech, who talked on the general topic of "Union among Colored People." Because of the absence of a majority of the Colored Methodist Episcopal Bishops during the session on the last day of the conference, Wayman offered a resolution regretting this situation, but hoping for the reassembly of the bishops of both conferences when a union could be brought about. All in all, it would seem that 1881-82 was a high point in efforts mounted from Baltimore to do much to unify the blacks on a national scale.[70]

Furthermore, in June 1882, the Sixteenth Encampment of the Grand Army of the Republic took place in

Baltimore and such local notables as Dr. H. J. Brown, William F. Taylor, Isaac Myers, John W. Locks, James T. Bradford, John H. Butler, and the Reverends J. A. H. Johnson and J. H. Reddick were prominently involved in handling those matters related to blacks from throughout the country who participated in the affair.[71]

Inasmuch as Baltimore welcomed the highest of black culture and achievement to the community, it was proper for it to send to other places evidence of its own cultural eminence. In the fall of 1884, Maryland blacks took part in an exhibition of black achievement at an affair held in New Orleans under the general charge of former U.S. Senator Blanche K. Bruce. Bishop Wayman drafted Reverend Adam B. Wilson to handle Maryland's section at which portraits by J. James Dungee were shown--one being a portrait of Bishop Wayman, himself. The Morning Herald office acted as a kind of collection station for items to be judged before being sent to the exposition.[72]

Several years later, Baltimoreans put out the welcome mat for another unusual occasion. A kindergarten opened in October 1886 by Mrs. Addie E. Jones, formerly of Boston, had a fund raiser in February 1887, at which the black historian George Washington Williams lectured. Located at Fremont Street and China Alley, the school, consisted of about forty pupils. Miss Jones was assisted by the daughter of Reverend C. Hedges of Grace Presbyterian Church. She also got valuable support from the Episcopalians and the A.M.E.'s as well.

This kindergarten was not the earliest one established in Baltimore, however, for by early 1884, the Episcopalians had opened two with the involvement of Reverend C. B. Perry and the school's president, Mrs. William H. Brune. Black laborers' children were taken care of at a cost of 10 cents per day per first child and 5 cents each additional one.[73]

In March 1887, the Colored Baseball League met at Douglass Institute to set their schedule for the season. It appears the League was first organized in the city with William S. Brown as League president of the six clubs located in Baltimore, New York, Louisville, Philadelphia, Pittsburgh, and Boston. This was to be one of the last major meetings of this sort at Douglass Institute.[74]

As early as May 1887, a meeting of blacks took place to raise $25,000 to erect another black hall, like the Douglass Institute. In February 1888, the Institute was sold to George H. Klank for $20,000. The selling was a result of petitions from heirs to stock and those who grew dissatisfied that the corporation had not paid any dividends recently. After being placed in receivership and eventually having been sold, after paying off debts, there was nothing left for those so eager to collect. Thus ended the life of one of the most valuable institutions the city ever had.[75]

Baltimore had justifiable rights to claim to be the most important black metropolis throughout most of the nineteenth century, whose men and women made her significant, "unofficially" the capital for black life in this time period. Ironically, it is interesting, as well as important, to view one aspect of Baltimore's significance vis-a-vis the nation's capital black society, itself.

Washington Episcopalians were under the direction of the Maryland Diocesan office and because of this, the closeness of the two black Episcopal communities can be evidently seen on many occasions. At the death of Rev. Harrison H. Webb in December 1878, rector of St. James Episcopal Church for many years and long active in the community, the eulogy was given by Alexander Crummell, founder and pastor of St. Luke's in Washington. Webb, born in 1804, had been ordained a deacon at St. James in April 1853. His elevation to the priesthood was at ordination services presided over by Bishop Whittingham in January 1856.

Before his elevation to the priesthood, Webb served effectively in the community as a teacher. In the later years of his life, Webb was only active occasionally and ended his priestly career assisting at St. Mary's Chapel. He was buried at Laurel Cemetery. Crummell, in his eulogy, said he had long known the deceased and spoke feelingly of his gentleness of deportment, his piety and boldness in preaching. Webb, according to Richard T. Greener, worked with his grandfather, Jacob Greener, against the American Colonization Society in the period around 1840.[76]

The interaction of Baltimore and Washington Episcopalians was evident on another important front. Washington Episcopalians made efforts to found, in May 1879, a private high school for boys under the headship of Reverend George C. Cranston, a graduate of Brown University in Rhode Island. The Board of Directors included such Washingtonians as Hon. Blanche K. Bruce, Joseph T. Rainey, Richard T. Greener, John W. Cromwell,

Alexander Crummell, I. T. Augusta, and such Baltimoreans as Dr. H. J. Brown, Isaac Myers, William H. Bishop, Sr., and James T. Bradford.

In June 1879, Crummell presided over a meeting to further implement plans for the high school. At this meeting was Rev. Calbraith B. Perry of St. Mary's in Baltimore under which the companion girls' school operated and to which Crummell sent his daughter. By September, the boys' high school program had to be cancelled due to the sudden illness of Reverend Cranston. It appears, however, that the boys' high school idea was revived again in 1880. In May 1880, Christopher C. Fleetwood, a parishoner of St. Luke's in Washington, performed a concert at the Samaritan Temple in Baltimore for the benefit of the proposed school.[77]

Several Baltimoreans, and those with roots in the city, moved to Washington after the Civil War. This class included Frederick Douglass, Richard T. Greener, William E. Matthews, Christopher C. Fleetwood, Daniel Murray, Henrietta Vinton Davis, and some others.

Frederick Douglass was the most famous of these ex-sons. His relationship with the city began in his days as a slave of seven or eight when he came to Baltimore around 1825 to wait and serve in the Auld family, then living in the Fells Point section. Baltimore's place in Douglass' heart as home was so, because there he met his lifelong friends, fell in love with Anna Murray, his first wife, and learned to read and write. Also, at Centennial Methodist Church, then known as Dallas Street Methodist Church, he was converted to the Christian faith and from its environs, resolved to take upon himself the burden of fighting for the rights of blacks.

Even when a resident of Washington, Douglass seemed to prefer Baltimore society. In fact, at least once, in dramatic fashion, he came to Baltimore to lay bare the sins of the nation's capital. He was sponsored by St. Paul Lyceum at an assembly held in Douglass Institute. At this time, as Marshall of the District of Columbia, when Douglass entered the hall, immediately a round of applause ensued. Music by a band followed, and the prayer said by Rev. James A. Handy, a friend of Douglass' from their years as caulkers in the shipyards of Baltimore. After an introduction by the Secretary of the Lyceum, W. J. Perkins, Douglass spoke.

Douglass initially indicated his reluctance to

speak on the subject, "The National Metropolis," especially as many thought this was a subject out of his ken of knowledge; in other words, it was not about slavery and the like. Nevertheless, he thought his several years' stay there entitled him to critique it. He started out with the good by noting the capital was the center of the best government in the world, a government "leading the world upward and onward" in the march of civilization and renown. He acknowledged the grandeur of its burgeoning architectural improvements, including Washington's monument nearing completion. He also defended the Board of Public Works, responsible for reforms in his view but considered by some as emanating from a band of thieves.

After these niceties, Douglass uttered the unthinkable. He said Washington had many a church with steeple, pointing heavenward, "but I fear that the place pointed to and Washington are far apart." These words were surely one of the reasons some Washingtonians demanded his resignation when he returned to Washington. Douglass, however, said he had drawn that conclusion, partly because of the easy relationship that had existed between the city and slavery and all its ills--and the after-effects of that relationship still lingered on, in his opinion. He said Washingtonians were basically lazy folk. A Washingtonian "walks, sits, talks, rides and gesticulates with a cane, and sometimes plays Cain." He further stated, "You can generally tell the character of a man by the way he wears his hat. On first sight you would think you were among a lot of thieves, by the manner in which they wear their hats in Washington. They wear them down over the eyes, which gives them a sombre, sinister appearance." One cannot imagine what Douglass supposed could be the reaction to such a painted word-picture when he left Baltimore to resume his position of public trust as Marshall of the District, especially as he had pointedly said Congressmen who controlled matters in the District were those who really set the style for roguish hat-wearing.

The movement to censure Douglass began immediately; petitions were circulated to be given to the President, demanding his removal. Columbus Alexander, one of those who stood behind Douglass' bondedness, wanted the courts to have his name withdrawn from that pledge. There was some concern that Douglass went out of his way to defend members of the Board of Public Works, some of whom were in charge when the Freedmen's Bank, with Douglass as president, went bankrupt. There was speculation Douglass' unusually harsh criticism of the capital may have been deliberatly done by him so people would not think that he took the U.S. Marshall's office to remain quiet, especially in the face of Hayes' apparent bargain with Southern Democrats, which resulted in the pulling of Federal Troops out of the South, leaving blacks even more unprotected before the rage of former rebels.

Yet, be this as it may, some blacks were also involved in expressing disapproval, if not calling for his removal. The effort to remove him was very serious and, because of this, Douglass felt called upon to defend himself, in a letter that was published in newspapers, in which he claims he was partly misquoted and that he made the speech, partly in jest.

Whatever be the truth with regard to Douglass' criticism of Washington, he continued to come to Baltimore to speak and to take part in services that had a personal meaning for him inasmuch as he seemed genuinely to consider the place home. Such occasions were the dedication of a new Centennial Methodist Church, or the celebration of that church's founding of its Sunday School, which Douglass had witnessed as a slave some forty-seven years before, and other such gatherings. Naturally he came back to lecture on various topics from "William, the Silent" to "John Brown." Then, too, he was honored on occasions as when a friend, Bishop Alexander Wayman, presented him with a gold-headed cane on behalf of black Baltimoreans in May 1890. A couple of years later, Douglass was prevailed upon by his friend, J. Murray Ralph, to purchase the old Dallas Street Church. He did so, and turned the property into houses, using the foundation and part of the structure to build five houses which still stand. The foundation of the building goes back to 1776. Of course, at his death, his many friends in Baltimore mourned his passing, and attended his funeral.[78]

Another resident of Washington who had deep roots in the city during the time Douglass was a slave in Baltimore was Richard T. Greener. Greener was the first black graduate of Harvard and, shortly after graduating, took charge of a high school in Philadelphia. After resigning his position in Philadelphia, he accepted a similar position in Washington in 1873. He later became Dean of Howard University's Law School and was a prominent member of the Fifteenth Street Presbyterian Church. Greener had an historical interest in his people, inasmuch as his grandfather, Jacob Greener, was an old associate of people like William Watkins, Benjamin Lundy, and William Lloyd Garrison.

Greener made known the considerable esteem he held for his Baltimore roots in a speech he gave in Hermitage Square on October 25, 1878, in the presence of Frederick Douglass, among others. At that moment, he had just finished campaigning in the South.

In 1879, Richard Greener was corresponding secretary of the Banneker Historical Society in Washington. In February 1882, he lectured on Banneker at an audience which included Frederick Douglass and William E. Matthews. Greener paid tribute to the Quaker abolitionists of Banneker's day and displayed several items of historical interest, such as a first-edition Banneker almanac and a facsimile of Banneker's letter to Jefferson. At this lecture, Greener spoke to the need to build a monument to Banneker, an idea seconded by William E. Matthews.

Greener was often called to speak before Baltimore audiences or lend his hand in some enterprise. Beginning in 1885, David D. Dickson and some others asked Greener, holder of a law degree, to open a law school in Baltimore. This move to establish a law school came about the time William E. Matthews' letter to the Sun about the race's progress in the law received quite a bit of comment from such people as Douglass and James T. Bradford.[79]

Another expatriate son of Baltimore in Washington, William E. Matthews, made good and he never forgot his Baltimore roots, either. He, too, often came back to speak. Matthews was a lawyer and investment banker. In June 1880, he gave the annual address to college societies at Wilberforce College in Ohio. His address was entitled "Young Manhood: Its Relation to a Worthy Future." Matthews made a trip to Europe, returned in the fall of 1889, and appeared at the Monmental Literary Association in Baltimore, speaking on "What I Saw and Felt Abroad." Some thought was given by him, while in Europe, to the necessity of blacks establishing an Afro-American League, a self-defense and self-preservation organization similar to that of The Order of Regulators idea promoted in Baltimore in 1882. In a letter to a newspaper pushing John M. Langston for presidency of such an organization, his opinion released quite a response throughout the country.

In a public exchange of letters that took place between Langston and Matthews in September 1889, Langston thanked Matthews for his confidence in him. Langston returned the compliment and talked of Matthews' experience in seeing various surroundings and knowing of what he spoke. The _Plain Dealer_ of Detroit heartily supported Matthews' scheme to establish his national organization in the states which, as Matthews thought, "would do much to give our brethren in the South hope and courage" to endure and fight, in a specific manner, the outrages being commited. Matthews concluded, however, that he did not know how long blacks would be pacific. His plans were also similar to those put forth a bit earlier by Thomas Fortune, a black newspaper man in New York, which were endorsed by J. C. Price from North Carolina, soon to become leader of the League Matthews advocated.[80]

Bishop Henry M. Turner, however, was one man who was not impressed that blacks would vigorously defend themselves. He seems to have been present when The Order of Regulators idea was taken up in Baltimore in the spring of 1882. Turner said of the new League:

> Does it propose to raise an army to put down the riotous condition that exists in the South? We will never do that, for we are too mean and stingy to erect a monument in honor of Charles Sumner which is a disgrace to every Negro in the United States.[81]

Turner also said, "Does it propose a Black man's party?" The answer here, too, was "no."

Nevertheless, the renewed interest in forming a national body, fostered by Matthews, blossomed into two organizations--The Afro-American League which organized in Chicago in January 1890 under the leadership of Thomas Fortune and J. C. Price, and the Negro National Protective Association which had Perry Carson in prominence at its organization at Metropolitan Church in Washington. Price was elected President of this organization, too.

That Perry H. Carson, known as the Black Oak of the Potomac, should have been in the fore in organizing the Negro Protective Association, is not too surprising. This native Baltimorean, born in January 1832, was a veteran of the Civil War. After the war, he settled among the contraband in Washington. There he led a band of blacks who violently resisted whites who attempted to compel blacks to remain in certain areas of the city. Afterward this display of determined self-defense, it was possible for blacks to travel safely in any part of the District of Columbia. Carson was quite a politician in the leadership of the area who even bested Douglass on several occasions.

Henrietta Vinton Davis, stepdaughter of George A. Hackett, was one woman who moved to Washington and established herself in that city, but who remained proud of her Baltimore heritage. In April 1883, she made her debut as the race's first national actress. Frederick Douglass introduced her to the audience. Davis was born in Baltimore on August 4, 1860, her father being Mansfield Davis, a distinguished musician in the city. A few days after her birth, Davis' father died and within about six months, her mother married George A. Hackett. Hackett provided his stepdaughter with such schooling as he could amply afford. A year after Hackett's death, Henrietta and her mother moved to Washington where her mother was employed by the Federal Government in the Treasury Department.

One of Henrietta's teachers in Washington, Miss Mary Bozeman, encouraged her to study elocution and, in a little time, this served as the basis for her acting career. In 1875, Henrietta passed the teachers' examination and taught somewhere in Maryland. She later went to Louisiana (perhaps her mother's home, Washington, Louisiana) to teach and remained there several years. She next came back to Washington because of her mother's declining health. In 1878 she was employed by the Recorder of Deeds as a copyist where she remained until 1884. In 1881, Frederick Douglass was elevated from Marshall to Recorder of Deeds.

Henrietta Davis' yearning for the stage while in the Recorder's office grew irrepressible. The widely and well-read Miss Davis then began taking lessons under Miss Marguerette E. Saxton, who was white and formerly from New York. In April 1883, after much preparation, she was introduced to the public by Frederick Douglass. Douglass had an additional reason to foster Davis' career; besides the fact of her being the stepdaughter of George A. Hackett, she had grandparents who lived on a farm adjoining that on which Douglass belong when he was a slave on the Eastern Shore.

Miss Davis was described at her first performance as being tall and slender and as "possessing a fine carriage which tends to make her a perfect figure. She is a moorish color, with beautiful large eyes. Her eyes were brown, hair as black as a raven with a countenance

300

of great mobility of expression." She performed "Briar Rose," a demanding piece which tested an artist's dramatic power. From there she did "The Jiners," a reading showing a person's irritation at being hounded to join or take part in the festivities of lodges and societies, such as the Galilean Fishermen and the Sons and Daughters of Abraham.

From there, Miss Davis did the speech of "Portia" in the Merchant of Venice. One critic said, ". . . but no lawyer defended his cause with more consummate skill than did Miss Davis deliver this argument which Shakespeare puts in Portia's mouth." She also did something from Romeo and Juliet. One critic said, "She needs but encouragement, the favoring circumstances of friendly criticism and fair patronage, to take an honored place on the American stage among her sisters of the other race." This writer also hoped that at her next performance more blacks would be present.

After her appearance in Washington that April 1883, Henrietta Davis toured the principal cities of the East and Midwest. But, before setting off north, she gave one more reading in Washington from Macbeth, as Lady Macbeth, which a critic did not particularly like. He said:

> . . . her reading no one will attempt to discount, but as an actress she lacks harmony in her voice and seemed to disregard the fact that too much declaiming don't make an actor or actress. In the conspiracy, where Lady Macbeth instigates Macbeth to murder Duncan, she failed to impress or to demonstrate her great anxiety to have Macbeth murder the King. Her business was to look at Macbeth and impress him and not the audience, which was the failure in all of her pieces except Parthenian in Ingomar (sic). Her great desire was it seemed to show her stature and declaim her part like a schoolgirl.[82]

When Henrietta Davis did set out on her tour, it seems she went with Hurle Bavardo, a Baltimorean, and a troup of other actors.

At one place she stopped, Cleveland, Ohio, she received a very large bouquet from George A. Myers, son of Isaac Myers. They were schoolmates together when in Baltimore, no doubt, attending Bethel's school. She later returned to Cleveland and was highly commended for her improvement in roles such as "Cleopatra" and "Zingeralia, The Gypsy Girl."

For a while, as she toured the Midwest, at the beginning of 1884, Miss Davis was managed by two Bostonians, W. H. Dupree, a station postmaster in Boston, and James M. Trotter, author of a book on black music and father of radical opponent to Booker T. Washington in the early 1900s, William M. Trotter. By April 1884, she came under the managment of Thomas T. Symmons of New York who had managed the Bohemian Dramatic Club. Symmons formed a dramatic company to support her. Afterward, her career blossomed even more; she received enthusiastic responses from both blacks and whites in New York State. The success under Symmons was such that by May 1884, the troup moved out of New York for a grand testimonial for Miss Davis in Philadelphia.

In October 1884, Henrietta V. Davis, accompanied by Symmons and a Mme. F. E. Ridgeway, performed at Centennial Methodist Church in Baltimore. While in the city, in October, she also performed at the Lyric. Her mother apparently accompanied her to Baltimore. Ironically, at about the time of Davis' triumphs on the national scene, the daughter of Francis E. W. Harper was about to embark on a career as an elocutionist. In one of her earliest performances in early December 1884, Mrs. Harper's daughter read before a Baltimore audience.

Apparently sometime in 1885, Davis formed her own company--The Davis Miller Concert and Dramatic Company which, in December 1885, exhibited its talents at a benefit for the Brotherhood of Liberty, a civil rights organization founded in Baltimore. All the principals of her company were Baltimoreans. By 1888, Davis was living in Chicago and continued to improve herself to the point of including comic pieces in her repertoire such as Paul Lawrence Dunbar's "When Malindy Sings." Sometime along the way of her many travels, she received the approval of Boston critic John Boyle O'Reilly and, by the 1890s, was acclaimed worldwide. Henrietta Davis continued performing up to about 1920.[83]

Another former Baltimorean who gained renown and who lived in Washington was Christopher Fleetwood. Fleetwood was a companion of William E. Matthews in his younger days, and was pampered as a child by a white woman for whom his father worked. He was given run of her library and subsequently trained in the office of Dr. James Hall, toward the day he would pursue a merchant's career in Liberia. He was sent to Lincoln University in Pennsylvania to further his preparation for going to Liberia. For some reason, however, he did not go to Liberia and continued to live in Baltimore at the outbreak of the Civil War. He was, along with some others, responsible for the Lyceum Observer, the organ for the Galbreth Society, and considered the first black newspaper to be published below the Mason-Dixon line.

As the Civil War took place, he joined the 4th Regiment U.S. Colored Troops, under General James Birney's leadership, where his exploits won him the Congressional Medal of Honor. After the Army, he settled in Washington, being employed in various clerical positions at various times at the U.S. Supreme Court, in the Freedmen's Bank, City Registry, Office of Tax Collector, and Freedmen's Bureau. He worked in the War Department also. He was thoroughly acquainted with music and had a baritone voice, which he used at benefit concerts free of charge. At one time he sang with the Fifteenth Street Presbyterian Church in Washington, but later he organized and led St. Luke's Episcopal Church choir. He served also as a promoter for various entertainment extravaganzas in the city and was responsible for organizing several black militia companies.[84]

Inasmuch as the fame of former residents and their travels abroad and their readiness to acknowledge a debt to the City of Baltimore did contribute to that continuing fame of the city in the latter part of the nineteenth century, in a similar vein the literary and intellectual output of some Baltimoreans did much to enhance the city's reputation. In Baltimore, literary societies had their beginning in the 1820s and the most famous of the era being that which had William Watkins, William Douglass, Lewis G. Wells, and a number of others as members. Isaac Myers said there were seven of these flourishing before the Civil War. It is known that even Frederick Douglass belonged to one. Of course, the most important ones straddling the periods of slavery and freedom were the Galbreth Lyceum and the one at Bethel Church. There is not too much information on these groups before the Civil War to give a true and full picture of their lives and activities.

After the Civil War, information about these kinds of societies becomes more available. Indeed, around the middle of the 1880s, there existed a union of the lyceums and literary societies in Maryland, which met in annual conventions. In Baltimore, however, by at least the 1870s there seemed to be two very important ones, that is two very active ones in addition to the Galbreth--The St. Paul's Lyceum and the Monumental Literary Association. The St. Paul Lyceum was founded in 1871 and had its headquarters on St. Paul Street. Two of its known presidents were William J. Bell and Warner T. Guinn. Solomon G. Brown, who belonged to the Galbreth once, gave this new group some items to encourage it in its endeavor. By 1880, the group had one thousand books in its library and quite an exhibition of animals and plants.

The other group, the Monumental Literary Association had its rooms opposite Bethel Church in the beginning. It seems, in fact, to have been the continuation of the old Bethel Literary Society under a new name. It was formally opened in August 1878 and at these ceremonies, George T. Watkins delivered the commencement address. In February 1879, a lecture at Bethel to benefit the Association was delivered by Richard H. Cain, a former member of Congress from South Carolina and an A.M.E. minister. After the speech, Bishop Wayman invited all to view the rooms of the society. By 1889, the Monumental Literary Association was meeting out of Madison Presbyterian Church. Its members of prominence, at that time, included Rev. William H. Weaver of Madison Avenue Presbyterian as president, John H. Murphy as vice president, and such dignitaries as Rev. R. F. Wayman, Dr. H. J. Brown, Rev. William Alexander, Lawyers E. J. Waring and J. S. Davis, and Dr. R. M. Hall.[85]

A good many of the presentations before Baltimore's literary societies were printed in the A.M.E. Review. There were articles in this Review from Baltimoreans which also seem not to have been presented before a literary society. Nevertheless, some of the more interesting pieces that were printed here came from the pens of former William Watkins students. A selection of the topics discussed and/or later printed dealt with such subjects as the black Exodus issue of 1879, "The Colored Man Before the Law," "The Recent Race Riots in the South," "What I Saw and Felt Abroad," "The Life of Nat Turner," "Sunday School Work," "Political Economy," Shakespeare, and other literary masters.

Rev. James H. A. Johnson, an A.M.E. minister, had his essay entitled "Plain Humanity" published in the A.M.E.Review. He was a former Watkins pupil and without question this piece is reminiscent of Watkins. The Watkins tone of deep sarcasm, apt quotation, and vivid language can be seen in the opening line. Johnson said, "The Negro now, more than anybody else in America is being made a subject for all kinds of criticism and misanthropic speculation. By some he is turned over all sides and looked at 'through a glass darkly.'" Johnson went further, "He is considered as though he was not a human being. Every virtuous element in him is blurred; all his good intentions are gainsaid; all his acts of kindness are discounted. The gloomiest foreboding are advanced against him; and the most heartless efforts are made to have him fixed in public opinion to be regarded as a bad dog."

Throughout the essay it is understandable why Johnson was referred to as being perhaps "the brainiest man" in the A.M.E. connection, for he quotes and mentions the most numerous variety of sources that hang together in such an elegant style. In the article, Johnson indicated he was in charge of a newspaper--The African Methodist, a fact that only partially explains his wide acquaintance with many things, because Watkins seems to have impressed on most of his most eager students the necessity of breadth and depth of knowledge together.[86]

In another essay published a few years later, Johnson expounded on "Female Preachers." There seemed to be a great cropping-up of them at the time and Johnson used Scripture and reasoning to defend his position that women were not physically or mentally suited to be preachers.[87]

William E. Matthews was another William Watkins' pupil to appear in the A.M.E. Review who, in the first year of the journal, 1884, wrote about "Money As a Factor in Human Progress." In the second paragraph, Matthews wrote, "Money is that element in human progress which supported all the others, and with it there could be no progress, no refinement, no literature and no liberal art." Civilization, as Matthews knew it, was based "on a division of labor, only made possible in the society that has money to allow each to do one thing in a chain that links and supports all, from shoemaker and cook to the scholar and preacher." Matthews was against those in the pulpit in the black community, who discouraged blacks from struggling to accumulate money; he said he agreed with Emerson, "The pulpit and the press have many commonplaces denouncing the thirst for wealth; but if men should take these moralists at their word, and leave off aiming to be rich, the moralist would rush to rekindle, at all hazard, this love of power in the people, lest civilization should be undone."

Matthews believed in private enterprise and "individual exertion" as a means of preventing "stagnation and death." He was opposed to socialism and state ownership of industries, the means of production. He admired the British way of doing things. Through the rest of the article, Matthews, too, evidenced that he had read deep in the literature of the day. In subsequent pieces, he displayed his skills as a writer, such as "A Summer Vacation in Europe" and "Pessimism, or a Plea for a Larger Faith and Hope."[88]

In addition to the many A.M.E. Review pieces by Baltimoreans or former Baltimoreans that enchanced the city's image, the black community indicated its intense interest in mental culture in other ways as well, as when Bishop Wayman was elected vice president of a Methodist Historical Society in Baltimore, representing the A.M.E. denomination. He continued a tradition in church history started by Bishop Payne, which several others who had been connected with the city were to do, such as when Bishops Benjamin Arnett and Henry M. Turner, both of whom served in Baltimore and became church historians of their denominations as Payne had been.

At the death of three nationally prominent blacks toward the end of the nineteenth century, the role of the city in the lives of these men was reechoed and in part, indicated the city was entitled to respect as the "black capital" in the nineteenth century. The three who died in the 1890s were Daniel Payne, Frederick Douglass, and Alexander Wayman. The funeral of Payne took place in December 1893. His body was transported from Wilberforce, Ohio, where he died, and placed on view at Bethel for two days. Several bishops were present and representatives from various conferences of the connection attended the last rites. The services were begun with the hymn, "Servant of God, Well Done," Scripture reading, then the song, "Lead Kindly Light" by the choir and the sermon by Bishop Wayman, successor to Payne as Senior Bishop of the African Methodist Episcopal Church, the most significant national black organization of the nineteenth century.

Wayman's text was from Matthews 25:21, "His Lord said unto him: Well done thou good and faithful servant; thou has been faithful over a few things, I will make thee ruler over many things, enter thou into the joy of thy Lord." Wayman said, if a man should be in Heaven, Payne should be there. Others to speak included Reverend James H. A. Johnson, Reverend C. S. Smith of the Sunday School Union and Mrs. Fannie Jackson Coppin, wife of Bishop Levi Coppin. Payne was buried in a vault at Laurel Cemetery. The following May a monument was raised over his remains at Laurel, as addresses were made by Rev. J. H. A. Johnson, Frederick Douglass, and Dr. W. B. Derrick of New York. The monument was unveiled by Bishop Henry M. Turner. This was to be the only monument to Payne, perhaps the most significant and active churchman throughout the breadth of the nineteenth century that blacks had produced.[89]

At the death of Frederick Douglass in February 1895, in Washington, Bishop Wayman issued a call that Baltimore blacks commemorate the former Sunday School scholar and teacher at Centennial. Wayman had known Douglass for fifty years or more. Indeed, Douglass' first wife, Anna Murray, lived with Wayman's parents before she married Douglass. He said he heard of Douglass while a youth in Caroline County in 1836, about the time Douglass tried to escape from his owner and was hauled off to jail with great publicity when his plans were discovered. Wayman said Douglass' last appearance in Baltimore was at the unveiling of the monument to Bishop Payne. He said, "He was the most genial and sociable man I ever met in my life."[90]

That November 1895, Bishop Wayman himself passed away. The three daily newspapers in Baltimore were even more laudatory about his personal worth to blacks in their progress than even of Bishop Payne's and Frederick Douglass' worth. Wayman lived in Baltimore for over thirty years after his elevation to the bishop's seat in 1864. He was a scholar and historian of the A.M.E. Church as well as one of the most active churchmen in establishing his denomination's influence throughout the country. It was said he traveled enough to belt the earth several times. Wayman was one of the more acceptable representatives of the race at integrated meetings in the city. The Baltimore and Ohio Railroad allowed his church, as one newspaper announced, to purchase in the most lenient manner, a camp meeting grounds at their Harman Station, fifteen miles out of the city on the railroad's tracks to Washington. The grounds, appropriately enough, were known as Wayman's Grove. This is just one example of the high regard in which he was held in the general community. Indeed, to him also, a monument was erected by black Baltimoreans as he was buried in Laurel Cemetery.[91]

With the continuity of history in the years of struggle for equality as represented in the lives of Elisha Tyson, William Watkins, George Alexander Hackett, Isaac Myers, and some others; and, in addition with the meaningful comings and goings of such greats as

Daniel Payne, Frederick Douglass, and Alexander W. Wayman to the city, it is no wonder that Baltimore shone so brightly in the nineteenth century, and deservedly is entitled to be known as the black capital city on the hills of the Patapsco.

Chapter VI

[1]*Weekly Anglo-African*, August 12, 1859, p. 2; *People's Advocate*, February 21, 1880, p. 3; February 28, 1880, p. 1;

[2]*Weekly Anglo-African*, August 20, 1859, p. 3.

[3]*Weekly Anglo-African*, September 3, 1859, p. 2.

[4]*Weekly Anglo-African*, September 12, 1859, p. 2.

[5]*Weekly Anglo-African*, October 1, 1859, p. 3.

[6]*Weekly Anglo-African*, December 10, 1859, p. 1.

[7]*Weekly Anglo-African*, December 24, 1859, p. 1.

[8]*Weekly Anglo-African*, January 7, 1860, p. 1.

[9]*Weekly Anglo-African*, February 18, 1860, p. 1.

[10]*Weekly Anglo-African*, March 31, 1860, p. 3.

[11]Baltimore County Land Records, W. B. 70, p. 523; Handy, *Scraps of A.M.E. History*, p. 14; Register of Certificates Granted by Clerk of Baltimore County to Negroes Free by Manumission in Virtue of an Act of Assembly Passed November Session 1805, Commencing on First of June 1806, pp. 90-91, Department of Legislative Reference, Bureau of Archives, City of Baltimore; *Federal Gazette*, July 15, 1815, p. 2.

[12]*Federal Gazette*, April 11, 1805, p. 3.

[13]Richard R. Wright, *The Encyclopedia of the African Methodist Episcopal Church* (Philadelphia: 1947), Second edition, p. 512; Letter, Daniel Coker to Bishop Thomas Kemp, n.d. c.a. 1824, Maryland Diocesan Archives, Maryland Historical Society; Baltimore City Wills 26, p. 192, of George A. Hackett.

[14]*San Francisco Elevator*, December 21, 1872, p. 2.

[15]E. A. Anderson, *Slavery and the Domestic Slave Trade in the United States* (Boston: Light & Stearns, 1836), p. 56; Handy, *Scraps of A.M.E. History*, p. 14; Plan of Appointment for Baltimore City Station, 1826-27, 1843-44, Lovely Lane Museum, Baltimore, Maryland; *Sun*,

July 8, 1859, p. 1; Christian Advocate, May 24, 1848, p. 1; Indianapolis Freemen, October 12, 1889, p. 1; James Watkins, Struggle for Freedom; or the Life of James Watkins (Manchester: James Watkins, 1860), p. 58.

[16]American, June 1, 1869, p. 4.

[17]Afro-American, August 17, 1895, p. 7.

[18]Anglo-African Magazine, October 1859, p. 4; African Repository December 1826, p. 298; Freedom's Journal, July 20, 1827, p. 74; American, November 17, 1884, p. 4; Sun, February 21, 1884, p. 4; American, December 1885; People's Advocate, June 7, 1879, p. 2; American, July 23, 1891, p. 6.

[19]American, July 13, 1878, p. 4.

[20]Weekly Anglo-African, January 14, 1860, p. 3; New York Globe, December 15, 1883, p. 3; American, March 19, 1881, p. 4; June 18, 1886, p. 4.

[21]Afro-American, December 24, 1898, p. 1; January 7, 1899, p. 1; Washington Bee, August 24, 1887, p. 2.

[22]Afro-American, November 17, 1906, p. 4; November 24, 1906, p. 4; February 16, 1918, p. 1.

[23]New York Age, December 19, 1885, p. 1; Edward W. Wilson, The History of Morgan State College (New York: Vantage Press, 1975), p. 174.

[24]Sun, December 20, 1861, p. 1; Maryland News Sheet, December 20, 1861, p. 1; Baltimore Clipper, December 20, 1861, p. 1; The Baltimore Republican, December 19, 1861, p. 4; Afro-American, November 2, 1912, p. 8.

[25]American, December 4, 1877, p. 4; December 6, 1877.

[26]Afro-American, May 30, 1896, p. 2; Sun, (Supplement), August 11, 1890, p. 4.

[27]American, July 5, 1889, p. 6; Washington Bee, April 28, 1894, p. 3; Indianapolis Freeman, February 23, 1889, p. 4.

[28]American, February 20, 1891, p. 6

[29]American, July 22, 1889, p. 6.

[30]Sun, July 3, 1883, p. 4.

[31]American, April 6, 1887, p. 4.

[32]American, January 17, 1885, p. 4; October 14, 1885, p. 4; Sun, October 12, 1885.

[33]American, August 7, 1888, p. 4.

[34]Fielding Lucas, Jr., Picture of Baltimore (Baltimore: Fielding Lucas, Jr., 1832), p. 1; American, March 1, 1843, p. 2; March 2, 1843, p. 2; Sun, March 3, 1842, p. 1; March 5, 1842, p. 1; February 16, 1844, p. 2; February 10, 1845, p. 2; February 20, 1846, p. 2; February 26, 1846, p. 2; March 4, 1846, p. 1.

[35]Sun, October 7, 1865; American, June 17, 1873, p. 4.

[36]Morning Herald, April 16, 1879, p. 4.

[37]People's Advocate, April 19, 1879.

[38]Morning Herald, August 15, 1879, p. 4; People's Advocate, August 23, 1879, p. 2; Afro-American, July 18, 1908, p. 4.

[39]American, September 13, 1876, p. 4.

[40]Morning Herald, January 24, 1876, p. 4; Afro-American, December 21, 1895, p. 4.

[41]Sun, December 6, 1886, p. 4; Afro-American, February 22, 1902, p. 8; Morning Herald, July 5, 1882, p. 4; July 15, 1882, p. 4; September 8, 1882, p. 4; September 21, 1886, P. 3.

[42]Afro-American, August 24, 1901, p. 3; September 12, 1903, p. 4.

[43]Sun, April 20, 1881, p. 1; May 9, 1881, p. 4.

[44]American, July 30, 1867, p. 1; August 26, 1867, p. 4; January 23, 1873, p. 4.

[45]American, May 7, 1873.

[46]Sun, June 1, 1875, p. 1.

[47]American, May 31, 1879, p. 4.

311

48Morning Herald, June 14, 1878, p. 4; December 6, 1878, p. 4; American, May 31, 1877, p. 4; May 31, 1881, p. 4.

49American, October 24, 1889, p. 6.

50American, August 5, 1881, p. 4; February 23, 1883, p. 4; Sun, October 23, 1885, p. 4; Afro-American, February 22, 1902, p. 8.

51Sun, May 20, 1870, p. 1; American, May 20, 1870, p. 1.

52Sun, August 22, 1867, p. 1.

53Sun, August 18, 1868, p. 4.

54Sun, February 14, 1873, p. 4.

55American, February 8, 1873, p. 4.

56American, March 6, 1874, p. 4.

57American, October 2, 1874, p. 4.

58Sun, May 1, 1875, p. 1.

59Sun, November 21, 1876, p. 4.

60Sun, June 23, 1877, p. 4; June 25, 1877, p. 4.

61Morning Herald, October 10, 1877, p. 4.

62American, January 11, 1878, p. 4; January 14, 1878, p. 4; January 15, 1878, p. 1.

63American, February 26, 1879, p. 4; April 27, 1880, p. 4; February 20, 1884, p. 4; Morning Herald, April 24, 1879, p. 4.

64American, June 20, 1879, p. 4.

65Sun, March 27, 1882, p. 4; December 19, 1883, p. 4.

66American, April 17, 1879, p. 4.

67Sun, January 4, 1881, p. 1.

68Morning Herald, April 17, 1881, p. 4.

[69]Morning Herald, December 16, 1881, p. 4; April 14, 1882, p. 4; May 1, 1882, p. 1; American, April 14, 1882, p. 4.

[70]American, May 20, 1882, p. 4; May 23, 1882, p. 4; Morning Herald, April 25, 1882, p. 1; April 27, 1882.

[71]Morning Herald, June 21, 1882; June 24, 1882, p. 3.

[72]Sun, October 25, 1884, p. 4; Morning Herald, October 24, 1884, p. 4; New York Age, October 13, 1888, p. 2.

[73]Sun, February 17, 1887, p. 4; New York Age, December 18, 1886, p. 4; Morning Herald, March 11, 1884, p. 4; January 31, 1887, p. 2.

[74]American, March 15, 1887, p. 4; Morning Herald, March 15, 1887, p. 2; March 16, 1887, p. 1.

[75]Sun, May 19, 1887, p. 4; New York Age, February 25, 1888, p. 1; Sun, February 14, 1888.

[76]American, December 16, 1878, p. 4; December 19, 1878, p. 4; Sun, December 17, 1878, p. 4.

[77]People's Advocate, May 24, 1879, p. 2; September 20, 1879; May 8, 1880, p. 1.

[78]American, May 9, 1877, p. 4; May 14, 1879, p. 2; Sun, May 9, 1877, p. 4; May 12, 1877, p. 1.

[79]People's Advocate, October 18, 1879, p. 3; February 11, 1882, p. 3; New York Globe, March 21, 1885, p. 1; April 11, 1885, p. 4; American, December 16, 1890, p. 8; December 17, 1890, p. 6.

[80]The Plain Dealer (Detroit), October 4, 1889, p. 1; October 11, 1889, p. 4; October 18, 1889, p. 4; October 25, 1889, p. 1; November 1, 1889, p. 1; February 7, 1890, p. 2.

[81]The Plain Dealer (Detroit), November 1, 1889, p. 1.

[82]People's Advocate, June 16, 1883, p. 2.

[83] Mary A. Hackett, RG 56 Entry 210, General Records Department of Treasury. Applications and Recommendations for Positions in the Washington, D.C. Office, 1830-1910. People's Advocate, April 28, 1883, p. 3; March 8, 1884, p. 3; Washington Bee, May 10, 1884, p. 3; April 28, 1884, p. 3; New York Age, March 29, 1884, p. 3; April 26, 1884, p. 3; May 3, 1884, p. 3; May 10, 1884, p. 4; Cleveland Gazette, February 2, 1884, p. 1; February 9, 1884, p. 1; March 1, 1884, p. 3; May 12, 1888, p. 1; April 28, 1894, p. 2; Afro-American, February 24, 1917, p. 6; New York Age, November 8, 1884, p. 1.

[84] Washington Bee, April 11, 1885, p. 2.

[85] Sun, October 14, 1885, p. 4; October 14, 1886, p. 4; New York Age, October 24, 1885, p. 1; People's Advocate, June 12, 1880, p. 2; June 19, 1880; June 26, 1880, p. 3; Morning Herald, August 23, 1878, p. 4; April 3, 1879, p. 4; April 10, 1879, p. 4; September 18, 1889, p. 2; Indianapolis Freeman, October 12, 1889, p. 4; November 30, 1889, p. 1; December 7, 1889, p. 1; March 29, 1890, p. 1; August 8, 1891, p. 1.

[86] James H. A. Johnson, "Plain Humanity Without Distinction," A.M.E. Review (1885), p. 158.

[87] James H. A. Johnson, "Female Preachers," A.M.E. Review (1884), pp. 102-108.

[88] William E. Matthews, "Money As A Factor in Human Progress," A.M.E. Review (1884), p. 321.

[89] Sun, December 5, 1893, p. 10; December 22, 1893, p. 8; February 10, 1894, p. 8; May 22, 1894, p. 7; American, December 6, 1893, p. 8.

[90] American, February 21, 1895, p. 4; February 22, 1895, p. 8.

[91] American, December 1, 1895, p. 4; December 2, 1895, p. 3; December 5, 1895, p. 8; Morning Herald, December 1, 1895, pp. 6, 7; Sun, December 2, 1895, p. 7.

SELECTED BIBLIOGRAPHY

Manuscripts

Friends' Library, Swarthmore College (Swarthmore, Pennsylvania), Moses Sheppard papers.

Hall of Records (Annapolis, Maryland), Maryland Quaker Records.

Haverford College Library (Haverford, Pennsylvania), Quaker Collection.

Historical Society of Pennsylvania (Philadelphia, Pennsylvania), Black Locater File.

Library of Congress (Washington, D.C.), American Colonization papers.

Maryland Historical Society (Baltimore, Maryland), Maryland Colonization papers.

Morgan State University Library (Baltimore, Maryland), Forbush Collection.

National Archives (Washington, D.C.)

Periodicals

African Repository, Washington (1827-1870).

A.M.E. Review, Philadelphia (1884-1900).

Baltimore American (1799-1895).

Baltimore Afro-American (1895-1955).

Baltimore Patriot (1815, 1817-1824).

Baltimore Daily Repository (1792-1793).

Federal Gazette, Baltimore (1794-1830).

Federal Republican, Baltimore (1808-1812).

Freedom's Journal, New York (1827-1829).

Friends' Miscellany, Philadelphia (1831-1842).

Indianapolis Freeman, Indianapolis (1885-1895).

Maryland Colonization Journal, Baltimore (1835-1855).

Maryland Gazette, Annapolis (1790-1824).

Maryland Gazette, Baltimore (1788-1791).

Maryland Journal, Baltimore (1785-1797).

Morning Chronicle, Baltimore (1819-1820, 1822-1823).

Morning Herald, Baltimore (1876-1895).

Niles Weekly Register, Baltimore (1810-1824).

People's Advocate, Washington (1876-1885).

Sun, Baltimore (1840-1895).

The Liberator, Boston (1831-1865).

The Genius of Universal Emancipation, Greenville, Tennessee, Baltimore (1821-1830).

The Telegraphe and Daily Advertiser, Baltimore (1795-1801).

Washington Bee, Washington (1880-1920).

Primary Sources

Bell, Howard Holman. Minutes of the Proceeding of the National Negro Conventions, 1830-1864. New York: Arno Press and The New York Times, 1969.

Lay, Benjamin. All Slave-Keepers that Keep the Innocent in Bondage. Philadelphia: Benjamin Lay, 1737.

Learned, Joseph D. A View of the Policy of Permitting Slaves in the States West of the Mississippi. Baltimore: Joseph Robinson, 1820.

Lewis, Evan. Address to the Coloured People of Philadelphia Delivered at Bethel Church on the Evening of 17th 3rd Mo. 1833. Philadelphia: John Richards for the Meeting, 1833.

Lovejoy, J. C. Memoir of Rev. Charles T. Torrey. Boston: John P. Jewette & Co., 1847.

Minutes of an Adjourned Session of the 19th Session of the American Convention for Promoting the Abolition of Slavery . . . . Philadelphia: Benjamin Lundy for the American Convention, 1826.

Minutes of the Adjourned Session of the 20th Biennial American Convention for Promoting the Abolition of Slavery . . . . Philadelphia: Samuel Parker for the American Convention, 1828.

Needles, Edward. An Historical Memoir of the Pennsylvania Society for Promoting Abolition of Slavery . . . . Philadelphia: Pennsylvania Society, 1848.

Norris, John Saurin. A Biographical Notice of the Late Moses Sheppard. n.p.: Board of Trustees of Sheppard Asylum, 1857.

Parrish, John. Remarks on the Slavery of the Black People. Philadelphia: John Parrish, 1806.

Pinkney, William. Speech of William Pinkney, Esq., in the House of Delegates of Maryland, at Their Session in November, 1789. Philadelphia: Joseph Crukshank, 1790.

Porter, Dorothy, ed. Negro Protest Pamphlets. New York: Arno Press and The New York Times, 1969.

Sharp, Granville. Letter from Granville Sharp, Esq., of London, to the Maryland Society for Promoting the Abolition of Slavery . . . . Baltimore: Society, 1793.

Townsend, Richard H. The Diary of Richard H. Townsend. 3 vols. Baltimore: Enoch Pratt Free Library, 1937.

Tyson, John Shoemaker. Life of Elisha Tyson, The Philanthropist. Baltimore: Benjamin Lundy, 1825

Vaux, Robert. Memoirs of the Lives of Benjamin Lay and Ralph Sandiford, Two of the Earliest Public Advocates for the Emancipation of the Enslaved African. Philadelphia: Solomon W. Conrad, 1815.

317

Secondary Sources

Articles

Abbott, Collamer M. "Isaac Tyson, Jr., Pioneer Mining Engineer and Metallurgist." Maryland Historical Magazine, 60 (March 1965):165-25

Allen, Robert R. "Count Rumford: Behavior Engineer." Social Science Review, 46 (December 1972):597-602.

Bernard, Ella K. "Elisha Tyson, Philanthropist and Emancipator (1749-1824)." The Journal of the Friends' Historical Society, 9 (April, 1912):108-112.

Brown, Kirk. "Friends Libraries in Maryland." The Journal of the Friends' Historical Society, 2 (November, 1905):130-132).

Cadbury, Henry J. "Negro Membership in the Society of Friends." Journal of Negro History, 21 (April 1936):151-213.

Calvert, Monte A. "The Abolition Society of Delaware, 1801-1807." Delaware History, 10 (October, 1963):295-320.

Coll, D. Blanche. "The Baltimore Society for the Prevention of Pauperism, 1820-1822." American Historical Review, 61 (October 1955):77-87.

Cooper, Frederick. "Elevating the Race: The Social Thought of Black Leaders, 1827-1850." American Quarterly, 24 (December 1972):604-625.

Davis, David B. "James Cropper and the British Anti-Slavery Movement, 1823-1833." Journal of Negro History, 46 (1961):154-173.

Davis, Lance E., and Pane, Peter L. "From Benevolence to Business: The Story of Two Savings Banks." Business History Review, 32 (Winter 1958):386-406.

Della, M. Ray, Jr. "The Problems of Negro Labor in the 1850's." Maryland Historical Magazine, 66 (Spring 1971):14-32.

Gardener, Betty J. "William Watkins: Antebellum Black Teacher and Anti-Slavery Writer." Negro History

Bulletin, (September/October 1976):623-625.

Hoyt, William D., Jr., ed. "Civilian Defense in Baltimore, 1814-1815: Minutes of the Committee of Vigilance." Maryland Historical Magazine, 39 (September 1944):199-224.

MacGavey, Charles J. "Daniel Raymond, Esquire, Founder of American Economic Thought." Maryland Historical Magazine, 44 (June 1949):111-122.

Miller, Randall M. "The Union Humane Society." Quaker History, 61 (Autumn 1972):91-106.

Mohl, Raymond A. "Humanitarianism in the Preindustrial City: The New York Society for the Prevention of Pauperism, 1817-1823." The Journal of American History, 57 (December 1970):576-599.

"Nat Turner's Insurrection." Atlantic Monthly, (1861):173-187.

Sowley, Patrick. "The North Carolina Manumission Society, 1816-1834." The North Carolina Historical Review, 42 (Winter 1965):47-69.

Wright, Edward N., ed. "John Needles 191786-1878): An Autobiography." Quaker History, 48 (Spring 1969):3-21.

Books

Adams, Alice Dana. The Neglected Period of Anti-Slavery in America (1808-1831). Boston: Ginn and Co., Publishers, 1908.

Adams, Herbert B., ed. The Life and Writings of Jared Sparks. 2 vols. Boston: Houghton-Mifflin Co., 1893.

Aptheker, Herbert, ed. "One Continual Cry." David Walker's Appeal to the Colored Citizens of the World (1829-1830): Its Setting and Its Meaning. New York: Humanities Press for A.I.M.S., 1971.

Arndt, Karl J. R. George Rapp's Harmony Society, 1785-1847. Philadelphia: University of Pennsylvania Press, 1965.

Bailyn, Bernard. The Ideological Origins of the American Revolution. Cambridge, Massachusetts: The Belknap Press of Harvard University Press, 1972.

Barnes, Gilbert Hobbs. The Antislavery Impulse, 1830-1844. New York: Harcourt, Brace & World, Inc., 1964.

Baxley, C. Herbert, ed. A History of the Baltimore General Dispensary Founded 1801. Baltimore: General Dispensary Foundation, Inc., 1963.

Bedini, Silvio A. The Life of Benjamin Banneker. New York: Charles Scribner's Sons, 1972.

Bell, Howard Holman. A Survey of the Negro Convention Movement, 1830-1861. New York: Arno Press and The New York Times, 1969.

Birney, William. James G. Birney and His Times. New York: D. Appleton and Co., 1890.

Bohner, Charles H. John Pendleton Kennedy: Gentleman from Baltimore. Baltimore: The Johns Hopkins Press, 1961.

Boyd, George Adams. Elias Boudinot: Patriot and Statesman, 1740-1821. Princeton: Princeton University Press, 1952.

Brackett, Jeffrey, R. The Negro in Maryland: A Study of the Institution of Slavery. Baltimore: The Johns Hopkins University Press, 1889.

Bridenbaugh, Carl. Cities in the Wilderness: The First Century of Urban Life in America, 1625-1842. New York: Alfred A. Knopf, 1955.

Brinton, Howard H. Friends for 300 Years. Wallingford, Pennsylvania: Pendle Hill Quakerback, 1965.

Brock, Peter. Pioneers of the Peaceable Kingdom. Princeton: Princeton University Press, 1968.

Brookes, George S. Friend Anthony Benezet. Philadelphia: 1937.

Brown, Letitia Woods. Free Negroes in the District of Columbia, 1790-1846. New York: Oxford University Press, 1972.

320

Bruchey, Stuart Weems. Robert Oliver, Merchant of Baltimore, 1783-1819. Baltimore: The Johns Hopkins Press, 1956.

Campbell, Penelope. Maryland in Africa: The Maryland State Colonization Society, 1831-1857. Chicago: University of Illinois Press, 1971.

Catterall, Helen T., ed. Judicial Cases Concerning American Slavery and the Negro. Vol. IV. Washington: The American Institution of Washington, 1936.

Christie, John W., and Dumond, Dwight L. George Bourne and the Book and Slavery Irreconcilable. Philadelphia: The Historical Society of Delaware and the Presbyterian Historical Society, 1969.

Clarkson, Paul S., and Jett, R. Samuel. Luther Martin of Maryland. Baltimore: The Johns Hopkins Press, 1970.

Cox, Joseph William. Robert Goodloe Harper: The Evolution of a Southern Federalist Congressman. Unpublished Ph.D. dissertation, University of Maryland, 1967.

Crummell, Alexander. Africa and America: Addresses and Discourses. New York: Negro University Press, 1969, c. 1891.

_____. The Future of Africa. New York: Charles Scribners, 1862.

Delaphine, Edward S. Francis Scott Key, Life and Times. New York: Biography Press, 1937.

Dillon, Merton Lynn. Benjamin Lundy and the Struggle for Negro Freedom. Urbana, Illinois: University of Illinois Press, 1966.

Douglass, Frederick. Life and Times of Frederick Douglass. New York: Collier-MacMillan Ltd., 1962, c. 1892.

Douty, Esther M. Forten, the Sailmaker: Pioneer Champion of Negro Rights. New York: Rand McNally & Co., 1968.

DuBois, William E. B. The Suppression of the African Slave Trade to the United States of America, 1638-

1870. Baton Rouge, Louisiana: Louisiana State University Press, 1969.

Dumond, Dwight L. Antislavery Origins of the Civil War in the United States. Ann Arbor, Michigan: University of Michigan Press, 1963.

Drake, Thomas E. Quakers and Slavery in America. Gloucester, Massachusetts: Peter Smith, 1965, c. 1950.

Dunlap, William C. Quaker Education in Baltimore and Virginia Yearly Meetings. Philadelphia: 1936.

Earle, Thomas. The Life, Travels and Opinions of Benjamin Lundy. Philadelphia: William D. Parrish, 1847.

Filler, Louis. The Crusade Against Slavery, 1830-1860. New York: Harper Torchbooks of Harper & Row, Publishers, 1963.

Finnie, Gordon E. The Antislavery Movement in the South, 1787-1836: Its Rise and Decline and Its Contribution to Abolition in the West. Ann Arbor, Michigan: University Microfilms, Inc.

Fladeland, Betty. Men and Brothers: Anglo-American Antislavery Cooperation. Urbana, Illinois: University of Illinois Press, 1972.

Foner, Philip S., ed. The Life and Writings of Frederick Douglass. 4 vols. New York: International Publishers, 1950.

Forbush, Bliss. Elias Hicks: Quaker Liberal. New York: Columbia University Press, 1956.

_____. A History of Baltimore Yearly Meeting of Friends. Sandy Spring, Maryland: Baltimore Yearly Meeting of Friends, 1973.

_____. Moses Sheppard: Quaker Philanthropist of Baltimore. Philadelphia: J. B. Lippincott, 1968.

Fox, Early L. The American Colonization Society, 1817-1840. New York: AMS Press, 1971, c. 1919.

Franklin, John Hope. From Slavery to Freedom. Third edition. New York: Vintage Books, 1969.

Frost, J. William. The Quaker Family in Colonial America: A Portrait of the Society of Friends. New York: St. Martin's Press, 1973.

Fuke, Richard P. Black Marylanders, 1864-1868. Ph.D. dissertation, University of Chicago, 1973.

Gara, Larry. The Liberty Line: The Legend of the Underground Railroad. Lexington, Kentucky: Kentucky Paperbacks, University of Kentucky Press, 1962.

George, Carol V. R. Segregated Sabbaths: Richard Allen and the Emergence of Independent Black Churches, 1760-1840. New York: Oxford University Press, 1973.

Gilchrist, David T., ed. The Growth of the Seaport Cities, 1790-1825. Charlottesville, Virginia: Published for the Elutherian Mills-Hagley Foundation by the University Press of Virginia, 1967.

Hallowell, Benjamin. Autobiography of Benjamin Hallowell. 2nd edition. Philadelphia: Friends' Book Association, 1884.

Harris, Sheldon H. Paul Cuffe: Black American and the African Return. New York: Simon and Schuster, 1972.

Harrison, J. F. C. Quest for the New Moral World: Robert Owen and the Owenites in Britain and America. New York: Charles Scribner's Sons, 1969.

Hart, Richard H. Enoch Pratt: The Story of a Plain Man. Baltimore: Enoch Pratt Free Library, 1935.

Hawke, David F. Benjamin Rush: Revolutionary Gadfly. New York: The Bobbs-Merrill Company, Inc., 1972.

Hoffman, Ronald. A Spirit of Dissension: Economics, Politics and the Revolution in Maryland. Baltimore: The Johns Hopkins University Press, 1973.

Holland, Ceclia M. Ellicott City, Maryland, Mill Town, U.S.A. Chicago: Ceclia M. Holland, 1970.

Hull, William I. William Penn and the Dutch Quaker Migration to Pennsylvania. Baltimore: Genealogical Publishing Co., 1970, c. 1935.

Innes, William. Liberia or the Early History & Single Preservation of the American Colony of Free Negroes on the Coast of Africa. 2nd edition. Edinburgh: Waugh & Innes, 1833.

Jacobs, Grace Hill. The Negro in Baltimore, 1860-1900. Master's thesis, Howard University, August 1945.

James, Sydney V. A People Among Peoples: Quaker Benevolent Eighteenth-Century America. Cambridge, Massachusetts: Harvard University Press, 1963.

Janney, Samuel M. Memoirs of Samuel M. Janney. Philadelphia: Friends' Book Association, 1881.

Littwack, Leon F. North of Slavery: The Negro in the Free States, 1790-1860. Chicago: The University of Chicago Press, 1961.

Locke, Mary S. Anti-Slavery in America from the Introduction of African Slaves to the Prohibition of the Slave Trade (1619-1808). Gloucester, Massachusetts: Peter Smith, 1965.

Lofton, John. Insurrection in South Carolina: The Turbulent World of Denmark Vesey. Yellow Springs, Ohio: The Antioch Press, 1964.

Luxon, Norwal Neil. Niles' Weekly Register: News Magazine of the Nineteenth Century. Baton Rouge: Louisiana State University Press, 1947.

Lynch, Hollis R., ed. Black Spokeman: Selected Published Writings of Edward Wilmot Blyden. London: Frank Cass & Co., Ltd., 1971.

Manakee, Harold R. Maryland in the Civil War. Baltimore: Maryland Historical Society, 1961.

Matthews, Donald G. Slavery and Methodism: A Chapter in American Morality, 1780-1845. Princeton: Princeton University Press, 1965.

May, Samuel Joseph. Memoir of Samuel Joseph May. Boston: Roberts Brothers, 1873.

Miller, John C. The Federalist Era, 1789-1801. New York: Harper & Brothers, Publishers, 1960.

Moore, Glover. The Missouri Controversy, 1819-1821.

Lexington: University of Kentucky Press, 1953.

Mosely, Thomas Robert. A History of the New York Manu-
mission Society, 1785-1849. Ph.D. dissertation,
New York University, 1963. Ann Arbor, Michigan:
University Microfilms, Inc.

Mullin, Gerald W. Flight and Rebellion: Slave Resistance in Eighteenth Century Virginia. New York:
Oxford University Press, 1972.

Ofari, Earl. "Let Your Motto Be Resistance." The Life
and Thought of Henry Highland Garnet. Boston:
Beacon Press, 1972.

Owens, Hamilton. Baltimore on the Chesapeake. Garden
City, New York: Doubleday, Doran & Co., Inc.,
1941.

Payne, Daniel. A History of the African Methodist Episcopal Church. Nashville: Publishing House of the
A.M.E. Sunday School Union.

_____. Recollections of Seventy Years. Nashville:
Publishing House of the A.M.E. Sunday-School Union, 1888.

Pease, Jane H., and Pease, William H. Bound with Them
in Chains: A Biographical History of the Antislavery Movement. Westport, Connecticut: Greenwood
Press, Inc., 1972.

Poole, William Frederick. Anti-Slavery Opinions Before
the Year 1800. Westport, Connecticut: Negro University Press.

Quarles, Benjamin. Black Abolitionists. New York: Oxford University Press, 1969.

_____. Blacks on John Brown. Chicago: University
of Illinois Press, 1972.

_____. Frederick Douglass. Washington, D.C.: The
Associated Publishers, Inc., 1948.

_____. The Negro in the American Revolution.
Chapel Hill, North Carolina

Raymond, Daniel. Thoughts on Political Economy. Baltimore: Fielding Lucas, 1820.

325

Richards, Leonard L. "Gentleman of Property and Standing," Anti-Abolition Mobs in Jacksonian American. New York: Oxford University Press, 1970.

Rothman, David J. The Discovery of the Asylum: Social Order and Disorder in the New Republic Boston: Little, Brown and Co., 1971.

Semmes, John E. John H. B. Latrobe and His Times, 1803-1891. Baltimore: The Norman, Remington Co., 1917.

Shyllon, F. O. Black Slaves in Britain. New York: Published for The Institute of Race Relations, London, by Oxford Press, 1974.

Smedley, R. C. History of the Underground Railroad in Chester and the Neighboring Counties of Pennsylvania. Lancaster, Pennsylvania: Office of The Journal, 1883.

Sogarin, Mary. John Brown Russwarm: The Story of Freedom's Journal, Freedom's Journey. New York: Lothrop, Lee, S. Sheppard, Co., 1970.

Standenraus, P. J. The African Colonization Movement, 1816-1865. New York: Columbia University Press, 1961.

Stuart, Charles. A Memoir of Granville Sharp. Westport, Connecticut: Negro Universities Press, 1970, c. 1836.

Sturge, Joseph. A Visit to the United States in 1841. New York: Augustus M. Kelley Publishers, 1969, c. 1842.

Tappan, Lewis. The Life of Arthur Tappan. New York: Arno Press and The New York Times, 1970, c. 1870.

Temperley, Howard. British Antislavery, 1833-1870. London: Longman Group Limited, 1972.

Thom, Helen Hopkins. Johns Hopkins: A Silhouette. Baltimore: The Johns Hopkins Press, 1929.

Thomas, John L. The Liberator: William Lloyd Garrison. Boston: Little, Brown and Co., 1963.

Thompson, Mack. Moses Brown: Reluctant Reformer. Williamsburg, Virginia: Institute of Early American

History and Culture and University of North Carolina Press, 1962.

Tyson, Martha E. A Brief Account of the Settlement of Ellicott's Mills. Baltimore: Maryland Historical Society, 1865.

Ullman, Victor. Martin R. Delany: The Beginning of Black Nationalism. Boston: Beacon Press, 1971.

Wade, Richard C. Slavery in the Cities: The South, 1820-1860. New York: Oxford University Press, 1964.

Ward, Samuel Ringgold. Autobiography. New York: Arno Press and The New York Times, 1968, c. 1855

Warner, Oliver. William Wilberforce and His Times. London: B. T. Batsford, Ltd., 1962.

Wayman, Alexander W. Encyclopedia of African Methodism. Baltimore: Methodist Episcopal Book Depositions, 1882.

Wikramanayake, Marina. A World of Shadow: The Free Black in Antebellum South Carolina. Columbia, South Carolina: For the South Carolina Tricentennial Commission by the University of South Carolina Press, 1973.

Wright, William C. The Secession Movement in the Middle-Atlantic States. Rutherford: Farleigh-Dickinson University Press, 1973.

Zilversmith, Arthur. The First Emancipation: The Abolition of Slavery in the North. Chicago: The University of Chicago Press, 1967.

329

333